CRITICAL APPROACHES TOWARD A COSMOPOLITAN EDUCATION

This book aims to reconceptualize teaching and learning in spaces with diverse populations of young people. Chapters focus on the schooling experiences and social and cultural adaptation issues of individuals who, through the meaning that they assign to their lived experiences, ascribe to multiple identity qualifiers. Contributors explore the impact of this cosmopolitan awareness on students, educators, and educational institutions, presenting issues such as curricular concerns around civic engagement, individual subjectivity versus social identity, and the convergence of context-specific policy and teaching environments on global dynamics in education reform. An emphasis on this understanding promises to better equip educators and policy-makers to plan instructional approaches and devise pedagogic resources that serve the needs and career aspirations of an expanding cohort of multifaceted learners.

Sandra R. Schecter is Professor of Education and Applied Linguistics at York University, Toronto, Canada

Carl E. James holds the Jean Augustine Chair in Education, Community and Diaspora in the Faculty of Education at York University, Toronto, Canada

CRITICAL APPROACHES TOWARD A COSMOPOLITAN EDUCATION

Edited by Sandra R. Schecter and Carl E. James

NEW YORK AND LONDON

First published 2022
by Routledge
605 Third Avenue, New York, NY 10158

and by Routledge
2 Park Square, Milton Park, Abingdon, Oxon OX14 4RN

Routledge is an imprint of the Taylor & Francis Group, an informa business

© 2022 selection and editorial matter, Sandra R. Schecter and Carl E.
James; individual chapters, the contributors

The right of Sandra R. Schecter and Carl E. James to be identified as the
authors of the editorial material, and of the authors for their individual
chapters, has been asserted in accordance with sections 77 and 78 of the
Copyright, Designs and Patents Act 1988.

All rights reserved. No part of this book may be reprinted or reproduced or
utilised in any form or by any electronic, mechanical, or other means, now
known or hereafter invented, including photocopying and recording, or in
any information storage or retrieval system, without permission in writing
from the publishers.

Trademark notice: Product or corporate names may be trademarks or
registered trademarks, and are used only for identification and explanation
without intent to infringe.

British Library Cataloguing-in-Publication Data
A catalogue record for this book is available from the British Library

Library of Congress Cataloging-in-Publication Data
A catalog record has been requested for this book

ISBN: 978-0-367-34764-2 (hbk)
ISBN: 978-0-367-34763-5 (pbk)
ISBN: 978-0-429-32778-0 (ebk)

DOI: 10.4324/9780429327780

Typeset in Bembo
by Deanta Global Publishing Services, Chennai, India

CONTENTS

List of Contributors	*viii*
Foreword	*xv*
Preface: Critical Approaches Toward a Cosmopolitan Education	*xix*
Acknowledgments	*xxx*

PART 1
Critical Cosmopolitanism in Contemporary Education   **1**

1 Subaltern Voices, Digital Tools, and Social Imaginaries   3
   Glynda A. Hull, Devanshi Unadkat, and Jessica Adams-Grigorieff

2 Race and Ethnicity within Cosmopolitan Theories of
   Spatiality and Temporality   22
   Carol Reid

3 Queering Hybridity: Relationality, Blending, and Appropriation   40
   Cris Mayo

4 Clashing and Converging Cosmopolitanisms: Reimagining
   Multiculturalism and the Question of Belonging   53
   Daniel A. Yon

vi Contents

PART 2
Schooling and the Development of Cosmopolitan Identities 67

5 Bringing Black Mixed-Race Pupils into Focus in British Schooling 69
Karis Campion and Remi Joseph-Salisbury

6 De- and Reterritorializing Identities: The Global Hip Hop Nation at Work in a Youth Hip Hop Recording Studio 86
Édouard Laniel-Tremblay and Bronwen Low

7 The Case Against Exoticism: Troubling "Identity" in Identity-Based Data Collection 101
Vidya Shah

PART 3
Forging Cosmopolitan Pedagogies 119

8 Translating Global Memory across Colonial Divides: Critically Contextualizing the Intimacies of Learning from Oral Histories of Colonial Violence 121
Lisa K. Taylor

9 Trilingual Instruction in an Indigenous Community in Northwestern Mexico: A Case for Cosmopolitanism from Below in Intercultural Education 138
María Rebeca Gutiérrez Estrada and Sandra R. Schecter

10 Race in Liminal Space: Youth Discourse in a Francophone School 155
Sara Schroeter

11 *Global Jinzai* and Short-Term Study Abroad: Expectations, Readiness, and Realities 172
Martin Guardado and Rika Tsushima

12 Playing and Making: Re-Fusing the Digital Divide 189
Jennifer Jenson

Contents **vii**

PART 4
Challenges for Cosmopolitan Education **207**

13 Students' Intercultural Experiences in an Internationalizing
University in China: A Critical Discursive Perspective 209
Yang Song and Angel M.Y. Lin

14 The Resistance to Getting Used to One Another 224
Ninni Wahlström

15 The Impact of Foreclosures on the Home Environments and
Education of Black Youth in the United States 238
Nemoy Lewis

16 Sheltered in Place: When Walls Trump Bridges 255
Suzanne de Castell

Index *273*

CONTRIBUTORS

Jessica Adams-Grigorieff is a doctoral candidate at the University of California, Berkeley's Graduate School of Education, Berkeley, USA, with a designated emphasis in New Media Studies. She holds an MA in education and a BA from UC Berkeley. She researches young adults' digital literacy practices from sociocultural and sociotechnical perspectives. Her dissertation, which is part of a design-based university-community partnership, focuses on how social media and educational platforms shape and interact with young adults' developing (critical) digital literacies.

Karis Campion is a Legacy in Action Research Fellow at the Stephen Lawrence Research Centre, De Montfort University, Leicester, UK. Her research interests span areas of (mixed) race/ethnic identity, geographies of race, intersectional inequalities, Black feminism, youth identities, antiracism, and institutional racism in education. She sits on the editorial board of the *Sociological Review* and the UKCGE Working Group on BME Participation in Postgraduate Research. Outside of academia she is a school governor and serves on the voluntary management committee of an adventure playground in Brixton, London.

Suresh Canagarajah is the Edwin Erle Sparks Professor of English, Applied Linguistics, and Asian Studies at Pennsylvania State University, State College, USA. He teaches courses in World Englishes, multilingual writing, language socialization, rhetoric/composition, and postcolonial studies. Suresh comes from the Tamil-speaking northern region of Sri Lanka. He taught earlier at the University of Jaffna, Sri Lanka, and the City University of New York. He was formerly the Editor of the *TESOL Quarterly* and President of the American Association of Applied Linguistics. His edited book *Routledge Handbook on Language and Migration*

(Routledge, 2017) won the 2020 best book award from the American Association of Applied Linguistics.

Suzanne de Castell is Professor Emerita in the Faculties of Education at Simon Fraser University, Burnaby, Canada, and at the University of Ontario Institute of Technology, Oshawa, Canada, where she has held professorial, administrative, and decanal roles. She has published widely on educational theory, literacies (both traditional and digital), research technologies, educational equity, and digital games and learning. She is currently Visiting Professor in the Faculty of Education at the University of British Columbia, Vancouver, Canada.

Martin Guardado is Professor of Applied Linguistics and Sociolinguistics at the University of Alberta, Edmonton, Canada. His research interests span several themes in applied linguistics with a current focus on the nexus between cosmopolitanism, global citizenship, and the internationalization of higher education. He has published broadly in these areas and given invited talks at universities in Canada and internationally. A leading scholar in heritage language socialization, he recently published a book on this topic (Blackwell, 2018), *Discourse, Ideology, and Heritage Language Socialization: Micro and Macro Perspectives*, where he dedicated two full chapters to the relevance of the notion of cosmopolitanism to learning spaces across contexts, including K–12, postsecondary, family, and community.

María Rebeca Gutiérrez Estrada is Associate Professor in the Department of Foreign Languages at Universidad de Sonora, Hermosillo, Mexico, where she also works in three graduate programs: Humanities, Linguistics, and History. Her main research interest is language policy and planning, focusing on English and minority (Indigenous) language teaching in northern Mexico. She has also studied the experiences of Mexican students abroad, particularly as these students develop their intercultural competence. She is a member of a nonprofit organization where she has developed a research project exploring empathy within citizenship education in elementary public schools in Mexico (https://monitoranticorrup cion.org/educacion-y-empatia-ee/).

Glynda A. Hull is Professor of Education at the Graduate School of Education, University of California, Berkeley, USA, and holds the Elizabeth H. and Eugene A. Shurtleff Chair in Undergraduate Education. The broad focus of her research has been literacy as a sociocultural process. More specifically, over the last 15 years, she has studied meaning-making in the context of, and in concert with, digital media and networked spaces, like social media and online courses. Glynda began her career in education by teaching middle and high school English in two small towns in Mississippi. A recipient of UC Berkeley's Distinguished Teaching Award, she offers undergraduate and graduate courses on literacy, digital media, and teaching in higher education.

x Contributors

Carl E. James holds the Jean Augustine Chair in Education, Community and Diaspora in the Faculty of Education at York University, Toronto, Canada, where he is also the Senior Advisor on Equity and Representation. He teaches in the Faculty of Education and in the graduate programs in Sociology and Social and Political Thought. For 17 years he was visiting scholar at Uppsala University in Uppsala, Sweden, where he taught in the Teacher Training Department. Carl's research interests include examination of the schooling experiences, educational performance, employment opportunities, career trajectories, and social achievements of racialized people—particularly Black youth. His recent publications include *"Colour Matters": Experiences, Education and Pursuits of Black Youth* (2021).

Jennifer Jenson is Professor of Digital Languages, Literacies, and Cultures in the Faculty of Education at the University of British Columbia, Vancouver, Canada. Her interest in research focused on media, communication, and education has led to her developing digital games research in Canada and internationally both as founder and as past president of the Canadian Game Studies Association and current Co-Editor of its journal *Loading*. Her publications on technologies and their application in K–12 schooling include a commissioned report for the Ministry of Education in Ontario, and articles on gender and gameplay, gender and technology, and multimodal, multilingual learning in journals such as *Feminist Media Studies*, the *Annual Review of Applied Linguistics, Learning, Media and Technology*, and the *Journal of Curriculum Theorizing*. She is currently Principal Investigator of an international research project, Re-Figuring Innovation in Games.

Remi Joseph-Salisbury is a Presidential Fellow in Ethnicity and Inequalities at the University of Manchester, Manchester, UK. He is the author of *Black Mixed-Race Men* and co-editor of *The Fire Now: Anti-Racism in Times of Explicit Racial Violence*. He has written widely on race and racism, with a particular focus on racism in education. His forthcoming work, with Dr. Laura Connelly, focuses on antiracist scholar-activism in UK universities and is being published as a book in 2021. Remi is active with a number of antiracist activist organizations and writes regularly for print and online media. He tweets at @RemiJS90.

Édouard Laniel-Tremblay is a MA student at McGill University, Montreal/ Tiohtià:ke, Canada. His research focuses on popular culture, most specifically Hip Hop, and how it fosters identities and belonging for youth in urban settings. His studies draw on critical race studies and translanguaging and multilingual theories.

Nemoy Lewis is Postdoctoral Research Fellow at the University of Toronto, Toronto, Canada. His PhD work explored the 2008 foreclosure crisis and its impact on racialized people in the United States. His current research explores the growing affordability and displacement problems impacting Black renters since the financialization of the rental markets in Toronto. Nemoy has co-authored an invited paper on race and urban politics in Ferguson, Missouri, in the leading geography journal *Environment and Planning D: Society and Space (2016)* and a book chapter for a special collection *Gentrification as a Global Strategy: Neil Smith and Beyond* (Routledge, 2018). He has also contributed a chapter to the edited volume *Neoliberal Chicago* (2017).

Angel M. Y. Lin is Professor and Tier 1 Canada Research Chair in Plurilingual and Intercultural Education at Simon Fraser University in Burnaby, British Columbia, Canada, where she teaches courses in the areas of classroom discourse analysis, sociocultural theories of language education, bilingual and plurilingual education, academic literacies, youth cultural and media studies, critical discourse analysis, and language-in-education policy and practice in postcolonial contexts. Her current research interests include: translanguaging and trans-semiotizing; languages, cultures, and literacies across the curriculum; content and language integrated learning (CLIL); languages and literacies in science and mathematics education; and social semiotics in plurilingual education contexts.

Bronwen Low is Associate Professor in the Department of Integrated Studies in Education at McGill University, Montreal, Canada. She has been leading and participating in research and program and curriculum development projects with a primary focus on how to best support socially marginalized young people. She studies the implications and challenges of popular youth culture, "urban arts," and Hip Hop culture for curriculum theory, literacy studies, pedagogy, and school transformation; translanguaging and the multilingual Montreal Hip Hop scene; life stories and human rights education. Her books include *Slam School: Learning through Conflict in the Hip-Hop and Spoken Word Classroom* (Stanford, 2011) and *Community-Based Media Pedagogies: Listening in the Commons* (Routledge, 2017), with Chloe Brushwood Rose and Paula Salvio.

Cris Mayo is Professor and Director of Interdisciplinary Studies in the College of Education and Social Services at the University of Vermont, Burlington, USA. In addition to being Editor-in-Chief of the *Oxford Encyclopedia of Gender and Sexuality in Education*, publications include *Gay Straight Alliances and Associations Among Youth in Schools* (Palgrave, 2017), *LGBTQ Youth and Education: Policies and Practices* (Teachers College Press, 2013), *Navigating Trans*+ and Complex Gender Identities* (with Jamison Green, Ashley Rhea Hoskin, and sj miller) (Bloomsbury, 2019), *Queer Pedagogies: Policy, Practice, Praxis* (co-edited with Nelson Rodriguez) (Springer, 2019), and *Queer, Trans, and Intersectional Theory in Educational Practice: Student, Teacher, and Community Experiences* (co-edited with Mollie Blackburn) (Routledge, 2020).

Carol Reid is a Sociologist of Education in the Centre for Educational Research at Western Sydney University, Penrith, New South Wales, Australia. Her research

xii Contributors

explores processes of globalization and mobilities on youth, ethnicity, and race and the intersections of these social identities with the changing nature of teachers' work. Current research projects include a longitudinal study of the settlement outcomes of Syrian and Iraqi conflict refugees in Australia with international partners from Canada, New Zealand, Sweden, the UK, Finland, and Germany; and knowledge translation to support early learning of refugee children and families in three states of Australia. Carol has published six books including *Global Teaching: Southern Perspectives on Teachers Working with Diversity* and *Compulsory Schooling in Australia*.

Sandra R. Schecter is Professor of Education and Applied Linguistics at York University, Toronto, Canada, where she teaches courses in language acquisition and pedagogy, urban education, and research methodology. An ethnolinguist, she conducts research on language and literacy education and learning, community-referenced pedagogy, language socialization, and language policy and planning in the context of multilingual societies. She has authored seven books, including *Language as Cultural Practice: Mexicanos en el Norte* (with Robert Bayley, Erlbaum), *Multilingual Education in Practice: Using Diversity as a Resource* (with Jim Cummins, Heinemann), and *Learning, Teaching and Community: Contributions of Situated and Participatory Approaches to Educational Innovation* (with Lucinda Pease-Alvarez, Routledge).

Sara Schroeter is Assistant Professor in the Faculty of Education at the University of Regina, Regina, Canada, where she teaches drama, arts, and antiracist education classes in French and English. For 20 years, she has worked as an informal educator with community and nongovernmental organizations and as a drama facilitator in schools across Canada. Her research focuses on the use of drama and applied theatre to examine differences of race, class, gender, and sexuality in multiracial schools. Her work exploring youth counternarratives, multimodal literacies, and the complexities of enacting social justice pedagogies in light of colonial relations and racialization has been published in *Race, Ethnicity and Education*, the *Journal of Adolescent and Adult Literacy*, the *Canadian Journal of Education*, and *Social Justice*.

Vidya Shah is Assistant Professor in the Faculty of Education at York University, Toronto, Canada, where she teaches in the Master of Leadership and Community Engagement program, as well as undergraduate and graduate level courses. In her research, as an educator, scholar, and activist committed to equity and racial justice, she explores antiracist and decolonizing approaches to leadership in schools, school districts, and communities and educational barriers to the success and well-being of Black, Indigenous, and other racialized students. She has worked in the Model Schools for Inner Cities Program in the Toronto District School Board (TDSB) and was a primary, junior, and intermediate classroom teacher in the TDSB.

Contributors **xiii**

Yang Song is Associate Professor in the Department of English Language and Literature at Fudan University, Shanghai, China. Her research interests include English as a medium of instruction in the context of internationalization of higher education in China, students' identity formation in relation to their lived experiences of interculturality, multilingual linguistic landscapes in urban China, translanguaging in digital communication, and digital literacies involved in the learning of online journalism. Her publications appear in journals such as *Journal of Multilingual and Multicultural Development, Multilingua, World Englishes, Asia Pacific Journal of Education*, and *English Today*. From 2021, she will serve as a Co-Editor of the Bloomsbury book series "Critical Perspectives of Language, Mobility and International Education."

Lisa K. Taylor is Professor in the School of Education, Bishop's University, Sherbrooke, Quebec, Canada. Her teaching, research, and film production explore the ethical, psychic, and sensorial dynamics of witnessing and historical memory of ongoing colonial violence and racial capitalism, mobilizing decolonial pedagogies in conversation with Indigenous ways of knowing and being in kinship and sacred ecologies. She is Co-Editor with Jasmin Zine of *Muslim Women, Transnational Feminism and the Ethics of Pedagogy* (2014) and with Lynne Davis, Jan Hare, Chris Hiller, and Lindsay Morcom of *Indigenization, Decolonization, and Reconciliation: Critical Considerations and Cross-Disciplinary Approaches in Post-Secondary Classrooms* (Canadian Journal of Native Education, 2018).

Rika Tsushima is a PhD candidate in the Department of Integrated Studies in Education at McGill University, Montreal, Canada, specializing in second language assessment. Her research interests include: formative assessment in ESL classrooms at the tertiary level; summative use of formative tests; short-term study abroad; heritage language development in interlingual families; and global citizenship and the internationalization of higher education. Rika worked as a manga artist and classroom teacher for many years in Japan.

Devanshi Unadkat is a PhD candidate at the Graduate School of Education at the University of California, Berkeley, USA. Her research interests focus on literacy, technology, and media in formal and informal educational spaces. Her dissertation seeks to explore pedagogical possibilities that emerge when using digital technologies and media in various local, national, and global contexts. Devanshi is also a faculty member in the Child Development Department at Santa Rosa Junior College. She is a former early childhood classroom teacher and special educator who has taught at schools in the United States and India.

Ninni Wahlström is Professor of Education at Linnaeus University, Växjö, Sweden. Her current research focuses on transnational and national policy discourses and their implications for national curriculum and classroom teaching from a

xiv Contributors

perspective of critical curriculum theory. Her research interests involve comparative policy studies in terms of exploring transnational educational policy in a time of conflicting trends of globalization and nationalism. A curriculum researcher within a cosmopolitanism framework, she has published "Cosmopolitanism as Communication? On Conditions for Educational Conversations in a Globalized Society" (*Scandinavian Journal of Educational Research,* 2016) and "Toward a Conceptual Framework for Understanding Cosmopolitanism on the Ground" (*Curriculum Inquiry,* 2014).

Daniel A. Yon's joint appointment to the Faculty of Education and Department of Anthropology at York University, Toronto, Canada, reflects his interest in the anthropology of education, and questions of youth, culture, and identity and the place of race and racism in subject formation and individual and collective identities. His *Elusive Culture* (SUNY, 2000) and related publications grapple with the importance of the contingency and fluidity of cultural assemblages for rethinking multicultural discourses and curriculum in urban education and the cosmopolis more generally. He has produced and directed three films, *One Hundred Men* (2008), *Sathima's Windsong* (2010), and *Mining Memory* (2018), that work with the sea to reflect on themes of memory and land/seascape, displacement, and belonging.

FOREWORD

Suresh Canagarajah

Sometimes it takes a pandemic to convey our shared human vulnerability and motivate us toward cosmopolitanism. I am reading the chapters in this book at a time when the onset of COVID-19 has suddenly made centuries of striving motivated by exceptionalism (whether human, national, or tribal) suddenly appear fragile. It is jarring to read about cosmopolitanism when we are all isolated by physical distancing and lockdown. Cityscapes across the globe, with skyscrapers and motorways flaunting our technological ingenuity, are eerily deserted and silent. Pundits and prophets provide different diagnoses for our predicament: that we violated nature and other species, harming the checks and balances in the ecosystem; that the walls we built around nation-states destroyed the trust among countries to collaborate in alerting others or fighting the infection; that social inequalities debilitated some and made them disproportionately vulnerable, and yet spread the virus without discrimination. It is possible to develop a narrative around the need for coexistence with the environment, other species, and different people as the moral of this tragedy.

While there are calls to rectify these imbalances and develop a social and environmental life based on dependency in the post-pandemic world, other signs suggest that our earlier strivings for exceptionalism also continue with renewed vigor. Nations are competing with one another to own the panacea that will define the next superpower. Racism informs our attempts to blame, exploit, or disadvantage others to appropriate limited resources. Funds for stimulus or compensation are shared unequally, profiting the privileged and making others destitute. Survival of the fittest prevails as institutions and groups that are bigger and stronger justify and exacerbate the precarity of others. Once again in a time of crisis, we witness the perennial swing between coexistence and exceptionalism, selflessness and self-interest, as nations and tribes look after their own. Perhaps the need for

xvi Foreword

self-protection and group identity is as strong as dependency and coexistence in human drives and motivations.

It is important, therefore, to address some of the criticisms pertaining to these competing drives that have been voiced against cosmopolitanism in recent times. Acknowledging the legitimate concerns of dissenting scholars might help develop a more complex orientation to social and educational practices. Critics have questioned: (a) the promotion of cosmopolitanism as a new and fashionable discourse in recent times; (b) its assumption of an idyllic homogeneity that is not desirable or even possible; and (c) its economic motivations, as neoliberal market forces use cosmopolitan discourses to expand profit-making purposes and worsen inequality.

Starting with the first concern, cosmopolitanism is not new and shouldn't appear exotic or start an academic bandwagon. It dates back at least to Diogenes in the 4th century BCE, who called himself *kosmopolitês* when people asked him which city-state he belonged to. Even earlier, Indigenous philosophies, including those of my Tamil-speaking community in South Asia, developed a worldview of nonduality, articulating the interdependence of all people, species, and nature. In our own time, postmodern geography and posthumanist physics have articulated that such entanglement of all natural and social actants is the stuff of life. The state of coexistence and interdependence, then, is ontological.

What is new is the role of cosmopolitanism as an epistemological lens at different points in history. In times and places where policies and institutions that favor exceptionalism are on the rise, it can be a source of challenge and resistance. Consider that since the advent of European modernity in the 17th century, discourses of exceptionalism have become more entrenched in social and educational institutions globally. Consider constructs such as methodological nationalism in our research and scholarship, which treat the nation as the unit of analysis for social life. On a smaller scale, the ethnic lens treats the community as the framework for analysis.

Along these lines, in education and language studies, we have treated labeled national languages as the grammatical unit of analysis or framework for competence. We have assumed the language ownership of native speakers and treated their norms as the target for everyone to aim at. These discourses are not just academic. They have become common sense and inform the ideologies of people everywhere. In this context, I consider cosmopolitanism a much-needed epistemological intervention in academic and educational circles, with the possibility of also pluralizing social discourses on how we look at life around us. Discourses are not mere words: they embody practices that help us interpret life, shape society, and transform conditions.

As a lens, cosmopolitanism doesn't obviate other concerns and discourses that are also important in our social life. Lenses are, after all, selective in what they represent. To move to the second criticism, then, the notions of global citizenship and a shared species identity don't exclude other types of community. There should be space for the struggles of Indigenous communities for their claims of sovereignty in their traditional lands, especially when they are motivated by their place-based identities. There is a need to affirm that minoritized groups, like Black lives, do matter.

What the cosmopolitan lens does, however, is expand our perspectives to diversify communities and identities. With the compression of time and space due to technological developments, digital media, and mobility, we form diverse affinity groups and communities of practice. These communities revolve like a kaleidoscope—constantly forming, reforming, and reconfiguring with diverse participants. They transcend skin, language, or place in their constitution and functions. Our community identities might thus be layered or overlapping in enriching ways. The cosmopolitan lens can even inform a healthier tribal or national identity. If we are able to acknowledge that all communities are not primordial but socially and historically constructed, then we will be able to enjoy our group identities without excluding other affiliations or questioning the legitimacy of other tribes and nations.

It is true that discourses such as cosmopolitanism, superdiversity, and translingualism are used by market forces to expand the reach of capital, as raised in the third criticism. For the profit motive, nothing is excluded. Even discourses of inclusivity and diversity are placed in the service of money-making. Consider how the promotion of English as a language that would facilitate intercultural communication creates new inequalities and divisions. Paradoxically, English becomes more powerful, "native speakers" enjoy social and economic capital, and other languages face extinction or marginalization. Or consider how chosen dispositions, typically from European traditions and values, are treated as facilitating cosmopolitan relations, inculcated among students, and rewarded in society and education. From these perspectives, cosmopolitanism may not be the great equalizer of all people, but spawn new configurations of inequality that transcend traditional national and class hierarchies.

Therefore, we have to be wary of celebrating cosmopolitanism as a disposition, idea, curriculum, or policy in product-oriented ways. If it is an essence or product, it can be wielded or waved around by anyone for their own ulterior motivations. I join some contributors in this book in treating *cosmopolitanization* as a form of practice. It is a way of framing the lens to intervene strategically in social relationships and expand forms of diversity, inclusivity, and equity. I draw an analogy from how postcolonial scholars struggled to correct notions of *hybridity* as an essence in favor of *hybridization* as a strategy. They conceived hybridization as always resisting attempts to stultify identities, communities, and texts into uniform and static essences.

In the same way, when schools introduce a nationalistic curriculum, we adopt a cosmopolitan lens to remind everyone of our dependencies beyond the local. When languages are taught as normative, we adopt a cosmopolitan lens to expand learning and communication to negotiate the diverse practices of others. When a few deny access to the many, we adopt a cosmopolitan lens to advocate that our

xviii Foreword

mutual dependency ensures a sharing of resources. When people ravage natural resources, we adopt a cosmopolitan lens to ask how sustainability can enhance human resilience. As a form of practice, then, cosmopolitanizing requires an ethical framework for its use. How we adopt this discourse will vary according to the ethics informing the people who use them. While some might use this discourse for profit-making purposes and self-interest, it is important for others to use this for diversity, inclusivity, and equity.

The excellent studies presented in this book reflect a shared concern for justice in education. The contributors examine how educational and pedagogical practices might expand possibilities for students through the adoption of a cosmopolitan lens. They explore the practices of teachers and students of different countries, ethnicities, and languages—and different configurations of these interactions in contact zones—to articulate the possibilities for a more diverse, inclusive, and equitable education. Rather than being dogmatic or imposing, they are honest in unveiling both the possibilities and the limitations—or promises and liabilities—of cosmopolitanizing. They use diverse lenses to attend to new areas of concern, allowing the cosmopolitan lens to collide with other lenses, such as intercultural communication, transnationalism, Critical Race Theory, intersectional analysis, decolonization, and gender studies, to reveal our blind spots. I wish every success for this book.

PREFACE

Critical Approaches Toward a Cosmopolitan Education

Sandra R. Schecter and Carl E. James, Editors

This edited volume brings together educational theorists, policy-makers, and critical practitioners engaged in (re-)conceptualizing teaching and learning in spaces that meet at the nexus of densely populated urban configurations, superdiverse racial and ethnic enclaves, and groups and individuals from around the globe who self-identify in multiple ways. It aims to provide informed portraits of the schooling experiences and civic participation issues related to individuals who inhabit cosmopolitan spaces, which through the meanings that participants derive from their instantiated experiences and intersectional identities signal globalizing processes that involve a range of mobilities (Appiah, 2006; De Costa & Jou, 2016; Dharwadker, 2001) and gesture to alternative ways of co-constructing the possibilities of intercultural relations (Beck, 2006; Delanty, 2009; Guardado, 2012). The essays in this volume explore the impact of these various sensibilities, or their notable absence, on students, educators, and educational institutions, as issues are presented that coincide with curricular concerns around civic engagement, transformative identities, and the influence of context-specific teaching and policy environments on global dynamics in education reform (Akiba, 2017).

Situating our Agenda

Over the past 15 years, with increased transnational migration, the notion of cosmopolitanism has found its way to the cutting edge of critical educational theory, as researchers take up issues associated with individuals or groups who display practices and values that gesture beyond the speech communities and ethnic enclaves with which others who may originate from similar backgrounds are associated or self-identify (Yon, 2000). These alternative ascriptions and appropriations suggest a re-visioning of the notion of diversity within a framework that

xx Preface

envisions cross-bordered communities (Blommaert & Rampton, 2011; García, 2009; Mignolo, 2010), where sites often localized within multilingual and multicultural societal contexts are considered to display a habitus of *superdiversity*, reflecting a host of characteristics associated with transnational, translinguistic, transcultural, and mixed-racial identities (Blommaert, 2013; Ibrahim, 2009; Vertovec, 2007, 2010). Idiosyncratic linguistic practices figure prominently within demographic clusters where diversification of languages, or plurilingualism, is available and where individuals may call upon multiple linguistic repertoires as they "cross borders either physically or virtually" (García, 2009, p. 54). Within a cosmopolitan frame of reference, these sociocultural appropriations reveal transformed social arrangements, where subjects rub up against monoglossic conceptions of norms that would regulate the ways in which they conduct their civic lives (Hull, Stornaiuolo, & Sahni, 2010), participate in social institutions (Thorne & Ivković, 2015), and situate their authentic selves (Love, 2017; Schecter, 2015).

Some researchers have emphasized fluidity and openness to new modes of being as part of their understanding of the cosmopolitan condition (Beck, 2006). Others voice an expectation that cosmopolitan spaces display significant interaction among individuals across ethnic and racial boundaries as well as indicators of openness to what may be qualified as a "global" perspective. One finds individuals within heterogeneous communities distancing themselves from the notion of a unified subjectivity, positioning the construct of "self" as alternately fluid, multiple, intersectional, and hybridized rather than as stable and autonomous (Kubota & Lin, 2009). In this alternative dimension, or "Third Space" (Bhabha, 1994; Kramsch, 1998), social actors, released from geographic boundedness, may appropriate, translate, or renegotiate different linguistic and cultural resources, as well as social identity repertoires, in the process of challenging dominant discourses of both their birth and host countries and privileging representation over a priori defining features (Hall, 1996).

It is therefore not surprising that the carwash attendant whom Suresh Canagarajah (2010) identifies in Brampton, Ontario, as Tamil-speaking on the basis of the first name projected on the chest pallet of his uniform and other signifying features, will have none of his linguistic assailant. The attendant is determined to elude the reductive identity that he assumes is entailed in the greeting in Tamil that Suresh foists upon him in relieved—at least initially—anticipation of meeting up with a fellow linguistic traveler in an unfamiliar locale. For Suresh has usurped his subject's autonomy by presuming to ascribe to him a linguistic and ethnic identity, and the attendant is quick to assert that this identity can only be instantiated through his own willing appropriation of it. Similarly, within such a participatory/relational perspective (Schecter, 2015), a subject's "community" cannot be established solely by means of survey data addressing questions related to demographic background, status at birth, and place of residence. Rather, individuals may achieve community by participating in activities and acquiring experiences associated with membership in certain groups (Ivanić, 2006), and by invoking discourse practices that are commensurate with these respective identities (Ortega, 2012; Pennycook, 2007). In this manner, identity may be understood as emergent from experience, and experience from participation and practice (Canagarajah, 2007; Norton, 1997).

Pennycook's (2007) preoccupation with "glocalization" (intersection of global and local), situated as part of a transcultural process that invites openness to diversity, is compatible with this participatory framework. In this process, individuals who may be considered members of cultural communities strive to transcend their sociocultural boundaries and reconfigure as hybridized cultural entities. Such goals often entail the command of a *lingua franca* that serves as a shared vehicle for subjects from diverse linguistic backgrounds and differing life experiences to negotiate norms associated with a common, locally referenced identity. Related discussions often reference the large-scale appropriation of English as a vehicle of transnational communication in emergent cosmopolitan contexts (e.g., House, 2003; Pennycook, 2010) as well as the "glocalization" of Mandarin in societies such as Hong Kong and Singapore in response to the need for individuals to develop multilingual competencies compatible with an evolving transcendent cultural identity that recognizes the dominance of China and the growth of Mandarin as an international language (Tong & Cheung, 2011).

Note that a cosmopolitan sensibility may be evidenced in socioeconomically differentiated strata (Vertovec, 2007)—from privileged transnational professionals to the less privileged individuals placed or dis-placed in the transnational space of the city, where one observes various uncertainties about citizenship, as people in lower-income brackets migrate from impoverished areas to urban hubs seeking work. However, at this time, work is often difficult to obtain and *re*tain; and this predicament negatively impacts bids for citizenship, rendering cities—such as Mumbai, for example—scenes of urban inequality, indeed, the urban as constitutive of inequality. These indignities are most visible with regard to housing, which in metropolitan areas is often scarce and oversubscribed (Chaudhuri, 2001). This precarity, in turn, gives rise to unauthorized, or illegal, practices that may violate local ordinances and promote the use of substandard goods and services. Amidst these shifting relationships between cash/capital and sanctioned/unsanctioned practices there continues an ongoing struggle for space, as inhabitants experience increased stress over their real and imagined uses and definitions of private and public spaces and increased uncertainty about the distinctions between primary, secondary, and tertiary networks, impacting, among others, but pointedly, the well-being of LGBT or other gender nonconforming individuals whose sexualities fall outside traditional norms (Love, 2017; Mayo, 2017).

Here we have arrived at the nub of our concerns with cosmopolitanism as it relates to equitable educational access. First, both editors acknowledge the enormous debt we owe to community-referenced approaches (cf. Ladson-Billings, 1995; Moll, Amanti, Neff, & Gonzalez, 1992) that encourage educators, especially those working in multiethnic, multilingual school environments, to create pedagogic

xxii Preface

content activities that center the intellectual, experiential, and cultural resources that inform and shape students' experiences (James, 2012; Pease-Alvarez & Schecter, 2005; Schecter & Cummins, 2003; Schecter & Otoide, 2010; Schecter & Sherri, 2009). A community-engaged approach calls on educators to acknowledge the worldviews and lived experiences, including privileges and hardships, that inform their "interactions with students [and] contributes to the exchange relationship that is teaching" (James, 2012, p. 128). However, for individuals and groups who inhabit overlapping, intermingled communities, issues related to educational provision cannot wholly be addressed through "culturally responsive pedagogy."

What, then, are the implications of the paradigm shift (Blommaert & Rampton, 2011) we have described for professional educators, educational researchers, and policy-makers? What can such a perspective teach us about the connections that students may form as they search for commonalities with other youth across linguistic, cultural, and territorial boundaries? What is the learning potential suggested in these contemporary social changes that may open the door to the negotiation of transnational and/or global connections, or dialogical cosmopolitanism (Canagarajah, 2013; De Costa & Jou, 2016), through new contexts in and through which people orient their interactions? What materiality (artifacts and objects, including technologically enabled resources) is produced in the service of cosmopolitan users (Aronin & Ó Laoire, 2012), and how can these artifacts be pressed into service for purposes of teaching and learning? These key questions, which have received insufficient attention from educational researchers (but see Guardado, 2012; Hansen, 2011; Hull & Stornaiuolo, 2014), are addressed by authors of the chapters in this volume.

Before continuing, we would observe how awkwardly the construct of race fits within the preceding theoretical refurbishing of social and individual identity. This awkward positioning was dramatically highlighted in the spring and summer of 2020, as this book was in preparation. First, the disproportionate impact of the COVID-19 pandemic on people with Black and Brown bodies in the United States and elsewhere has laid bare racial inequities in a way that is impossible to ignore. Second, the rise of an international mass movement has focused attention on the need, not yet fully addressed, to acknowledge structurally that some lives do indeed matter.

Whereas through the lenses of language and culture, hegemonies associated with the dynamics between certain groups and individuals may be critically contested through the assertion of individual agency, race presents a more formidable challenge for "the cosmopolitan treatment of difference" (Beck, 2006, p. 48). Indeed, in narratives of how race as an identifier is taken up for racialized people, we find confirmations of Gouldner's (1957) not-yet-outdated hypothesis that people "impute to a person certain characteristics" that are "interpreted according to a set of culturally prescribed categories." If, in the cases of language, culture, and religion, identity has been viewed increasingly "as an activity, not a thing" (Appiah, 2018), when it comes to race, identity is, arguably, still significantly dependent on the way that physical traits are perceived by others (James, 2008).

Such is the perspective of Critical Race Theory (CRT), which maintains the significance of race and the "primacy of racism" (Gillborn, 2006, 2015) within contemporary society. In asserting the intercentricity of race and racism within educational processes (Ladson-Billings & Tate, 1995; Yosso, 2005), scholars within CRT and Antiracism Education, using methodologies that privilege the experiential knowledge of racially diverse and marginalized students (e.g., DeCuir & Dixson, 2004; L. Taylor, 2000, 2008), underscore the manner in which particular racial classifications elicit responses that render certain individuals' public lives difficult (Caballero, Haynes, & Tikly, 2007; Matsuda, Lawrence, Delgado, & Crenshaw, 1993; Wardle, 2000).

These researchers bear witness to how racial labels, including Black/white binaries used to describe "mixed-race" people, instantiate identities (Mahtani, 2002; L. Taylor, 2017) that continue to be used as commodities to serve the needs of those who would maintain their hegemonic grip on the diminishing resources available on an overused planet (Lewis-McCoy, 2014; D. Taylor, 2014). "Educational theory and practice are used to subordinate certain racial and ethnic groups" (Solorzano & Yosso, 2001) while perpetuating systems of power and privilege (James, 2010). Within institutional structures such as schooling, mixed-race individuals become trapped within essentialized racial and ethnic categories, alternatively linked to stereotypes associated with one or another monoracial polarity (Mahtani, 2002) or deficits ascribed to identity confusion where racially mixed people are assumed to be trapped between worlds (Caballero et al., 2007). And while some multiracial individuals emphasize the possibilities embedded in ambiguous identities for breaking free of domination and control, it would be imprudent to read these multiracial bodies as signals of a postracial society (Mahtani, Kwan-Lafond, & Taylor, 2014). Even acknowledging the intersectionality of race with other axes of oppression such as gender, class, and disability, within the critical cosmopolitan perspective presented here, we want to recognize the particular impact of race and advocate for resistance to any form of racial oppression.

We would all (contributors to this volume) agree that the issue of how difference is acknowledged and treated poses a serious challenge for a critical approach to schooling in contemporary society. Additionally, we view race, language, ethnicity, gender, class, and sexual orientation as indispensable components of the dialogue on cosmopolitanisms and education because in modern societies schools constitute primary sites of tensions in which different principles and orientations toward the recognition of differences related to these components are played out. In bringing these various elements together here for discussion and analysis, we proclaim our faith in the learning that can accrue from the sharing of these diverse narratives, each concerned with their representation of alterity, or "the truth of others" (Beck, 2006, p. 50).

xxiv Preface

The Volume

Critical Approaches Toward a Cosmopolitan Education is intended as both a heuristic and support text for university scholars, students, policy-makers, and teacher-researchers who are conducting research related to the teaching and learning practices of individuals and groups who inhabit diverse landscapes characterized by complex social formations and high levels of exchange of knowledge among cultures. Through this volume of essays, grouped under four thematic umbrellas— "Critical Cosmopolitanism in Contemporary Education," "Schooling and the Development of Cosmopolitan Identities," "Forging Cosmopolitan Pedagogies," and "Challenges for Cosmopolitan Education"—we have created a resource in which teachers, policy-makers, and educational researchers can see refracted aspects of their own students' and colleagues' issues and aspirations. Our goal here is to better equip educators and education policy-makers to plan instructional approaches and strategies and devise pedagogic resources that serve the needs and career aspirations of an expanding cohort of diverse, multifaceted learners.

Glynda Hull, Devanshi Unadkat, and Jessica Adams begin Part 1, "Critical Cosmopolitanism in Contemporary Education," with a reimagined account of the evolution of the cosmopolitan idea. They then examine a virtual reality story-telling exchange between young women in India and youth in California within the complementary frames of cosmopolitanism and translanguaging (Chapter 1). In Chapter 2, Carol Reid compares the insights of cosmopolitan theory with those of multiculturalism, postcolonialism, and Critical Race Theory in relation to two research projects in Australia, one involving students in a diverse area of Sydney and the other involving globally mobile teachers. In Chapter 3, Cris Mayo looks at the intersection of hybridity and queerness, exploring the possibilities of queer transnational hybridities but also recognizing the dangers of inappropriate appropriation. Focusing on Toronto in Chapter 4, Daniel A. Yon suggests that a cosmopolitan lens provides a more flexible and dynamic view of the city than the fixed categories of cultural pluralism and sees cosmopolitan ideas as tools for thinking about curriculum that transcend the familiar categories of nation, ethnicity, religion, gender, and race.

Part 2, "Schooling and the Development of Cosmopolitan Identities," opens with Karis Campion and Remi Joseph-Salisbury's exploration of the schooling experiences of Black mixed-race students in the UK. Detailing the racism these students undergo from other students, from teachers, and in the curriculum, they find that these experiences largely parallel those of monoracial Black students, with some elements that are particular to mixed-race students (Chapter 5). Édouard Laniel-Tremblay and Bronwen Low focus on a youth Hip Hop recording studio in the highly diverse Côte-des-Neiges neighborhood of Montreal, examining its place in the neighborhood community, the city, and the Global Hip Hop Nation. Their case study (Chapter 6) illustrates how racialized nonmainstream youth can carve out a place for themselves where they feel

Preface **xxv**

comfortable within a diverse society. In Chapter 7, Vidya Shah views the collection of identity-based data (IBD) in Ontario through the lens of Critical Race Theory and Critical Whiteness Studies. She finds that while IBD processes can contribute to reducing educational inequities for racialized and marginalized students, this will happen only if students, families, and communities whose realities illuminate the data in meaningful and authentic ways are included at every stage of these processes.

To begin Part 3, "Forging Cosmopolitan Pedagogies," Lisa K. Taylor analyzes the varied responses of high school students in a superdiverse urban classroom to a course unit that addresses the Rwandan genocide against the Tutsis by focusing on survivor testimony (Chapter 8). In Chapter 9, María Rebeca Gutiérrez Estrada and Sandra R. Schecter offer a case study of "cosmopolitanism from below" in a school in an Indigenous community in the Mexican state of Sonora. Here teacher agency is a major factor in the successful implementation of an initiative to teach three languages: the Indigenous language (Mayo), the societal language (Spanish), and the global language (English). In Chapter 10, Sara Schroeter discovers that drama-in-education (DiE) can be valuable, but also has limitations, in illuminating the meanings and significance of race. The context is a social studies unit on first contact between European colonizers and First Nations in a superdiverse francophone secondary school in British Columbia. Martin Guardado and Rika Tsushima examine a short-term study abroad program for Japanese students at a Western university. They find that the program's effectiveness in achieving its goal of fostering global competence is hindered by inadequate preparation, unrealistic expectations, and the commodification of higher education (Chapter 11). Jennifer Jenson's study (Chapter 12) confirms the importance of bringing students in inner-city schools into the global technocultures of digital game making and playing, while also stressing the need to address "digital divides" along lines of economic class, immigrant status, and gender.

Part 4 explores a variety of "Challenges for Cosmopolitan Education." Yang Song and Angel Lin's ethnographic study of international and Chinese students at a university in Shanghai (Chapter 13) finds that institutional discourses limited the extent to which students were able to develop a critical cosmopolitan mindset. In Chapter 14, Ninni Wahlström tests the ideas of John Dewey, Kwame Anthony Appiah, and others through the story of a disagreement between a graduating high school student in Sweden and her mother, who had immigrated decades earlier from Iraq, over whether to display the Swedish or the Iraqi flag on the student's graduation cap. Nemoy Lewis demonstrates the extent to which economic realities impede the goal of mobility and equity across fluid transnational spaces and boundaries in his study (Chapter 15) of the impact of home foreclosures on the educational and social lives of Black children in Jacksonville, Florida. Suzanne de Castell rounds out the volume (Chapter 16) with a researcher's story of frustration in trying to manage the "partnership" between a university-based research team and a regional school board in a digital literacies project in a high-needs school

xxvi Preface

district. She finds that the educational bureaucracy undermined the intent of the original project by repeatedly shifting their interpretation of equitable access and concludes that efforts to overcome educational inequality need to begin by addressing poverty.

We intend that the chapters contained in this volume will support the development of information networks and pedagogic resources that are responsive to the needs and aspirations associated with individuals inhabiting interconnected landscapes within an evolving global economy. We envision that the perspectives we have assembled will better equip teachers and administrators to plan instructional approaches and devise curricular resources that serve the needs and life goals of a diverse cohort of learners, through enhanced sensitivity to the convergence of context-specific pedagogic and policy environments on global dynamics in education reform. But mostly, we hope that this information will serve in the spirit of developing student thinkers who are open to engaging in intersubjective dialogue with one another as they explore alternative viewpoints on how different forms of inequality, perceptions of identity, and movements of people interrelate in and across different contexts.

References

Akiba, M. (2017). Editor's introduction: Understanding cross-national differences in globalized teacher reforms. *Educational Researcher, 46*(4), 153–168.

Appiah, K. A. (2006). *Cosmopolitanism: Ethics in a world of strangers*. New York: Norton.

Appiah, K. A. (2018). *The lies that bind: Rethinking identity*. New York: Liveright.

Aronin, L., & Ó Laoire, M. (2012). The material culture of multilingualism: Moving beyond the linguistic landscape. *International Journal of Multilingualism, 1*(11), 221–253.

Beck, U. (2006). *The cosmopolitan vision*. Cambridge, UK: Polity Press.

Bhabha, H. (1994). *The location of culture*. New York: Routledge.

Blommaert, J. (2013). *Ethnography, superdiversity and linguistic landscapes: Chronicles of complexity*. Clevedon, UK: Multilingual Matters.

Blommaert, J., & Rampton, B. (2011). Language and superdiversity. *Diversities, 13*(2), 175–195.

Caballero, C., Haynes, J., & Tikly, L. (2007). Researching mixed race in education: Perceptions, policies and practices. *Race, Ethnicity and Education, 10*(3), 345–362.

Canagarajah, S. (2007). Lingua franca English, multilingual communities, and language acquisition. *Modern Language Journal, 91*(s1), 923–939. doi: 10.1111/j.1540-4781.2007. 00678.x

Canagarajah, S. (2010). Achieving community. In D. Nunan & J. Choi (Eds.), *Language and culture: Reflective narratives and the emergence of identity* (pp. 41–49). New York: Routledge.

Canagarajah, S. (2013). *Translingual practice: Global Englishes and cosmopolitan relations*. London, UK: Routledge.

Chaudhuri, U. (2001). Theater and cosmopolitanism: New stories, old stages. In V. Dharwadker (Ed.), *Cosmopolitan geographies: New locations in literature and culture* (pp. 171–196). New York: Routledge.

De Costa, P., & Jou, Y. (2016). Unpacking the ideology of cosmopolitanism in language education: Insights from Bakhtin and systemic functional linguistics. *Critical Inquiry in Language Studies, 13*(2), 73–97.

DeCuir, J., & Dixson, A. (2004). "So when it comes out, they aren't that surprised that it is there": Using Critical Race Theory as a tool of analysis of race and racism in education. *Educational Researcher, 33*(5), 26–31.

Delanty, G. (2009). *The cosmopolitan imagination: The renewal of critical social theory* (1st ed.). Cambridge, UK: Cambridge University Press.

Dharwadker, V. (2001). *Cosmopolitan geographies: New locations in literature and culture.* New York: Routledge.

García, O. (2009). Education, multilingualism and translanguaging in the 21st century. In T. Skutnabb-Kangas, R. Phillipson, A. K. Mohanty, & M. Panda (Eds.), *Social justice through multilingual education* (pp. 140–158). Bristol, UK: Multilingual Matters.

Gillborn, D. (2006). Critical Race Theory and education: Racism and anti-racism in educational theory and praxis. *Discourse: Studies in the Cultural Politics of Education, 27*(1), 11–32.

Gillborn, D. (2015). Intersectionality, Critical Race Theory, and the primacy of racism: Race, class, gender, and disability in education. *Qualitative Inquiry, 21*(3), 277–287.

Gouldner, A. (1957). Cosmopolitans and locals: Toward an analysis of latent social roles. *Adminisrative Science Quarterly, 2*(3), 281–306.

Guardado, M. (2012). Toward a critical multilingualism in Canadian classrooms: Making local inroads into a cosmopolitan identity. *TESL Canada Journal, 30*, 151–165.

Hall, S. (1996). Introduction: Who needs identity? In S. Hall & P. du Gay (Eds.), *Questions of cultural identity* (pp. 1–17). London, UK: SAGE.

Hansen, D. T. (2011). *The teacher and the world: A study of cosmopolitanism as education.* New York: Routledge.

House, J. (2003). English as a lingua franca: A threat to multilingualism? *Journal of Sociolinguistics, 7*, 556–578.

Hull, G., & Stornaiuolo, A. (2014). Cosmopolitan literacies, social networks, and "proper distance": Striving to understand in a global world. *Curriculum Inquiry, 44*(1), 15–44.

Hull, G., Stornaiuolo, A., & Sahni, U. (2010). Cultural citizenship and cosmopolitan practice: Global youth communicate online. *English Education, 42*(4), 331–367.

Ibrahim, A. (2009). Operating under erasure: Race/language/identity. In R. Kubota & A. M. Y. Lin (Eds.), *Race, culture and identities in second language education: Exploring critically engaged practice* (pp. 176–194). New York: Routledge.

Ivanić, R. (2006). Language, learning and identification. In R. Kiely, P. Rea-Dickens, H. Woodfield, & G. Clibbon (Eds.), *Language, culture and identity in applied linguistics* (pp. 7–30). London, UK: Equinox.

James, C. E. (2008). "Armed and dangerous"/"known to police": Racializing suspects. In C. Brooks & B. Schissel (Eds.), *Marginality and condemnation: An introduction to critical criminology* (pp. 378–403). Halifax, NS: Fernwood.

James, C. E. (2010). *Seeing ourselves: Exploring race, ethnicity, and culture* (4th ed.). Toronto, ON: Thompson Educational Publishing.

James, C. E. (2012). *Life at the intersection: Community, class and schooling.* Black Point, NS: Fernwood.

Kramsch, C. (1998). *Language and culture.* Oxford, UK and New York: Oxford University Press.

Kubota, R., & Lin, A. M. Y. (Eds.). (2009). *Race, culture, and identities in second language education: Exploring critically engaged practice.* New York: Routledge.

xxviii Preface

Ladson-Billings, G. (1995). Toward a theory of culturally relevant pedagogy. *American Educational Research Journal, 32,* 465–491.

Ladson-Billings, G., & Tate, W. (1995). Toward a Critical Race Theory of education. *Teachers College Record, 97*(1), 47–68.

Lewis-McCoy, R. (2014). *Inequity in the promised land: Race, resources, and suburban schooling.* Stanford, CA: Stanford University Press.

Love, B. (2017). A ratchet lens: Black queer youth, agency, hip hop, and the Black ratchet imagination. *Educational Researcher, 46*(9), 539–547.

Mahtani, M. (2002). Interrogating the hyphen-nation: Canadian multicultural policy and "mixed race" identities. *Social Identities, 8*(1), 67–90.

Mahtani, M., Kwan-Lafond, D., & Taylor, L. (2014). Exporting multiculturalism? Canadian mixed race identities and multicultural policy. In R. King-O'Riain, S. Small, M. Song, P. Spickard, & M. Mahtani (Eds.), *Global mixed race* (pp. 238–262). New York: New York University Press.

Matsuda, M., Lawrence, C., Delgado, R., & Crenshaw, K. W. (1993). *Words that wound: Critical Race Theory, assaultive speech, and the First Amendment.* New York: Routledge.

Mayo, C. (2017). Queer and trans youth, relational subjectivity, and uncertain possibilities: Challenging research in complicated contexts. *Educational Researcher, 46*(9), 530–538.

Mignolo, W. (2010). Cosmopolitanism and the de-colonial option. *Studies in Philosophy and Education, 29*(2), 117–127. doi: 10.1007/s11217-009-9163-1

Moll, L. C., Amanti, C., Neff, D., & Gonzalez, N. (1992). Funds of knowledge for teaching: Using a qualitative approach to connect homes and classrooms. *Theory Into Practice, 31*(2), 132–141.

Norton, B. (1997). Language and identity: Special issue. *TESOL Quarterly, 31,* 431–450.

Ortega, L. (2012, March). *Ways forward for a bilingual turn in SLA.* Paper presented at American Association for Applied Linguistics annual meeting, Boston, MA.

Pease-Alvarez, L., & Schecter, S. R. (Eds.). (2005). *Learning, teaching, and community: Contributions of situated and participatory approaches to educational innovation.* New York: Routledge.

Pennycook, A. (2007). *Global Englishes and transcultural flows.* London, UK: Routledge.

Pennycook, A. (2010). English and globalization. In J. Maybin & J. Swann (Eds.), *The Routledge companion to English language studies* (pp. 113–121). Abingdon, UK: Routledge.

Schecter, S. R. (2015). Language, culture and identity. In F. Sharifian (Ed.), *The Routledge handbook of language and culture* (pp. 196–208). New York: Routledge.

Schecter, S. R., & Cummins, J. (Eds.). (2003). *Multilingual education in practice: Using diversity as a resource.* Portsmouth, NH: Heinemann.

Schecter, S. R., & Otoide, L. (2010). Through parents' eyes: An activist visual literacy project. *International Journal for Cross-Disciplinary Subjects in Education, 1*(1), 43–52.

Schecter, S. R., & Sherri, D. (2009). "Value added?": Teachers' investments in and orientations toward parent involvement in education. *Urban Education, 44*(1), 59–87.

Solorzano, D. G., & Yosso, T. J. (2001). From racial stereotyping and deficit discourse toward a critical race theory in teacher education. *Multicultural Education, 9*(1), 2–8.

Taylor, D. (2014). *Toxic communities: Environmental racism, industrial pollution, and residential mobility.* New York: New York University Press.

Taylor, L. (2000). Black, white, beige, other? Memories of growing up different. In C. E. James (Ed.), *Experiencing difference* (pp. 59–70). Halifax, NS: Fernwood.

Taylor, L. (2008). Looking north: Exploring multiracial experiences in Canadian context. In K. A. Renn & P. Shang (Eds.), *Biracial and multiracial college students: Theory, research, and best practices in student affairs* (pp. 83–91). San Francisco, CA: Jossey-Bass.

Taylor, L. (2017). Race, color and family: Exploring possibilities of school engagement. In C. Monroe (Ed.), *Race and colorism in education* (pp. 181–192). New York: Routledge.

Thorne, S. L., & Ivković, D. (2015). Multilingual eurovision meets plurilingual YouTube: Linguascaping discursive ontologies. In D. Koike & C. Blyth (Eds.), *Dialogue in multilingual, multimodal, and multicompetent communities* (pp. 167–192). Amsterdam, The Netherlands: John Benjamins.

Tong, H., & Cheung, L. (2011). Cultural identity and language: A proposed framework for cultural globalisation and glocalisation. *Journal of Multilingual and Multicultural Development, 32*(1), 55–69.

Vertovec, S. (2007). Super-diversity and its implications. *Ethnic and Racial Studies, 30*(6), 1024–1054.

Vertovec, S. (2010). Towards post-multiculturalism? Changing communities, contexts and conditions of diversity. *International Social Science Journal, 61*(199), 83–95.

Wardle, F. (2000). Children of mixed race—no longer invisible. *Educational Leadership, 57*(4), 68–71.

Yon, D. (2000). *Elusive culture: Schooling, race and identity in global times.* Albany, NY: State University of New York Press.

Yosso, T. (2005). Whose culture has capital? A Critical Race Theory discussion of community cultural wealth. *Race, Ethnicity and Education, 8*(1), 69–91.

ACKNOWLEDGMENTS

This project has grown out of a professional and personal collaboration that has developed over a period of more than 20 years. We wish to acknowledge the role of York University in providing a context in which two individuals from different disciplinary traditions, ethno-racial backgrounds, and social and cultural experiences could come together to think deeply about what is entailed in working toward educational equity in an increasingly diverse society structured by inequitable power relations. We also would acknowledge how gratifying this collaboration has been.

We thank the contributors to this volume for entrusting their work to us and for their goodwill in responding to our multiple editorial suggestions. We hope that *Critical Approaches Toward a Cosmopolitan Education* justifies their faith in our capacity to produce a coherent and timely collection that will prove useful to students, teachers, parents, scholars, and activists in these unsettled times.

To our friends and colleagues—especially those in the Faculty of Education—we extend our gratitude for their continued support and counsel. We are also grateful to the students from whom we have learned, and whose interest in our work has contributed not only to the formation of this project but also to its completion.

We are indebted to Matthew Friberg, Jessica Cooke, Nitesh Singh, and the team at Routledge for their enthusiasm for the project from the outset, and their care and attention in the production of this volume. Special thanks go to Bob Chodos for his assistance in editing the manuscript. His attention to detail and capacity to enhance clarity and consistency while respecting authors' intended meanings have helped ensure a polished final product. Finally, as always, we thank our respective families for their inspiration and understanding, and for knowing the importance of this work, and work in general, to us.

PART 1
Critical Cosmopolitanism in Contemporary Education

1

SUBALTERN VOICES, DIGITAL TOOLS, AND SOCIAL IMAGINARIES

Glynda A. Hull, Devanshi Unadkat,
and Jessica Adams-Grigorieff

Can the Subaltern Speak?

Three decades ago, the postcolonial theorist Gayatri Spivak (1988) asked a question about the dispossessed of the world that rocked the academy and reverberates still: *Can the subaltern speak?*[1] This striking question raised to consciousness the great divide between Western academics and people elsewhere, particularly "migrants in the metropolis," most often women, rendered invisible and voiceless. Spivak's short answer was "no," the subaltern cannot speak, because the gap between the subaltern and the rest is too wide, and the West cannot hear, being deaf to its own complicity in the world's problems and the injurious effects of "projecting oneself or one's world onto the Other" (Spivak, 2002, p. 6). Now, decades past Spivak's essay, the West continues to exert outsized political, economic, and epistemological influence in an increasingly globalized world where inequalities still abound and gaps still separate people and indeed grow wider. Global legacies of colonialism continue to mute conversations and understandings across differences and stymie the social futures of a majority of the world's population.

In this chapter, we describe a small project, one in a decade-long line of research (e.g., Hull, Jury, & Sahni, 2014; Hull & Scott, 2013; Hull & Stornaiuolo, 2014) that bears on speaking and hearing across geopolitical and ideological divides, even when the distance is great and the barriers high. We argue for the importance and necessity of embracing the educational and ethical imperative of ensuring that subaltern voices are heard, especially in an age when public discourse is characterized by rising incivility and compassion appears in short supply. Drawing on a reinvented account of cosmopolitanism, and appropriating the communicative power and human reach of stories fashioned for a digital age, we provide a somewhat different answer to Spivak's question: strongly affirming her concerns

DOI: 10.4324/9780429327780-1

4 Glynda A. Hull et al.

for rights and capacities to speak and be heard, we want to demonstrate that educational opportunities can be designed and deployed to connect across distance and difference, to cultivate semiotic acts of imagination, empathy, and trust, and to mitigate communicative and representational inequalities.

At the heart of our work is a desire to reframe the notion of *worlding the world*, which to Spivak meant the domination of the rest by the West, through the unreflective projection of a particular view of reality onto other people and their own differently figured worlds. Instead of this imperialist take on relationships and meaning-making, we appropriate the notion of worlding the world to describe the social practices of youthful subalterns who are engaged in representing their own lived experiences—in sharing their own takes on their own worlds—in relation to understanding the lived realities of others. These acts of perspective-offering and perspective-taking we see as quintessential critical cosmopolitan capacities for a global era—an era in which, as Appadurai (1996) explained, flows of people, texts, media, and capital continually challenge the boundaries of nation-states, providing the raw material for imagining ourselves in relation to the local, national, and global. Especially important are the linguistic and semiotic aspects of these imaginings, seen in the ways that youth world their worlds by marshaling symbolic resources that cross and blend languages, modes, and media. In so doing, they engage in translingual and transmedia practices (Canagarajah, 2013) that challenge the hegemony of bounded notions of national language (cf. Poza, 2017) as well as logocentric notions of texts (Lizárraga, Hull, & Scott, 2015).

To be sure, optimism about the permeability of national borders, and the ease and alacrity of the mobility and interconnectedness implied, have been tempered (cf. Appadurai, 2006). Rising populism and authoritarianism the world over, not to mention pandemics and other disasters on a global scale, seem to have greatly discouraged and diminished capacities to look outward and welcome inward with generosity and compassion, while logocentric conceptions of language, literacy, and learning persist, especially in school contexts (Canagarajah, 2011; Lizárraga et al., 2015; May, 2014). Yet, we would argue, the imagination remains—human beings' generative capacity to see, take the measure of, creatively engage with, and influence different worlds, a capacity potentially amplified through digitally mediated contact. Appadurai (1996) notes, "the work of the imagination … is neither purely emancipatory nor entirely disciplined but is a space of contestation in which individuals and groups seek to annex the global into their own practices of the modern" (p. 4). We agree, and thus we ask, how do youthful subalterns world the world, deploying their imaginations to assemble, curate, remix, and circulate multimodal meanings that are impactful, that are heard (cf. New London Group, 1996; O'Connor & Penuel, 2017)?

Who is Cosmopolitan?

For a long time, for centuries in fact, the prominent philosophical starting place for theorizing proper interaction with others' worlds has been the ancient idea of cosmopolitanism, with its emphasis on global as well as local allegiances, affiliations, and relationships. But it has been the last quarter-century that has witnessed the biggest uptake across most disciplines of cosmopolitan ideas, in tandem with the rapid transformation of space and time, and of consciousness and sociality, associated with processes of globalization. As social, political, economic, and cultural worlds compress and collide, the movement of media, capital, ideas, and people brings distant places and different realities within perceptual reach, making the challenge and need to understand one another through and across our difference all the more crucial. Philosopher Kwame Appiah (2006), who wrote in the aftermath of the 9/11 destruction of New York City's World Trade Center, argued that now our responsibilities as citizens must perforce go beyond "kith and kind" (p. xv). He optimistically offered, as a response to things that divide, dialogue and conversation "across the boundaries of race, religion, tribe, and nationality"—conversations not for the purpose of agreeing but for "getting to know each other in ways that mean we can share the world precisely without agreement" (p. 272; cf. Canagarajah, 2013). Writing at the same time as Appiah, and in response to the same cultural, economic, and geopolitical ruptures, communications scholar Roger Silverstone (2006) likewise theorized cosmopolitan identities, but specifically in relation to the omnipresence of media. Since the globe appears to us now largely through liquid crystal displays—the ubiquitous screens of computers, phones, and televisions—Silverstone recognized the importance of treating media as a symbolic *moral space*—largely fractious and cacophonous, but offering, as well the possibility, indeed the obligation, for the cosmopolitan individual "to recognize not just the stranger as other, but the other in oneself. In political terms," Silverstone (2006) wrote, cosmopolitanism "demands justice and liberty, In social terms, hospitality. And in media terms … an obligation to listen" (p. 14).

Appiah's and Silverstone's ideas about cosmopolitanism were pivotal for our own early projects on multimodal literacy and global citizenship (Hull & Stornaiuolo, 2014; Hull, Stornaiuolo, & Sahni, 2010); they helped us explore interactions among global youth, differently positioned geographically, economically, ideologically, and linguistically, and how they might be productively fostered, especially when mediated through digital narratives shared across digital networks. But even as Appiah, Silverstone, and others were appropriating cosmopolitanism to speak to the social and political conditions of the early 21st century, those conditions themselves continued to shift, erupt, and realign, as did scholarship on belonging, identity, language, and citizenship. Literatures began to speak in less static and bounded ways regarding ethnicity, embracing, for example, the notion of "superdiversity" in an effort to signal social dynamics and configurations that are increasingly complex, riven, and unequal (Creese & Blackledge, 2018; Vertovec, 2007, 2019). Simultaneously, scholars of coloniality offered analyses of global capitalism, laying bare both the subjugation of subaltern groups and their shared resistance across geographic, linguistic, and racial lines (e.g., Mignolo, 2011). This work has amplified and challenged older conceptions of who is considered

6 Glynda A. Hull et al.

cosmopolitan and what it means to be a global citizen, and it has enlivened and sharpened debates about what constitutes a meaningful education for subaltern youth (e.g., de los Rios & Seltzer, 2017; Harshman, 2018).

Robbins and Horta (2017) reframed cosmopolitanism as plural, as evoking "any one of many possible modes of life, thought, and sensibility that are produced when commitments and loyalties are multiple and overlapping, no one of them necessarily trumping the others" (p. 3). The emphasis here, then, is not only on multiple and plural selves but also on the complexity of the identities (Blommaert, 2012) that develop through the variegated roles and relationships emerging in superdiverse contexts, animated as well by shifts in consciousness that are occurring everywhere. Steger (2017), for example, referred to a developing *global imaginary*, the palpable sense that we all inhabit a broader world, with its differences and its samenesses, in addition to the time-honored imaginaries of neighborhood, town, and nation. Social imaginaries for subaltern youth can extend beyond the cultural and the geographic to include and embrace the political, resulting in their *ideological becoming*, to borrow Bakhtin's (1986) phrasing. We are especially interested in how young people, interconnected via a visual popular culture circulated through new media technologies, develop senses of self in critical relation to the local, the national, and the global.

The new plural cosmopolitanism does not aim to index, as in olden days, the experiences of elites, perpetuating the longstanding exclusivity of the privileged traveler who is free from personal and local obligations. It repels as well pernicious anti-Semitic associations (cf. Gelbin & Gilman, 2017) and Eurocentric stances of who is considered human, being ever mindful of the mechanism of colonialism through which processes of globalization emerged. The new plural cosmopolitanism embraces those who are not cosmopolitan by choice but have "had cosmopolitanism thrust upon them by traumatic histories of dislocation and dispossession" (Robbins & Horta, 2017, p. 3). To wit, Silviano Santiago's (2017) conceptualization of the *cosmopolitanism of the poor*. These repositioned conceptions gesture toward a recognition of the historical and continued violence of fashioning conceptions of humanity on adopted European ideals and a single universalism and move us closer to a decolonial or postcolonial cosmopolitanism—one fashioned from below or cultivated on border zones of difference and constructed by those who necessarily live with multiple commitments and loyalties. In such cases, an identity as a cosmopolitan does not so much bestow a privilege as call out an injustice or a challenge. Thus, subaltern youth are cosmopolitans too. What might we learn from them about their relationship to the global?

In the new cosmopolitanisms, while acknowledging, as Appiah (2006) does, the importance of dialogue, there is also the recognition that when people from different cultures and positionings, representing asymmetrical power relations, bump up against one another, there must be space for disagreement, misunderstanding, and discord, captured by Mary Louise Pratt (1991) in the term *contact zones*. A pedagogy appropriate for contact zones provides means and opportunities for subaltern youth, not to be heard in the patriarchal sense of the more powerful bestowing the gift of attention, but to dialogue as coequals engaged in worlding. A rethought cosmopolitanism thus benefits from an examination of linguistic and semiotic practices, rights, and responsibilities. In that regard, it benefits from a perspective on language and pedagogy that assumes and encourages subaltern interlocutors, particularly emergent bilingual and multilingual youth, to bring to bear, as they exercise their right to speak, any and all linguistic and semiotic resources that they have on hand: languages, to be sure, but other symbol systems and their sociotechnical systems as well.

Worlding through Translanguaging

The last quarter-century has witnessed a vast increase in people's mobility, through forced migration as well as voluntary movement and relocation, and through the capacity to connect via digital networks across distance and diasporas. Worldwide migration, along with other social, political, and economic ruptures, has disturbed sedentary academic paradigms too, such as how we conceptualize language. "Rather than working with homogeneity, stability and boundedness as the starting assumptions," Blommaert and Rampton (2011) explain, "mobility, mixing, political dynamics and historical embedding are now central concerns in the study of languages, language groups and communication" (p. 4).

For a long time in language education, particularly bilingual education in the United States, the major principle for imagining instruction has been the separation of languages, the cordoning off a learner's home language(s) from a school's target language, on the assumption that such an approach aids in learning English, the language of instruction, as quickly as possible. The tables have been turned of late as researchers of language, taking into account superdiverse contexts, have challenged the boundedness and naturalization of languages like English and Spanish and Hindi. In their everyday lives, people who are multilingual draw on their diverse meaning-making resources from multiple named languages. According to a translingual perspective, these resources constitute a single, complex, dynamic repertoire that people use to communicate, understand, and negotiate meanings with others. Calling out the performative quality of translanguaging, Canagarajah (2011, p. 5) labels it "creative improvisation" and "interactive achievement," which recalls Bakhtin's (1986) emphasis in his theorization of language and human activity on the considerable importance of *addressivity*, or "the quality of turning to someone" (p. 99).

Supporting translanguaging practices promotes learning and communication in classrooms, as abundant scholarship shows (e.g., García, Johnson, & Seltzer, 2017; García & Kleyn, 2016; García & Wei, 2014). But translanguaging scholars go further still, highlighting the ways in which translanguaging is a means of creating, performing, and asserting transgressive identities. Subaltern youth, such as Latinx populations in the United States who figure prominently in the translanguaging

8 Glynda A. Hull et al.

literature, are more often than not othered, viewed as linguistically different and deficient, as lacking, as lesser—injurious beliefs born of imperialist legacies of racism and classism. In such sociohistorical contexts, where people must cope every day with the aftermath of legacies of colonialism, translanguaging becomes a great deal more than a pedagogical orientation that helpfully builds on everyday linguistic and communicative practices. It also anchors, if you will, youthful subalterns' worlding of the world, serving as "a tool for .... questioning and subverting hegemonic linguistic norms" (Poza, 2017, p. 117) and for embracing the legitimacy of self (Anzaldúa, 1987). "If you really want to hurt me," Gloria Anzaldúa wrote, "talk badly about my language. ... As long as I have to accommodate the English speakers rather than having them accommodate me, my tongue will be illegitimate" (p. 59). Translanguaging becomes a primary means, García and Leiva (2014) claim, of "liberating the voices of language minoritized students" (p. 200).

Most work on translanguaging to date has focused on language to the exclusion of other semiotic systems, and oral forms more often than written ones, which is an understandable choice given their prominence in scholarship and teaching. But calls have increased to acknowledge how bilingual learners draw from their entire semiotic repertoires, including digital technologies and sociotechnical systems, and how teachers can exploit these broader toolsets in classrooms (Vogel, Ascenzi-Moreno, & García, 2018). Canagarajah (2013) in fact suggests "translingual practice" as an umbrella term, covering the range of communicative modes and signaling the field's epistemological shift from a monolingual bias, while Lin (2015) offers the concept of "trans-semiotics" to highlight the role in human communication of the visual, the oral, and the embodied (cf. García & Wei, 2014). The recent transliteracies framework in literacy studies makes a similar move to rethink existing paradigms that situate and bound their object of study, literacy, and it instead views literacy through a lens of movement and stasis across "social and material relationships."

The transliteracies framework retheorizes literacy as "critical and creative social semiotic practices arising within complex ideological networks and characterized by the movement of people and things" (Stornaiuolo, Smith, & Phillips, 2017, p. 72). We appreciate these shifts in naming, conceptualizing, and studying translanguaging and especially support the inclusion of multimodal language and literacy practices in this mix. Such practices have been part and parcel of humans' communicative repertoires for a long time (Canagarajah, 2013; Finnegan, 2014), but their use has intensified and transformed of late through the mediation of digital tools and connectivities, wherever these resources are available. For most youth, including subaltern youth, digital practices—the thread running through their social lives—take center stage.

A translanguaging perspective, especially one broadened to include a panoply of semiotic resources, can helpfully go hand in glove with a new cosmopolitan perspective. Indeed, we suggest that these frameworks on communication, citizenship, belonging, and identity need each other, each filling the other's lack.

Cosmopolitanism, though it is posited on dialogue, empathy, and connectivity, largely eschews any direct engagement with the nitty-gritty of everyday communication and contact through which shifts in relationships can occur. Translanguaging, while embracing an analysis of micromoments of conversation and interconnection in global contact zones, largely privileges the positive outcomes for emergent bilinguals of claiming a voice and authorizing an identity as agentive and creative. This is not to diminish the dominant agendas of either framework but to suggest the theoretical amplification that could occur by a closer linkage of literatures that have generally remained apart.

As we think of an alliance of cosmopolitan perspectives with translanguaging in a global world, we are especially interested in the affordances of visual narratives, or digital stories that combine language, image, and video. In earlier work, we have documented the promise and challenge of linking youth around the world through the exchange of digital stories (Hull & Stornaiuolo, 2014; Hull et al., 2010), but this work, though it connected youth from different linguistic, geographic, and cultural backgrounds, largely relied on English as a lingua franca (for an exception, see Lizárraga et al., 2015), or the visual to communicate outside a sole reliance on language, rather than a combination of multiple linguistic and semiotic resources in the spirit of translingualism.

In our current work, we are additionally interested in exploring the power of new forms of visual narrative, in particular 360-degree stories or forms of virtual reality (VR) storytelling. It is claimed that these give authors greatly expanded tools for embodied expression, and viewers a sense of physical presence or immersion (Riggs, 2019). Interestingly, VR has also been heralded as an *empathy machine*, as having the capacity to embody the viewer in someone else's experience. Journalists have attempted as much, with award-winning VR stories that feature, for example, a 12-year-old refugee in Jordan (Milk, Arora, & Pousman, 2015), Los Angeles citizens at a food bank (de la Peña, 2012), and Iraqi forces at war (Pirog & Solomon, 2016). It is important to note that, in all of the current literature on and practice of 360-degree storytelling and other forms of VR of which we are aware, the authors are always technical experts, privileged creators who depict others' worlds and circulate to broader audiences the representations they have constructed. The worlding that happens here, to our mind, is the old variety that we want to avoid, whereby someone from the West discursively names a subaltern's reality. We are interested instead in positioning youthful subalterns to world their own worlds, especially through the use of the most cutting-edge tools, like 360-degree storytelling.

Of course, simple exposure to diversity does not provide a clear path to a critical cosmopolitan orientation, even within more immersive environments such as VR storytelling. Rather, the author who leverages the immersive affordances of VR, as well as the reader who engages in embodied viewing, must be primed to engage with their own positionality and listen and hear. What is required, along with a willing and intentional engagement, is a critical orientation toward self and

10 Glynda A. Hull et al.

interlocutor, as befits one's sociohistorical circumstances. Both of these preconditions can be cultivated in classrooms, as we will illustrate next.

Cosmopolitan Translanguaging

The youthful subalterns whose voices and VR stories we share in this chapter are young women from Prerna Girls School[2] in Lucknow, India. Prerna's curriculum is rooted in a critical feminist pedagogy that seeks to promote gender justice (Sahni, 2017). Founded to empower girls and young women who are frequently forced into child marriage, Prerna serves the most vulnerable of India's young people: girls who must negotiate a patriarchal society, many of them also hailing from India's historically disadvantaged castes, and all of them coming from low-income communities. Prerna is renowned for its transformative curriculum that cultivates an ethic of care, respect, and responsiveness. Through a critical feminist curriculum, Prerna's youthful subalterns discover the power to speak, the authority of having a voice, and the confidence and self-worth to know their stories are worth telling and sharing in their school, community, and society. Moreover, the identities they develop include a collective sense that they as women have been disempowered and disenfranchised, that this is wrong, and that they can join together, in the context of their supportive school network, to right this wrong. So positioned, it was a straightforward, if complex and potentially fraught, next step to extend opportunities to the young women of Prerna to tell their stories to the world and, using a range of semiotic resources, to reach and understand across distance and difference.

Our work over the last ten years, in collaboration with Prerna Girls School in India as well as schools in North America and other parts of the world, explored how to support young people in developing transnational connections, identities, and literacies that position them to be critical participants in and shapers of their worlds (Hull & Scott, 2013; Hull & Stornaiuolo, 2014; Hull et al., 2010; Lizárraga et al., 2015; Scott, Hull, & DiZio, 2018). We wanted to open up digital spaces for subaltern youth to be able to world their worlds by speaking across differences, dialoguing, using digital tools (like social networks), and employing a palette of symbol systems: not only named written languages but also spoken words, images, and movies, including new narrative forms for storytelling. Working with local educators and researchers, we adapted our curriculum at each site, paying attention to local contextualization, meanings, and goals. In particular, we wanted to guard against acts of educational colonization, of merely imposing Western ideologies, values, practices, and tools. We guarded against such an outcome by building relationships intended to endure, through our collaboration with Prerna leaders, teachers, researchers, and students, with visits sustained over a period of years. Working with teachers at Prerna, rather than offering a decontextualized project, we situated our joint work within the school's larger empowerment curriculum.

At the same time, we offered access to new media technologies that are global in reach and that we expected would be appropriated in service of local purposes.

Our work on digital storytelling spans three different projects that subsequently built from one another in the tradition of design-based research (Barab & Squire, 2004) and in the spirit of reflexive ethnography (Burawoy, 2011). In 2008, we began a social media exchange among youth in the United States, South Africa, Norway, and India, who created and shared digital stories online by means of a private social networking platform. The intent of this project was to expand young people's communicative repertoires (e.g., Hull & Stornaiuolo, 2014) and to foster "cosmopolitan" literacy practices of reading, writing, and remix (cf. Silverstone, 2006), connecting youth across time and space so that they could converse with distant audiences of peers. We *revisited* (Burawoy, 2011; Sefton-Green & Roswell, 2014) this earlier work in 2012, examining the impact of the introduction of digital storytelling at Prerna School and the circulation of those media for civic-minded purposes (Hull, Jury, & Sahni, 2014). In 2017, the project reported here, we revisited Prerna again, this time to learn with young women about the affordances of 360-degree storytelling.

Through each iteration of the project, there were instances in which the Prerna girls' stories and those of other youth in the network transcended language, geography, and culture to connect and understand (Hull & Stornaiuolo, 2014). We traced the often striking, potent influence of individual digital stories on network youth, following an artifact from country to country, program to program, and author to viewers, documenting how it was received and reappropriated (Hull et al., 2010). In our revisits with the young women, we explored how digital practices functioned within the feminist, critical practices that were central to Prerna School's pedagogy. In conjunction with other forms of advocacy and the critical pedagogy characteristic of Prerna, we found that digital media practice served as a "civic fulcrum," providing young women with a public means to call attention to their points of view and their right to dignity, education, equality, and lives that extend beyond the home into the public sphere.

In the project, we connected a group of high school students in the Bay Area of northern California with high school students at Prerna. Students in the Bay Area watched digital stories made by students in earlier iterations of the project, including young authors from Prerna, and created two digital stories that centered on showcasing their own everyday lives through depictions of their school[3] and the surrounding neighborhood. Neither film employed a specific script or narrative, allowing viewers an *open* (Eco, 1979; Hull, Stornaiuolo, & Sterponi, 2013) interpretation of the scenes depicted. Students at Prerna viewed and discussed these stories and created narratives about themselves with a global audience in mind, particularly their peers in the Bay Area, whose stories they had just viewed and discussed. Responding to the Bay Area students' depictions of their school and community, the Prerna students created a film featuring their school's critical

12 Glynda A. Hull et al.

feminist curriculum, its focus on gender equality, and its insistence that daughters are equal to sons. They also incorporated the voices of family members and others from their community who similarly resisted patriarchal discourses and promoted gender equality.

The subaltern women at Prerna navigated multiple identities as they simultaneously responded to others' worlds and demonstrated their own understandings and aspirations. Each day they navigated being daughters, students, friends, leaders, learners, aspiring professionals, and bilingual speakers, among other things—no one identity "necessarily trumping the others" (Robbins & Horta, 2017, p. 3). Moreover, the interplay of their worlds, as they instantiated what we recognized as orientations consistent with tenets of new cosmopolitanisms, appeared in several ways. Predisposed to challenge inequality on the basis of their personal experiences with the critically turned curriculum at Prerna School, the students recognized how practices of engaging in reflections and actions upon their worlds empowered them to confront the tensions of straddling different roles laden with conflicting ideologies. They navigated identities that, on the one hand, demanded conformity to patriarchy and, on the other, inspired them to discover their agency. In engaging with their global peers, the students desired to be heard and to "teach," as they put it. At the same time, they showed a willingness to learn from others reflexively—local members of their community as well as distal peers.

We were especially interested in how the Prerna girls worlded the world through translingual semiotic practice. To be sure, their linguistic and semiotic choices were situated within complex social, political, and economic influences on language use in multilingual India. For example, in India, there is interest in learning English for purposes of social mobility, despite its colonial origins, but the turn to English can also represent a means of resistance to Hindi, since Hindi is viewed by some as a marginalizing language.[4] The roles that English plays in India, then, have contours that are shaped by particular historical and political contexts, which, in turn, influence the nature of translingual practice.

Translanguaging was apparent in the semiotic practices of Prerna students. Not only did the young women have a range of digital and nondigital resources with which to communicate their stories, but they also drew upon their rich multilingual and multimodal repertoires to communicate specific meanings. They all spoke Hindi fluently and English with varying levels of confidence, and some knew a third language. Additionally, through their schooling at Prerna, they each had experience in engaging with multiple genres of communicative practice, including drama, dance, storytelling, and music. For their visual narrative, the students incorporated images alongside 360 films, depicting their school, families, and teachers and the younger generation of Prerna girls. They also recorded and embedded a song that advocated for valuing girls and boys as equals: *nahin kisee par bojh betiyan*, or daughters are not burdens on anyone, a message conveyed directly through song midway through their video. Their narration was primarily in Hindi, the first language of most of the students in the group, but in another

Subaltern Voices **13**

translingual gesture, they eventually planned to include English subtitles for more global viewers.

When creating their 360 films, the students at Prerna leveraged emergent insights about the affordances of VR. As they grappled with and reflected on the semiotic potential of immersive digital storytelling, they remarked that "stories are fun to hear and watch only when you live in them." Whereas viewers of traditional digital stories, they suggested, might "forget it [the story] in the matter of a few blinks," VR "makes a human being feel involved, compels them to give their views," allowing authors to create "involvement [so] that people learn things, people teach things."[5] Such emergent insights—to use VR to "involve" viewers and make them feel that they are "living" in stories to support the purposes of teaching and learning—guided their composition and translanguaging practices.

The students drew from semiotic repertoires developed from years of digital storytelling (though at times traditional digital storytelling practices conflicted with the immersive modality[6]). In their story's opening scene, for example, the students emphasized the communal practices of their school by depicting a series of school activities that filled the entirety of the 360 landscape (see Figure 1.1).

(a)

(b)

FIGURE 1.1 Prerna 360 scenes.

14 Glynda A. Hull et al.

This sequence of visuals, borrowed from their deep history with digital storytelling, included a square-framed image of the school, a voiceover narrative in Hindi, and quick cuts between immersive video. Their opening sequence emphasized a key message: Prerna fostered a supportive school community. This sense of community was felt by several Bay Area students who later experienced the VR video; one student reflected that the Prerna video reminded her of her own school: "close and friendly and just fun."

Depending on the goals and purposes of each scene in their film, the Prerna girls made choices to use a combination of several semiotic resources: English and Hindi languages, traditional square-frame images, 360-video footage, and different narrative strategies to create a powerful experience for the viewer. We considered such displays of meaning-making practice instances of cosmopolitan translanguaging, characterized by reflection, experimentation, and multisemiotic resourcefulness, geared toward communicating with others. Additionally, the exchange between subalterns in India and students in the Bay Area suggests that the critically turned young women at Prerna felt empowered to speak to their global peers, knowing that they could draw on their repertoires to persuasively communicate the work they engage in on a daily basis to challenge oppressive structures in their community, and expecting to inspire distally located peers to similarly reflect and act upon their own worlds as well.

Prerna's ideology and pedagogy played a central role in our students' cosmopolitan sensibilities, specifically in the ways that they spoke and listened to others. For example, guided by their critical feminist curricula, the young women displayed cosmopolitan sensibilities through reflecting on LGBT equality highlighted by the Bay Area students' videos and used this reflection to identify unexamined injustices in their own society and their capacity to subvert this form of oppression. The subaltern women admired the symbols of equality depicted by rainbow flags and sidewalks in the Bay Area students' "bike ride" video, captured as a student rode through a community historically known for its LGBTQIA activism. Inspired by the iconic displays on streets and windows of business and residences, the Prerna students considered the experiences of members of the hijra community in India, which includes transgender and intersex people. The girls wished that Indian society would adopt a humanizing view that treated hijras as not so "different from themselves" and as equal members of society. The acts of hearing displayed by these subaltern women was a capacity nourished by Prerna's critical feminist pedagogy.

We were met with difficulties as well as successes in engaging Bay Area students' capacity to hear across differences. In terms of challenges, we noticed that when we shared the Prerna story with our Bay Area students, they at times called attention to stereotypical or unfamiliar imagery rather than the Prerna students' message, such as remarking on their accents, cows mooing in the background of key scenes, and the bare feet of family members in interviews. Yet there were many noteworthy instances of translingual hearing, which were supported by scaffolded reflections on meaning and cultural similarities and differences; viewing the videos across media, including iPads, computers, and immersive head-mounted displays; and using the videos to inspire conversations about their own communities and selves. Discussions about the "impact" of the Prerna video led some students to take a keener interest in the Prerna students' fight for women's equality and inspired Bay Area students' creation of stories about mental illness and sexuality.

We were not surprised by such difficulties at hearing the subaltern, since past iterations of our project revealed similar challenges. In our revisit in 2011, for example, we learned that the digital stories, which gave material form to feminist values and elevated their importance—and, by extension, women's right to have their say—via local and global circulation, turned out to be difficult for some parents, local community members, and distal peers to hear, but even more difficult to ignore. One Prerna student recalled her parents' shifting reactions to the publicity surrounding a video she had created on the topic of how sons are favored over daughters and how daughters can resist[7]:

> Aunty, initially, they got angry. For example, my mother wanted to get me married in grade 6 as they were afraid of all the problems they had seen. But I refused. Because of this, at that time, they became very angry. However, when they saw this movie, they realized and accepted that, "Yes, it was our fault." Now, I do all the household chores, like going to the bank, getting gas [traditionally male roles], getting admission [to school] for my brother. Now you know what my mom says, Aunty? She now says that "the day you get you married, I do not know what is going to happen to this house, and who will watch this house." Now she tells my brother to learn from me, and tells me to teach him so that he will be able to take over.[8]
>
> *(Hull, Jury, & Sahni, 2014, p. 99)*

Like speaking, hearing the other and engaging in dialogue are practices that are developed and molded over time. Our work shows both that subaltern youth can in fact speak, not only because of the ambitious spirit and communicative expertise displayed by Prerna students but also because, as educators, we can develop the capacity for our students to hear.

Worlding the World: The Subaltern Speaks

Since Spivak's powerful rendering of the silencing of subaltern subjects, much remains the same in the world, or has worsened: material inequalities, forced movement and migration due to armed conflict and economic necessity, and, of course, environmental and health disasters on a global scale. But one thing that has changed and carries with it Janus-faced potential is radical connectivity, instantiated through the internet and digital media and providing the capacity for the creation and

16 Glynda A. Hull et al.

circulation of many points of view and representations of the world. Such capacities, critically practiced, are important above all for subaltern youth and the educators who aspire to position them to claim their places to listen intensely and speak persuasively, worlding the world. We hope the theorizations we have reviewed and the project we have described illustrate one compelling example of this aspiration.

Throughout the chapter, we have appropriated the term *worlding the world* for subaltern youth's acts of meaning-making. We have done so, first, to turn on its head the belief that the West worlds the rest, and second, to emphasize what is at stake for subaltern youth as they articulate and thereby assert their rights as local and global citizens with particular concrete visions for their own social futures, their own social imaginaries. In an information-saturated world, with multiple symbolic modes at the ready, it is more important than ever to equip subaltern youth to wield their imaginations, critical capacities, and technical know-how to launch their own meanings and interpretations and to take part with confidence and aplomb in negotiating those meanings and interpretations with others. We hope that our use of *worlding the world* will prove a generative term for this crucial activity.

To theorize the capacities that for us are at the heart of worlding the world, we juxtaposed the plural cosmopolitans literature with scholarship on translanguaging, believing that they comprise two sides of the same coin. The former positioned us to consider and learn from youthful subalterns as cosmopolitans—still a rare perspective in the wide-ranging literatures on cosmopolitanism—while the latter helped us think more precisely about the nature and character of communication between "others." Our case study of Prerna girls' creation of a 360-degree story, a nascent version of virtual reality storytelling, showed the power of a translingual perspective when interlocutors' communicative repertoires include not only languages but also technologies. As we would expect from a translanguaging perspective, we saw evidence of how these youth, in making their 360-degree story, drew on a single, complex, dynamic repertoire consisting of named languages (Hindi, English) but also sociotechnical systems and tools such as videography and photographs. Interestingly, their efforts to draw on previous digital practices from their extant digital stories bumped up against the current constraints of 360 storytelling, which does not easily incorporate other visual modalities. This mismatch resulted in a stretched and distorted depiction in the girls' 360-degree movie, but what it illustrated for us was not a failure of execution but rather the generative capacity these composers brought to bear as *emergent translinguals* (Lizárraga et al., 2015) who drew broadly from their semiotic repertoire, in addition to their linguistic resources.

We chose in this project to introduce youthful subalterns to 360-degree storytelling, a kind of virtual reality narrative, and to introduce them to it not as consumers of commercially available examples, such as Google Expeditions, but as makers and composers of their own immersive stories of their own lives, setting forth their own social imaginaries. This is a crucial distinction. VR technologies

Subaltern Voices **17**

are still new, expensive, and cumbersome, and researchers are only beginning to study the potential of such immersive environments and to explore the affordances of embodied communication. Certainly, claims about VR being an empathy machine are overstated, and much work remains to be done to understand and develop the interesting possibilities of new forms of narrative where authors more radically relinquish control of their storylines. However, when inventive technologies for communication, creativity, thinking, and learning come to the fore, our position is that we owe youthful subalterns and their teachers access to these new sociotechnical systems, along with the opportunity, in the Vygotskian sense of internalizing powerful psychological tools, to deploy them and shape their uses (Freedman, Hull, Higgs, & Booten, 2016).

According to a postcolonial perspective, subalterns can speak only when their interlocutors can hear. Perhaps the greatest challenge in our work to date has been enabling hearing, as Spivak would predict. Sometimes the difficulty can be accounted for by the width of a cultural or linguistic divide; sometimes it has to do with an apparent ideological incapacity to engage with the other; and sometimes it is just a matter of youthful inattention that will resolve over time. As we have thought about fostering dialogue between youth in the Global North and South, between the subaltern and the rest, it is worth recalling Silverstone's (2006) words about the centrality of a moral vision for media in the enterprise:

> Insofar as they [the media] provide the symbolic connection and disconnection that we have to the other, the other who is the distant other, distant geographically, historically, sociologically, then the media are becoming the crucial environments in which a morality appropriate to the increasingly interrelated but still horrendously divided and conflictual world might be found, and indeed expected.
>
> *(p. 8)*

We witnessed in Prerna School acts of imagination, creativity, and trust that enabled quintessential subalterns to speak and to hear. Now our task is to harness the power of a similarly moral pedagogical vision for digital media, driven by cosmopolitan aims and translingual means, that can empower other youth around the globe both to speak and to hear.

Notes

1 We gratefully acknowledge the sponsorship of the Berkeley Education Global Initiative. We thank Urvashi Sahni, founder of Study Hall Educational Foundation and Prerna Girls School, whose collaboration made our project possible. We thank John Scott, who designed the activities for our 360-degree storytelling project and led our fieldwork. We are grateful for the commentary and assistance provided by our colleagues: Sam Finn, Danièle Fogel, Matt Hall, Emily Hellmich, Adrienne Herd, José Lizárraga, Catherine Park, Jeeva Roche, Amy Stornaiuolo, Gever Tulley, and the Write4Change

18 Glynda A. Hull et al.

research team. Finally, we thank the teachers at Prerna School and the youth who shared their stories with us and taught us much about communication and understanding in a global world. Previous versions of this chapter were presented at meetings of the Comparative International Education Society, the American Educational Research Association, and the Literacy Research Association.

2 Prerna Girls School is part of the Study Hall Educational Foundation (SHEF). Additional information about Prerna can be found on the SHEF website: www.studyhallfoundation.org/about_shef.php

3 One group of Bay Area students created a story that depicted their unique school with its explicit focus on tinkering and making as a means to learning. This 360-degree video takes a viewer on a tour of the school from the perspective of someone walking around the space. Another group of Bay Area students created a film depicting the neighborhood surrounding their school from the perspective of a person on a bike. A 180-degree camera affixed to the helmet that a student wore as he cycled through the streets gave viewers the sense of *being* the bike rider. This video captured vibrant rainbows on streets, sidewalks, and houses in the neighborhood, known for its rich history and vocal support of LGBTQIA rights.

4 India is a historically multilingual country where the politics of language use is influenced by colonial and religious histories of oppression. Although English was introduced in India through the indirect rule of colonial policy, its status as a lingua franca stems from its position not only as a worldwide means toward economic and social mobility (Bhattacharya, 2017; Singal, 2017) but also as a resistance to the imposition of Hindi, which many parts of the Indian population view as a form of religious and ethnic hegemony since its practice is rooted predominantly in the northern regions of the country and is associated with religious Hinduism (Khan & Khan, 2018; Singal, 2017). Thus, some Indians view English as a language of their own and perceive Hindi as a marginalizing language (Khan & Khan, 2018; Singal, 2017).

5 Interviews were conducted in English and Hindi, whichever language the girls chose in the moment, by a member of our research team who was fluent in both English and Hindi. Much of their video was narrated in Hindi; in presenting the video to students in the United States, we provided an English translation.

6 For example, while the students wished to integrate still images into their story, these images appear distorted because, as they were rendered, they stretched across the 360-degree landscape. The traditional semiotic resources of digital storytelling—video, image, etc.—thus did not seamlessly mesh with immersive modal aesthetics.

7 This story, entitled "Change," depicted a series of scenes in which the young female protagonist of the video roped her brother into helping her with the household chores she was assigned so that both siblings could share household responsibility and have time to spend on schoolwork

8 This interview was conducted in Hindi and translated into English.

References

Anzaldúa, G. (1987). *Borderlands/La frontera: The new mestiza.* San Francisco, CA: Aunt Lute Books.

Appadurai, A. (1996). *Modernity at large: Cultural dimensions of globalization.* Minneapolis, MN: University of Minnesota Press.

Appadurai, A. (2006). *Fear of small numbers.* Durham, NC: Duke University Press.

Appiah, K. A. (2006). *Cosmopolitanism: Ethics in a world of strangers.* New York: W. W. Norton.

Bakhtin, M. M. (1986). *Speech genres and other late essays* (V. W. McGee, Trans.). Austin, TX: University of Texas Press.

Barab, S., & Squire, K. (2004). Design-based research: Putting a stake in the ground. *Journal of the Learning Sciences, 13*(1), 1–14.

Bhattacharya, U. (2017). Colonization and English ideologies in India: A language policy perspective. *Language Policy, 16*, 1–21.

Blommaert, J. (2012). *Complexity, accent and conviviality: Concluding comments.* Tilburg Papers in Culture Studies, 26. Tilburg, The Netherlands: Tilburg University.

Blommaert, J., & Rampton, B. (2011). Language and superdiversity. *Diversities, 13*(2), 1–21.

Burawoy, M. (2011). Revisits: An outline of a theory of reflexive ethnography. *American Sociological Review, 68*(5), 645–679.

Canagarajah, S. (2011). Translanguaging in the classroom: Emerging issues for research and pedagogy. *Applied Linguistics Review, 2*(1), 1–27.

Canagarajah, S. (2013). *Translingual practice: Global Englishes and cosmopolitan relations.* London, UK: Routledge.

Creese, A., & Blackledge, A. (Eds.). (2018). *The Routledge handbook of language and superdiversity.* New York: Routledge.

de la Peña, N. (Writer, Producer, & Director). (2012). *Hunger in Los Angeles* [Video]. United States: Immersive Journalism. Retrieved from https://docubase.mit.edu/project/hunger-in-los-angeles/

de los Rios, C. V., & Seltzer, K. (2017). Translanguaging, coloniality, and English classrooms: An exploration of two bicoastal urban classrooms. *Research in the Teaching of English, 52*(1), 55–76.

Eco, U. (1979). *The role of the reader: Explorations in the semiotics of text.* Bloomington, IN: Indiana University Press.

Finnegan, R. (2014). *Communicating: The multiple modes of human interconnection* (2nd ed.). London, UK: Routledge.

Freedman, S., Hull, G., Higgs, J., & Booten, K. (2016). Teaching writing in a digital and global age: Toward access, learning, and development for all. In D. H. Gitomer & C. A. Bell (Eds.), *Handbook of research on teaching* (5th ed., pp. 1389–1450). Washington, DC: American Educational Research Association.

García, O., Johnson, S. I., & Seltzer, K. (2017). *The translanguaging classroom: Leveraging student bilingualism for learning* (1st ed.). Philadelphia, PA: Caslon.

García, O., & Kleyn, T. (Eds.). (2016). *Translanguaging with multilingual students: Learning from classroom moments.* New York: Routledge.

García, O., & Leiva, C. (2014). Theorizing and enacting translanguaging for social justice. In A. Blackledge & A. Creese (Eds.), *Heteroglossia as practice and pedagogy* (pp. 199–216). Dordrecht, The Netherlands: Springer.

Garcia, O., & Wei, L. (2014). *Translanguaging: Language, bilingualism, and education.* New York: Palgrave Macmillan.

Gelbin, C. S., & Gilman, S. L. (2017). *Cosmopolitanisms and the Jews.* Ann Arbor, MI: University of Michigan Press.

Harshman, J. (2018). Developing global citizenship through critical media literacy in the social studies. *Journal of Social Studies Research, 42*, 107–117.

Hull, G. A., Jury, M., & Sahni, U. (2014). "Son enough": Developing girls' agency through feminist media practice. In B. Kirschner & E. Middaugh (Eds.), *#Youthaction: Becoming political in the digital age* (pp. 81–105). Charlotte, NC: Information Age Publishing.

20 Glynda A. Hull et al.

Hull, G. A., & Scott, J. (2013). Curating and creating online: Identity, authorship, and viewing in a digital age. In K. Drotner & K. C. Schrøder (Eds.), *Museum communication and social media: The connected museum* (pp. 130–152). New York: Routledge.

Hull, G. A., & Stornaiuolo, A. (2014). Cosmopolitan literacies, social networks, and "proper distance": Striving to understand in a global world. *Curriculum Inquiry, 44*(1), 15–44.

Hull, G. A., Stornaiuolo, A., & Sahni, U. (2010). Cultural citizenship and cosmopolitan practice: Global youth communicate online. *English Education, 42*(4), 331–367.

Hull, G. A., Stornaiuolo, A., & Sterponi, L. (2013). Imagined readers and hospitable texts: Global youth connect online. In D. Alvermann, N. Unrau, & R. Ruddell (Eds.), *Theoretical models and processes of reading* (6th ed., pp. 1208–1240). Newark, DE: International Reading Association.

Khan, I., & Khan, A. A. (2018). Historical overview of language politics in post-colonial India. *Global Journal of Human Social Sciences: G Linguistics & Education, 18*(4), 21–24.

Lin, A. (2015). Egalitarian bi/multilingualism and trans-semiotizing in a global world. In W. E. Wright, S. Boun, & O. García (Eds.), *The handbook of bilingual and multilingual education* (1st ed., pp. 19–37). Hoboken, NJ: John Wiley & Sons.

Lizárraga, J. R., Hull, G., & Scott, J. M. (2015). Translingual practices in a social media age: Lessons learned from youth's transnational communication online. In D. Mole, E. Sato, T. Boals, & C. Hedgspeth (Eds.), *Multilingual learners and academic literacies: Sociocultural contexts of literacy development in adolescents* (pp. 105–132). New York: Routledge.

May, S. (2014). *The multilingual turn: Implications for SLA, TESOL, and bilingual education.* New York: Routledge.

Mignolo, W. (2011). *The darker side of Western modernity.* Durham, NC: Duke University Press.

Milk, C. (Author), Arora, G. (Author & Director), & Pousman, B. (Director). (2015). *Clouds over Sidra* [Video]. United States: VRSE Works. Retrieved from https://www.with.in/watch/clouds-over-sidra

New London Group. (1996). A pedagogy of multiliteracies: Designing social futures. *Harvard Educational Review, 66*(1), 60–93.

O'Connor, K., & Penuel, W. (2017). From designing to organizing new social futures: Multiliteracies pedagogies for today. *Theory into Practice, 57*(1), 1–15.

Pirog, J. (Producer), & Solomon, B. C. (Writer & Director). (2016). *The fight for Falluja* [Video]. United States: New York Times. Retrieved from https://www.facebook.com/watch/?v=10150869720464999

Poza, L. (2017). Translanguaging: Definitions, implications, and further needs in burgeoning inquiry. *Berkeley Review of Education, 6*(2), 101–128.

Pratt, M. L. (1991). Arts of the contact zone. *Profession,* 33–40.

Riggs, S. (2019). *The end of storytelling: The future of narrative in the storyplex.* London, UK: Beat Media Group.

Robbins, B., & Horta, P. L. (2017). Introduction. In B. Robbins, K. A. Appiah, & P. L. Horta (Eds.), *Cosmopolitanisms* (pp. 1–20). New York: New York University Press.

Sahni, U. (2017). *Reaching for the sky: Empowering girls through education.* Washington, DC: Brookings Institution.

Santiago, S. (2017). Cosmopolitanism of the poor. In B. Robbins, K. A. Appiah, & P. L. Horta (Eds.), *Cosmopolitanisms* (pp. 21–39). New York: New York University Press.

Scott, J., Hull, G. A., & DiZio, J. (2018). Remixing meanings, tools, texts, and contexts: Digital literacy goes to school. In J. Sefton-Green & O. Erstad (Eds.), *Learning beyond the school: International perspectives on the schooled society* (pp. 151–173). New York: Routledge.

Sefton-Green, J., & Rowsell, J. (Eds.). (2014). *Learning and literacy over time: Longitudinal perspectives*. New York: RoutledgeFalmer.

Silverstone, R. (2006). *Media and morality: On the rise of the mediapolis*. Cambridge, UK: Polity.

Singal, P. (2017). The rise and growth of English language in India and its perceived relation vis-à-vis the sense of identity among young adults. *Language in India*, *17*(6), 323–344.

Spivak, G. C. (1988). Can the subaltern speak? In C. Nelson and L. Grossberg (Eds.), *Marxism and the interpretation of culture* (pp. 271–313). Basingstoke, UK: Macmillan Education.

Spivak, G. C. (2002). *Righting wrongs*. Unpublished manuscript. Retrieved from http://www.law.columbia.edu/law:culture/Spivak Paper.doc

Steger, M. (2017). *Globalization: A very short introduction* (4th ed.). Oxford, UK: Oxford University Press.

Stornaiuolo, A., Smith, A., & Phillips, N. C. (2017). Developing a transliteracies framework for a connected world. *Journal of Literacy Research*, *49*(1), 68–91.

Vertovec, S. (2007). Super-diversity and its implications. *Ethnic and Racial Studies*, *30*(6), 1024–1054.

Vertovec, S. (2019). Talking around super-diversity. *Ethnic and Racial Studies*, *42*(1), 125–139.

Vogel, S., Ascenzi-Moreno, L., & García, O. (2018). An expanded view of translanguaging: Leveraging the dynamic interactions between a young multilingual writer and machine translation software. In J. Choi & S. Ollerhead (Eds.), *Plurilingualism in teaching and learning: Complexities across contexts* (pp. 89–106). London, UK: Taylor & Francis.

2
RACE AND ETHNICITY WITHIN COSMOPOLITAN THEORIES OF SPATIALITY AND TEMPORALITY

Carol Reid

For some time, the interface between globalization and equity in education has occupied my thinking—partly in terms of policy networks (Ball, 2012; Lingard, 2010), but also in relation to the growing inequities surrounding the culturally diverse population in schools in southwestern Sydney (SWS), Australia. Globalizing processes involving a range of mobilities—people, ideas, policy—have shaped the region. Increasingly segregated schooling results in hierarchies of resourcing, curriculum limitations, and geospatial clustering of ethnic groups, particularly among low-socioeconomic-status families and along gender lines, but also among the increasingly large middle class where people compete for selective schools and private schooling. Private schools have grown considerably since the mid-1990s when then Prime Minister John Howard supported these schools with a form of middle-class welfare. The state of New South Wales now has a highly segregated schooling system, and it is growing nationally as well.

These effects have been well documented elsewhere (Campbell, 2009; Smyth, 2014; Windle, 2017) but have not been scrutinized using cosmopolitan theories. Globalization in a neoliberal context not only creates inequalities but also produces multiple cosmopolitanisms. If we are living the "cosmopolitan condition," as Beck (2007) argues, then there are some inescapable realities produced in this context. These realities are documented in contested meanings of cosmopolitanism, demonstrated in the broad array of literature discussing various cosmopolitans such as elite and vernacular (Werbner, 2006); plebeian and patrician (Gidwani & Sivaramakrishnan, 2003); forced and abject (Nyers, 2003); pragmatic and dedicated (Weenink, 2008); and Indigenous (Forte, 2010; Papastergiadis, 2011). There are many others, and they traverse disciplinary boundaries. Each is constructed to harness particular contexts and situated practices (Sobe, 2009), so as to make complex what is seemingly self-evident. Early models of cosmopolitan theory

DOI: 10.4324/9780429327780-2

recreated powerful discourses of truth from another place, usually a colonizer, and thus lacked a connection to place and people, and to the local (Appadurai, 1996). Being mobile, colonialists with the means to do so produced an unethical individualism and an elitist view of the world for those who could access opportunity.

After a discussion of more recent approaches to cosmopolitan theory, its potential for providing different explanations in educational research will be canvassed, followed by the ways in which this analysis builds on or departs from multiculturalism, postcolonialism, and Critical Race Theory.

Theoretical Background

Recent cosmopolitan social and education theories have moved away from an elitist understanding of the rootless and detached globally mobile citizen. These theories focus on cosmopolitanism that is associated with transformative identities where authenticity is not bound up with static, remote, and racialized phenotypes (Reid, 2014a). Openness to new modes of being, as Werbner (1999) has argued, may be embodied by workers on oil rigs who negotiate lives with others who speak another language and move in new circles of influence (Ros I Solé, 2013). Werbner considers such cosmopolitans from a "bottom-up" perspective.

Gidwani and Sivaramakrishnan (2003), in examining the mobility of workers in India, offer a tentative theory of rural cosmopolitanism. They discuss the regional movement of people and suggest a multiscalar cosmopolitanism where "patrician" transnational cosmopolitans run businesses moving between regional areas and the metropolis. Young women from local villages in these regions— "plebeian cosmopolitans"—work as domestics in businesses and in doing so their experiences and identities are refashioned. This means power is reconstituted, in part as a result of socioeconomic differentiation and legal stratification, leading to an associated ambivalence regarding the idea of building collective strategies based on cultural particularism. This has some relevance to the problematic nature of liberal multiculturalism in Australia, which focused on group boundaries (Leeman & Reid, 2006), because it highlights the ways in which traditional group identity politics are unsettled by new ethnoscapes, finascapes, technocapes, mediascapes, and ideoscapes (Appadurai, 1996). This critique is not new. James (2012) in Canada and Hage (2012) in Australia have argued that liberal multiculturalism concealed power through a focus on the racialized other.

Another important consideration in the debate around cosmopolitanism is how it might relate to Indigenous populations. There is a body of work keen to move forward from static views of indigeneity. Forte (2010) in Canada and Papastergiadis (2011) and Grant (2016) in Australia provide some interesting analyses. Stan Grant, an Indigenous (Wiradjuri) journalist, academic, and television personality in Australia, argues that, like migrants who came to Australia, Indigenous Australians are also an economic migration story. He states:

24 Carol Reid

> From the fringes of the frontier, Indigenous people started to connect with the colonial economy. Like migrants everywhere, they were marooned by the tides of history, the products of upheaval and violence, forced from their homes like refugees.
>
> *(Grant, 2016, p. 14)*

In other words, they had agency, as well as being victims of racialized policies and practices. Forte (2010) in Canada also traces the ways in which indigeneity can be associated with mobility and transformation rather than being seen as place-centered (i.e., fixed) and unchanging. Another myth is that inability to change led to culture being wiped out. According to Papastergiadis (2011), Papunya Tula artists in the center of Australia, through an act of cultural translation, developed a new symbolic process—a new art form that constituted Indigenous cosmopolitanism.

Other cosmopolitanisms emerge in new and old processes of globalization, including those related to refugees, a particularly pertinent issue for our time. The situatedness of refugees is rooted among local and global assemblages. It must be understood politically, as a critical cosmopolitan stance (Delanty, 2006), rather than only through transnational hybrid identities (Nyers, 2003; Sobe, 2009; Werbner, 2006). Refugees are located in multiple places and, from a bottom-up perspective (Werbner, 2006), imagine a future working across linguistic, cultural, and physical boundaries (Reid & Al Khalil, 2013). They engage with processes of cultural translation (Papastergiadis, 2011) through displacement. As abject cosmopolitans—those who create anxiety and fears (Nyers, 2003)—refugees are potential sites for critical cosmopolitanism in "how they contest and reshape traditional forms of political community, identity and practice" (Nyers, 2003, p. 1070).

Refugees are often positioned as lacking agency. Various claims are made, such as they are a drain on government resources and they need to escape their circumstances. Stories of trauma also dominate. Their cosmopolitan dispositions are in their situatedness, their rootedness in dispossession. They share dispossession with others in the same situation, yet also develop cultural repertoires through observing the host culture. This presents challenges for cosmopolitan education. and some of these are taken up in Part 4 of this book. Drawing again on Sobe (2009), the focus is not so much on their transnational border crossings but on their situated practices such as "strategies for knowing forms of belonging connected with estrangement, displacements, and/or distance from the immediate local" (Sobe, 2009, p. 6).

While there are many more ways of theorizing cosmopolitans, the rest of this chapter will examine research in education using cosmopolitan theory, then compare and contrast this to other approaches.

Harnessing Cosmopolitan Theory in Educational Analysis

This section contains a discussion of two important research initiatives I have undertaken. They will be used as vehicles to explore how cosmopolitan theories can be harnessed in the analysis of education. One of these projects was located in SWS, while the other was national. The context is described for those who are not familiar with Australia, while links to other contexts are made where appropriate and significant.

The 2016 Australian census shows that 49% of the population are either first- or second-generation migrants. The remaining 51% are at least third generation, including 2.8% who are Indigenous (Australian Bureau of Statistics, 2017). In the 2016 census, for the first time, most people born overseas were from Asia, not Europe. As of 2015, Australia stood ninth in the world in terms of the number of people born outside the country. At 26%, the proportion of its population born outside the country was ahead of that of New Zealand (23%) and Canada (22%), among many other countries. Most overseas-born Australians (61%) lived in New South Wales and Victoria, though there has been a notable increase in the proportion in Queensland (from 9.5% to 16.5%) and Western Australia (from 9.3% to 12.9%) between 1966 and 2016. Western Sydney in New South Wales is a very diverse region and most of Sydney's migrants live in this region.

Western Sydney is home to people from all corners of the globe and consequently is characterized by linguistic, religious, cultural, and class diversity. SWS is the inner area of this region, with a denser population. Most of Sydney's Islamic communities reside in SWS, along with Chinese and many other ethnic groups. It is a product of the global interaction between Sydney and the world. The region has been transformed by globalization and neoliberalism: immigration, reduced tariff protection, deregulation of finance, privatization of industry including

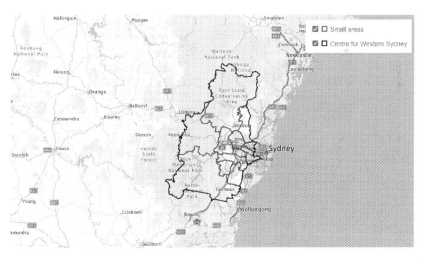

FIGURE 2.1 Map of Greater Western Sydney region. Source: Australian Bureau of Statistics (2016).

education, and increased mobilities. Neoliberalism is ontoformative, changing the very nature of the family (Connell, 2011), and this is evident in the lives of young people in local schools. In addition to these social and economic relations, the spatial dynamics of SWS are intrinsic to the opportunities made available. To use a term located in the spatial turn in social theory, these dynamics produce *scales of opportunity*, which are related to local industry, social networks, transport, government policy, politics, gender, ethnicity, race, and parents' involvement in their children's schooling. Such dimensions reveal how power operates in the contested urban and periurban terrain of this area where resource allocation conceals privilege (Westwood, 2001).

The Impact of the New Compulsory Schooling Age

An example of these dynamics emerged in a project I carried out in SWS examining the 2010 change in compulsory schooling age in New South Wales from 15 years, where it had stood since 1943, to 17 years. Network policy analysis (Ball, 2012) revealed a policy disjuncture that created major tensions (Reid & Young, 2012). This disjuncture resulted from a long-term policy of school choice that had produced residualized schools, limiting the touted positive impacts of increasing the number of years of schooling, which broadly encompass personal benefits through to community cohesion and national competitiveness (Reid & Young, 2012). This policy disjuncture—*school choice* alongside the *new compulsory schooling age*—shows that public high schools in SWS are residualized for several reasons, including cultural and religious conventions around the separation of the sexes, community perceptions about the value of a particular school, and removal of academically inclined students to selective schools.[1] The policy disjuncture can be summarized as follows:

- Choice leads to residualized schools for the most disadvantaged students.
- Residualized schools have less staff, less curriculum diversity, and different or less social and cultural capital.
- The new compulsory schooling age requires all the above.

While raising the minimum school-leaving age to increase school retention has, arguably, successfully addressed issues around minority education and social disadvantage in the United States, this is not so straightforward in Australia. Australia has a highly selective immigration program in which many immigrants have very good outcomes, although this is not uniform across ethnic groups, religions, or social classes (Windle, 2004).

The impact of the new compulsory schooling age in New South Wales was examined in 21 high schools from a wide cross-section of suburbs in the SWS region. Data collection focused on identifying issues concerning retention in the new compulsory senior year among students of diverse ethnic backgrounds, the strengths and limitations of responses to these issues, and whole-school strategies. The schools represented a range of contexts including (a) predominantly English as an Additional Language or Dialect (EAL/D); (b) predominantly Anglo with Aboriginal students; (c) traditional comprehensive working-class with employed parents, demographically mixed; (d) comprehensive middle-class; and (e) gendered and class dynamics that interplay with issues of ethnicity.

The study found that larger schools were better able to cope with changes to curriculum and timetabling since they have more students to enable sufficient numbers to create classes in additional subjects. That is, while the traditional focus of senior years was academic, more vocational subjects are now required with a more diverse student population staying on at school longer. There are differences in the situations of students depending on their gender and ethnicity. Most students from high-EAL/D communities attend small schools, particularly recently arrived immigrants. Both boys' schools were small, and all of the girls' schools medium-sized. Single-sex schools for girls are generally very popular in New South Wales, and thus none are small.

There were strong patterns of highly gendered choices in girls' and boys' schools (Reid, 2014b), ethnic concentrations of poverty and success (Reid & Young, 2012), growing designations of "at-risk" youth related to alternative forms of schooling (Moustakim, 2011), and spatial differences (Gulson & Symes, 2007) such as concentrations of Anglo-Celtic communities in periurban areas and ethnic minorities in old suburban working-class areas (Reid, 2014b).

Using Bourdieu as a theoretical frame, the initial focus was on the extent to which social and cultural capitals emerged as constraints in the negotiation of changed social conditions in the lives of students, and their families and school communities (Bourdieu, 1986). In this study, those with the least economic capital also had *different* cultural and social capitals and were clustered in very disadvantaged schools. Emphasizing different family capital acknowledges that policy decisions build on the preferred capital of some communities and not on others in education. For example, trade training centers were placed in schools and tradespeople were available in the local community to offer apprenticeships. Bourdieu's concepts were limiting, however, and have increasingly been misused and overused (Reay, 2004), representing a hegemonic approach that does not reveal a lot about agency, tending to focus on what is missing among communities and families. What this means is that in concentrating on what is missing in terms of various capitals, the actual practices that are outside of dominant social relations are overlooked or misrecognized. Navarro (2006) explains that misrecognition

> embodies a set of active social processes that anchor taken-for-granted assumptions into the realm of social life and, crucially, they are born in the midst of culture. All forms of power require legitimacy and culture is the

28 Carol Reid

> battleground where this conformity is disputed and eventually material-
> ises amongst agents, thus creating social differences and unequal structures.
> *(p. 19)*

As discussed below, young men were engaged in a range of practices that sat outside of standard school-to-work processes and were due to family connections.
However, while these are cultural practices, the structures creating inequalities are
profound.

A proliferation of choices in schooling has emerged that makes it hard to
decide what may be the best in terms of interest, future pathways in education
and training, and pathways to work. The impact on schools of floating student
populations and staffing formulas unattuned to these vagaries multiplies problems.
In discussions with teachers, it is not that these contextual factors do not emerge
but that they remain disconnected from what might be done. In other words, they
do not focus on the situated practices (Sobe, 2009) of young people. Instead, there
develops a process of ethnicization whereby the pathologizing of young people
(in the main young men) from Islamic or refugee backgrounds occurs. Their
ethnicity was invoked when they did not fit some ideal or norm in schooling.
For example, their mobility was a problem, and their communities were "outside"
of an imagined Australian community, as this teacher's comment at a boys' high
school demonstrates:

> That's indicative of some of the parents, I feel like they're so far removed
> from the society which they live in. They go to Lebanon; they have their
> normal … they still live in the same communities here.

A cosmopolitan approach acknowledges global connections or geopolitics in the
identities of immigrant families and sees this as a resource or an opportunity for
the exchange of knowledge and new ways of seeing the world. Young Muslim
males were pathologized for visiting their parents' home country while overseas
experience is valued for others. Travel is seen as an "interruption" rather than a
valuable experience. Their cosmopolitan dispositions and experiences are invisible.

Another way of harnessing cosmopolitan theory is to focus on transformation
rather than fixed identities. Young Muslim males in the small boys' high schools
were seen to be uninterested, absent, or tired from working in family businesses
late into the night. In a sense, these young men were marking time until they were
17 and could legally leave school. A number commented on the work they did:

P1: I was thinking about leaving at 16, getting a mechanics job or working with
my dad. He's an ex-mechanic. [School's] boring, getting harder every year;
got to do assignments and exams.

P2: There are people who know they want to leave, when they're 16 or whatever,
they're just wasting a year of their life for nothing.

P3:Yes, I did leave ... I did leave, I was working, but then I came back to school. I was just working with my brother in carpentry, part-time, but we have to come back to school.

These young men were not fitting into the senior years of schooling, which had an academic focus. The regulations stated they must have ongoing education linked with qualified employers (certificates obtained and recognized in Australia, which rarely happens) if they were to leave before 17. As one teacher at Station Boys High School said,

> They used to have all these plumbers and tilers and, you know, electricians. They were going into these and all this because of their uncles and all that. But now with the new guidelines, they can't—they have to do the proper registration [with a licensed tradesperson].

Almost without exception, the plumbers, electricians, bakers, and so on in their communities, did not have these pieces of paper. In their villages, they had learned their trade by being apprenticed to a family member or family friend. Current capacities in education are important, but overwhelmingly they focus on a deficit discourse as if young people are empty vessels. Many young people participating in the research tended to work with families. So, first- and second-generation immigrants in low-socioeconomic-status communities are more likely to work in small and medium enterprises. Yet these situated practices are invisible in thinking about what might be done. In addition, given the global market in labor, the connections they are establishing with distant networks may be their future opportunities. Not to engage with these connections productively is to privilege only the elite's global networking, which occurs through transnational "experiences" with volunteers abroad, study tours, and international baccalaureates. Linking to the actual practices of the students who participated in our research would include providing pathways in technical education or building on their skills and practices in school.

Globally Mobile Teachers

Another project (Reid, Collins, & Singh, 2014), this one national in scope, examined the movement of teachers into and out of Australia. This research found that globally mobile teachers' knowledge and skills were not recognized. For immigrant teachers, the focus was on integration/assimilation into "our way" (Collins & Reid, 2012), and for emigrant teachers, the knowledge they brought back was invisible (Reid & Collins, 2013). Indeed, they had to do professional development if they had been absent for more than five years. In the developed world, policies of accountability and standards are rendered through the discourse of the quality teacher and its converse, "a strong discourse of derision" (Robertson, 2012, p. 11).

30 Carol Reid

This can be seen in the nonrecognition of the professional capital globally mobile teachers bring.

To provide some insight into these experiences, one dimension of cosmopolitan theory, *disposition* (Delanty, 2006; Holton, 2009), is useful because it gestures toward a reflexive engagement with the locality as a necessary element of professional capital. Place-making then becomes an important part of being globally mobile because the local, and particular, need to be acknowledged without losing sight of the global. This has political and critical aspects, including the recognition of global belonging, responsibility, and involvement (Rizvi, 2009). It is important to acknowledge that this does not mean everything is acceptable: dispositions are not consistent across fields because there are multiple (Woodward, Skrbis, & Bean, 2008) or partial (Appiah, 2006, p. xvii) cosmopolitans. The key is self-transformation, and this occurs through a process of cultural translation—connecting, comprehending, and evaluating—as a consequence of finding oneself in a "void" (Papastergiadis, 2011) but also resulting from a concern for the world as if it is one's *polis* (Benhabib, 2004, pp. 174-175).

Two examples from the project are included here to highlight dispositions that lead to the professional capital of critical cosmopolitans. The first concerns emigrant teachers: those from Australia educated in Australian institutions for whom English is increasingly a passport to mobility. A number of our informants had experience teaching English in China, one of the largest markets for English language teachers. Women found it much harder than men, and they also experienced the cultural binary that positioned Westerners as "Hollywood-like" foreigners (Stanley, 2013, p. 125) who have to perform. Stacy from South Australia commented on similar experiences in Japan:

> In the beginning it was really daunting and then I got the hang of it. I realized that I wasn't so much a teacher as a circus ringleader, actress, movie star, more of an entertainer, and it was about coming up with silly things you know?

And she developed a sense of humor to deal with local street interactions:

> Also … you would be walking down the street and you hear, "Will you be my hot girl?"—or something. Well [and I'd say], "If you speak English, yes!"

Others first felt their "whiteness," as Melinda said commenting on her early experience in Malaysia:

> I mean, I felt a little uncomfortable, you know, when you had 800 little heads careening out the window because … yeah … "There goes that white chick!" You know my teacher said, "Don't be offended if they call

you 'putih'"—and they said it just means "white"; it's a rude way of saying "white." "Don't be offended by it, they're just curious."

Remembering the isolation of being a foreigner and using this knowledge to understand how immigrant teachers might feel in Australia, Jane from South Australia commented:

> I think one of the problems with migrant teachers coming here is the lack of interest in their background experience in schools, by other teachers in the school, and I think most people would really have no idea what it has been like for me.

Immigrant teachers (we surveyed and interviewed 230 across four states in Australia) often found themselves in hard-to-staff schools as a result of demographics or location. In tough schools, immigrant teachers also needed to develop a sense of humor as their accents (like the Australian accents in China and elsewhere) were derided. Most did this through an understanding of the power they had over young people. In general, they could deal with the young people, understanding their own location as different and needing to reveal themselves and their identities over time. In remote areas, place-making was heightened, particularly in a mining town in a remote part of Western Australia (Reid, 2016). One teacher from Kenya said,

> If you don't get involved and you don't want to become part of the town you get isolated, and that's true to the word because I feel I am a part of this community, I feel accepted and I go to any social engagement, and I think something else that really helps is the fact that there's no one single person who can lay claim on the town. We are all of us coming and going from somewhere and going somewhere else, so we can build a community around ourselves and our jobs.

In terms of immigrant teachers and Aboriginal communities, there was a range of dynamics to negotiate. In another regional town in Western Australia, a group of high school teachers discussed the complexities of working in a school where staff were highly mobile and there was a large Aboriginal population. Without immigrant teachers, the school would not be able to function. The group was very critical of their induction regarding the Aboriginal students and variously commented that it rested on stereotypes, gave excuses for the students to underperform, and didn't fit because some of them had a bit of "white" in them. Many of their comments rested on a view of Aboriginality as static, primordial, and non-agentic. However, there was some truth in their concerns, in that the induction attempted to prepare them for working with Aboriginal students through a culturalist framework. Some found this framework useful, especially in terms

32 Carol Reid

of connecting to the community as part of a necessary place-making process. Others revolted against the romantic stereotypes of the noble savage when faced with less malleable and often downright resistant students. Some drew parallels with other marginalized students to understand the context, taking a more politically critical position. In this discussion, the teachers were comparing, contrasting, and comprehending (Papastergiadis, 2011), using the imaginaries they brought to understand the place (Buscher & Urry, 2009).

In these two short examples from large research projects, cosmopolitan theory allows a focus on situated practices in the context of power relations considering agency, place-making, and situatedness, cultural translation and global connectedness. These are concepts and analytical tools that enable understanding of new conditions. In the next section, these are compared with more traditional forms of analysis in terms of understanding ethnicity and race in education.

Comparing Cosmopolitan Theory to Multiculturalism, Postcolonialism, and Critical Race Theory

In the following section, I move from the meso level to macro societal analyses to provide an understanding of multiculturalism, postcolonialism, and Critical Race Theory. This overview can by no means take up a thorough argument of each strand, but elements of divergence and symbiosis are raised to move the debate forward without throwing everything out. All have something to offer, and all emerged from particular contexts. The construction of nation has been important in this process, along with parallel challenges that unsettle homogenizing and exclusionary policies and practices. The first strand discussed is multiculturalism since this has been hegemonic in Australia and Canada for some time. Its strengths and weaknesses are briefly canvassed and compared with cosmopolitan theory. Following this discussion, postcolonial theory is examined, exploring the similarities and differences with cosmopolitan theory. This is important since cosmopolitanism in an earlier period was married to the idea of a free colonial going out into the world. Then the final strand, Critical Race Theory, is outlined, exploring the context of its emergence and its strengths and limitations in a rapidly globalizing world.

Multicultural societies such as Australia, Canada, the United Kingdom and the United States have taken very different positions on multiculturalism as ideology and policy initiatives. Of course, all societies are demographically multicultural, but these are not often named as such. Instead, the focus is placed on the nation as unified around some core values. Indonesia is arguably one of the greatest multicultural countries on earth, but this is not a term employed when defining what unites it as a nation.

Canada and Australia have adopted strong multicultural agendas—Australia more so in the past—and these were defined very much in relation to the nation. The search for a postmulticultural agenda in both countries is indicative of the changing context and discourses surrounding multiculturalism (Vertovec, 2018). Vertovec quotes Hall (2001) in charting diverse policies and practices, including conservative, liberal, plural, commercial, and corporate in many countries. One could also add critical to this list as educational critiques sought to reframe multiculturalism in the face of growing complexities and inadequacies in policy and practice (May & Sleeter, 2010). These included the tendency to essentialize the curriculum, the prevalence of a politically agnostic ideology, and an overwhelming focus on the ethnicity of the "other" in Australia and elsewhere (Leeman & Reid, 2006)—including the United States and Canada (James & Schecter, 2000)—undermining the possibilities for socially just outcomes.

The limitations of a multicultural approach are evident in the first research project outlined, where an overwhelming focus on the ethnicity of the students concealed how their practices were connected to new conditions. Cosmopolitan theory, on the other hand, focuses on these new conditions and agency, while a critical cosmopolitan view connects their worlds to global relationships without neglecting issues of power (Rizvi, 2009). Cosmopolitan theory in teacher education (Reid & Sriprakash, 2012; Rizvi, 2009) would highlight these factors without losing some key elements that involve respect for diversity and pluralistic provisions. The focus on superficial differences limits the capacity for multicultural education to respond to complex times, and despite long-term investment in education and the broader social sphere, racism and inequalities persist (Vertovec, 2018).

While multicultural approaches have been dominant in education policy and practice, there have also been attempts to move beyond these approaches, using more fluid constructions of identity. Postcolonial theory has provided the notion of the liminal third space, a place of hybridity and a challenge to the notion of authenticity or static identities (Bhabha, 2013). This body of theory has not found much traction in educational practice and is more usually applied to analysis in research. However, the influence of postcolonial theory can be found in critical cosmopolitan multicultural approaches in education (Roxas, Cho, Rios, Jaime, & Becker, 2015) where it is used to suggest that non-elites are forced cosmopolitans through various oppressions (p. 231). This not only fails to recognize diverse cosmopolitan identities but risks removing agency. Indeed, Dabashi (2015) talks of moving beyond postcolonialism and asks: "Can non-Europeans think?" Dabashi argues that postcolonialism as a body of theory has served us well but that a "particular mode of thinking, even in its most critical aspects, after a while exhausts its epistemic possibilities" (Shackle, 2015). The central argument is that ideas of marginalization and oppression assimilate all knowledge back to European thought. In postcolonial theories, there is a tendency to be oppositional and focused on binary relations of dominant/oppressed. Drawing on debates in the sociology of knowledge, Connell (2011) argues, citing Hountondji (1996), that oppositional accounts of knowledge and identity lead to silo approaches to knowledge and the possibility of change.

34 Carol Reid

Connell also notes that oppositional claims to knowledge can lead to some equally inequitable outcomes that have consequences of their own.

Building on the strengths of postcolonialism using cosmopolitan insights leads to a decolonial process, including in education (Mignolo, 2010). Mignolo argues for a decolonial cosmopolitanism that allows for untold histories and stories, such as those of the young Muslim males and the emigrant and immigrant teachers discussed in the last section, to emerge. In harnessing cosmopolitan social and education theory, the focus is on interconnectedness. This represents a shift from separate and distinct knowledge systems to a new sociology of knowledge—southern theory, which is not a recipe for how to "do knowledge" but an approach to how knowledge is formed in processes of exchange (Connell, 2007). It does not dwell in an anticolonial space, recognizing the colonial in the erasure of history but also recognizing the transformative possibilities, always framed in relations of power. In this particular epoch, neoliberalism is not only ontoformative, but as Karatani (2011) suggests, ideologically similar to imperialism. The key notions deployed in neoliberalism—"self-help," "free competition," "winners," and "losers"—are no different from those of Social Darwinism in the heyday of colonialism. Decolonial cosmopolitanism refers to these global processes and conceptualizations delinking from both neoliberal globalization and liberal cosmopolitan ideals (Mignolo, 2010).

The final comparison to consider when moving forward with cosmopolitan theory in education is with Critical Race Theory, which emerged in the United States in the context of highly racialized and unequal social relations (Gillborn, 2006) between Black and white populations. This was a direct consequence of slavery, and the impact of these policies and practices continues to this day. In a sense, it is also part of the colonial matrix of power and shares some epistemological elements with postcolonial theory. Critical Race Theory is based on an "ontology of skin" (Leonardo, 2013) but this has the problematic of centering "whiteness," just as Dabashi suggests postcolonial theory references Europe. This differs from cosmopolitan theories in the sense that they are about finding a language for mediating racism, that of mutual knowledge exchange and new knowledge out of the void through processes of cultural translation. Critical Race Theory seeks to focus on state-based power, and in the UK, it also arose from a critique of liberal multiculturalism (Gillborn, 2006) and an effort to move beyond deficit constructions of Blackness. The hermeneutic trap, of course, is that whiteness is at the center of this process. Looking away from this racial binary and at actual practices, it is possible to see agency, as in the example of the Papunya Tula artists in central Australia (Papastergiadis, 2011) who made a new form of art out of the void of colonial oppression, cultural loss, and cultural translation.

While Critical Race Theory has explanatory power, the global context of increasing superdiversity (Vertovec, 2018) and neoliberalism drives the necessity for new ways of understanding. State power is central to the struggle in Critical Race Theory, and this in itself is a form of methodological nationalism (Chernilo,

Race and Ethnicity **35**

2006). If technoscapes, mediascapes, ideoscapes, ethnoscapes, and finascapes (Appadurai, 1996) are transforming our lives, then the national container framing our analysis and practice also needs to be critically appraised. This presents opportunities for knowledge exchange. A cosmopolitan antiracism has communicative deliberation at its core with a model of mutual learning (Delanty, 2009, p. 153) and a focus on "alterity"—the quality of the unknown unclassifiable other (Nava, 2007, p. 158). Mutual learning is of course conditional on understanding power and the ways that misrecognition manifests in inequities.

Teaching Cosmopolitan Antiracism through a Mutual Learning Model

The epistemological links between the sociology of knowledge and multicultural/antiracist education are of interest. The rise of sociology as a discipline corresponded with the rise of the bounded nation-state and rejection and skepticism of the notion of a free cosmopolitanism once associated with exiles and elites (Delanty, 2009, p. 52). Liberal multiculturalism has focused on group rights within the nation-state and assumed separateness and boundedness (Delanty, 2009, p. 154).

Cosmopolitan theory acknowledges global connections or geopolitics in identities and sees this as a resource or an opportunity for an exchange of knowledge and new ways of seeing the world. It represents not a simple openness to the world but an engagement with it. In the few examples given in this chapter, cosmopolitan theory provides a way of focusing on the agentic moves of subjects by examining situated practices that lead to transformation. In critical approaches, this does not mean eliding questions of power, but it also does not mean assuming *a priori* that race or colonial thinking is the source of this power. A multiscalar cosmopolitanism is attuned to complex, nonlinear spatialities and temporalities: temporary, circular movements of people and multiple belongings. These can be harnessed for more equitable outcomes, as in the case of the young Muslim males who were invisible in terms of their own practices. Cosmopolitanism challenges neoliberalism because the collective strategies and new knowledge practices that are generated may not be contained. Climate change is but one example of cross-border allegiances along with mobile populations seeking safety. Refugees in camps set up businesses and schools and in their state of statelessness create new conditions for living. Climate activists engage through social media, and influence institutions such as pension funds to invest their money carefully. There are many aspects of globalization that open up new strategies and practices leading to the cosmopolitan condition.

As Appiah (2006, p. xvii) argues, this is not a moral imperative since local perspectives might mean people are partial cosmopolitans, who have the ability to live everywhere, but under certain circumstances bring their previous cultural conditioning with them as an entrenched component of their habitus,

36 Carol Reid

consequently limiting their tolerance of the other (see Wahlstrom, this volume). The aim is not to appeal to some simplistic universalism but to understand the struggle and transformation that emerge from cultural translation and new forms of knowledge.

Note

1 ˙ Selective schools in New South Wales select academically high-performing students at the end of their primary schooling and channel them into high schools with similar students. Originally, there were around nine of these schools across New South Wales, two of which were devoted to agriculture. Since the late 1980s and early 1990s, there has been an explosion in numbers. There are now 21 selective schools, along with 24 partially selective high schools with streams for students in enrichment classes. There are also selective sports (1) and creative and performing arts (12) high schools. In many ways, the public system has developed these schools to compete not only with the private sector but also among themselves to be the best and brightest.

References

Appadurai, A. (1996). *Modernity at large: Cultural dimensions of globalization*. Minneapolis, MN: University of Minnesota Press.

Appiah, K. A. (2006). *Cosmopolitanism: Ethics in a world of strangers*. New York: W. W. Norton.

Australian Bureau of Statistics. (2016). *Census of population and housing*. Map compiled and presented in profile id by ID Informed Decisions. Retrieved March 18, 2021, from https://profile.id.com.au/cws

Australian Bureau of Statistics. (2017). Cultural diversity in Australia, 2016. *2071.0—Census of population and housing: Reflecting Australia—stories from the census, 2016*. Retrieved from https://www.abs.gov.au/ausstats/abs@.nsf/Lookup/by Subject/2071.0~2016~Main Features~Cultural Diversity Article~60

Ball, S. J. (2012). *Global Education Inc.: New policy networks and the neo-liberal imaginary*. London, UK: Routledge.

Beck, U. (2007). The cosmopolitan condition: Why methodological nationalism fails. *Theory, Culture & Society, 24*(7–8), 286–290. doi: 10.1177/02632764070240072505

Benhabib, S. (2004). *The rights of cultures: Aliens, residents and citizens*. Cambridge, UK: Cambridge University Press.

Bhabha, H. (2013). In between cultures. *New Perspectives Quarterly, 30*(4), 107–109.

Bourdieu, P. (1986). The forms of capital. In J. Richardson (Ed.), *Handbook of theory and research for the sociology of education* (pp. 241–258). New York: Greenwood.

Buscher, M., & Urry, J. (2009). Mobile methods and the empirical. *European Journal of Social Theory, 12*(1), 99–116.

Campbell, C. (2009). *School choice: How parents negotiate the new school market in Australia*. Crows Nest, NSW: Allen & Unwin.

Chernilo, D. (2006). Social theory's methodological nationalism: Myth and reality. *European Journal of Social Theory, 9*(1), 5–22.

Collins, J., & Reid, C. (2012). Immigrant teachers in Australia. *Cosmopolitan Civil Societies Journal, 4*(2), 38–61. doi: 10.5130/ccs.v4i2.2553

Connell, R. (2007). *Southern theory: The global dynamics of knowledge in social science*. Sydney, NSW: Allen & Unwin.

Connell, R. (2011). *Confronting equality: Gender, knowledge and global change*. Sydney, NSW: Allen & Unwin.

Dabashi, H. (2015). *Can non-Europeans think?* London, UK: Zed Books.

Delanty, G. (2006). The cosmopolitan imagination: Critical cosmopolitanism and social theory. *British Journal of Sociology, 57*(1), 25–47.

Delanty, G. (2009). *The cosmopolitan imagination: The renewal of critical social theory* (1st ed.). Cambridge, UK: Cambridge University Press.

Forte, M. C. (Ed.). (2010). *Indigenous cosmopolitans: Transnational and transcultural indigeneity in the twenty-first century* (1st ed.). New York: Peter Lang.

Gidwani, V., & Sivaramakrishnan, K. (2003). Circular migration and rural cosmopolitanism in India. *Contributions to Indian Sociology, 37*(1–2), 339–367.

Gillborn, D. (2006). Critical Race Theory and education: Racism and anti-racism in educational theory and praxis. *Discourse: Studies in the Cultural Politics of Education, 27*(1), 11–32.

Grant, S. (2016). *The Australian dream: Blood, history and becoming*. Quarterly Essay No. 64. Melbourne, VIC: Black Inc.

Gulson, K. N., & Symes, C. (2007). *Spatial theories of education: Policy and geography matters*. New York: Routledge.

Hage, G. (2012). *White nation fantasies of white supremacy in a multicultural society*. Hoboken, NJ: Taylor and Francis.

Hall, S. (2001). *The multicultural question*. Pavis papers in social and cultural research. Milton Keynes, UK: Open University, Pavis Centre for Social and Cultural Research.

Holton, R. J. (2009). *Cosmopolitanisms: New thinking and new directions*. London, UK: Palgrave Macmillan.

Hountondji, P. J. (1996). *African philosophy: Myth and reality*. Bloomington, IN: Indiana University Press.

James, C. E. (2012). *Life at the intersection: Community, class and schooling*. Halifax, NS: Fernwood.

James, C. E., & Schecter, S. R. (2000). Mainstreaming and marginalization: Two national strategies in the circumscription of difference. *Pedagogy, Culture & Society, 8*(1), 23–41.

Karatani, K. J. (2011). *History and repetition* (S. M. Lippit, Ed.). New York: Columbia University Press.

Leeman, Y., & Reid, C. (2006). Multi/intercultural education in Australia and the Netherlands. *Compare, 36*(1), 57–72.

Leonardo, Z. (2013). *Race frameworks: A multidimensional theory of racism and education*. New York: Teachers College Press.

Lingard, B. (2010). Policy borrowing, policy learning: Testing times in Australian schooling. *Critical Studies in Education, 51*(2), 129–147.

May, S., & Sleeter, C. E. (2010). *Critical multiculturalism: Theory and praxis*. New York: Routledge.

Mignolo, W. (2010). Cosmopolitanism and the de-colonial option. *Studies in Philosophy and Education, 29*(2), 111–127.

Moustakim, M. (2011). Reproducing disaffection. *International Journal on School Disaffection, 8*(2), 14–23.

Nava, M. (2007). *Visceral cosmopolitanism: Gender, culture and the normalisation of difference*. Oxford, UK: Berg.

Navarro, Z. (2006). In search of a cultural interpretation of power: The contribution of Pierre Bourdieu. *IDS Bulletin, 37*(6), 11–22.

Nyers, P. (2003). Abject cosmopolitanism: The politics of protection in the anti-deportation movement. *Third World Quarterly, 24*(6), 1069–1093. doi: 10.1080/01436590310001630071

38 Carol Reid

Papastergiadis, N. (2011). Cultural translation and cosmopolitanism. In K. Jacobs & J. Malpas (Eds.), *Ocean to outback: Cosmopolitanism in contemporary Australia* (pp. 68–95). Crawley, WA: UWA Publishing.

Reay, D. (2004). "It's all becoming a habitus": Beyond the habitual use of habitus in educational research. *British Journal of Sociology of Education. 25*, 431–444.

Reid, C. (2014a). Cosmopolitanism and rural education: A conversation. *International Journal of Inclusive Education, 19*(7), 721–732.

Reid, C. (2014b). Girls can and boys can't?: The factors shaping choice and the new compulsory schooling age in single sex, ethnically diverse south-western Sydney high schools. In S. Gannon & W. Sawyer (Eds.), *Contemporary issues of equity in education* (pp. 38–54). Newcastle upon Tyne, UK: Cambridge Scholars Publishing.

Reid, C. (2016). Teachers' work in the age of migration: A cosmopolitan analysis. In D. R. Cole & C. Woodrow (Eds.), *Super dimensions in globalisation and education* (pp. 191–205). Singapore: Springer.

Reid, C., & Al Khalil, A. (2013). Refugee cosmopolitans: Disrupting narratives of dependency. *Social Alternatives, 32*(3), 14–19.

Reid, C., & Collins, J. (2013). "No-one ever asked me": The invisible experiences and contribution of Australian emigrant teachers. *Race, Ethnicity and Education, 16*(2), 268–290.

Reid, C., Collins, J., & Singh, M. J. (2014). *Global teachers, Australian perspectives: Goodbye Mr Chips, Hello Ms Banerjee*. Singapore: Springer.

Reid, C., & Sriprakash, A. (2012). The possibility of cosmopolitan learning: Reflecting on future directions for diversity teacher education in Australia. *Asia-Pacific Journal of Teacher Education, 40*(1), 15–29.

Reid, C., & Young, H. (2012). The new compulsory schooling age policy in NSW, Australia: Ethnicity, ability and gender considerations. *Journal of Education Policy, 27*(6), 795–814.

Rizvi, F. (2009). Towards cosmopolitan learning. *Discourse: Studies in the Cultural Politics of Education, 30*(3), 253–268.

Robertson, S. L. (2012). Placing teachers in global governance agendas. *Comparative Education Review, 56*(4), 584–607.

Ros I Solé, C. (2013). Cosmopolitan speakers and their cultural cartographies. *Language Learning Journal, 41*(3), 326–339.

Roxas, K., Cho, J., Rios, F., Jaime, A., & Becker, K. (2015). Critical cosmopolitan multicultural education (CCME). *Multicultural Education Review, 7*(4), 230–248.

Shackle, S. (2015). Can non-Europeans think? An interview with Hamid Dabashi. Retrieved from https://newhumanist.org.uk/articles/4912/can-non-europeans-think-an-intervi ew-with-hamid-dabashi#nav

Smyth, J. (2014). *Becoming educated: Young people's narratives of disadvantage, class, place and identity.* New York: Peter Lang.

Sobe, N. W. (2009). Rethinking "cosmopolitanism" as an analytic for the comparative study of globalization and education. *Current Issues in Comparative Education, 12*(1), 6–13.

Stanley, P. (2013). *A critical ethnography of "Westerners" teaching English in China: Shanghaied in Shanghai.* London, UK: Routledge.

Vertovec, S. (2018). Towards post-multiculturalism? Changing communities, conditions and contexts of diversity. *International Social Science Journal, 68*(227–228), 167–178.

Weenink, D. (2008). Cosmopolitanism as a form of capital: Parents preparing their children for a globalizing world. *Sociology, 42*(6), 1089–1106.

Werbner, P. (1999). Global pathways: Working class cosmopolitans and the creation of transnational ethnic worlds. *Social Anthropology, 7*(1), 17–35.

Werbner, P. (2006). Vernacular cosmopolitanism. *Theory, Culture & Society, 23*(2–3), 496–498.

Westwood, S. (2001). *Power and the social.* New York: Routledge.

Windle, J. (2004). The ethnic (dis)advantage debate revisited: Turkish background students in Australia. *Journal of Intercultural Studies, 25*(3), 271–286.

Windle, J. (2017). The public positioning of refugees in the quasi-education market: Linking mediascapes and social geographies of schooling. *International Journal of Inclusive Education, 21*(11), 1128–1141.

Woodward, I., Skrbis, Z., & Bean, C. (2008). Attitudes towards globalization and cosmopolitanism: Cultural diversity, personal consumption and the national economy. *British Journal of Sociology, 59*(2), 207–226.

3

QUEERING HYBRIDITY

Relationality, Blending, and Appropriation

Cris Mayo

Critical work on transnational queer and trans identities discusses how border crossings complicate local forms of LGBTQ+ subjectivity. Queernesses, like hybridities, are derived from problematizing the normative contours and borders of subjectivities and practices; queering the concept of hybridity highlights how hybridity is already the contestation and refusal of stable and clear borders. Like other work on cosmopolitanism and transnational subjectivities, queer theories look for possibilities that emerge in new connections, understanding that this means a focus on movement across borders and sharing ideas among cultures as well as understanding how local formations affect queernesses that circulate globally. Many of the arguments surrounding queerness relate to discussions of cosmopolitanism that both vaunt the potential of border-crossing and caution against overly grandiose claims about what such crossings mean. Some caution, in other words, pervades discussions of cosmopolitanism and discussions of queerness. Caution is necessary, too, in recognizing and thinking about the queer hybridities that emerge from transnational immigration and cultural circulation. This queer caution can push us to rethink how we might teach more queerly about hybridity and cosmopolitanism in general.

Queer hybridities also provide normative challenges, however tentative and contingent, for thinking about exchanges within and across differences in contexts of unequal forms of power. These hybrid formations engage differences beyond gender and sexuality—racialization, class-related processes, and global positioning all complicate queer hybridities. Sorting out how such exchanges affect definitions and practices of sexuality and gender is complex. Some transnational/cosmopolitan forms begin to displace more local forms of same-sex attraction and gender complexity, bringing potentially problematic ideas about liberal equality and disrupting local practices (King, 1992). In some situations, antagonisms may

DOI: 10.4324/9780429327780-3

develop between longstanding local practices, however partially respected they may be, and those local people who embrace global/Western definitions that seem to bring with them different assertions about meaning and rights (Azhar, 2017).

Local and cosmopolitan definitions may even coexist in contradictory ways—but people make sense of theoretical contradictions through equally complicated practices, playing at the edges of consistency or working through contradictions by deploying the kind of ambiguities that have been central to queer practice (Khan, 2016). Because queerness is a process of critique and learning, thinking through the normative challenges associated with how practices interact, merge, and experience historical and contemporary forces are all part of the educational shaping of queer communities.

This chapter begins with a discussion of the normative potentials and challenges raised by cosmopolitanism in general and queer transnational hybridities in particular. I then take each complication separately, although in practice they may not be entirely separate—relational, blended, and appropriated forms of queerness may be judged from different perspectives, especially from different power-laden positionalities. So all queer formations might be scrutinized from each of the perspectives I am suggesting are key here: (a) the relational cross-constitution of concepts; (b) the blended playfulness of travel among concepts (Lugones, 1987); and (c) the potential abuses related to the appropriation of cultural forms. In conclusion, I return to the queer normative challenges of queering hybridity, posing the reverse problem of hospitality and the perpetual difficulty of being and even tentatively knowing the other.

Relational Hybridities Happen, but Not in Conditions of Their Own Making

Attention to queer hybrid relationality explores how queernesses or similar nonnormative formations are emergent within cultures, and how histories and contemporary power imbalances shape all such queered hybridities. In part, pushed by colonialism and imperialism, Western forms of homosexuality and gender diversities may also be experienced as syncretic with the gender, spiritual, and sexuality-related traditions that preceded forced cultural changes. Queerness may be a project of empire in some ways, but even in colonial nations, it remained on the periphery for most people. In addition, recognizing gender- and sexuality-related normativities and nonnormativities that did not arise from late-20th-century queerness likely means recognizing things that late 20th-century queerness derived itself from. Borrowings are not neutral, but neither are the origins of things—queerness included—pure.

Hybridities are relationalities, sometimes pushed by external forms of oppression and sometimes emergent in resistant practices opposing those external forms. Sometimes, too, queer hybridities may start as gestures of resistance and miss their

42 Cris Mayo

complicity in the circulation of colonial appropriations. Since queerness has never sought innocence, complicity may simply be a part of queer critique: if we understand power as not only a top-down process, the constant criticality of our actions and subjectivities needs to be part of how we take responsibilities for appropriations and borrowings that continue oppressive practices. Hybridity happens in conditions not of our own making, but how we reflect on those conditions matters. Queer practices of critique may call for a queer methodology of transnational and hybrid formations.

However related the project of thinking through queer hybridities and cosmopolitanism may be, there are differences between queer borrowings and the travel, consumption, and cross/multicultural practices associated with cosmopolitanism. Usually without generationally based forms of cultural reproduction easily at hand, queers copied, circulated, and altered forms of subjectivity and community that had gone before them. And as with any form of such copying and hybrid formations, they borrowed in ways that exacerbate the economic inequalities related to colonialism. Further, because queerness is an intentionally subversive process of rearticulating gender and sexuality, queerness enters relational understandings of gender and sexuality to blend, alter, and contest.

In many ways, then, queerness is already indebted to hybrid reconfigurations and reterritorializations of gender- and sexuality-related subjectivity, but national and cultural border-crossing highlights power imbalances in these formations. However, queerness also cannot do without hybridity. All queer and trans communities have built with, on, and over formations that came before or from somewhere else. This chapter seeks to reckon with these constitutive crossings while problematizing the asymmetrical costs of such hybridities. The problems of appropriation, the close cousin of hybridity, complicate how to think of subjectivity as ownership and what constitutes borrowing. Being attentive to these power-laden dynamics is not especially easy, nor is returning to our own culture a possible response. Cautious queer hybridities, wary of their debts but unable to stay still or pure, may provide a way into the fray. As King (2002) puts it, "'queer' … in its productive instabilities, is implicated in the struggles for universals that can mobilize global activism and yet can honor particularisms of meaning and action" (p. 36).

Cosmopolitanism, Normative Negotiations, and Queer Dilemmas

The methods whereby this contested balance can be politically and normatively navigated are challenging. In their introduction to *Queer Globalizations*, Arnaldo Cruz-Malavé and Martin F. Manalansan (2002) position queer work against the more baldly material understanding of transnational flows of capital and people. Subjectivities also flow, they say, and need to be the site of theoretical investigation (Cruz-Malavé & Manalansan, 2002). Their thoughtful introduction sets out cautionary limits to those subjective flows, seeing at once the traces of crossings

Queering Hybridity **43**

and mergings in how transnational queers might define themselves but also pointing out the hard lines of colonial appropriation in at least one white queer question (Cruz-Malavé & Manalansan, 2002). They show the difficulties of prying subjectivities away from historical and contemporary global inequities and the challenges to making clear distinctions between how colonialism and capital have shaped subjectivities and the additional work that subjectivities may do beyond material circuits (Cruz-Malavé & Manalansan, 2002). In other words, while subjectivities develop in excess of controlling forms of power, colonial possession follows subjectivities around too.

In some sense, the dilemmas of queer transnationalism are also core problems of cosmopolitanism. Queer subjectivities, communities, and practices push against the normative powers defining borders between concepts like gender, sexuality, and sex. The normative limitations of cultures and nations are the context in which queer communities move, stay, hide, flourish, and grow. Queer people and communities push against normativities, recover traces of queerness within cultures, and, yes, take hints from pasts or presents in their own and other places. But such innovations also run up against the potential for uncredited appropriation. This difficulty may be more easily seen in its commodified versions, where clear profit is made from copying cultural formations. There may be a commonsense calculus: if the one doing the appropriation has more cultural and economic power than the one being appropriated from, the appropriation is unjust. But such calculuses become complicated by queer theory and poststructuralism's attention to interstitial spaces of power and subversive repetition.

Further, for queers, the local may not always offer much in the way of support, and even if resources in that local provide sustenance in other ways or provide the substrate for queer innovations to emerge, going somewhere else is sometimes necessary. How to navigate that somewhere else and how to begin to flourish in translocal and transnational spaces without appropriative blendings are core ethical questions, all reliant on particularities of context. Cosmopolitan, hybrid, and postcolonial spaces are not singular, and none are easily generalized—each space is a collection of local and relational practices. Thinking and acting on these relationalities require a methodological approach that might assume, at the outset, that the inequities that generated relationalities and forced movements in local and transnational spaces always leave their trace in even the most resistant practices. So it may be best to assume that all connections are potentially exploitative but also not to assume that all blending and seeking refuge is the same. Sassen (1999) has suggested that this cosmopolitan mindset, this tendency to think beyond one's seemingly home culture, has been facilitated by the growth of international markets, interest in human rights, and technological changes that facilitate greater transnational communication. At the same time, however, she emphasizes that such resource-based changes are not equally available to everyone.

Cosmopolitanism and queered globalizations are everywhere, and the queer theoretical move to examine how subjectivities and communities develop within

44 Cris Mayo

cosmopolitan circuits, as well as to call for responsibilities to history and trespass, show the more "mundane cosmopolitanism" (Beck, 2016) of lived connections. Although queer theorists have been reluctant to set out normative criteria prior to the political formations that would motivate them, queer communities are rife with disputes over authenticity and appropriation. The gestures of inclusion within the practice of queer argumentation are related to thinking something like democracy, something like representation, and definitely keenly interested in critiquing even the norms that subtend such ideals. Queer communities' conversation, then, encompassing transnational queers and others, has something in common with the more democratic hopes for a pragmatic, lived, and shared sense of community.

Waldron (2006) sees the hope of cosmopolitanism in the daily democracy of the "dense thicket of rules that sustain our life together," thinking about letters, personal interactions, and even potentially the kind of cultural borrowing and appropriation that might be related to queer issues, although he does not discuss queerness in particular. It might be argued that one part of the hybridity of queer cultures, for all their shyness about normative critique, is their tendency to develop this interpretive thicket, continually contesting key definitions and practices.

However, the potential elitism of even mundane cosmopolitanisms continues to pose challenges for thinking about what happens when the local offers insufficient support and global movement is coerced and coercive. On the one hand, the hope of cosmopolitan ethics is that exclusionary xenophobia will be challenged, and on the other hand, the problem is, as always, whose potentially normative framework will make that challenge. Beck (2016) calls on cosmopolitan researchers to replace "ontology with methodology" (p. xii), but if our methods—research-wise or community-wise—are still shaped by histories of extraction and conflict, how can we acknowledge the appropriations that motivated our subjective positionalities and communities while also endeavoring to not replicate their exclusions? This ambiguity between host and hostility, the dilemma of hospitality set by Derrida, motivates Bonnie Honig's (2006) suggestion that cosmopolitan politics will remain in the space of ambiguous and constant action and "wariness."

Queer Hybrid Relationality

In a more specifically queer transnational context, Lisa Weems (2010) approaches this problem in relation to queerness by juxtaposing a queer sense of camp with the displacements of the refugee camp. She argues that queers need to become attentive to the neocolonial knowledges and global circuits in which queer practices are situated and carefully interrogate all processes implicated in globalized inequities. In this sense, Weems (2010) argues for a critical queer transnational ethos, a kind of spatialized and temporalized approach to what queer does and thinks. Her approach to thinking queerly sits at the intersection of queer theory and decolonizing

Queering Hybridity **45**

transnational theory, rooted in material as well as cultural critique. By keeping concepts of camp in relation, Weems (2010) remaps how educators and others might think about how our words and practices signal other words and practices. Weems (2010) uses this relational assemblage to problematize discourses of safety in schools, exploring the differences in what camp means in the safety of going to a summer camp, the subversive practices of gay camp, and dislocated spaces of refugee camps. She reassembles the disconnections immanent in queer theory that are seemingly disavowed when LGBTQ+ politics seek spaces of safety.

Emphasizing the responsibilities all queers have for those who are dislocated, Weems literally shifts the scene of queer critique into a relationship with decolonizing projects. All queer spaces are partial and transient (Weems, 2018). Weems (2018) provides tools to connect the struggles of US-based queers, particularly queers of color, with decolonizing projects that move beyond national borders. Entangling Sandoval, Foucault, Deleuze, and Butler, she analyzes relationality across categories and spaces, suggesting such "contact zones" provide an opening to rethinking (in her example) school-based practices seeking an unproblematic notion of safety. Educational (and other) institutions are not safe spaces—they have been designed to make distinctions and to emphasize difference. Looking to institutions to fix the problems they are designed to have is not possible. For Weems (2018), making connections across spaces and temporalities is not a simple form of appropriation but signals practices of solidarity, while also signaling that struggles that may seem distant to those who are not paying attention are also happening locally.

Blending and Borrowing

When I do trainings in K–12 schools to resituate their understandings of LGBTQIA+ people, I caution against appropriation but also caution against keeping the discussion only situated in the contemporary moment and a particular US context. I discuss how US-dominant cultural practices displaced Indigenous understandings of sex and gender beyond the binary, while also cautioning against cultural appropriation. The point simply is that how "we" think we do things is not the only approach to sex and gender, so we ought to think about how ideas about gender were borrowed across cultures—not exactly translated or translatable, but also not without influence (Davis, 1993). This complicated relationship across time, space, cosmopolitanism, and localism is evident in conversations in Pakistan between traditionally recognized Khwaja Sira people (including three subcategories) and Pakistani transpeople, groups whose practices of nonbinary gender are situated differently and yet also in connection. The two communities, which are not always discontinuous, show tensions between what might be considered local formations of gender that have been understood and practiced for centuries and the more possibly Westernized, liberal-rights-related understanding of gender articulated by contemporary transpeople.

46 Cris Mayo

Those conversations are sometimes adversarial, at least in some situations where the groups consider themselves to be distinct from one another. But they may also not be a full account of how to draw the line between internal gender diversity and external gender formations. Pakistan has approved the designation of a third gender identity on official documents for those whose subjectivity conforms with traditional third-gender options (there is more than one "third" gender so *third* operates in some ways here as a term that indicates more than two but not necessarily three). At the same time, even those within recognized categories do political work that pushes against gender normativity, although it does so through deflection and ambiguity (Khan, 2016). Khan (2016) argues that Khwaja Sira activists' decisions not to answer questions directly and to turn questions of love and sexuality back onto all categories of people signal political work intent on subtly undoing normative genders and sexualities.

Geeta Patel (2003) thinks through her interest in hijras, third gender communities in India, which she sees as having a connection to queer formations and traditional gender formations. Both connections signal that there is more to gender than the binary and that time and space are crucial to our understandings of complex practices. Patel (2003) also calls for queerness to hybridize those categories that dominate the center and thus to dismantle normativity, not as a direct project but as one that introduces mixture and complexity into conversations and practices. The governmentality of gender, then, is undone in subtle forms of internal and hybrid action. Her process of looking at the dailiness of such activities within the home and within mundane conversations creates a sense of queer hybridity in contrast to the queer spectacles of parades and protests (Patel, 2003). As she puts it (2003), "Queerness then becomes a way to make the center ambivalent, hybridize it, so that hybridity and queerness no longer sit in for 'otherness,' but … unsettle the self" (p. 410).

That process of unsettling extends to those in normatively gendered positions who have to recognize the limits of their normativity when more than normative categories present themselves. Khan (2016) notes the fascination with Khwaja Sira activists, but also how such fascination becomes intrusive and reinforces normativity. Tense encounters and shared discourses create a different hybrid tension between more Westernized trans community members in Pakistan and Khwaja Sira approaches to gender. The kind of public discourse deployed by Khwaja Sira activists that deflects questions about body parts and sexual activities (Khan, 2016) is also similar to trans accounts of embodiment described in Manaal Farooqi's (2019) account of the disjunctures between the predominately elite and possibly Westernized transpeople in Pakistan and the largely less elite Khwaja Sira community. One transperson Farooqi interviewed would rather, much like Khwaja Sira activists discussed by Khan (2016), have discussions about their spiritual sense of themselves and what they can be, instead of discussing what transitions entail and other details related to embodiment.

Each group, traditional third gender or trans (groups that also overlap) gives an account that indicates some understanding of some forms of acceptance may seem to favor traditional third gender or new trans subjectivities. But neither group (and, again, there are those who identify with both) indicates that either nonbinary formation is completely accepted. Like the complicated discussions between transpeople in the United States, including those whose identification may fit something like a normalized formation (for instance, supportive families, official diagnosis, normative treatment, and stealth identity), normativity is yet to be fully accomplished, and the ebb and flow of identifications and disidentifications with other forms of gender nonnormativity also continues apace. The connection may be in Patel's (2003) formulation, related to hijras in Mumbai: "they bring difference to your house" (p. 418).

The queer hybridities that these complicated inter- and intra-community discussions raise also work against the governmentality of border-assessing subjectivities. While the discussions above may not seem to directly address cosmopolitanism, they do disavow the elitist tendencies of its material processes: what Pheng Cheah calls "the globalization of biopolitical technologies of governmentality" (Hui, 2011). In his interview, Cheah (Hui, 2011), suspicious of how the normative can be so closely tied to the governmental and exploitable, connects the discourse of capabilities with the development of human resource capital. As queer, trans, and beyond-binary gendered people think through their relations to one another—including decisions to blend and borrow discourses, and their potential solidarities—border-related critiques may also need to be wary of their quasi-nationalist tendencies in figuring what part of subjectivity and nonnormative or nonbinary or nonheterosexual cultural expression "belongs" to whom. Queer hybridities point to debts owed to others, but also reinforce the queer and hybrid critique of border patrols.

Inappropriate Appropriations

The governmentality, for instance, in decisions about which performances of nonnormative gender are proper to a given Gay Pride March and which are appropriative show the problem of appropriation and the problem of governmentality. Claims for drag as an inherent form of queer culture run up against claims that dressing in one's gender is the purview of transpeople. In the 2010s, for instance, pride festivals were divided over whether drag was part of gay culture or an appropriation of trans culture that was insulting to the trans community. If drag performances have long been part of gay communities, queer communities, and/or trans communities, the lines between cultures may not be entirely always clear. Arguments that seek that clarity, certain that their cultural experience of cross-dressing and performance ought to be generalized, may be, on the one hand, a longstanding form of queer abrasive culture or, on the other hand, the

48 Cris Mayo

beginnings of the sort of thicket of regulatory practices discussed previously. The less salutary side to that formation, though, is the development of governmentality that mimics the judgment of the state and regulates the contours of a community. Governmentality, in other words, may run both ways, albeit not with the same material force—subcultural policing of what kind of expression is appropriate and what kind is appropriative may be either an expression of critical queer ethos or a mimicking of nationalism. Or might it be suggested that queer and trans governmentality is inherently queer, aimed as it is at normativizing practices?

If drawing lines around membership might be problematic, taking what others value as sustaining aspects of their culture and commodifying them is even more so. To return to Honig's (2006) discussion of the ambiguousness of cosmopolitan gestures—or Gloria Anzaldúa's (1990) mestiza consciousness—queerness at its best is cognizant of its debts and wary of its trespasses. But the problem of appropriation—transnational, cosmopolitan, or internal—is a complicated one. Seeking to fix inequities is a perpetual necessity. Knowing the origins of practices and meanings with too much certainty may be a more complicated issue, albeit one related to cultural inequities. We need to consider the responsibilities of developing communities in the midst of flows of people, capital, and cultural expressions, while also not embracing a purity that knows who owns every practice. But taking without care for the others from whom one takes is the gesture of colonialism and not, one hopes, queerness. Further, queer hybridities need to take care that queer does not become a "sovereign discourse" (Spurlin, 2006), displacing particularities of place and community. Spurlin (2006) works against appropriation but also cautions against a queerness that ignores how nonnormativity inheres in diverse locations and practices. In other words, queer hybrid ethics cannot ignore other nonnormativities in its attempt to repress its desire to take from other places. It is too idealistic just to think of queer acts as those that are simply antinormative. Queer acts have to carefully encourage critique without installing a colonizing queer nationalism. For Spurlin (2006), this sort of queer decolonization is a necessary struggle:

> The processes of decolonization must involve ongoing engagement with the lived, everyday experience of marginality and its transgression so that better sense can be made of the effects of new sites of imperial and hegemonic domination so as to avoid any simplistic opposition between national and transnational spheres.
>
> *(p. 144)*

Theories and pedagogies of queer hybridities then also need to recognize that within daily life practices emerge in resistance to demanded crossings. Agency, even seen as a form of oppositionality within constricting forces, may assert sovereignty in a space, from a space.

Whether unrooted by colonialism or transnational movement, people have that "homing desire" that Avtar Brah (1996, p. 180) discusses. Such desires, Brah (1996) maintains, are not necessarily always a desire for the home that has been left (although arguably that may be a difference between people who willingly leave, people forced to leave, and people whose land was taken from them) but for what that home would have been had they not had to leave or what a sense of newly constituted home could be like. Living in colonized spaces and picking up the pieces again after colonialism means enhancing narratives from before and reconnecting them to current practice (Weems, 2018). Cosmopolitan practices, especially those in which diasporic tensions work against racializations or positioning of sexuality and gender, may reshape practices and interpretations. Diaspora, of course, literally means scattering, and that transnational sense of scattering means picking up pieces afterward, reassembling them in new contexts, and changing their meaning but still desiring some kind of movement toward comfort.

If even queer assembled comforts tread on other people's sense of sovereignty or similar homing desires, there needs to be some kind of recognition and reckoning. Recognition is not always an external relationship but may also highlight intracultural tensions that were there but become more apparent on later reflection, in other locations. Patel (2003) talks about the "familiar but unremembered" understandings of hijras and nonnormative gender that began to fade as she lived in the United States. She recounts, "This array of no-longer forgotten led me to questions about the production of diasporic identities at the nexus of power/ knowledge, in the guise of an unremarked reorganization of memories" (Patel, 2003, p. 412). Queer hybridities need to take responsibility for what emerges in locations and from locations. This queer hybrid knowing and memory, too, requires knowing more about what queerness can do and has done, but it also requires knowing that ultimately there are limits to such knowledges.

Queer Problems

The simplest point here is that queer hybridities have always moved locally but in ways that affected those beyond the local, or globally in ways that potentially impact local contours. That movement is not just elitist cosmopolitanism (although gay elitism definitely remains a problem), but also movement born of being pushed out of recognition as belonging in spaces and into practices that have to borrow and connect. Relationality may turn out to be blending; blending may be critiqued as appropriation. When the push to continue to live and think in ever-changing contexts of differences leads those with more historical and institutional power to make mistakes, or those who did not intend to take what was not theirs to realize they have, those errors invite rethinking against the grain of appropriation. The more relationality and blending are recognized, one

50 Cris Mayo

hopes, the more appropriation will be understood as an unwelcome and dangerous practice that harms others, even if it inevitably happens. Taking responsibility even for perhaps inevitable mistakes (most definitely for intentional appropriation) needs to be part of the queer hybrid project, as much as it also needs to be part of cosmopolitan ethics.

Like Weems's (2010) discussion of the refugee camp, queer hybridities are, in their best forms, working against power inequities and making connections across struggles. Some of these gestures of connection may run into other difficulties. Queer hybridity, mestizaje, world traveling, cosmopolitanism, and other relational crossings should not lead to the erasure of Indigenous peoples and communities who are seeking to preserve themselves from appropriation and destruction and for whom what looks like "relationality" is, in fact, only a continuation of conquest (Grande, 2000; Weems, 2018). Nor should attempts to settle debts and be respectful too readily reconcretize others into only the bearers of their culture (Gregoriou, 2003) and suggest that those who embrace cosmopolitanism and hybridity are the ones who can see beyond provincial cultural limits.

Queer problems remain, undercutting all the talk of taking responsibility and accounting for borrowings. Subjects are not knowable, to themselves or by others. Nor are others knowable. The origins and originary moments within cultures are also unknowable (Balaram, 2018). Attempts at connection, even relationality and borrowing, are the start of thinking about inequities, but ought not to be the start of reimposing borders that are not themselves knowable. This ends with the dilemma of queer hybridities seeking to be hypercritical and responsible but also needing to recognize the same complexities, indefiniteness, and responsibilities in others. As Gregoriou (2003) puts it, cosmopolitanism does not lead to simple educational lessons, a clear list of responsibilities, and a sense of well-defined diversities to respect. Cosmopolitanism, especially in its educational iterations, leads instead to aporia:

> Aporia, as "the coming without a pass," would not mean paralysis between incommensurable values or tasks but the continuous negotiation of contradictory duties: the unconditional welcoming of the Other and the necessary condition to organize educationally this hospitality, which means laws, rights, conventions, borders. Such an antinomy is not an ethical impasse but the condition for responsibility and decision, what prevents ethical thinking from sliding to good conscience and praxis to technical application. It means to cultivate respect for the Other and accept the possibility of a certain assimilation by the Other.
>
> *(p. 264)*

That "continuous negotiation of contradictory duties" is the ambiguous key to queer hybrid criticality, whether assessing its own complicated situatedness

Queering Hybridity **51**

in histories of gender difference or diversity of sexualities or acting against its tendencies to take from other cultures, even if other cultures too have internal contradictions with which to reckon. Thinking through the queerness of hybridity and the hybridity of queerness raises the ethical stakes of cosmopolitan and transnational relationships. Those processes require us to see interconnectedness as sustaining, as difficult, and simply as how subjectivities have emerged, even if that acknowledgment of complex debt has not always been actively pursued. Nelson Rodriguez and I (Mayo & Rodriguez, 2019) have argued that queer pedagogies follow the general queer route of wanting more. Bringing queer hybridities into cosmopolitan education also requires this attention to more: more complexity, more possibility, and more criticality.

References

Anzaldúa, G. (1990). La conciencia de la mestiza: Towards a new consciousness. In G. Anzaldúa (Ed.), *Haciendo caras: Making face, making soul* (pp. 377–389). San Francisco, CA: Aunt Lute Books.

Azhar, M. (2017, July 29). Pakistan's traditional third gender isn't happy with the transgender movement. *The World*. Retrieved from https://www.pri.org/stories/2017-07-29/pakistans-traditional-third-gender-isnt-happy-trans-movement

Balaram, A. (2018). (Re)theorizing hybridity for the study of identity and difference. *Social and Personality Psychology Compass*, *12*(10), 1–10.

Beck, U. (2016). Foreword. In M. Rovisco, M. Nowicka, & R. Holton (Eds.), *Cosmopolitanism in practice* (pp. xi–xiv). London, UK: Routledge.

Brah, A. (1996). *Cartographies of diaspora: Contesting identities*. New York: Routledge.

Cruz-Malavé, A., & Manalansan, M. F. (2002). Introduction: Dissident sexualities/alternative globalizations. In A. Cruz-Malavé & M. F. Manalansan IV (Eds.), *Queer globalizations: Citizenship and the afterlife of colonialism* (pp. 1–10). New York: New York University Press.

Davis, N. Z. (1993). Iroquois women, European women. In M. Hendricks & P. Parker (Eds.), *Women, "race," and writing in the early modern period* (pp. 243–258, 349–361). London, UK: Routledge.

Farooqi, M. (2019, March 29). The transgender and Khawaja Sira communities: Shared struggles and tensions. *Wear Your Voice*. Retrieved from https://wearyourvoicemag.com/lgbtq-identities/trans-khawaja-sira

Grande, S. (2000). American Indian identity and intellectualism: The quest for a new red pedagogy. *Qualitative Studies in Education*, *13*(4), 343–359.

Gregoriou, Z. (2003). Resisting the pedagogical domestication of cosmopolitanism: From Nussbaum's concentric circles of humanity to Derrida's aporetic ethics of hospitality. In K. Alston (Ed.), *Journal of philosophy of education 2003* (pp. 257–266). Urbana, IL: Philosophy of Education Society.

Honig, B. (2006). Another cosmopolitanism? Law and politics in the new Europe. In R. Post (Ed.), *Another cosmopolitanism: Hospitality, sovereignty, and democratic iterations* (pp. 102–126). Oxford, UK: Oxford University Press.

Hui, Y. (2011, March 17). That which cannot be recognized as human: Interview with Pheng Cheah on cosmopolitanism, nationalism and human rights. *Theory, Culture & Society*. Retrieved from https://www.theoryculturesociety.org/interview-with-pheng-cheah-on-cosmopolitanism-nationalism-and-human-rights/

Khan, F.A. (2016). Khwaja Sira activism: The politics of gender ambiguity in Pakistan. *Trans Studies Quarterly, 3*(1–2), 158–164.

King, K. (1992). Local and global: AIDS activism and feminist theory. *Camera Obscura, 10*(1), 78–99.

King, K. (2002). "There are no lesbians here": Lesbianisms, feminisms, and global gay formations. In A. Cruz-Malavé & M. F. Manalansan IV (Eds.), *Queer globalizations: Citizenship and the afterlife of colonialism* (pp. 33–45). New York: New York University Press.

Lugones, M. (1987). Playfulness, "world"-traveling, and loving perception. *Hypatia, 2*(2), 3–19.

Mayo, C., & Rodriguez, N. (2019). Introduction: Wanting more: Queer theory and education. In C. Mayo & N. Rodriguez (Eds.), *Queer pedagogies: Theory, praxis, politics* (pp. 1–12). New York: Springer.

Patel, G. (2003). Home, homo, hybrid: Translating gender. In H. Schwarz & S. Ray (Eds.), *Companion to postcolonial studies* (pp. 410–427). New York: Wiley.

Sassen, S. (1999). *Globalization and its discontents: Essays on the new mobility of people and money*. New York: New Press.

Spurlin, W. J. (2006). *Imperialism within the margins: Queer representation and the politics of culture in southern Africa*. New York: Palgrave Macmillan.

Waldron, J. (2006). Cosmopolitan norms. In R. Post (Ed.), *Another cosmopolitanism: Hospitality, sovereignty, and democratic iterations* (pp. 83–100). Oxford, UK: Oxford University Press.

Weems, L. (2010). From "home" to "camp": Theorizing the space of safety. *Philosophical Studies in Education, 29*(6), 557–568.

Weems, L. (2018). *Staging dissent: Young women of color and transnational activism*. New York: Routledge.

4

CLASHING AND CONVERGING COSMOPOLITANISMS

Reimagining Multiculturalism and the Question of Belonging

Daniel A. Yon

> At one stage I thought of myself as a Black person and that limits me because as a Black person there are things that I am suppose[d] to be. So I had to shed that. I am not just Black. I am also a woman, and that limits me as well … If I think that I am limited, then I don't dare risk anything or try to do anything. So bust being Black and bust being a woman.
>
> —*Margaret, high school student, Maple Heights*

> I became fascinated with the concept of cosmopolitanism as being a challenge, an ideal, a sentiment and even a collision with other education and political ideals. This push and pull sits well within my own inner clashings and ideas of uniqueness as [a] Muslim female graduate student versus the somewhat universal experience and identity of being an immigrant to Canada. I was grateful for a flexible framework, inspired by cosmopolitanisms, compared with the more indoctrinated biomedical approaches of my own discipline.
>
> —*Kashmala, doctoral candidate, York University*

More than two decades separate the time of my conversation with Margaret and that of Kashmala's reflections. Margaret was a student at Maple Heights, a Toronto public high school, the ethnographic site for *Elusive Culture* (Yon, 2000a). Kashmala was a student in my 2019 interdisciplinary graduate seminar "Cosmopolitanisms: Reimagining Multiculturalism and the Question of Belonging". One of the difficulties students encounter in this course is the problem of definitions, or the lack thereof, of what we're talking about when we're talking about *cosmopolitanism* or, as we insist on the plural, *cosmopolitanisms*. Some find definitions and attempt to work with them, but while definitions facilitate, they also constrain, overdetermining

DOI: 10.4324/9780429327780-4

54 Daniel A. Yon

what can and what cannot be conceived as cosmopolitan or cosmopolitanism. The intense interest, debates, and attendant burgeoning literature on the subject in recent times ensure that the concept is far from one-dimensional and does not conjure up a singular worldview. The "difficulty" is further complicated because cosmopolitanism is for many an aspirational idea, and for some still "a practice ... awaiting realization" (Breckenridge, Pollock, Bhabha, & Chakrabarty, 2002, p. 1).

Accordingly, in *reimagining multiculturalism and the question of belonging*, we proceed with the understanding of cosmopolitanisms as multiplex ideas, as *sentiments and ideals* as well as practices, brought into the conversation to formulate multifaceted lenses through which we might reflect upon the social world, and in particular the city of Toronto, championed as one of the most diverse cities in the world. We ask, for example, what cosmopolitan perspectives might enable us to see and how they might enable us to reimagine the city beyond the restricted lens of *cultural pluralism* and *multiculturalism*. Cultural pluralism leads to a view of the city as a proliferation of seemingly distinct cultures, ethnic and otherwise, coexisting and converging, delineating the spatial dimensions of the city into so-called ethnic communities. While facilitating a way of envisioning the city, this vision limits possibilities for engaging practices and ways of being that exceed pluralism.

A key aim of this chapter, therefore, is to ask how the lens of cosmopolitanism might enable other visions of the city. These visions are not reducible to the familiar categories of nation, ethnicity, religion, and gender, as we see both Margaret and Kashmala embodying a cosmopolitan sense of the limitations of fixed and singular identification even as those identifications recognize their "traces of difference." Despite coming together in the space of the city of Toronto to make a life together rather than living "a form of apartheid or separatism," people still want to retain something of their histories and distinctiveness in carving out home in a new space (Hall, 2002, p. 25). However, inherent in both students' talk of identity, belonging, and living and working with cultural differences are the sentiments of antagonism and dissonance. I argue in this chapter that such sentiments are central to the propagation and aspirations of cosmopolitanisms and to thinking about cosmopolitan education.

I met Margaret in the early days of my year-long research project, focusing on what I loosely describe as a study of the question of identity among youth in a Toronto high school in global times. I used *global times* to engage with the cultural and social manifestations of globalization, the "time-space compressions" (Giddens, 1984) ushered in by advances in technology that enabled the largely immigrant student population at Maple Heights to be both *here and there* in the way they imagined their lives in the high school. Two decades later, it is an understatement to say that connectivity and time-space compressions have been superseded by the multiplication of online platforms, new digital social media, and cyber worlds in which young people live their lives. The possibilities of the cell phone provoke new imaginaries and relationships; new assemblages, cyber communities, and fleeting

Clashing and Converging Cosmopolitanisms **55**

identifications that variously challenge the premises of multiculturalism and insist upon cosmopolitan and cosmopolitical ways of thinking and being in the world.

When I started writing this chapter, I was mindful of the urgency of *cosmopolitics* in the face of global warming, a politics in which young people are playing a key role globally, raising consciousness and concerns about their futures and the future of the planet itself. As I complete the chapter, a novel coronavirus ravages the globe without regard for boundaries or borders, geographical or otherwise, forcing reflections through the prism of the cosmopolitan sentiment of "the world as a whole" (Robertson, 1992, p. 2). But paradoxically, at the same time, we witness the resurgence of nationalist rhetoric, demonizing racist discourses of *the* immigrant, racializing the virus itself, and a reassertion of boundaries. COVID-19 is, in fact, the disease of the connected world, simultaneously uniting and fracturing the *world as a whole*. For students, these times intensify what Nussbaum (2002) describes as the "international nature of the world around them" (p. 295). In these times, cosmopolitanism becomes a critical concept for thinking about the contemporary world as the concept signals renewed attention to the complex ways in which globalization, connectivity, nationalism, citizenship, multiculturalism, and belonging are variously linked.

Since my first conversation with Margaret took place in the early days of my research project, I was struck by the passion of her political and social engagement within the school. She was one of the founding and leading members of a club of female students called the African Queens, whose project was to confront the intersections of racism and sexism in the school. In the course of that conversation, I was taken aback by Margaret's sudden talk of "busting" the very categories through which she lived and with which she worked every day. I was struck by her strategic deployment of identity—working with the possibilities of categories while simultaneously throwing their constraints to the wind. I saw in this a desire for group recognition and justice coexisting with a desire for freedom beyond a politics of recognition and identity. I also saw the interplay of two modes of freedom invoked by Fanon: the desire for freedom and liberation from the racism suffered by the "wretched," as in the *Wretched of the Earth* (Fanon, 1963), and the desire for existential freedom, a freedom from objectification, as in *Black Skin, White Masks* (Fanon, 1967). Accordingly, while locally rooted, Margaret's commitment to antiracism and antisexism is indicative of a politics that is also global, rooted in the histories of antiracisms while foreshadowing, for example, Black Lives Matter and the making of what Warner (2007) describes as a cosmopolitanism forged around the idea of a *black globality*. The sensibilities that underpin Margaret's words demonstrate how cosmopolitan aspirations are situated and arise out of and are implicated in local projects.

Kashmala echoes comparable sentiments in her talk of "push and pull" and "inner clashings," sentiments that she embraces as she claims the categories *Muslim woman* and *immigrant*. Kashmala holds onto the dialectical tensions between these

56 Daniel A. Yon

two categories rather than opting for one over the other, as individual subjectivity is in tension with external objectifications. There are oscillations between subjective inner worlds and assumptions about the universals of the outer world, assumptions in which Islam in the West becomes synonymous with *immigrant*. Kashmala embraces the "collisions," the ideals and challenges of cosmopolitanism, as well as the conflicting ideas of education. Aware of Derrida's *aporia* (Derrida, 2001; Verdeja, 2004), she resists the temptation to stake out a position, once and for all, opting instead for the impossibility of resolving what are otherwise logical contradictions. In so doing, she holds onto "a state of constant dilemma with no general or final solution" (Wang, 2005, p. 45). But, as will become clear below, this impossibility of resolution suggested by Derrida's aporia is ironic, because far from generating an impasse it generates new possibilities for thinking about cosmopolitanism and education. Aporic thinking—that is, grappling with seemingly incommensurate ideas and claims without easy recourse to resolution—is, I argue, a necessary complement to cosmopolitanism and the execution of cosmopolitics.

While Margaret's concerns took place against a backdrop of anti-Black racism, Kashmala's dilemmas are in the context of a post-9/11 world marked by pervasive discourses of securitization, heightened value-laden talk of immigration, increasing Islamophobia, and what might be termed the *decosmopolitanization* (Appadurai, 2000, p. 628) or *anticosmopolitanism* (Shapcott, 2010) of these times. Both students articulate much of what is now commonly understood (though not commonly championed) in educational research: that there is no neat coherence between the categories of multiculturalism's discourses of inclusion, on the one hand, and how students live their lives and imagine themselves in relation to these dominant discourses, on the other. This tension is not always championed in theory and pedagogy, in part because it undermines assumptions of multiculturalism that invoke a pedagogy premised upon self-affirmation as opposed to critique, as in claims to curriculum provision that "reflects the diversity" of the student body.

From Multiculturalism to Cosmopolitanism

In *Elusive Culture* (Yon, 2000a), ambiguity, ambivalence, contradiction, and even satire and parody variously stand in for coherence. Students such as Margaret transcend the categories through which discourses of multiculturalism perceive them as they shuttle back and forth between what Gianni Vattimo (1992) terms "belonging and disorientation"—sometimes the causes of these categories, sometimes their effects. In these oscillating processes, there is estrangement, but the estrangement is not pathological. Instead, estrangement opens up cosmopolitan possibilities. To embrace estrangement is to recognize that while there is value in *knowing one's culture* (culture-as-property), which is one of the cornerstones of multiculturalism, there is also value in cultural estrangement—that is, of getting beyond oneself and one's culture in the pursuit of other values, including cosmopolitan aspirations to *planetary consciousness* and *conviviality* (Gilroy, 2005). To

Clashing and Converging Cosmopolitanisms **57**

acknowledge, counterintuitively, the value of estrangement is to also acknowledge what should be a basic principle in talk of inclusivity: that it is through engagement with the other that one gets to know the self. Estrangement, in this context of multiculturalism, is also a key dimension of cosmopolitanism.

Resistance to cultural reductionism emerged as a dominant theme in my study at Maple Heights, and the concept *elusive culture* is meant to capture the sense in which young people in the school were in a continual process of *making* culture: an understanding of culture as always emergent, as a domain that is impermanent, fluid, shifting, inconsistent, and open to surprises. The *culture* of elusive culture is both noun and verb. The verb, *culture-as-process*, challenges or "busts" popular multiculturalist engagements with culture as a stable object, as in *my* culture and *your* culture. Elusive culture is also attentive to what emerges, and is made noun, from the encounters between purportedly different cultures. Thus, the cosmopolitan sensibilities that were once assumed to come from travel are present in daily encounters with difference, not only in the differences within the school itself but also in that which is mediated through cyberspace (Saul, 2010, 2014).

In resisting the cultural reductionism of multiculturalism, students at Maple Heights opted for metaphors to describe themselves. They talked and wrote about being "sponges in the pool of life," "jigsaw puzzles," "coconuts," "rivers whose depth and direction cannot be discerned"; they parodied and sometimes ridiculed the categories through which they were *known*; they did so in performances in drama classes and videos of themselves, and in their everyday interactions. Students at Maple Heights did not discuss their desires, worries, views, and aspirations by settling upon a neat definition of identity, culture, or race. Instead, these concepts constantly emerged as shifting combinations of first- and second-hand memories, changing geographies, and desires for community as well as desires to resist the constraints of community. In this context, the markers of race also shifted, such that a student who in one context was described as "Black" was seen as "white" in a different context, because the signifiers of race are the cultural meanings and performances attached to the body rather than the unmediated body itself.

There were few attempts to conceal the *chaos* evident in the contradictory practices and talk of identity at Maple Heights. One exception to this rule was found in conversations with a self-identified member of a white nationalist organization who, in talk of her history, politics, and identity, held onto what Vergès (2005) called a "fantasized purity of the colonial racial order" by constantly attempting to patch up the contradictions and inconsistencies in her narrative for the sake of coherence and moral certainty. Significantly, it appeared that students who lived their lives through the messiness of *culture-making* seemed more at-home, more cosmopolitan, than those who made efforts to hold onto identity as a fixed, knowable, and stable object.

The students at Maple Heights, in their recourse to poetics and metaphors, art and aesthetics, gesture to the idea of *aesthetic cosmopolitanism* (Cicchelli, Octobre, & Riegel, 2020; Papastergiadis, 2019) to get at a sense of themselves in the world, with the

58 Daniel A. Yon

metaphors representing an approximation rather than a mirror image of who they are and what they are becoming. This observation does not disregard the persistence of specific histories, or racism, marginalization, and violence in the present. On the contrary, my ethnographic work served as a reminder of the surprising ways in which history constantly returns to mark the present. In this context, Zelia Gregoriou's (2003) observation is significant. She writes that what cosmopolitanism needs to borrow from culture is the "ethical passion of endurance … not the familiarity with and mutual respect for the other's difference but the difference of an impossible codification and representation of the other in our familiar categories" (p. 257).

Theories and practices of multiculturalism have been widely and extensively debated, appraised, and critiqued. I will not review the range of critiques here except to state what is indicated above: that debates on cosmopolitanism, as theory and practice, can usefully be brought into dialogue with current understandings and applications of multiculturalism. Thus, for example, while Kymlicka (2001) advocates multicultural diversity and pluralism to protect and perpetuate minority rights and group cultures, others view cosmopolitanism as a challenge to the kinds of identity politics associated with multiculturalism in which cultural preference is presented as nonnegotiable and the individual is reduced to a "mere epiphenomenon" of their culture (Beck, 2002, p. 37).

Conversations between multiculturalism and cosmopolitanism raise epistemological as well as ontological questions—questions of explanation, and also of affect. "Actually existing cosmopolitanism" (Malcomson, 1998; Robbins, 1998) complicates models of multiculturalism and spatial understandings of identity. Identity is seen not simply in terms of location but, crucially, as also about displacement and relocation, multiple attachments, attachments at a distance, and plural loyalties (Cohen, 1992; Nussbaum, 1996). *Cultural pluralism*, the image of the city as coexisting discrete cultures, gives way to a more complex vision of the city as cultural practices that are at times overlapping while at other times divergent, as often ambivalent relationships interact with other forms of belonging, such as national belonging, rather than replacing them. It needs to be kept in mind, however, that in making the case for multiculturalism I am not suggesting a displacement of one set of lenses by another. And here James Donald's (2007) remarks on the subject are important. He writes,

> The multiculturalist reminds the cosmopolitan of the thickness and stickiness of culture … the cosmopolitan reminds the multiculturalist of the contingency and historicity of affect and moral communities … [and] the lethal consequences of giving culture precedence over politics … even while acknowledging the partiality of all universalisms.
>
> *(p. 306)*

In imagining Maple Heights and its place in the multicultural city of Toronto, conversations with teachers and other parties hint at perceptions of the school as what I describe as a site for "the battles of multiculturalism" (Yon, 2000a, p. 38).

Thus, there was talk and a lament of "immigrant waves" changing the school; of "vacuums created by the departures of old immigrants"; of "multiculturalism disadvantaging us" (read: white Canada); of "the dominant culture becoming the minority culture"; of "Black culture becoming mainstream cool"; of "the ethnic thing going too far"; of Canada being "taken advantage of" (Yon, 2000a). In these perceptions of change, the school is frequently enmeshed in discourses of resentment, popular conservatism, and new racism: *they* are now taking advantage of *us*.

But there are also inconsistencies and contradictions in these conversations. The city is, on the one hand, celebrated as a place of *multi-cultures* (read: opportunities to consume "ethnic foods" and become immersed in, or entertained by, "different cultures"). On the other hand, it is damned as the place of degeneration wherein *they* now threaten *our* identity, disabling Canada's efforts to recognize itself. The *battles of multiculturalism* are perceived through the lens of cultural pluralism, whereby educators may have difficulty separating out their own anxieties about the urban change, and the shifting demographics may be equated to the rise of crime, personal disorientation, and urban degeneration. What educators might have cared about, as in what the school "used to be," is gone, and there is a divide between them and the students who are passionate about different things.

Chaosmopolis and Pluriverse

Elusive Culture (Yon, 2000a) attempts to posit a different conceptualization of the school and community, one that sees Toronto as a site of profound movement and difference, which make the school while the school makes the movement and difference. In *Elusive Culture* (Yon, 2000a), I noted that

> by the beginning of the twenty-first century what are now named "visible minorities" will indeed be the "visible majority" in Toronto, and our theories of dominant and minority culture will have to be revised to reflect and engage these demographics.
>
> *(p.30)*

Twenty years later, one-half of the entire population of Toronto is foreign-born. What might it mean to revise our theories of cultural pluralism by putting those theories, and the lens through which we see the city, into conversation with a large and growing body variously described as *new cosmopolitanisms* (Hollinger, 2001)? What might it mean to see the city in ways that reflect the chaos and disorderliness of identity, indicated not only in coherence but also in "clashing" and "busting" identifications? How might Conley's (2002) notions of *chaosmopolis* aid our thinking?

To think with Conley (2002) about the city and its sprawling suburbs as a cosmopolis runs against the grain of the sentiments discerned in talk of urban changes at schools such as Maple Heights in Toronto. The cosmopolis, Conley

60 Daniel A. Yon

notes, is composed of *cosmopolites*, who extend hospitality to others, including refugees, postcolonial subjects, and other migrants. The migrants and immigrants are transformed by their presence in the city as at the same time the city is transformed by their presence (Conley, 2002 p. 130). This *double transformation* ensures that both hosts and guests are transformed, both within their respective groupings but also as a result of contact with each other. The cosmopolis becomes a place for "thinking towards the horizon" (Conley, 2002 p. 131) instead of fixating on ossified patterns of what things used to be like, which ends up being a selective reading of the past.

Subsequently, the connections and networks that are forged within the school and across the city resonate with the metaphoric *rhizome*. The rhizome's spread and reach are horizontal, interconnecting across the surface of the soil. In this way it is unlike *roots*, which are vertical, rooting the plant deeply in the soil and, metaphorically, communities in their histories. Instead of privileging multiculturalist notions of "knowing your roots" as a reified object, the rhizome is cognizant of *routes* and of culture-as-process, hybridity, creolization, and mestizaje. Cosmopolites, Conley suggests, make connections across differences to form *always temporary, partial assemblages*, in contrast to assumptions about communities as continuous and intrinsically stabilized by their roots. The temporary and partial nature of the assemblages challenges ideas of the cosmopolis as "stable, well-ordered and harmonious," as it becomes (with Conley borrowing from Felix Guattari) a *chaosmos* whose citizens are chaosmopolites that "see themselves as part of an ever-evolving 'chaosmopolis,' a world-as-city where every configuration is but temporary and ongoing negotiations are necessary" (Conley, 2002, p. 135). Thus, the creation and practice of the cosmopolis are always a process (p. 135). For Conley, then, "Chaosmopolities practice and invent a world that is neither pre-existent nor a totality but always partial, constantly being created and recreated" (p. 136).

When, some years ago, I convened a series of talks titled "Beyond Multiculturalism; Back to Cosmopolitanism(s)," a colleague asked, "But whose cosmos and whose polis?" Her question reflected a familiar anxiety about, and even disdain for, contemporary interest in the cosmopolitan concept. In large part, this disdain is premised upon the commonly understood elitist and privileged meaning of the term *cosmopolitanism*—embodied, for example, in ideas about the globetrotting academic. James Donald (2007) describes this privileged understanding of cosmopolitanism as those cosmopolites who "can see through the fictions of cultural loyalties while the rest of us remain dopily seduced by them" (p. 291).

Such notions of cosmopolitanisms are grounded in Europe's beliefs about its own universalism and assumptions about reason. Veteran anthropologist Joel S. Kahn (2006), however, notes the deceptive nature of such notions of universalism. He writes, "It is certainly possible to argue that Kant's notion of a cosmopolitan imperative was also inevitably eurocentric, and hence not universal at all" (p.

Clashing and Converging Cosmopolitanisms **61**

160). The universalists, he argues, assume that only the West is capable of generating universalist thought and value. Accordingly, such assumptions have come to underpin beliefs about a supposed clash between Islam and the West as a clash between universalist Western values and particularistic, traditionalist, and even "fundamentalist" Islamic values. Kahn (2006) criticizes such assumptions about a singular universalism, arguing instead for multiple universals, thus acknowledging different kinds of cosmopolitanisms. Others, taking up the challenge to think about the world as not a universe but a *pluriverse*, write about the necessity to think beyond the idea of the universal to the *pluriversal* (Hutchings, 2019). They caution against tendencies to see cosmopolitanism as a concept and strategy for bringing harmony to dissonance in pursuit of a dialogic democracy (Todd, 2010).

In Glick Schiller and Irving's (2014) edited collection *Whose Cosmopolitanism? Critical Perspectives, Rationalities and Discontents*, contributors all variously voice concern about the dangers of universalist claims and how such claims often become screens for practices of assimilation, new kinds of imperialism, and unrestrained capitalist incorporation. Thus, Glick Schiller (2014) critiques the familiar *citizen of the world* concept for not taking power difference into account and for insinuating that to appreciate otherness also assumes "the power to define who and what is different and to grant or not grant the humanity of others" (p. 32). Importantly, these writers argue that a cosmopolitan worldview is also about admitting to feelings of conflict, alienation, and resentment as well as moments of shared humanity (Stacey, 2014, pp. 35–36), and that cosmopolitan encounters with otherness and difference also include feelings that are both disconcerting and disorienting (Spencer, 2014, p. 38).

In their special issue on cosmopolitanism in *Public Culture*, the editors Sheldon Pollock, Homi Bhabha, Carol Breckenridge, and Dipesh Chakrabarty (2000) make the case that cosmopolitanism should not be reduced to a predefined, prefigured entity with a clearly prescribed content and character. Rather, it should be seen as a practice awaiting realization. Like contemporary feminism, contemporary interests in cosmopolitanism emphasize the situated rather than the universal subject, and they argue that cosmopolitanism must struggle with a universal discourse. Subsequently, in this special issue of *Public Culture*, the contributors look to new archives (beyond the privileged location of Europe) in order to revision histories that capture a wide range of practices that have existed in times past. In so doing, they undermine notions of the absolute universalism of Western cosmopolitanism. They call attention to global historic practices that epitomized cosmopolitanism long before the concept came into popular use in the late 19th century. They variously highlight the idea of "living at home abroad or abroad at home" (Pollock et al., 2000, p. 587) as ways of inhabiting multiple places at once and of being different simultaneously.

Thus, cosmopolitan sensibilities suggest that cosmopolitanism is not just an idea, or a prefigured entity, but relates to multiple ways of being, and that these ways of being are often threatened by modernist work—as in multiculturalism—of

62 Daniel A. Yon

separating and purifying different realms that have never been separate and pure. It also suggests an aspiration, as opposed to a clearly delineated model, that might predicate our thinking about curriculum, as discussed below.

Following the *cosmopolitan turn* (Harvey, 2009), there is an understanding among those who write on the subject that cosmopolitanism should be referred to in the plural to stress the multiple, diverse, and sometimes contentious ways of being, acting, and belonging in the world and relating to democratic projects of inclusion (Chakrabarty, 2000). Thus, for example, scholars describe a *new* cosmopolitanism that reconciles otherwise national and universal concerns (Appiah, 2006; Hollinger, 2001). Beck (2002) uses *cosmopolitanization* as a framework for thinking about the local and internal working of globalization; Mignolo (2000) uses *critical cosmopolitanism* for exploring and mediating difference; and the term *discrepant cosmopolitanisms* (Clifford, 1998) signifies multiple and uneven encounters, negotiations, and affiliations that challenge simplistic understandings of cultures or identities within identity politics and multicultural discourses, as discussed previously.

The differing iterations of the cosmopolitan concept also complicate spatial understandings of identity, as viewed in terms not simply of location but also of displacement and relocation (Robbins, 1998). These various concepts of cosmopolitanism and cosmopolitan politics and practices interrogate the line between singular universalist, humanist cosmopolitanism, patriotism, and nationalism, as they point to overlapping spheres of influence and interference and serve as advocates for *vernacular cosmopolitanism* (Werbner, 2006). Importantly, they remove the focus from the elite cosmopolitan toward multiple, "ordinary," and vernacular cosmopolitans, who include exiles, working-class immigrants, refugees and "abject" cosmopolitans, and diasporic dwellers who exhibit a variety of forms of being situated-in-displacement (Featherstone, 2002; Lamont & Aksartova, 2002 Nyers, 2003; Werbner, 1999). The "banal cosmopolitanism" of the millions of refugees, some of whom appear on television screens, stuck at borders, do not embrace the cosmopolitan sentiments of openness to strangers, conviviality, and engagements the difference out of choice but out of sheer necessity and the need for survival (Agier, 2016).

Resisting Pedagogical Domestication

At the start of this chapter, I mentioned the initial challenges, posed in my course "Cosmopolitanism: Rethinking Multiculturalism and the Question of Belonging," of thinking about cosmopolitanisms as multifaceted as opposed to thinking with a singular definition. A lesser challenge came from participants wedded to a specific notion of the applied. This question is expressed in the question "But what do we do with all this?" and especially "What do we do with Derrida's aporia?"—a question that appears to assume that thinking is not itself a doing. However, in thinking about the question of curriculum and education through the broad lens accorded by the cosmopolitan turn or the new cosmopolitanisms, I too, with Gregoriou (2003), want to *resist the pedagogical domestication of cosmopolitanism* in the same way that *Elusive Culture* is an appeal to resist desires to domesticate the inconsistencies, ambivalence, and dialectics of belonging and estrangement, dissonance and harmony for the sake of theoretical coherence as well as the desire to "know" the cultures of youth (Yon, 2000b).

One of the lessons I take from Margaret and Kashmala is to see the duality of dissonance and harmony, the interplay of *shared humanity* and *alienation*, in their reflections as a cosmopolitanism that affirms belonging and estrangement as a dialectic that is generative. Accordingly, I advocate for the multiplex ideas and the various lenses accorded by the literature on cosmopolitanism as tools to think with and about curriculum, especially a humanities curriculum, that seeks to transcend the confines of the familiar categories of nation, ethnicity, religion, gender, race, and so on. Resisting pedagogical domestication means taking seriously observations regarding multiple universals—the world as a pluriverse—and the challenges of aporia that insist upon continually grappling with opposing ideas and contradictory voices. No single model for cosmopolitan education "prevents ethical thinking from sliding to good conscience and praxis to technical application," as Gregoriou (2003, p. 264) puts it.

Resisting pedagogical domestication also entails grappling with, while retaining, the challenges of "difficult knowledge" without necessary recourse to resolution (Britzman, 1998; Yon, 1999). It does not stand in opposition to the passion and promise of a humanities curriculum built around Nussbaum's (1997) *narrative imagination* notions of concentric circles, reaching inwards and outwards while aspiring to a sense of belonging to humanity *as a whole*. But while Nussbaum's model aspires to the sentiments of harmony and peace that underpin how cosmopolitanism has been historically imagined, Sharon Todd's (2010) work on *agonistic cosmopolitics* is important for its critical engagement with the dissonance of the contemporary world and for cautioning against claims of universality. She notes, "An agonistic cosmopolitics is mindful of pluralism without romanticizing or vilifying it," as it also entails "continual self-interrogation about our claims of universality" (p. 226).

This brings us full circle back to the pedagogical question of "what to do with it." The *multiplex lens* accorded by the *sentiments and ideals* and aspirations of cosmopolitanisms is a shifting one that insists on treating the question of "what to do" as not simply a question of epistemology and application but also a question of ontology, one that raises questions about the virtues and effect of cosmopolitical thinking on the self and the imaginaries and possibilities such ideas and thinking might incite for questions about our pedagogical efforts and concerns.

References

Agier, M. (2016). *Borderlands: Towards an anthropology of the cosmopolitan condition*. Cambridge, UK: Polity.

Appadurai, A. (2000). Spectral housing and urban cleansing: Notes on millennial Mumbai. *Public Culture, 12*(3), 627–651.

Appiah, K. A. (2006). *Cosmopolitanism: Ethics in a world of strangers*. New York: W. W. Norton.

Beck, U. (2002). The cosmopolitan society and its enemies. *Theory, Culture & Society, 19*(1–2), 17–44.

Breckenridge, C. A., Pollock, S., Bhabha, H. K., & Chakrabarty, D. (Eds.). (2002). *Cosmopolitanism*. Durham, NC: Duke University Press.

Britzman, D. (1998). *Lost subjects, contested objects: Toward a psychoanalytic inquiry of learning*. Albany, NY: State University of New York Press.

Chakrabarty, D. (2000). Universalism and belonging in the logic of capital. *Public Culture, 12*(3), 653–678.

Cicchelli, V., Octobre, S., & Riegel, V. (Eds.). (2020). *Aesthetic cosmopolitanism and global culture*. Leiden, The Netherlands: Brill.

Clifford, J. (1998). Mixed feelings. In P. Cheah & B. Robbins (Eds.), *Cosmopolitics: Thinking and feeling beyond the nation* (pp. 362–270). Minneapolis, MN: University of Minnesota Press.

Cohen, M. (1992). Rooted cosmopolitanism: Thoughts on the left, nationalism, and multiculturalism. *Dissent, 39*, 478–483.

Conley, V. A. (2002). Chaosmopolis. *Theory, Culture & Society, 19*(1–2), 127–138.

Derrida, J. (2001). *On cosmopolitanism and forgiveness* (M. Dooley & M. Hughes, Trans.). New York: Routledge.

Donald, J. (2007). Internationalisation, diversity and the humanities curriculum: Cosmopolitanism and multiculturalism revisited. *Journal of Philosophy of Education, 41*(3), 289–308.

Fanon, F. (1963). *The wretched of the earth*. New York: Grove Press.

Fanon, F. (1967). *Black skin, white masks*. New York: Grove Press.

Featherstone, M. (2002). Cosmopolis: An introduction. *Theory, Culture & Society, 19*(1–2), 1–16.

Giddens, A. (1984). *The constitution of society: Outline of the theory of structuration*. Berkeley, CA: University of California Press.

Gilroy, P. (2005). *Postcolonial melancholia*. New York: Columbia University Press.

Glick Schiller, N. (2014). Whose cosmopolitanism? And whose humanity? In N. Glick Schiller & A. Irving (Eds.), *Whose cosmopolitanism? Critical perspectives, relationalities, and discontents* (pp. 31–33). New York: Berghahn Books.

Glick Schiller, N., & Irving, A. (Eds.). (2014). *Whose cosmopolitanism? Critical perspectives, relationalities, and discontents*. New York: Berghahn Books.

Gregoriou, Z. (2003). Resisting the pedagogical domestication of cosmopolitanism: From Nussbaum's concentric circles of humanity to Derrida's aporetic ethics of hospitality. In K. Alston (Ed.), *Journal of philosophy of education 2003* (pp. 257–266). Urbana, IL: Philosophy of Education Society.

Hall, S. (2002). Reflections on "Race, Articulation and Societies Structured in Dominance." In P. Essed & D. T. Goldberg (Eds.), *Race critical theories* (pp. 449–454). Malden, MA: Blackwell.

Harvey, D. (2009). *Cosmopolitanism and the geographies of freedom*. New York: Columbia University Press.

Hollinger, D. (2001). Not universalists, not pluralists: The new cosmopolitans find their own way. *Constellations, 8*(2), 236–248.

Hutchings, K. (2019). Decolonizing global ethics: Thinking with the pluriverse. *Ethics & International Affairs, 33*(2), 115–125.

Kahn, J. S. (2006). *Other Malays: Nationalism and cosmopolitanism in the modern Malay world*. Singapore: Singapore University Press.

Kymlicka, W. (2001). *Politics in the vernacular: Nationalism, multiculturalism and citizenship*. Oxford, UK: Oxford University Press.

Lamont, M., & Aksartova. S. (2002). Ordinary cosmopolitanisms: Strategies for bridging racial boundaries among working-class men. *Theory, Culture & Society, 19*(4), 1–25.

Malcomson, S. L. (1998). The varieties of cosmopolitan experience. In P. Cheah & B. Robbins (Eds.), *Cosmopolitics: Thinking and feeling beyond the nation* (pp. 233–245). Minneapolis, MN: University of Minnesota Press.

Mignolo, W. D. (2000). The many faces of cosmo-polis: Border thinking and critical cosmopolitanism. *Public Culture, 12*(3), 721–748.

Nussbaum, M. C. (1996). Patriotism and cosmopolitanism. In M. C. Nussbaum & J. Cohen (Eds.), *For love of country: Debating the limits of patriotism* (pp. 2–20). Boston, MA: Beacon Press.

Nussbaum, M. C. (1997). *Cultivating humanity: A classical defense of reform in liberal education*. Cambridge, MA: Harvard University Press.

Nussbaum, M. C. (2002). Capabilities and social justice. *International Studies Review, 4*(2), 123–135.

Nyers, P. (2003). Abject cosmopolitanism: The politics of protection in the anti-deportation movement. *Third World Quarterly, 24*(6), 1069–1093.

Papastergiadis, N. (2019). Aesthetic cosmopolitanism. In G. Delanty (Ed.), *Routledge international handbook of cosmopolitan studies* (pp. 198–210). London, UK: Routledge.

Pollock, S., Bhabha, H. K., Breckenridge, C. A., & Chakrabarty, D. (2000). Cosmopolitanisms. *Public Culture, 12*(3), 557–589.

Robbins, B. (1998). Introduction part 1: Actually existing cosmopolitanism. In P. Cheah & B. Robbins (Eds.), *Cosmopolitics: Thinking and feeling beyond the nation* (pp. 1–19). Minneapolis, MN: University of Minnesota Press.

Robertson, R. (1992). *Globalization: Social theory and global culture*. London, UK: SAGE.

Saul, R. (2010). Kevjumba and the adolescence of YouTube. *Educational Studies, 46*(5), 457–477.

Saul, R. (2014). Adolescence and the narrative complexities of online life: On the making and unmaking of YouTube's AnonyGirl1. *Digital Culture and Education, 6*(2), 66–81.

Shapcott, R. (2010). *International ethics: A critical introduction*. Cambridge, UK: Polity.

Spencer, R. (2014). Whose cosmopolitanism? Postcolonial criticism and the realities of neocolonial power. In N. Glick Schiller & A. Irving (Eds.), *Whose cosmopolitanism? Critical perspectives, relationalities, and discontents* (pp. 37–38). New York: Berghahn Books.

Stacey, J. (2014). Whose cosmopolitanism? The violence of idealizations and the ambivalence of self. In N. Glick Schiller & A. Irving (Eds.), *Whose cosmopolitanism? Critical perspectives, relationalities, and discontents* (pp. 34–36). New York: Berghahn Books.

Todd, S. (2010). Living in a dissonant world: Toward an agonistic cosmopolitics for education. *Studies in Philosophy and Education, 29*(2), 213–228.

Vattimo, G. (1992). *The transparent society*. Cambridge, UK: Polity.

Verdeja, E. (2004). Derrida and the impossibility of forgiveness. *Contemporary Political Theory, 3*(1), 23–47.

Vergès, F. (2005). One world, many maps. *Interventions, 7*(3), 342–345.

Wang, H. (2005). Aporias, responsibility, and the im/possibility of teaching multicultural education. *Educational Theory, 55*(1), 45–59.

Warner, R. (2007). *Battles over borders: Hip Hop and the politics and poetics of race and place in the new South Africa* (Unpublished doctoral dissertation). York University, Toronto, ON.

66 Daniel A. Yon

Werbner, P. (1999). Global pathways: Working class cosmopolitans and the creation of transnational ethnic worlds. *Social Anthropology, 7*(1), 17–35.

Werbner, P. (2006).Vernacular cosmopolitanism. *Theory, Culture & Society, 23*(2–3), 496–498.

Yon, D. A. (1999). Pedagogy and the "problem" of difference: On reading community in The Darker Side of Black. *International Journal of Qualitative Studies in Education, 12*(6), 623–641.

Yon, D.A. (2000a). *Elusive culture: Schooling, race, and identity in global times.* Albany, NY: State University of New York Press.

Yon, D. A. (2000b). Urban portraits of identity: On the problem of knowing culture and identity in intercultural studies. *Journal of Intercultural Studies, 21*(2), 143–157.

PART 2

Schooling and the Development of Cosmopolitan Identities

5

BRINGING BLACK MIXED-RACE PUPILS INTO FOCUS IN BRITISH SCHOOLING

Karis Campion and Remi Joseph-Salisbury

According to Bhabha (1994), the third space represents a site for new forms of cultural meaning, a challenge to the limitations of fixed racialized boundaries and national identities. People of mixed ethnic backgrounds are perhaps among the most explicit signifiers of this third space, often appropriated as symbols of the dissolution of such boundaries and the "cosmopolitan condition" that structures our increasingly heterogeneous communities (Beck, 2007). In this chapter, we consider how mixed-race school pupils, the poster children of diversity discourse, experience their identities within their schooling. We trace how their difference has been acknowledged or ignored historically within educational settings to highlight the need for approaches to schooling that recognize and value the diversity of Black schooling experiences, as well as the nuances of contemporary cosmopolitan identities in British schools.

The median age of the mixed-race population in the UK is 18 (Government of the United Kingdom, 2018), and figures suggest that the number of mixed-race school pupils is rising rapidly. The size of Black/white mixed-race groups in schools is particularly pronounced. While the Mixed White and Black Caribbean group is the second largest of all the mixed ethnic groups in English schools (105,408 or 27%),[1] the Mixed White and Black African group has experienced the fastest growth of all, up by 243% between 2003 and 2017, to 51,404 (13% of the total population of mixed-race pupils) (Lewis & Demie, 2019, p. 2066). To date, and with exceptions, the schooling experiences of this group of students have remained largely underconsidered. Mixed-race pupils have often been subsumed into broader monoracial categories in school data, reporting, policies, and academic scholarship. However, as mixed-race populations continue to grow, it becomes ever more important that British schools duly consider their specific needs and experiences. Indeed, any attempt to shift toward more cosmopolitan

DOI: 10.4324/9780429327780-5

forms of education that recognize the nuances of multiethnic identities within the ever-growing "superdiversity" of our classrooms must give due recognition to mixed-race identities (Vertovec, 2007).

Given that Critical Mixed-Race Studies is still an emergent area of scholarship, and that mixed categories were only included on the census for the first time in 2001 (Thompson, 2012), it is perhaps unsurprising that mixed pupils have not, historically, been treated as a distinct ethnic group by policy-makers. Furthermore, Black mixed-race students and Black monoracial students do share similar schooling experiences across a range of indicators. Both Black and Black mixed-race pupils are found to be awarded relatively low grades (Government of the United Kingdom, 2019), are overrepresented in school exclusions (Government of the United Kingdom, 2020), are vulnerable to low teacher expectations (Joseph-Salisbury, 2016), and express dissatisfaction with the curriculum (Caballero, Haynes, & Tikly, 2007; Doharty, 2019; Joseph-Salisbury, 2017).[2]

While we recognize these very similar experiences over time, in this chapter, we indicate important points of divergence in their schooling experiences. To date, relatively little analysis has highlighted specifically where, how, and why particular points of divergence emerge. One example where we see this divergence emerges from some small insights into the conditions in the 1960s. At this time, schools were routinely used as a site through which to enforce the British state's assimilationist project (Carby, 1982; Tomlinson, 2008). The "West Indian" child, like the (so-called) "coloured immigrant" child, was persistently constructed as a threat to British schooling in need of being integrated.

These Black pupils were victims of aggressive policy recommendations such as "busing," which—in response to protests of white parents—saw Black and brown children sent to schools with higher numbers of white British pupils to facilitate integration and reduce levels of overconcentration (Esteves, 2018).[3] This policy had a plethora of negative stigmatizing implications, with "immigrant" children feeling a sense of being "segregated rather than integrated," and reportedly being "educated" in separate parts of their new schools (Child Immigrants, 2017). The policy created conditions for racist abuse and violence, and ultimately led to the racist murder of Shakil Malik in 1975 (Butler, 2012). Many Black mixed-race pupils in schools with high numbers of Black and brown children were implicated by these policies. Nevertheless, by virtue of having one white *British* parent and one "immigrant" parent, the place of mixed-race school children in the official definitions of what constituted the "immigrant child" was sometimes complex and unclear (Tomlinson, 2008, p. 31; Ydesen & Myers, 2016, p. 8).

These patterns of discrimination over time suffered by the "Black," "Black mixed-race," "immigrant," and "West Indian" child lay the foundation to our chapter. We aim to center the pernicious effects of anti-Black racism in the lives of Black mixed-race pupils. Simultaneously, however, we argue for a closer reading of some of the categories that mixed-race pupils have historically been written into

Black Mixed-Race Pupils in British Schools **71**

and out of, and to highlight the persistence of essentialist discourses of race that exist even within our contemporary cosmopolitan condition (Beck, 2007). In so doing, we seek to better recognize the complexities of Black mixed-race experiences within the broader existing narratives of Black schooling in the UK and add to emergent literatures that complicate homogenous and reductive understandings of Black schooling experiences (Ali, 2003; Caballero et al., 2007; Haynes, Tikly, & Caballero, 2006; Joseph-Salisbury & Andrews, 2017; Lewis & Demie, 2019; Tikly, Caballero, Haynes, & Hill, 2004). Centering Black mixed-race pupils' schooling experiences, this relatively small body of work has pointed toward particular and specific mixed-race experiences that sit alongside (and overlap) those shared with monoracial Black peers. These include, but are not limited to, issues related to the implications of ethnocentric curricula that lack positive references to specifically *mixed-race* people, and vulnerability to continuous negative stereotypes that pertain specifically to racial mixedness (for example, notions of "identity confusion" and "fragmented" family lives).

In this chapter, we endeavor to bring the analytical weight of Critical Mixed-Race Studies to bear on discussions around cosmopolitan education. We draw upon primary data from three studies. First, we utilize research in which Karis Campion (2017) conducted qualitative interviews with 37 people of mixed white and Black Caribbean heritage, aged between 20 and 56, in the UK city of Birmingham (hereafter referred to as Study A). Second, we draw upon qualitative interview data from Joseph-Salisbury's (2013, 2016, 2017) research on the schooling experiences of 20 Black/white mixed-race men between the ages of 16 and 21 in the UK (hereafter Study B). Third, we consider data from Joseph-Salisbury's (2016, 2018) research with Black mixed-race men, who were all 16–25 years old. While this was a UK/US study, we draw only on data from the 14 Black mixed-race men in the UK (hereafter Study C). The use of these three data sets means that we draw upon a considerable sample size for qualitative research, enabling us to draw out a picture over time. With this in mind, we also draw upon wider literatures throughout.

We start by considering the transition from primary to secondary school, to trace how Black mixed-race pupils experience a loss of innocence through encounters with explicit forms of interpersonal racism and racial microaggressions.[4] We argue that Black mixed-race people are better able to recognize these experiences of racism as they are coming of age in secondary school. We then go on to trace the various ways in which racism has permeated the schooling experiences of Black mixed-race pupils over time, in the form of low expectations and prejudice from teachers, interpersonal racism from peers, and ethnocentric curricula. We conclude the chapter by arguing for a more nuanced analysis of Black experiences and then by highlighting methods for resisting the erasure of Black mixed-race experiences of school. This disposition, we maintain, has to be fundamental to contemporary cosmopolitan education.

Primary School

Primary school[5] serves as an important site of socialization outside of the home and family. These early encounters can be highly influential for a pupil's sense of self, and—given the white supremacist underpinnings of UK education (Gillborn, 2008)—this is pertinent for racially minoritized students (Archer & Yamashita, 2003; Gillborn, 2008; Tikly et al., 2004). A number of participants across all of our studies were able to identify assertions of difference made by fellow pupils at primary school that could make them feel othered. However, as young children, they recalled not having the language or frameworks at the time to understand and articulate what the interactions they were experiencing meant. Many did not necessarily understand their encounters in explicitly racialized terms. The quote from Maya (Study A) below succinctly demonstrates how this could play out. She explains that as early as six years old, as a primary school pupil in the mid-1990s, she learned that her body was *out of place* (Puwar, 2004):

> At [primary] school I don't think I've articulated it in those words but I guess I wanted to be white … I hated my hair … everyone used to tell me it was frizzy. Like, I was the butters [ugly] friend at that school (laughs) … I remember one day being in PE [Physical Education] and wearing the same shorts as … my best friend … and she was looking at her shorts and looking at my shorts and mine were tight and she was like "*Why is your bum so big?*" And I remember just really feeling … why is my bum so big? It's disgusting.

Maya's anecdote adds to the extensive literature that has traced how Black bodies are made to feel unruly and out of place in white spaces (Joseph-Salisbury, 2019b; Puwar, 2004). The othering from her white peer prompts Maya to reject and despise her Black body. As a young girl, Maya did not recognize this interaction as informed by the pervasive ideology of anti-Blackness that underpinned the practices and processes of the school, and indeed the society which she moved through. This inability to name racism for what it was meant that at primary school it was often something that was felt but not "known" (Ali, 2012, p. 97). This was true even for those who encountered quite explicit racial slurs, as Cassandra (Study A) did in the early 1990s:

> Yeah so before going into junior school … quite young … 5 or 6 kind of, maximum, I remember kids calling me Paki or blackie. … I just knew it wasn't a nice thing to be called and I didn't like it. … It was almost like you know some kids get called, "oh you're a ginger," "you're fat," you're this, you're that … to me, that was what I got called but … I couldn't really remember it making any sort of sense.

Although these two excerpts are quite explicit examples of racist sentiment, it is interesting that Maya and Cassandra seem to convey an understanding of *racialization* rather than *racism* in these encounters at primary school. That is, they clearly see that "blackie" and "big bum" are references to racialized differences, but they do not recognize the unequal power that allows the white pupils to use *these* particular differences to subjugate them. Nevertheless, whether read as racism or not, the pain that these slurs inflict is clear and is indicative of how interpersonal racisms are experienced from an early age in the multiculture of British schools (Pérez Huber & Solorzano, 2015). The point here is that, although racism might be less recognized in primary schools, this does not mean that it is absent. Rather, as is evident across all of our studies, from primary school onward, racism slowly emerges as an explanatory framework to help Black mixed-race people make sense of their (minoritized) positions (Troyna & Hatcher, 1992).

School Transitions and the "Loss of Innocence"

For many of the participants in our studies, the move from primary to secondary school[6] was a transformational experience and represented an important coming-of-age process. Although many had experienced feeling othered at primary school, it was mostly at secondary school that they were able to identify and articulate more clearly the racism that was the driving force behind the prejudice they had previously experienced. Malcolm (Study A) explained, "As a kid you don't see it because you're not looking for it. [There was a] loss of innocence in growing up and … starting senior school." Others from Study A expressed similar experiences, Morgan explained: "At primary school age … I can't remember being called anything at all. My only experience of racism as a child was in secondary school." Upon entering secondary school, the pupils were no longer Black children but Black *youth*.[7] Accordingly, they would start to become vulnerable to many of the stereotypes that have been ascribed to this racialized group in British schools over time. It was during these formative years that many participants seemed to develop an increasing awareness of the possibility that secondary schools could be racist institutions (Gillborn, 2005). Here we turn to consider racism and prejudice from peers, racism from teachers, and racism in the curriculum.

Racism from White Pupils

As with their primary school experiences, many participants across our studies—and thus, across time periods—could identify being othered by their peers. By secondary school age, however, they became better equipped to draw out the nuances of the interactions. By the time they entered secondary school, many of them had developed a sense of *double consciousness* (Du Bois, 1903/2007; Yancy, 2017)—seeing oneself through the white gaze—which made them acutely aware of the anti-Black racisms that implicated their experience. By this age, and perhaps reflecting

74 Karis Campion and Remi Joseph-Salisbury

this double consciousness, many participants had come to recognize themselves as Black *and* mixed-race. This multilayered identification, we argue, is reflective of the overlapping but distinct experiences of Black mixed-race students. In the first instance, much of the racism experienced by Black mixed-race pupils is predicated on explicit anti-Blackness and is similar to that documented in studies of monoracial Black students. From being called "nigger, coon, Black bastard, or whatever" (Luke, Study B) to being subject to racialized sexual stereotypes, or "jokes" about hair, there was an abiding sense among most participants that they were *primarily* interpellated (and stereotyped) as monoracially Black. This was certainly the case for Theo (Study C), who recalled a violent encounter with a white peer:

> He was like "I'm not your mate you Black cunt get back to your own country" and I was like "who the fuck are you talking to?" and he grabbed me up against the wall and he was like "yeah, you Black this, you Black that, fuck off back to your own country," strangling me.

In this incident, Theo's interlocutor seeks to degrade him through specifically anti-Black racism. He reminds Theo of the old adage "There ain't no Black in the Union Jack" (Gilroy, 2013). Theo attended school well into the 2000s and even into the early 2010s. Contrary to the popular assumption that explicit racism in the UK only occurred in the distant past, his account is reflective of the persistence of explicit racism within the cosmopolitan context, adding to the evidence base which challenges claims that the ever-growing diversity of our societies has moved us toward the "postracial" (Goldberg, 2015).

There was also a sense among some participants that they were subject to more generalized white racism from peers. That is, they were subject to forms of racism that were aimed at all nonwhite students. In other cases, an inability to racialize Black mixed-race pupils meant that they were misrecognized in the racism they received from white pupils. This was the case in the following account from Chris (Study A), who, in the mid-1980s, started traveling from his ethnically diverse inner-city area in Birmingham to attend his new secondary school in a majority white area in the south of the city:

> [White pupils] didn't even understand where I was coming from. [They] were identifying me with something that had *no, no* correspondence with who I was, you know they're calling me a Paki. So, you're saying I'm from Pakistan, you're saying I'm Asian, you know it's anything that's not white. … Because I wasn't fully Black, because I was brown, I think they just associated brown with erm … Pakistanis or whatever it was, do you get what I mean?

In this account, Chris recalls experiencing racism commonly targeted at South Asian people in the UK ("Paki"). He attributes this to his interlocutor's inability

Black Mixed-Race Pupils in British Schools **75**

to recognize his identity as mixed-race. While Chris would undoubtedly ask for better solutions than his aggressors using the "correct" racial epithet, his account shows that—even at the level of interpersonal racism—Black mixed-race identities are often subsumed under monoracial categories. Although we might be tempted to see this as a consequence of the relative absence of discourses on racial mixedness in this historical period (for example, the absence of mixed-race categories on the national census), accounts from Study B and C show the endurance of these forms of erasure across time.

In addition to being misrecognized through explicit racist slurs, mixed-race pupils could also be subject to other more implicit misunderstandings about their identities. In a number of cases, these misunderstandings could be specifically predicated on the mixed-race identity of participants. For instance, Jake (Study B), who went to secondary school in the 2000s, lamented "people not being able to understand that I'm not adopted despite being told." He went on to reason, "Some people in the South-West find it rather difficult to comprehend interracial relationships." Seemingly, Jake and his family do not fit the archetypal same-race setup that he perceives as characterizing the region where he lives and goes to school. Such experiences can be impactful as they deny the legitimacy and reality of mixed-race families. In the context of a Black-white racial dichotomy, these experiences pose a particular threat to the schooling and well-being of Black mixed-race students. As Reece (Study B, also schooled in the 2000s) put it, conveying his frustrations at being assumed to be unrelated to his mother, "It's like fuck me?! It's cringe. It's really awkward, really awkward."

As Johnston and Nadal (2010, p. 126) argue, mixed-race people may be subject to interpersonal racisms predicated on Blackness as well as (simultaneously) being subject to forms of racism that are specifically related to their mixed-race identities. These examples signify how mixed-race pupils can simultaneously be hypervisible and invisible, as Black children in white-centered schools and as mixed-race children within the persistent Black-white racial dichotomy. That these complex experiences of erasure and visibility are not unique to one particular age cohort is indicative of the longevity of the racisms that have confronted mixed-race people in British schools and, until now, have been relatively unaccounted for.

Prejudice from Black Peers

Across our three studies, in addition to encounters with racism from white pupils, there were examples of prejudice from Black peers. Gabrielle (Study A, schooled in the late 1990s and early 2000s) explained the dynamics within her friendship group when she was at school: "My main majority of friends … were Black … I still kind of felt *in* with the Black kids but they still used to take the piss and call me zebra." In line with existing literature that suggests Black mixed-race young people *tend* to be in Black friendship groups (Campion, 2019; Lewis & Demie, 2019; Sims & Joseph-Salisbury, 2019),[8] Gabrielle was "in" with the Black kids.

However, her status within the group could seemingly come into question at times through jovial interactions and teasing. Robert, also from Study A, described a similar experience, of being simultaneously within *and* outside the boundaries of the Black peer group at his secondary school through the early-to-mid-1980s:

> Black people ... we were still a minority ... mixed-race we were even a smaller minority than the Blacks. ... At one stage it was a bit awkward because Blacks didn't accept us so we were in the middle. Like, "what would you do if there was a race war?" Because you're not Black and you're not white and you're on your own and there's only a couple of you.

In his reference to "we" Black people, Robert comfortably claims membership in the Black community. However, he also identifies himself as part of a mixed-race community in school that he perceives as constituting a minority *within* a minority at that time. The nuances of the Black mixed-race experience are clear from the "race war" question that, he recalls, would sometimes be posed by his peers, including Black counterparts. The question provides a momentary ultimatum, in that it requires an answer from him that signifies an allegiance to one racialized group as opposed to the expression of a hybridized positioning (Joseph-Salisbury, 2018). Further to this, the question serves as a manifestation of the historical pathological stereotypes that have emphasized the problematic position of mixed-race subjects as stuck *in between* two (or more) ethnic and/or racial categories, marginalized as a result, and unable to align with or reconcile these competing aspects of their racial selves (Aspinall, 2013; Christian, 2008; Stonequist, 1937).

Similar to the earlier example in the previous section, relating to the misunderstandings about family relations that can arise because of phenotypical differences within mixed-race families, there were some examples in our studies of Black mixed-race people specifically having "relations" to their *Black* family members scrutinized. This experience emerged as a point of contention for lighter-skinned Black mixed-race people in particular, who could sometimes "pass" as white at school. These participants gave specific examples of how other Black pupils would sometimes question their relation to *Black* parents, which could result in their claims to a Black identity and heritage being scrutinized (Campion, 2019). Janice (Study A, schooled in the 1990s and into the early 2000s) explained:

> I remember a guy asking me ... a Black guy ... at school ... he come up to me and he tapped me on the shoulder and was like "is your dad Black?" I was like "yeah," he was like "oh all right then."

Such disbelief about family connections is indicative of peer curiosities around mixed-race identities and can risk the threat of identity erasure for Black mixed-race pupils (Joseph-Salisbury, 2018). The threat of identity erasure was particularly high for pupils like Janice, who had rather "white" phenotypical features that could result in her Black heritage being "unseen" by peers. For Janice, her skin tone served as a primary marker of her ethnicity (Brunsma & Rockquemore, 2001):

> Erm, there was an incident actually when I was at secondary school, I think I was about 13—back in them days you was allowed to go out at lunchtime. … We was going to the chip shop … me … erm, another friend of mine who was Black, who I grew up with … another friend who was white … an Asian girl, a friend … we all was friends at school. And I was stopped by … a Black girl and a Black boy … and … basically they took our dinner money off of us … and I remember her saying to my Black friend, well "we're not gonna trouble you cuz you're one of us" … but *that's* the bit that stuck with me. I wasn't bothered they took the money off me … but when she said "you're one of us," I thought *wow*.

Janice's experience of not being recognized as Black speaks to Song and Aspinall's (2012) concept of "racial mismatch," which explains the disjuncture between *observed* and *expressed* identities that mixed-race subjects can encounter. It is clear that, when considering interactions with peers, Black mixed-race students can be subject to racism from white peers and prejudice from Black peers.[9] While our respondents generally felt white racism was more harmful (perhaps because of the power it accrues from its structural positioning), Black prejudice, at times, can harm Black mixed-race students (Campion, 2019). Much of the racism our respondents experienced came in the form of microaggressions (everyday—often deniable—articulations of structural racism), oftentimes metacommunicating the erasure of mixed-race identities. This has to be a consideration for schools and educators hoping to foster more cosmopolitan environments that recognize and embrace the multiplicity of identities present in contemporary British schools.

Racism from Teachers

As research has shown, for better or for worse, schoolteachers play a key role in shaping the schooling experiences of Black mixed-race students (Joseph-Salisbury, 2016; Tikly et al., 2004; Williams, 2011). A recurrent theme in our studies was that of racialized and racist low teacher expectations. As Aaron (Study C) put it, "They don't expect mixed-race pupils to do well." In this sense, the experiences of Black mixed-race students are again akin to those of their Black peers. In many cases, we found that those low expectations were based on anti-Black discourses that enveloped Black mixed-race pupils as part of a pathologized Black monolith. Participants from across the range of age groups gave examples of this experience, which indicates the persistence of anti-Black sentiment in British schools over time. The racism from teachers seemed particularly acute and explicit for older participants like Isabelle (Study A), who attended secondary school through the late 1970s and early 1980s,

> Schools were extremely racist ... they put Black children to the back of the class ... they never believed you wanted to learn. If you showed any interest in anything, it wasn't pursued *at all* ... they weren't putting Black kids forward for anything, only sport. ... If you ask a lot of Black and mixed parentage children, you know, "what do you want to do when you grow up?" ... they would already decide for you, what you were going to do ... you were gonna be a cleaner ... you weren't gonna be a lawyer or doctor.

Evidently, "the lingering pseudo-scientific beliefs in the intellectual inferiority of Black children," which had consistently characterized educational policies and the culture of British schools and teachers, negatively implicated Black mixed-race trajectories in a very similar vein to their Black counterparts (Tomlinson, 2008, p. 40). However, as was the case with racism from white peers, there was also evidence of low teacher expectations that were based on stereotypical views of mixed-race identities. For instance, Taylor (Study B, schooled in the late 1990s and early 2000s) spoke of teachers acting as if he "was troubled," "confused," and from a broken family. He attributed this specifically to his interpellation as mixed-race. Simultaneously, therefore, our participants felt that they were subject to anti-Black stereotypes of being loud, disruptive, and "educationally subordinate" (Coard, 1971) and mixed-race-specific stereotypes of identity "confusion" and fragmented home lives (Haynes et al., 2006). It is clear, therefore, that while overlapping with Black peers and other mixed-race groups, "Blackness and mixedness interact to create unique and specific barriers" in the lives of Black mixed-race pupils (Joseph-Salisbury, 2016, p. 155).

It bears stating that the negative stereotypes that threaten to surround Black mixed-race students are not only enacted by individual teachers but manifest throughout society, and particularly in media and political discourses. For instance, as Chairman of the Commission for Racial Equality in 2007, Trevor Phillips spoke problematically of mixed-race people growing up "marooned between communities" (Caballero & Aspinall, 2018, p. 6). It is apparent, therefore, that the challenges facing Black mixed-race students in schools extend beyond the immediate confines of the school and are a surface-level articulation of the white supremacy underpinning British society and its institutions. This has to be a significant consideration for any interventions that cosmopolitan forms of education seek to make. While many Black mixed-race students found ways to overcome the negative perceptions of their teachers (Joseph-Salisbury, 2019a), it is worth heeding the following assertion from Aaron (Study C):

> I don't think that should take the emphasis away from the schools and the teachers. It still should be the schools that make changes to accommodate the students. Not the other way around.

As well as the low expectations, there was evidence across our studies of teachers engaging in racially microaggressive acts toward racially minoritized students generally, and toward Black mixed-race students particularly. For instance, Leon (Study B, schooled in the 2000s) incredulously recalled a teacher telling him, in response to his handwriting mistake, that, "*in this country* we put dots over our i's." As Leon declared of his being rendered as an outsider in the country, "That is really racist." Participants across our studies also conveyed a sense that teachers lacked racial literacy (Twine, 2004)—it is damning that there was little sense of improvement across the accounts of those in Study A (schooled between the 1960s and 2000s) and those in studies B and C (schooled in the late 1990s and early 2000s). This meant that teachers could both be the perpetrators of racism in schools and be ill-prepared to deal with racist incidents when they arose. The inability to deal confidently with racism in schools is a woeful inadequacy in teaching, insofar as it hinders teachers' ability to exercise a duty of care to racially minoritized students, as in the example below. Levi (Study A), started secondary school in the early 1980s:

> Teachers wouldn't really challenge it. … I remember once somebody wrote "Everett nigger" on my desk and I pointed it out to the teacher and she just says, "Oh, I'll clean it up after." … I was like, "Okay, I don't really want it cleaned up, I want whoever's done this to be told about it."

This type of willful ignorance by teachers, in response to racisms at school, also featured in some of the more contemporary accounts across our studies. The ineffective response of teachers and the school created a sense of vulnerability for Black mixed-race students. In some cases, where students felt compelled to take things into their own hands (as a consequence of school failures), this had negative disciplinary implications (such as exclusion) for the Black mixed-race student who was the victim of a racist incident.

While issues with teachers are worthy of attention, it is important to see these as structural and institutional problems that are, in part, the consequence of a lack of training, the absence of school-level antiracist policies, and a general lack of institutional (and societal) commitment to improving the experiences of racially minoritized students (Doharty, 2019; Gillborn, 2005). In this sense, interventions must be structural and institutional, and—importantly—must not inadvertently erase mixed-race experiences. The lack of institutional commitment we observe in the context of teaching is also manifest clearly in the curriculum.

Racism in the Curriculum

The majority of our Black mixed-race participants were incredibly disappointed and frustrated by their school curricula, and this was cited as a key barrier facing Black mixed-race students (Tikly et al., 2004). Reflecting on his schooling in the early 2000s, Taylor (Study C) exemplified this sense of urgency around the curriculum: "The curriculum should be the starting point. It's so central to everything and it's so bad, so white, that's where I'd start." Expressions of dissatisfaction with the ethnocentricity of the national curriculum have been a consistent concern for Black mixed-race pupils historically. Ezra (Study A) recalled his frustration with the content being delivered in his class in the late 1980s:

> Why are you teaching us about drawbridges and castles? Why ain't you teaching us about slavery? … We don't wanna know about … the Battle of Hastings. We wanna know about the Middle Passage, we wanna know how we got here.

These revisionist histories in the curriculum mean that students too often fail to grapple with the realities of the British Empire and remain ill-informed about the realities and long histories of the Black presence in the UK (Atkinson et al., 2018). As participants conveyed, this ethnocentricity also manifests in the erasure of the achievements and contributions of Black communities (in which and with which many Black mixed-race students identify). However, while participants called for greater Black representation, some also suggested that this should include a recognition of mixed-race identities. On this point, Craig (Study C, schooled in the late 1990s and early 2000s) reasoned that "some might get that from a curriculum targeted at Black kids, but why not include mixed-race stuff too?" Jamie (Study C, schooled in the early 2000s) also explicitly referenced mixed-race people when he argued:

> If people want racial equality, everyone to have equal chances, then there has to be a drive to represent all minority groups in the curriculum and mixed-race people need to be a part of that. If the curriculum is just designed for white people and to include white people then it is going to advantage white people.

Jamie makes an important set of points here that reflects several of the accounts across our study. First, he argues for the importance of representation in the curriculum. This intervention has been widely posited in existing antiracist education scholarship. Yet, Jamie's position is antithetical to recent shifts in British education. The British curriculum has become increasingly narrow and insular owing to the broader pushback against multicultural educational policies that has sought to promote so-called "fundamental British values" in recent years (Alexander, Weekes-Bernard, & Arday, 2015; Habib, 2018). Mostly introduced as a response to anxieties about "terrorism" and "extremism" in schools, instead of recognizing the cosmopolitanism of 21st-century Britishness these "values" flatten out differences. Disguised under the banners of tolerance, integration, and cohesion, the problematic teaching of "fundamental British values" is deeply reminiscent of the nascent assimilationist approaches within schools that sought to bring "immigrant" children in line with so-called British culture by erasing their own (Tomlinson, 2008).

In noting the general absence of racially monitored groups in curricula, Jamie also calls for a specific focus on mixed-race identities within the overall project of increased representation. Without such a focus, the inclusion of some (monoracial) groups can act to further the exclusion of other (mixed-race) groups. Thus, in the absence of a consideration of mixed-race students, what appear to be progressive interventions can in fact constitute forms of *monoracism* (Johnston & Nadal, 2010).[10] We contend that the seeds for the inclusion of mixed-race students are already in place with figures like Mary Seacole and Bob Marley (as well as, for example, Jackie Kay, W. E. B. Du Bois, Malcolm X, and Huey P. Newton) providing perfect opportunities to explore the interconnectedness and fluidity of Black and Black mixed-race identities (Joseph-Salisbury & Andrews, 2017). It is important that this representation, however, does not become mere tokenism, as it so often has in the history of British education.

Conclusion

This chapter intervenes at a point when mixed-race populations are rapidly growing but in-depth considerations of mixed-race lives are often lacking. For this reason, this chapter has drawn upon three studies to center the experiences and specific needs of Black mixed-race students. We show that many of the challenges that Black mixed-race students face endure over time. Thus, progress and change are too slow. We have argued that antiracist changes aimed at improving education need to incorporate a consideration of racial mixedness. Given that Black mixed-race student experiences often overlap with racially minoritized students generally, and Black students particularly, more general interventions can benefit Black mixed-race students. However, without a specific focus on racial mixedness, there is simultaneously a danger that such interventions can intensify the marginalization of mixed-race students. In this regard, we echo Williams (2011, p. 17), who argues:

> There are times when it is expedient to view black and mixed-race as one group, as there are some obvious and pertinent connections to be made with pupils of black British heritage. However, common stereotypes and assumptions made about mixed-race pupils should mean there are also distinct strategies employed for the mixed-race group.

Arguing that Black mixed-race students seem to recognize racism as racism in their secondary school years, we have highlighted three particular areas where racisms manifest: racism from teachers, racism from peers, and racism in the curriculum. Although there are other sites worthy of concern (school policies, for instance), we argue that these three areas should be seen as key sites for interventions aimed

82 Karis Campion and Remi Joseph-Salisbury

at raising the attainment of—and improving the experiences of—mixed-race students. While mixed-race identities often embody the plurality that cosmopolitan approaches to education seek to capture, as our participants make clear, this perspective has to be undergirded by a commitment to visibilizing and dismantling white supremacy.

Notes

1 The "Other Mixed" group is the largest of all the mixed groups in schools, which speaks to the ever-growing diversity of mixed ethnicities in the UK.
2 It is worth noting that there is some variation within the Black and "Black mixed-race" categories. This manifests in higher attainment and lower exclusion for "Black African" and "White and Black African" students in comparison with their respective "Black Caribbean" and "White and Black Caribbean" counterparts.
3 Unlike the US equivalent, busing in the UK was "one-way traffic," meaning the onus was entirely on "immigrant" children to be bused (Butler, 2012). In the UK, there was a political consensus that there should be no more than 30% of "immigrant" children in any one school.
4 In this chapter, we take our understanding of racial microaggressions from Pérez Huber and Solorzano (2015) who show that everyday racisms are not abstract phenomena but are mediated by institutional racisms and macro-level white supremacy.
5 In the UK, *primary school* generally refers to schooling for children from age 5 to 11.
6 *Secondary school* in the UK generally refers to compulsory schooling from age 11 to 18.
7 "Black youth" have been the subject of various racialized and racist moral panics in the UK.
8 This is not to say that there is no variation among Black mixed-race people, or to ignore the reality that Black mixed-race people form a range of relationships (Joseph-Salisbury, 2018), but merely to reflect a common pattern.
9 We use the terms Black *prejudice* and white *racism* to reflect the role that power plays in constituting racism, and to account for the *disempowered* structural locations of Black communities. That is, Black people do not occupy a structural position of power that enables them to be racist to Black mixed-race people.
10 Johnston and Nadal (2010, p. 125) define *monoracism* as "a social system of psychological inequality where individuals who do not fit monoracial categories may be oppressed on systemic and interpersonal levels because of underlying assumptions and beliefs in singular, discrete racial categories."

References

Alexander, C., Weekes-Bernard, D., & Arday, J. (2015). Introduction: Race and education—contemporary contexts and challenges. In C. Alexander, D. Weekes-Bernard, & J. Arday (Eds.), *The Runnymede school report: Race, education and inequality in contemporary Britain* (pp. 4–5). London, UK: Runnymede Trust.

Ali, S. (2003). *Mixed-race, post-race*. Oxford, UK: Berg.

Ali, S. (2012). The sense of memory. *Feminist Review, 100*(1), 88–105. doi: 10.1057/fr.2011.71

Archer, L., & Yamashita, H. (2003). Theorising inner-city masculinities: "Race", class, gender and education. *Gender and Education, 15*(2), 115–132. doi: 10.1080/09540250303856

Aspinall, P. J. (2013). The social evolution of the term "half-caste" in Britain: The paradox of its use as both derogatory racial category and self-descriptor. *Journal of Historical Sociology, 26*(4), 503–526. doi: 10.1111/johs.12033

Atkinson, H., Bardgett, S., Budd, A., Finn, M., Kissane, C., Qureshi, S., ... Sivasundaram, S. (2018). *Race, ethnicity & equality in UK history: A report and resource for change*. London, UK: Royal Historical Society.

Beck, U. (2007). The cosmopolitan condition. *Theory, Culture & Society, 24*(7–8), 286–290. doi: 10.1177/02632764070240072505

Bhabha, H. (1994). *The location of culture*. New York: Routledge.

Brunsma, D. L., & Rockquemore, K. A. (2001). The new color complex: Appearances and biracial identity. *Identity, 1*(3), 225–246. doi: 10.1207/S1532706XID0103

Butler, V. (2012, October 4). Advocates of bussing should learn from British history and not just the US. *HuffPost*. Retrieved from https://www.huffingtonpost.co.uk/vicki-butler/bussing-uk-segregation_b_1938803.html

Caballero, C., & Aspinall, P. (2018). *Mixed race Britain in the twentieth century*. London, UK: Palgrave Macmillan.

Caballero, C., Haynes, J., & Tikly, L. (2007). Researching mixed race in education: Perceptions, policies and practices. *Race, Ethnicity and Education, 10*(3), 345–362. doi: 10.1080/13613320701503389

Campion, K. (2017). *Making mixed race: Time, place and identities in Birmingham* (Unpublished doctoral dissertation). University of Manchester, Manchester, UK.

Campion, K. (2019). "You think you're Black?" Exploring Black mixed-race experiences of Black rejection. *Ethnic and Racial Studies, 42*(16), 196–213. doi: 10.1080/01419870.2019.1642503

Carby, H. V. (1982). Schooling in Babylon. In Centre for Contemporary Cultural Studies (Ed.), *The empire strikes back: Race and racism in 70s Britain* (pp. 183–211). London, UK: Hutchinson & Co.

Child immigrants "bussed" out to school to aid integration. (2017, January 30). *BBC News*. Retrieved from https://www.bbc.co.uk/news/uk-england-leeds-38689839

Christian, M. (2008). The Fletcher report 1930: A historical case study of contested Black mixed heritage Britishness. *Journal of Historical Sociology, 21*(2–3), 213–241. doi: 10.1111/j.1467-6443.2008.00336.x

Coard, B. (1971). *How the West Indian child is made educationally sub-normal in the British school system*. London, UK: New Beacon Books.

Doharty, N. (2019). "I FELT DEAD": Applying a racial microaggressions framework to Black students' experiences of black history month and black history. *Race, Ethnicity and Education, 22*(1), 110–129. doi: 10.1080/13613324.2017.1417253

Du Bois, W. E. B. (2007). *The souls of Black folk*. Oxford, UK: Oxford University Press. (Original work published 1903)

Esteves, O. (2018). Babylon by bus? The dispersal of immigrant children in England, race and urban space (1960s–1980s). *Paedagogica Historica, 54*(6), 750–765. doi: 10.1080/00309230.2018.1521451

Gillborn, D. (2005). Education policy as an act of white supremacy: Whiteness, Critical Race Theory and education reform. *Journal of Education Policy, 20*(4), 485–505.

Gillborn, D. (2008). *Racism and education: Co-incidence or conspiracy?* London, UK: Routledge.

Gilroy, P. (2013). *There ain't no Black in the Union Jack* (Routledge Classics, 2nd ed.). London, UK: Routledge. (Original work published 1987)

Goldberg, D. T. (2015). *Are we all postracial yet?* Cambridge, UK: Polity Press.

Government of the United Kingdom. (2018). Age groups. *Ethnicity facts and figures*. Retrieved from https://www.ethnicity-facts-figures.service.gov.uk/uk-population-by-ethnicity/demographics/age-groups/latest

Government of the United Kingdom. (2019). GCSE English and maths results. *Ethnicity Facts and Figures*. Retrieved from https://www.ethnicity-facts-figures.service.gov.uk/education-skills-and-training/11-to-16-years-old/a-to-c-in-english-and-maths-gcse-attainment-for-children-aged-14-to-16-key-stage-4/latest#by-ethnicity

Government of the United Kingdom. (2020). Pupil exclusions. *Ethnicity Facts and Figures*. Retrieved from https://www.ethnicity-facts-figures.service.gov.uk/education-skills-and-training/absence-and-exclusions/pupil-exclusions/latest

Habib, S. (2018). *Learning and teaching British values: Policies and perspectives on British identities*. London, UK: Palgrave Macmillan.

Haynes, J., Tikly, L., & Caballero, C. (2006). The barriers to achievement for white/Black Caribbean pupils in English schools. *British Journal of Sociology*, *27*(5), 569–583. doi: 10.1080/01425690600958766

Johnston, M. P., & Nadal, K. L. (2010). Multiracial microaggressions: Exposing monoracism in everyday life and clinical practice. In D. W. Sue (Ed.), *Microaggressions and marginality: Manifestation, dynamics, and impact* (pp. 123–144). New York: John Wiley & Sons.

Joseph-Salisbury, R. (2013). *Black mixed-race male identity in the UK* (Unpublished master's thesis). University of Leeds, Leeds, UK.

Joseph-Salisbury, R. (2016). *Black mixed-race men, hybridity, and post-racial resilience*. Leeds, UK: University of Leeds.

Joseph-Salisbury, R. (2017). Black mixed-race male experiences of the UK secondary school curriculum. *Journal of Negro Education*, *86*(4), 449–462.

Joseph-Salisbury, R. (2018). *Black mixed-race men*. Leeds, UK: Emerald.

Joseph-Salisbury, R. (2019a). Black mixed-race men and the Black monster: Challenging the axiom of self-fulfilling prophecies. In S. N. J. Blackman, D. A. Conrad, & L. I. Brown (Eds.), *Achieving inclusive education in the Caribbean and beyond: From philosophy to praxis* (pp. 121–132). Cham, Switzerland: Springer Nature.

Joseph-Salisbury, R. (2019b). Institutionalised whiteness, racial microaggressions and Black bodies out of place in higher education. *Whiteness and Education*, *4*(1), 1–17.

Joseph-Salisbury, R., & Andrews, K. (2017). Locating black mixed-raced males in the black supplementary school movement. *Race, Ethnicity and Education*, *20*(6), 752–765. doi: 10.1080/13613324.2016.1248838

Lewis, K., & Demie, F. (2019). The school experiences of mixed-race white and Black Caribbean children in England. *Ethnic and Racial Studies*, *42*(12), 2065–2083. doi: 10.1080/01419870.2018.1519586

Pérez Huber, L., & Solorzano, D. G. (2015). Racial microaggressions as a tool for critical race research. *Race, Ethnicity and Education*, *18*(3), 297–320. doi:10.1080/13613324.2014.994173

Puwar, N. (2004). *Space invaders: Race, gender and bodies out of place*. Oxford, UK: Berg.

Sims, J. P., & Joseph-Salisbury, R. (2019). "We were all just the Black kids": Black mixed-race men and the importance of adolescent peer groups for identity development. *Social Currents*, *6*(1), 51–66. doi: 10.1177/2329496518797840

Song, M., & Aspinall, P. (2012). Is racial mismatch a problem for young "mixed race" people in Britain? The findings of qualitative research. *Ethnicities*, *12*(6), 730–753. doi: 10.1177/1468796811434912

Stonequist, E. (1937). *The marginal man: A study in personality and culture conflict*. New York: Russell and Russell.

Thompson, D. (2012). Making (mixed-)race: Census politics and the emergence of multiracial multiculturalism in the United States, Great Britain and Canada. *Ethnic and Racial Studies*, *35*(8), 1409–1426. doi: 10.1080/01419870.2011.556194

Tikly, L., Caballero, C., Haynes, J., & Hill, J. (2004). *Understanding the educational needs of mixed heritage pupils*. Research reports RR549. London, UK: Department for Education and Skills.

Tomlinson, S. (2008). *Race and education: Policy and politics in Britain*. Maidenhead, UK: Open University Press.

Troyna, B., & Hatcher, R. (1992). *Racism in children's lives: A study of mainly-white primary schools*. London, UK: Routledge.

Twine, F. W. (2004). A white side of Black Britain: The concept of racial literacy. *Ethnic and Racial Studies*, *27*(6), 878–907. doi: 10.1080/0141987042000268512

Vertovec, S. (2007). Super-diversity and its implications. *Ethnic and Racial Studies*, *30*(6), 1024–1054. doi: 10.1080/01419870701599465

Williams, D. (2011). *Mixed matters: Mixed-race pupils discuss school and identity*. Leicester, UK: Matador.

Yancy, G. (2017). *Black bodies, white gazes*. Plymouth, UK: Rowman and Littlefield.

Ydesen, C., & Myers, K. (2016). The imperial welfare state? Decolonisation, education and professional interventions on immigrant children in Birmingham, 1948–1971. *Paedagogica Historica*, *52*(5), 453–466. doi: 10.1080/00309230.2016.1192207

6

DE- AND RETERRITORIALIZING IDENTITIES

The Global Hip Hop Nation at Work in a Youth Hip Hop Recording Studio

Édouard Laniel-Tremblay and Bronwen Low

Discourses of many kinds—legal, political, media—separating a "*nous*" from "*vous*" often shape lived experience in Quebec, the Canadian province in the unusual situation of having its (French-speaking) dominant population be a minority in the rest of the country. At the time of writing, these discourses were particularly present and heated, fed and formed by interventions from the recently elected Coalition Avenir Québec (CAQ) government including a "secularism" law banning the wearing of religious symbols in the public sector; a mandated "values test" for newly arrived immigrants; and guidelines restricting access to English-language services in the province.[1] While such discourses and policies can cause great harm (see Shah, this volume), producing multiple and intersecting forms of exclusion, discrimination, and harassment for those identified as other, racially and culturally marginalized Québécois continue to find ways of creating alternate communities of belonging. These ways transcend identification with a specific culture. As Anthias (2011) describes, belonging involves more than claiming membership in a particular group, and is articulated through "practices" that "give rise to our sense of belonging" (p. 208), and through "the social places constructed by such identifications and memberships" as well as "the emotional and social bonds that are related to such places" (p. 209).

To better understand how racialized youth in Montreal are creating alternate communities of belonging, this chapter explores a particular social place that is very popular with local teenagers, with attendant emotional and social bonds and practices, where youth challenge and "rub up against monoglossic conceptions of norms" (Editors' Preface, this volume). NBS is a recording studio for youth, most of whom are deeply invested in Hip Hop culture (see NBS Studio, n.d.-a, for photos, audio, and video clips). The quality of NBS Studio's facilities and equipment, combined with the director's artistic and interpersonal skills and profound

DOI: 10.4324/9780429327780-6

commitment to empowering youth, have made this free-access studio a focal point for emerging artists in the Montreal Hip Hop community. While Quebec and Canadian master narratives, grounded in the settler-colonial project (Smith, 2014), can mark the migrant subject "for perpetual estrangement or conditional inclusion as supplicants" (Thobani, 2007, p. 6), racialized youth take center stage at NBS.

NBS is located at the Chalet Kent youth center in the Côte-des-Neiges neighborhood of Montreal. Côte-des-Neiges is one of the most diverse neighborhoods in the city and indeed the country: residents have origins in more than 35 countries, 40% self-identify as visible minorities, 77% of the population is identified as immigrant or first-generation, and more than 40% of the population was initially educated in a language other than French or English (Ville de Montréal, 2018). However, such statistics, in their reliance on information about countries and languages of origin and ethnicity, reproduce the diversity discourse that theorists of superdiversity have shown to be limited in understanding the "multiplication of significant variables that affect where, how and with whom people live" (Vertovec, 2007, p. 1025), ignoring the "mobility, complexity, and unpredictability" (Blommaert, 2013, p. 6) of contemporary social patterns, shaped by mass migration and the rise of the internet.

For the youth in our study, a key variable shaping how they live is their deep engagement with Hip Hop culture, supported via their participation in NBS Studio. This culture is deeply local, tied to the NBS Studio space in Chalet Kent and to the vibrant Hip Hop scene in Montreal, and transnational, connected to the Global Hip Hop Nation; technology is integral to both. In previous work on the Montreal Hip Hop community, Low and colleagues have focused on the role of language and language mixing in its constitution. We explored, for instance, how Hip Hop artists rapping in and across multiple languages flatten and rework dominant language hierarchies (Low, Sarkar, & Winer, 2009), defy prescriptivist monolingual mindsets (Low & Sarkar, 2014), fly in the face of official linguistic identities (francophone, anglophone, and allophone—this last a "none of the above" category invented in Quebec) through translanguaging (García, Bartlett, & Kleifgen 2007), and challenge the hierarchies of whiteness and French language variety that shape who is understood to be Québécois (Sarkar, Low, & Winer, 2007).

Other theorists have also noted Quebec Hip Hop culture's political charge, describing lyrics that are "critical responses to and interventions in xenophobia and nationalist debates and discourses of belonging" (Leppänen & Westinen, 2017, p. 3). Directly and indirectly challenging traditional approaches to framing, managing, and policing diversity in the province, these artists point to the inadequacies of the fixed and reductive concepts of language and culture undergirding official intercultural and language policies. In this way, they echo critics of multicultural policies and practices reliant on "definite, static, ahistorical and essentialist units of 'culture' with fixed boundaries and with little space for growth and change" (Anthias, 2011, p. 207) that can reproduce and reify binaries of "us" and "them."

In our earlier attention to complex, hybrid linguistic and identity work in Hip Hop in Montreal, we did not consider the spaces that foster it or the non-linguistic practices that produce and sustain alternate communities of belonging grounded in Hip Hop culture for youth. This study of NBS Studio extends this earlier work, with a focus on a particular location whose bonds and practices are both local and transnational, real and virtual. It brings spatial concepts of de- and reterritorialization into this collection's discussion of superdiversity and cosmopolitanism. Our analysis of NBS draws upon interviews with youth participants, our observations and fieldnotes, and examples of its social media activity and creative output.[2]

De- and Reterritorialization

Deterritorialization, according to Papastergiadis (2000), describes "the ways in which people now feel they belong to various communities despite the fact that they do not share a common territory with all the other members" (p. 115). Deterritorialization understands culture under conditions of globalization—shaped by global capitalism, processes of mobility, displacement, and migration, and new media and communication technologies—as hybrid, networked, and mobile, in contrast to traditional anthropological models of culture embedded within a "given territory" (Papastergiadis, 2000, p. 103). Deterritorialization can produce a critical distance from social norms and instrumental and controlling forms of culture, as in Braidotti's (1994) association of deterritorialization with "a critical consciousness that resists settling into socially coded modes of thoughts and behaviour"[3] (in Papastergiadis, 2000, p. 117).

Coexisting with deterritorialization is reterritorialization, which Papastergiadis (2000) describes as "an exilic search for home" regained through thought and feeling (p. 118) and Plüss (2006) envisions as "changing the ethnic identities of migrants by rooting them in their current place of abode" (p. 658). De- and reterritorialization are overlapping processes that produce and sustain multiple relations and affiliations. Both processes help us to understand the "glocal" (Alim & Pennycook, 2007) nature of Hip Hop culture; our study offers insight into how youth can experience these processes, which can be different from adults' experience (Hörschelmann & van Blerk, 2011, p. 126).

Hip Hop Traditions and Technologies

At the moment when Hip Hop, as an irruption, interrupts and distorts what is—the order of things—it formulates and incarnates an ontological critique. It besieges the foundation of things and categories, because it imposes itself from the ex nihilo capacity for affirmation, and did not wait

De- and Reterritorializing Identities **89**

for the assent of … or recognition of … Because it does not only invite one to desire something else, but to desire otherwise.

—Néméh-Nombré, 2018, p. 41, our translation

Irruption and distortion are key elements of Hip Hop culture's emergence, including the 1970s block parties in African American and Latinx communities in the South Bronx whose sound systems were hotwired to street lights (Rose, 1994), a musical sound created through the "specific mis-use and desecration of the artifacts of technology and the entertainment media" (Dery, 1994, p. 73), and lyrics, often politically charged, which broke the rules and tested the limits of free speech (Rose, 1994). The protest tradition of Hip Hop, shaped in part by roots in the Civil Rights and Black Power movements (Rabaka, 2013), is key to Hip Hop's political and cultural spread across the globe (Alim, Ibrahim, & Pennycook, 2009; Forman & Neal, 2012; Hill Collins, 2006; Mitchell, 2001). What gets called the Global Hip Hop Nation (GHHN) is a deterritorialized one, an "imagined" and "a multilingual, multiethnic" nation with "a fluid capacity to cross borders, and a reluctance to adhere to the geopolitical givens of the present" (Alim, 2009, p. 3). To "keep it real" (Low, Tan, & Celemencki, 2013; McLeod, 1999), a core Hip Hop postulate that privileges authenticity, Hip Hop traditions are often articulated with regional particularism, including local languages (Krims, 2000; Pennycook, 2007). Hip Hop is thus a strong example of how "cultures are simultaneously deteritorrialised and reterritorialised in a world 'on the move'" (Höorschelmann & van Blerk, 2011, p. 126).

The important role of African Americans, Latinx, and other people of color in the emergence of Hip Hop in the United States and France (whose Hip Hop scene is second only to that of the US in scale), and as trendsetters more generally (Kitwana, 2005, p. 95), helps explain the rhizomatic evolution, and irruption, of Hip Hop culture through the racialized communities of Montreal in the early 1980s (Lamort, 2017; Sarkar et al., 2007). Hip Hop centers Blackness, and the hypervisibility of Black and other racialized artists within Canadian Hip Hop can act as an ontological critique by challenging the historical marginalization and invisibility of nonwhite people within public space (Campbell, 2014; D'Amico, 2015). In the Quebec context, music by white rappers often needs first to be legitimized through statements of appreciation by members of racialized communities before being recognized by the community at large (Chamberland, 2006, p. 2). These processes around prestige and legitimacy in Hip Hop in Quebec can reverse the direction of dominant dynamics of power because of the symbolic weight that Hip Hop holds for this generation, making it an important player in the ongoing contestation of narratives and patterns of social exclusion (Arbour-Masse, 2017).[4]

Just as technologies (and their distortion) were key to Hip Hop's emergence, technology continues to be integral to Hip Hop, including production and recording software and hardware, online platforms for broadcasting and listening, and social media sites that help craft and disseminate rapper identities. As a deterritorialized culture, the GHHN is shaped and fueled by the internet, which enables its spread and fosters its vitality, including the resemiotization of Hip Hop cultural production and consumption as the youth rework (mixing, borrowing, sampling, and modifying) and thus appropriate Hip Hop cultural content in their own fashion (Varis & Blommaert, 2015). One example of how technology fosters innovation was the Piu Piu community or movement of beatmakers whose instrumental creations, shared online, helped forge the Quebec Hip Hop community while minimizing the importance of language to the form (Boudreault-Fournier & Blais, 2016). In this way, Piu Piu bypassed the cultural orthodoxy and colonial dichotomy that one was either a francophone or anglophone rapper (White, 2019, p. 6). Piu Piu both de- and reterritorialized the Quebec Hip Hop scene by devaluing the importance of locality—one's specific place of residence or origin—as a marker of identity, while at the same time revaluing the urban (Boudreault-Fournier & Blais, 2016). This angle of analysis helps to position the Hip Hop community at the forefront of challenges to traditional Quebec language and identity politics.

Inside NBS Studio: The Feel, Sights, and Sounds of Belonging

To enter NBS Studio, you must take the stairs to the basement of Chalet Kent youth center and cross the martial arts room and then a former bathroom converted into an impromptu digital audio station. You now come to a door. Open it and you have entered a sanctuary of youth and sound. Its three audio recording stations, stocked with professional equipment (some pieces donated, others purchased through grants), are always busy; here young producers, many trained at the studio, work with teens who have come to create and record their music— rehearsing raps and songs, laying down instrumental tracks, and creating beats. In the winter of 2019, Laniel-Tremblay conducted semi-structured individual interviews with nine youth. The participant group consists of six young men and three young women, aged 18–21, with origins in Chile, the Dominican Republic, France, Haiti, Lebanon, Madagascar, the Philippines, Senegal, and Vietnam.[5] All of these youth have grown up in multilingual households and have moved between neighborhoods or countries at some point. Five were born outside Canada. These movements contribute to the youths' feelings of deterritorialization and thus their openness to, and indeed need for, nongeographic and more abstract sources and strategies of belonging and identity.

"I Feel Different, No Matter Where I Go"

While each participant has a unique life trajectory influenced by the socioeconomic status of their family, their gender, their cultural background, and the

De- and Reterritorializing Identities **91**

languages they speak, similarities emerge among them, such as feeling othered and in-between cultures. In interviews, many NBS youth participants shared feelings of ambivalence both with respect to their identity construction as Québécois or Canadians and in relation to the cultures of origin of their parents. For instance, one female participant noted that "I feel a part that identifies me to each [the country of origin of her parents and Montreal], but at the same time, I feel that like, there is not really one that totally identifies me."[6] Another explained:

> I cannot define a place where I can call home, because I feel different no matter where I go. Like when I'm here it's like you're not a Canadian-Québécois because you're not pale. When I go to [country of family origin in Africa] well it's like I'm too pale to be from the place and then I get dressed differently, I speak differently, so that there is not really a place where I feel I belong.

This young person's identity seems suspended between cultures and places, limited by the racial dynamics of national membership. Her point about whiteness as a criterion for inclusion in Canada and Quebec reflects Day's (2016) argument that racialized people will always be excluded at some level from dominant Canadian society. In her family's country of origin, skin color is also a grounds for belonging or exclusion, reflecting the complex legacies of colonial pigmentocracies. Similar to the mixed-race youth in Campion and Joseph-Salibury's study (this volume), the impossibility of relying on traditional markers of national or ethnocultural identity, given their foundations in othering and discrimination, has the effect of encouraging these youth to look for other points of reference. Their passion for music brought them to Hip Hop culture.

"It Leads to a Kind of State of Mind, We Are All Together"

Clear from the interviews is that youth attend NBS in large part for the personal relationships and community—we witness youth achieving "community by participating in activities and acquiring experiences associated with membership in certain groups" (Editors' Preface, this volume). According to the youth participants, the studio is a space that fights social isolation. It allows them to reteritorrialize their identities within its walls via strong affective bonds; many of the youths described NBS as one of the first places where they felt that they really belonged to something, and where they experienced less stigma than elsewhere. In discussing this stigma, one participant described feeling hypervisible when he left the Island of Montreal. Another reported being the victim of racial profiling by the police (and although only one participant mentioned this in the interviews, youth at the center regularly describe profiling as part of their lived reality in the neighborhood). The population of youth attending the studio is very diverse and most of the youth are racialized, which offers the possibility of shared lived experience; a number of the youths described how the majority of their friends outside the studio are also racialized. This is not only a product of their diverse neighborhoods and schools but also a defensive strategy against othering, in which racialized bodies are experienced as sites of struggle within the Canadian colonial project (Mugabo, 2019; Néméh-Nombré, 2018; Walcott, 2001).

A tie that binds is a love of Hip Hop. One participant described how

> Hip Hop helped me get into a community, that's for sure. I started meeting more rappers, more people who share the same vision as me. I thought I was the only one, but in fact there are many who share the same vision as me about music.

The community and shared vision are enacted via collaboration, as this participant explained: "Even if the music is not deep, the process behind is, like, time spent at the studio, kind of helping each other all the time." It seems that the creative process is sometimes more appreciated than the final product and that relationships with others are integral. Another youth recounted,

> When we are here, we are a dozen, we are all there, well when there is enough room. There are people who are doing instrumentals, then wow! We are congratulating them, I have the impression that we are all united. It leads to a kind of state of mind, we are all together.

That sense of unity, forged through mutually supportive relations as well as space (as the youths squeeze themselves into the studio room), was echoed by another studio participant who said, "I consider every single rapper like family, you know?" This feeling of family, of all being together in a shared project, drives the peer mentorship model that shapes all aspects of the studio. As the studio director, Jai Nitai Lotus, describes, NBS is "teaching youth so they can teach each other." This philosophy is evidenced by the number of former youth participants employed as studio interns and staff.

"I Really Consider Myself a Montrealer but Not So Much a Québécois"

Some of the reterritorializing moves made by the youths include identifying with Montreal rather than Quebec or Canada. On many occasions in interviews, youths highlighted the distinction between the identity category *Québécois*, corresponding to white francophones, and *Montrealer*, which appears to these youths relatively more open to difference, including other identity affiliations (e.g., anglophones, racialized people). One participant describes this by saying, "I really consider myself a Montrealer but not so much a Québécois; Montreal because I'm

De- and Reterritorializing Identities **93**

from an ethnic minority and, like, if you identify with Quebec as such it's really the Québécois."

It seems that the French-English duality that historically characterized Montreal's cultural life and linguistic landscape, at least officially—since members of other cultures or speakers are lumped together as "cultural communities" or allophones—seems to be mutating for this generation toward a division between French-speaking white "Québécois" and multicultural and multilingual urban "Montrealers" (see Burman, 2007, for a discussion of Montreal as "multicultural" despite Quebec's policy of interculturalism, and in contrast with Toronto as a "diasporic city"). This distinction might have origins in the realization of young people that the identity category *Montrealer* is less hermetic than *Québécois*, and these young people feel a greater (though not ideal, as the comments about racial profiling made clear) sense of belonging in Montreal. Because of the ethnic diversity that second- and third-generation immigrant children bring into the Montreal cultural mix, one participant draws parallels with what happens in Toronto:

> In recent times, because of the second generation of immigrants, we have developed our own culture that is truly just Montrealers. Like a little bit like Toronto? ... In Montreal, we have our own culture so I really identify with Montreal.

This youth seems to envision Toronto as a kind of inclusive cosmopolitan ideal, something new and distinct forged through immigration, which does not take into consideration the realities of racism in Toronto (see Shah, this volume).

This division between Montreal and Quebec also affects participant understandings of the Hip Hop scene. As one youth noted:

> There is a big distinction because rap, ... it splits into two categories: Montreal rap and Quebec rap. The Montreal rap really comes from the city, the immigrants who came here. There are many influences from France ... and the United States.

By contrast, Quebec rap designates the rap of the white francophones. By identifying with Montreal and Montreal Hip Hop, these youths flip the social hierarchy that values white francophone culture over all others.

"We Out Here Live": De- and Reterritorializing Via Social Media

While the live relationships at NBS reterritorialize the identities of our participants in the time and place of the youth center, the Côte-des-Neiges neighborhood, and the city of Montreal more widely, feelings of belonging and affective ties are also fostered virtually via NBS's very lively social media presence—not surprising since social media are a principal identity construction tool for members of Generation Z (Seemiller & Grace, 2019, p. 10). The young people attending the studio are very active on platforms like Instagram, Snapchat, and to a lesser extent Facebook, regularly posting and sharing stories of their creative activities with photos, videos, and livestreamed broadcasts. Moreover, the youths move almost seamlessly between offline and online conversations; this blurring of boundaries can also include their real-life and artistic personas. By sharing music through a social media post or an Instagram or Snapchat story, they build their reputations as artists and members of the Montreal Hip Hop community. Their avatars on social media are an integral part of this artistic identity construction, complementing their lyrics, music, and their presence on stage.

An example of how NBS creates a strong collective sense or mythology of itself through cultural production shared online is the series of visual stories filmed by the young artists that they have named "We Out Here Live" (NBS Studio, n.d.-b). These stories showcase original NBS music tracks; yet, as in the interviews, much of the emphasis in the videos is on collaborative processes. The "We Out Here Live" videos are mostly set inside the studio, complemented by occasional shots of the Côte-des-Neiges neighborhood. They have a handheld-camera aesthetic and often integrate footage from cell phones; the low-tech, improvised style of the videos is a deliberate choice that feels authentic to the teens. In one clip featuring a young artist called "Bronko," the rapper is lit by a circle of cell phones held by youths surrounding him, both symbolically and actually placing him in the spotlight. In the "We Out Here Live" stories, performers are never alone. They are sometimes accompanied by live musicians and at other times by appreciative listeners, moving in time to the beats and lyrics. Through this series and NBS social media activity more generally, the youth and staff ground themselves in a particular place rich with meaning, creating a sense of locality as they repeatedly document the particularities of the studio, the larger youth center, and the surrounding neighborhood. The coexistence of the real and the virtual as the youth take space and make themselves visible both on- and offline suggests the importance of both for a generation that often communicates through social networks (Dovchin, Pennycook, & Sultana, 2018) but also seemingly values live connections in a physical space. Pragmatically, the social media presence of the NBS studio community has contributed to the local credibility of the studio, which has resulted in increased studio attendance, invitations to perform at public events across the city, and the recording of numerous tracks by young artists across the city.

NBS's reterritorialization of identity and community through social media is also a deterritorializing move, given that its online audience is not limited by geography—through their stories of self and place the youths inscribe NBS as an important creative hub within the larger Global Hip Hop Nation. These social media practices of NBS Studio thus make clear that the youths' identity practices

De- and Reterritorializing Identities **95**

are simultaneously local and global, an instance of glocalization in which the participants draw upon the international codes of Hip Hop culture while "keepin' it real" by hybridizing these codes within their lived realities in Montreal.

Creating a Montreal "Hiphoplect": Moving Between the Local and Global

These lived realities include the multilingual language practices of the youths' families and neighborhoods. As in our previous data on Hip Hop artists in Montreal, what Schecter and James (Preface, this volume) describe as "idiosyncratic linguistic practices" remain a powerful strategy mobilized by youth at NBS for crafting identities and community. In this section, we explore this Hip Hop language use, what we are calling a *hiphoplect*, as a tool for both de- and reterritorializing belonging. Take, for instance, the first creative collaboration between NBS Studio and Espace Paris Jeunes Mahalia Jackson, a similar youth center program in Paris. The two studios are creating a shared "mixtape," prompted by their common interest in building connections with Hip Hop youth programs elsewhere. The teams are currently sending beats and lyrics back and forth to be combined, extended, and remixed. To begin, NBS shared several tracks created by youth; the Paris group selected one with beats and a rapped chorus with blank spaces for additional vocals, and then rapped and sang into it. The lyrics annotated in Table 6.1 are from the first track, entitled "Oulala," featuring the chorus created by a young man from Côte-des-Neiges who mixes French and words borrowed from Maghrebi Arabic, Haitian Creole, English, and Hip Hop English.

The first line, equivalent to the common Hip Hop address "What's up?" (Doeff, 2016), establishes this artist's familiarity with both the codes of Hip Hop and a piece of Montreal slang popular with youth regardless of their cultural origins, and also with France's *racaille* (or thug) style of Hip Hop. Another common

TABLE 6.1 Lyrics from "Oulala" on the Montreal-Paris mixtape

Lyrics	*English translation*
Wesh wesh **sa ka fetè**,	What's up, what's up
C'est <u>today</u> que j'ferai ta fête	I will "roast" you today
Ils se sont mis à quatre pattes,	They got down on four legs
Aujourd'hui i'mangent des pâtes	Today they eat pasta
T'as trop compté sur tes **pats**,	You rely too much on your friends
Résultat t'es cuit comme un rat	So that your "goose is cooked"
Tu leur as fait croire qu't'étais un G,	You make them believe you were a gangsta
Va pas s'mentir ouais t'es *zabi*	We won't lie yeah, you're a piece of shit

Coding: Quebec French / *Maghrebi Arabic* / **Haitian Creole** / <u>English</u> / HIP HOP ENGLISH

96 Édouard Laniel-Tremblay and Bronwen Low

variation in Quebec French is the elision of a vowel to merge words (e.g., *j'ferai* instead of *je ferai* or *qu't'étais* instead of *que tu étais*), contributing to the localization. When asked about the use of multiple languages, the author, whose background is Northwest African, responded, "It's normal, because it is the language I've grown up with and use all the time." The term "G" also signals the artist's familiarity with Hip Hop terminology in English, while "pats," short for the Haitian Creole *patnè* (Séraphin, 2017), flags the important role of Haitian Creole in Montreal French Hip Hop expressions.

When played to a group of people at an annual assembly at Chalet Kent for the first time, the chorus invoked cries of delight from youth who seemed to appreciate hearing this mix of their current linguistic expressions. The rest of the track features the youth from Paris rapping the song's verses in French, and at one point singing in Arabic, in response to the chorus from Montreal. It is a vivid illustration of the dynamism of the *francophonie*, and in particular, what we are thinking of as a *francophonie des jeunes et de la rue* (a francophone community of youth and the street), as these teens in two different countries create together in French mixed with the other languages spoken in their neighborhoods. As an overt international collaboration, "Oulala" performs what is already present in much of the glocal music created at NBS, as microlocal (e.g., NBS Studio), local (e.g., Montreal), and national (e.g., Canada, Quebec) references are in constant dialogue with the transnational flows of Hip Hop (Alim et al., 2009).

Part of the reason these lyrics, representative of much of what gets created at NBS, build a sense of community for the youth is that they index the language of racialized people in Montreal. In accordance with the "keepin' it real" motto of Hip Hop, the youth intuitively draw upon the multilingualism and translanguaging practices found in their homes and neighborhoods. This Montreal hiphoplect challenges Quebec's official monolingual language policies (as one of the youths pointed out sarcastically, "Montreal, which does not mix languages!"), celebrating language standards from the ground up. In the process, these youths create linguistic referents with high social and cultural prestige for members of a generation that highly values Hip Hop (Arbour-Masse, 2017).

NBS: Anchor and Pivot

By drawing upon Hip Hop referents, the youth at NBS are able to counter and undermine the values of the nation-state (Papastergiadis, 2000, p. 109), while creating a home for themselves that is responsive to their collective, cross-bordered histories and their ongoing, dynamic gestures toward an emancipatory cosmopolitan identity. Through our analysis of the interviews, the "We Out Here Live" social media series, and the first track in the Paris-Montreal mixtape, we see participants seeking and enacting belonging through place, practices, feeling, and sight and sound. In interviews, the study participants expressed an ambiguous, incomplete sense of belonging to Quebec, Canada, and/or their parents' countries of origin. Youth counter the limited identity options they see made available to them by claiming as their own the space and place of NBS Studio firmly established in Côte-des-Neiges and the Montreal Hip Hop scene. NBS studio thus acts as an anchor and pivot point for young emerging Hip Hop artists in Montreal, grounding the relatively abstract identity of the Montreal Hip Hop community in local spaces and values, defined in its own terms, and connecting it to the wider Hip Hop community. The youth can start small, begin to experiment in the safety of NBS Studio, and then use its platforms to reach out when ready through social media to wider audiences and communities. The concepts of deterritorialization and reterritorialization help us to understand the dynamic movement NBS allows between the local and the global, as the youth mobilize micro and macro cultural references and communities while developing their identities and sense of belonging. By documenting their art and space on social media, and using a specifically Montreal hiphoplect in their lyrics, artists from NBS are indexing their identities to their neighborhood, their city, and local and global Hip Hop culture. Because Hip Hop is a prestige culture developed by Black and racialized communities in North America and internationally, it can act as a powerful ontological critique of Quebec and Canadian dominant narratives of belonging.

Notes

1 The Coalition Avenir Québec government passed Bill 21 restricting religious symbol wearing for any member of the public service seen as having power over others in June 2019 (Quebec, 2019); the values test was introduced in January 2020 as part of the immigration process; an election promise to cut immigration numbers by 20% had been exceeded by 5% in the first year of the CAQ mandate (Bruemmer, 2019; Sucar, 2019)
2 Although as a white graduate student and a white university professor we are in many ways outsiders to the largely racialized community of youth and facilitators at Chalet Kent, Laniel-Tremblay conducted the interviews during the winter of 2018–2019 after a year of relationship building at NBS Studio, and at the time of writing, Low has been on the board of Chalet Kent for 15 years, 12 of these as president. These ties are integral to our access and our confidence in our interpretations, which have also been checked with center and studio staff.
3 That said, deterritorialized identities are not necessarily progressive or liberatory, and Papastergiadis (2000) also invokes Appadurai's work on culture and modernity in which he argues that diasporic communities can also be deeply traditional, including retreating to fundamentalist visions for their homelands.
4 However, Hip Hop in Quebec is also afflicted by manifestations of anti-Blackness, as in the invisibilization of its Black ethos when it accesses Quebec's mainstream public space (Néméh-Nombré, 2018). As well, intertwined dynamics of plurilingualism, race, and gender can also undermine access to public space, as demonstrated in Lesacher's (2014) intersectional analysis of the challenges faced by female Haitian rap artists in Montreal.
5 In order to share NBS Studio's identity via its social media sites, giving interested readers a visual and auditory glimpse into the space and its practices while still protecting participant confidentiality, we are not creating specific profiles.
6 Translations of interviews from French to English are Laniel-Tremblay's.

References

Alim, H. S. (2009). Introduction. In H. S. Alim, A. Ibrahim, & A. Pennycook (Eds.), *Global linguistic flows: Hip Hop cultures, youth identities, and the politics of language* (pp. 1–22). New York: Routledge.

Alim, H. S., Ibrahim, A., & Pennycook, A. (Eds.). (2009). *Global linguistic flows: Hip Hop cultures, youth identities, and the politics of language*. New York: Routledge.

Alim, H. S., & Pennycook, A. (2007). Introduction to the special issue: Glocal linguistic flows: Hip-Hop culture(s), identities, and the politics of language education. *Journal of Language, Identity, & Education, 6*(2), 89–100.

Anthias, F. (2011). Intersections and translocations: New paradigms for thinking about cultural diversity and social identities. *European Educational Research Journal, 10*(2), 204–217.

Arbour-Masse, O. (2017, September 27). Comment le rap queb est-il devenu la musique de l'heure? *Rad*. Retrieved from https://www.rad.ca/dossier/rap/6/comment-le-rap -queb-est-il-devenu-la-musique-de-lheure

Blommaert, J. (2013). *Ethnography, superdiversity and linguistic landscapes: Chronicles of complexity*. Clevedon, UK: Multilingual Matters.

Boudreault-Fournier, A., & Blais, L. K. (2016). La comète piu piu: Nouveaux médias et nationalisme en mutation. *Anthropologie et Sociétés, 40*(1), 103–123. doi: 10.7202/1036373ar

Braidotti, R. (1994). *Nomadic subjects: Embodiment and sexual difference in contemporary feminist theory*. New York: Columbia University Press.

Bruemmer, R. (2019, November 26). CAQ targets newcomers with more restrictions on access to English services. *Montreal Gazette*. Retrieved from https://montrealgazette .com/news/quebec/caq-targets-newcomers-with-more-restrictions-on-access-to-en glish-services

Burman, J. (2007). Divergent diversities: Pluralizing Toronto and Montreal. In J. Sloan (Ed.), *Urban enigmas: Montreal, Toronto, and the problem of comparing cities* (pp. 255–273). Montreal, QC: McGill-Queen's University Press.

Campbell, M. (2014). The politics of making home: Opening up the work of Richard Iton in Canadian Hip Hop context. *Souls, 16*(3), 269–282. doi: 10.1080/10999949. 2014.968978

Chamberland, R. (2006). Le paradoxe culturel du rap québécois (P. Roy, Trans.). In S. Lacasse & P. Roy (Eds.). *Groove: Enquête sur les phénomènes musicaux contemporains: Mélanges à la mémoire de Roger Chamberland* (pp. 1–16). Quebec, QC: Presses de l'Université Laval.

D'Amico, F. (2015). "The mic is my piece": Canadian rap, the gendered "cool pose," and music industry racialization and regulation. *Journal of the Canadian Historical Association, 26*(1), 255–290. doi: 10.7202/1037204ar

Day, I. (2016). *Alien capital: Asian racialization and the logic of settler colonial capitalism*. Durham, NC: Duke University Press.

Dery, M. (1994). Black to the future: Interviews with Samuel R. Delany, Greg Tate, and Tricia Rose. In M. Dery (Ed.), *Flame wars: The discourse of cyberculture* (pp. 179–222). Durham, NC: Duke University Press.

Doeff, J. (2016, May 6). Wesh. *Urban Dictionary*. Retrieved from https://www. urbandictionary.com/define.php?term=Wesh

Dovchin, S., Pennycook, A., & Sultana, S. (2018). *Popular culture, voice and linguistic diversity: Young adults on- and offline*. Cham, Switzerland: Palgrave Macmillan.

Forman, M., & Neal, M. (Eds.). (2012). *That's the joint!: The Hip-Hop studies reader* (2nd ed.). New York: Routledge.

García, O., Bartlett, L., & Kleifgen, J. A. (2007). From biliteracy to pluriliteracies. In P. Auer & L. Wei (Eds.), *Handbook of multilingualism and multilingual communication* (pp. 207–228)). Berlin, Germany: Mouton de Gruyter.

Hill Collins, P. (2006). *From black power to hip hop: Racism, nationalism, and feminism.* Philadelphia, PA: Temple University Press.

Hörschelmann, K., & van Blerk, L. (2011). *Children, youth and the city.* New York: Routledge.

Kitwana, B. (2005). *Why white kids love Hip-Hop: Wankstas, wiggers, wannabes, and the new reality of race in America.* New York: Basic Civitas Books.

Krims, A. (2000). *Rap music and the poetics of identity.* Cambridge, UK: Cambridge University Press.

Lamort, K. (2017). *Les boss du québec: R.a.p. du fleur de lysée (Analyse socio-historique et sociologique du Hip-Hop dans la société québécoise)* (2nd ed.). Montreal, QC: Production noire.

Leppänen, S., & Westinen, E. (2017). Migrant rap in the periphery: Performing politics of belonging. *Aila Review, 30,* 1–26.

Lesacher, C. (2014). Rap, langues, « québéquicité » et rapports sociaux de sexe : pratiques et expériences de rappeuses montréalaises d'origine haïtienne. *Diversité urbaine, 14*(2), 77–95. doi: 10.7202/1035426ar

Low, B. & Sarkar, M. (2014). Translanguaging in the multilingual Montreal Hip-Hop community: Everyday poetics as counter to the myths of the monolingual classroom. In A. Creese & A. Blackledge (Eds.), *Heteroglossia as practice and pedagogy* (pp. 99–118). Dordrecht, The Netherlands: Springer.

Low, B., Sarkar, M., & Winer, L. (2009). "Ch'us mon propre bescherelle": Challenges from the Hip-Hop nation to the Quebec nation. *Journal of Sociolinguistics, 13*(1), 59–82. doi: 10.1111/j.1467-9841.2008.00393.x

Low, B., Tan, E., & Celemencki, J. (2013). "Keepin' it real" in the classroom: The discourse of authenticity and challenges for critical Hip-Hop pedagogies. In M. L. Hill & E. Petchauer (Eds.), *Schooling Hip-Hop: New approaches to based education* (pp. 187–216). New York: Teachers College Press.

McLeod, K. (1999). Authenticity within Hip-Hop and other cultures threatened with assimilation. *Journal of Communication, 49*(4), 134–150. doi: 10.1111/j.1460-2466.1999. tb02821.x

Mitchell, T. (2001). *Global noise: Rap and Hip-Hop outside the USA.* Middletown, CT: Wesleyan University Press.

Mugabo, D. (2019). Black in the city: On the ruse of ethnicity and language in an antiblack landscape. *Identities, 26*(6), 631–648. doi: 10.1080/1070289X.2018.1545816

NBS Studio. (n.d.-a). nbs.studio. Retrieved from https://www.instagram.com/nbs.studio/?hi=en

NBS Studio. (n.d.-b). We out here live. Retrieved from https://www.instagram.com/stories/highlights/18028157710166174/

Néméh-Nombré, P. (2018, Autumn). Le Hip-Hop avec des gants blancs. *Liberté, 322,* 39–44.

Papastergiadis, N. (2000). *The turbulence of migration: Globalization, deterritorialization, and hybridity.* Cambridge, UK: Polity Press.

Pennycook, A. (2007). Language, localization, and the real: Hip-Hop and the global spread of authenticity. *Journal of Language, Identity, and Education, 6*(2), 101–115.

Plüss, C. (2006). Becoming different while becoming the same: Re-territorializing Islamic identities with multi-ethnic practices in Hong Kong. *Ethnic and Racial Studies, 29*(4), 656–675.

Quebec. (2019). *An act respecting the laicity of the state.* Statutes of Quebec, 2019, c. 12. Quebec, QC: Quebec Official Publisher. Retrieved from http://www2.publicationsd uquebec.gouv.qc.ca/dynamicSearch/telecharge.php?type=5&file=2019C12A.PDF

Rabaka, R. (2013). *The Hip Hop movement: From R & B and the Civil Rights movement to rap and the Hip Hop generation*. Lanham, MD: Lexington Books.

Rose, T. (1994). *Black noise: Rap music and Black culture in contemporary America*. Hanover, NH: University Press of New England.

Sarkar, M., Low, B., and Winer, L. (2007). "Pour connecter avec le peeps": Québéquicité and the Quebec Hip-Hop community. In M. Mantero (Ed.), *Identity and second language learning: Culture, inquiry and dialogic activity in educational contexts* (pp. 351–372). Charlotte, NC: Information Age Publishing.

Seemiller, C., & Grace, M. (2019). *Generation Z: A century in the making*. Abingdon, UK: Routledge. doi: 10.4324/9780429442476

Séraphin, P.-D. (2017, March 2). Créole haïtien 101. *Urbania*. Retrieved from https://urbania.ca/article/creole-haitien-101/

Smith, A. (2014, June 20). The colonialism that is settled and the colonialism that never happened. *Decolonization: Indigeneity, Education & Society*. Retrieved from https://decolonization.wordpress.com/2014/06/20/the-colonialism-that-is-settled-and-the-colonialism-that-never-happened/

Sucar, D. (2019, August 17). CAQ kept its promise to reduce immigration: Study. *Montreal Gazette*. Retrieved from https://montrealgazette.com/news/caq-kept-its-promise-to-reduce-immigration-study

Thobani, S. (2007). Multiculturalism and the liberalizing nation. In S. Thobani (Ed.), *Exalted subjects: Studies in the making of race and nation in Canada* (pp. 143–175). Toronto, ON: University of Toronto Press.

Varis, P., & Blommaert, J. (2015). Conviviality and collectives on social media: Virality, memes, and new social structures. *Multilingual Margins, 2*(1), 31–45.

Vertovec, S. (2007). Super-diversity and its implications. *Ethnic and Racial Studies, 30*(6), 1024–1054.

Ville de Montréal. (2018). Profil sociodémographique recensement 2016: Arrondissement de Côte-des-Neiges–Notre-Dame-de-Grâce. Retrieved from http://ville.montreal.qc.ca/pls/portal/docs/PAGE/MTL_STATS_FR/MEDIA/DOCUMENTS/PROFIL_SOCIOD%C9MO_CDN-NDG%202016.PDF

Walcott, R. (2001). Caribbean pop culture in Canada; or, the impossibility of belonging to the nation. *Small Axe, 5*(1), 123–139.

White, B. W. (2019). *Franglais* in a post-rap world: Audible minorities and anxiety about mixing in Québec. *Ethnic and Racial Studies, 42*(6), 957–974.

7

THE CASE AGAINST EXOTICISM

Troubling "Identity" in Identity-Based Data Collection

Vidya Shah

Context

The collection, analysis, and reporting of identity-based data (IBD) processes are essential structures for reducing disparities and the disproportionate representation of particular groups of students in schooling outcomes on the basis of social identities. In the elementary and secondary schooling context, data on student achievement, well-being, experience, and engagement can be disaggregated by IBD to identify achievement, opportunity, and well-being gaps. These gaps can then inform school- and district-level changes in programming, policies, and structures to intervene and eliminate barriers to full student participation and success. However, if approached with uncritical, ahistorical, and apolitical lenses, IBD processes further reinforce harmful narratives and structural oppression. Collecting, analyzing, and reporting IBD are therefore both *necessary and potentially dangerous structures* for schools and districts committed to better meeting the needs of historically marginalized student populations.

Disaggregating demographic data occurs internationally and notes significant achievement gaps. Over 75 countries participate in the Programme for International Student Assessment (PISA), a standardized test offered by the Organisation for Economic Co-operation and Development. The 2018 report *Equity in Education: Breaking Down Barriers to Social Mobility* reports a strong link between a school's socio-economic profile and students' performance, with more socioeconomically advantaged schools performing better in PISA (Organisation for Economic Co-operation and Development, 2018a). In many countries, there are clear achievement gaps on the basis of ability, gender, race/ethnicity, and measures of poverty (Organisation for Economic Co-operation and Development, 2018b). Similar trends are found in the 2016 UNESCO report *Educating for*

DOI: 10.4324/9780429327780-7

102 Vidya Shah

People and Planet: Creating Sustainable Futures for All (UNESCO, Global Education Monitoring Report Team, 2016), which also names educational disparities such as caste and religious minority status as well as living in rural areas. The importance of collecting identity-based data is highlighted in the 2015 United Nations report *Transforming our World: The 2030 Agenda for Sustainable Development*, which outlines a global commitment to monitor progress using data disaggregated "by income, gender, age, race, ethnicity, migratory status, disability, geographic location, and other characteristics relevant to national contexts" (United Nations, 2015, p. 27).

Unlike the United States and the United Kigdom, which have been collecting IBD for decades, Ontario is only now beginning to collect school district data that explore the connections between identity and achievement/opportunity gaps in standardized test scores, school grades, graduation rates, postsecondary outcomes, and career tracking. Conversations about achievement gaps in Ontario have been influenced by conversations in the United States and have come to include understandings of opportunity gaps, which are uneven distributions of resources and learning opportunities (Johnson-Ahorlu, 2012; Milner, 2012), and to a lesser extent education debts, which are a collection of historical, economic, sociopolitical, and moral debts accrued against marginalized and racialized people and children (Ladson-Billings, 2006). Ontario classrooms are filled with diversity on the basis of race, ethnicity, faith/creed/spiritual worldview, language, gender, gender identity, sex, sexual orientation, place of birth, social class, citizenship, immigration status, age, disability, family status, and more. Similar to global education patterns, historical and contemporary structural barriers to equitable schooling have resulted in achievement and opportunity gaps on the basis of many of these social identities, whether officially measured or not.

In Ontario, the commitment to the collection and reporting of IBD has been most influenced by the structures and policies of the Toronto District School Board (TDSB), which has collected identity-based data since the 1970s to explore patterns and trends in student achievement, and later well-being, perception, and experience across diverse populations. Toronto is one of the most diverse cities in the world with close to three million people. The 2016 Canadian Census notes that there has been a 25% increase in the Indigenous population between 2011 and 2016, from about 37,000 to just over 46,000 people (City of Toronto, 2018). The 2016 Canadian Census indicates that close to half of Toronto's population is made up of immigrants and 75% of the population are first- and second-generation Canadians (Arora, 2019). Arora also notes that there are over 160 languages spoken in the city and almost half the homes speak both English and another language. However, increased diversity does not translate into increased inclusion. Arora notes that income disparities, housing challenges, and experiences of discrimination are all higher for immigrants than for Canadian-born residents and there has been a significant rise in hate-related crimes based on race and religion since 2016.

The Case Against Exoticism **103**

With the introduction in 2017 of the Ontario Ministry of Education's Education Equity Secretariat and the Equity Action Plan (Ontario Ministry of Education, 2017), more Ontario school districts are committing to IBD processes, which include the collection, integration, and reporting of IBD to identify and close achievement and opportunity gaps. As with other structural changes aimed at educational equity, discomfort and unwillingness to acknowledge and respond to racism often render race invisible in conversations about IBD processes. This chapter intentionally theorizes IBD processes through the frameworks of Critical Race Theory (CRT) (Ladson-Billings & Tate, 2017; Lynn, Yosso, Solórzano, & Parker, 2002) and Critical Whiteness Studies (Bonilla-Silva, 2009; Picower, 2009; Sleeter, 2001), with a recognition that CRT both centers race in its analysis and considers intersections with other identities.

Theorizing Race and Whiteness in Identity-Based Data Processes

Through examinations of racism and Indigeneity, CRT explores the normalization of race and the entrenchment of white supremacy in cultures, systems, and structures that simultaneously render it invisible to white people while adversely impacting racialized people (Delgado & Stefanic, 2001). The historical context for the causes of sustained achievement and opportunity gaps is largely unknown to educators and ignoring history and social context serves to maintain racist views of students and families (E. Taylor, 2006). CRT challenges the idea of color-evasiveness (DeCuir & Dixson, 2004) established in liberal individualistic notions of neutrality, objectivity, and meritocracy (Giroux, 2003), which maintain achievement gaps by promoting equal opportunity over equality of outcomes, despite an unlevel playing field. Interest convergence (Bell, 1980), which suggests that white elites will advocate for improvements for Black and other ethnic minorities only when there are benefits to those white elites, is an aspect of CRT.

A historical view highlights the permanence of racism (Bell, 1995), complete with periods of seeming progress and subsequent backlash as whites reassert their dominance (E. Taylor, 2006). The permanence of racism is evident in the entrenchment of racial achievement gaps for decades in both the United States (E. Taylor, 2006), the United Kingdom (Gillborn, 2015), and other countries. CRT challenges the ideology of whiteness as a universal norm that creates the basis of white privilege (Bonilla-Silva, 2009). It simultaneously critiques the construction of whiteness as passive, in favor of understanding it as intentional acts of structural domination (Leonardo, 2004). In the 1990s, CRT explored the ways racialized students were constructed and counted (or not) and the problematic mechanisms by which racialized students had, or were denied, access to white knowledge and their own histories (Ladson-Billings & Tate, 1995).

Closely connected to CRT, Critical Whiteness Studies sheds light on the social construction of whiteness. It recognizes that antiracist efforts must include an

104 Vidya Shah

examination and critique of how whiteness operates at the institutional, ideological, and cultural levels to challenge the protection of racial hierarchies and associated unearned and unacknowledged white privileges (Bonilla-Silva, 2009; Kincheloe & Steinberg, 1997). Whiteness is defined as "a set of assumptions, beliefs and practices that place the interests and perspectives of White people at the center of what is considered normal and everyday" (Gillborn, 2015, p. 278). Student achievement, success, opportunity, engagement, and well-being are defined in relation to whiteness, rendering the interests and perspectives of non-white students and families irrelevant, othered, deviant, and invisible.

Identity-Based Data in Other Contexts

There is much to learn from the mistakes and misuse of IBD in the United States and the United Kingdom. In her 2008 study of achievement gaps in mathematics, American scholar Rochelle Gutiérrez (2008) explores a phenomenon known as gap gazing, an excessive focus on the achievement gap to the exclusion of other educational issues. Gutiérrez (2008) notes several dangers of gap gazing. First, most gap studies offer a static picture of inequities that are ahistorical and decontextual, resulting in analyses that identify unreasonable levers for changes such as family income. Second, given the absence of normative and political analysis, longitudinal studies that demonstrate a widening or narrowing of gaps do little to determine causality because causes of gaps are based on inferences that are often limited by omitted variables. Third, many gap studies focus on technical or behavioral causes (e.g., pedagogy, teacher knowledge) and do not account for larger, systemic factors such as investments in education, overworked teachers, and the effects of standardized testing. Finally, a focus on achievement gaps leads to a narrow view of learning and the purpose of education and detracts from critical thinking and civic engagement.

As part of a larger neoliberal movement of accountability, achievement gaps are often based on standardized test scores that lead to narrow notions of literacy and numeracy that fail to account for creativity and multiple ways of knowing and learning (Shah, 2016). American scholar Linda Darling-Hammond (2004) warns that there must be limits to the accountability movement when advancing equity reforms to guard against "teaching to the test," creating a depoliticized citizenry, reinforcing deficit thinking, and placing far too great an emphasis on preparing students for the workforce. This can be partially mitigated by collecting a wide range of data on student engagement, opportunity, well-being, and experience in addition to achievement data. It is also important to examine how achievement and opportunity gaps are influenced by structural and ideological considerations such as inequities in funding and resource allocation, policies and practices, access to high-quality teaching, and access to decision-making for students, families, and communities (Shah, 2018).

In the UK, critical race scholar David Gillborn (2008) suggests that the permanence of racism results in locked-in inequality in social, economic, political, legal, and educational realms that consistently disadvantage racialized people. Gillborn (2008) explores the means by which "Gap Talk" creates the illusion of reforms for equity in the English education system, which negates the more fundamental and structural changes needed to overcome educational inequities. Gap talk—the intentional misrepresentation of positive impacts of gap-closing efforts while disguising persistent and deep-seated racial inequities—serves to hide entrenched inequality in the systems that actively maintain those inequities by creating the illusion of progress (Gillborn, 2008). Therefore, IBD processes can serve to disrupt whiteness and white supremacy, or they can create new mechanisms to maintain whiteness as the norm. Given the potential dangers of IBD processes, school districts and governments/departments that oversee education are encouraged to relate to identity data as Kumashiro (2004) suggests we relate to knowledge—in troubled and paradoxical ways. As such, even as school boards and governments use IBD processes to close achievement and opportunity gaps for historically racialized and other marginalized populations, they can continue to interrupt the ongoing intentional and unintentional oppression that comes from the partiality of what they know regarding data and identity, and how they come to know.

Troubling Identity in Identity-Based Data Collection

IBD processes can fall short of capturing the complexity and nuance of student identity in several significant ways. First, notions of identity among critical scholars have evolved over time from what Grande (2009) describes as "the comparatively static notion of identity as a relatively fixed entity that one embodies" into "the more fluid concept of subjectivity—an entity that one actively and continually constructs" (p. 186). Subjectivities destabilize essentialist analyses of difference and are highly dependent on social discourse, institutions, and structures (Grande, 2009). The construction of identity in IBD processes aligns with previous oversimplified interpretations of identity that create oppressive binary oppositions such as Black/White (Mahtani, 2002) and male/female and fixed categories of race, gender, social class, and sexual orientation, among others. These categories limit understanding of the complexities of students' multiracial, multilingual, multifaith, and transnational realities. This approach to identity results in oppositional polarities and fixedness based on principles of exclusion, essentialism, and purity (Ashcroft, Griffiths, & Tiffin, 1995).

In the context of race, the oversimplification of race and racial categories in the IBD process can lead one to believe that there are inherent or natural differences between ethno-racial groups (E. Taylor, 2006). IBD processes also fail to account for the importance of context and history in understandings of identity, which suggests that different aspects of our identities matter at different times on the basis of the material consequences they afford to our bodies (hooks, 2000).

106 Vidya Shah

For example, the schooling experiences of a student marginalized by low income whose family may have experienced historical barriers to economic opportunity and security are very different from those of a racialized student who is new to Canada and whose parents cannot secure accreditation for professional designations from their country of origin. Yet another student may be experiencing situational marginalization, with low income due to a particular life circumstance (e.g., eviction, precarious work, changes to labor laws, wage freezes, death in the family). These students may all be "coded" similarly in IBD processes unless the measurement tools are sensitive enough to capture these nuances. In these cases, race may not be a factor in how student experiences are conceptualized, given that discussion of social class tends to be color-evasive. Community input is essential in understanding the range of student and family experiences to support more sensitive and reliable measurement tools.

A second challenge for IBD processes is the focus of relational approaches to identity on intersubjectivity, or how individuals occupy liminal spaces as they navigate multiple worlds (Kubota & Lin, 2009; Schecter, 2015). Postcolonial theorists such as Homi Bhabha, Frantz Fanon, Gayatri Spivak, and Edward Said speak to notions of hybridity, in which "transnational actors can appropriate, translate or renegotiate different linguistic resources and social identity repertoires, ... challenging dominant discourses of both their birth and host countries" (Schecter, 2015, p. 201). Hybridity is a postcolonial concept that guards against multicultural exoticism (Bhabha, 1994), in which peoples, places, and cultural practices are depicted as perpetual foreigners under the Western gaze (Said, 1978). IBD processes run the risk of thwarting understandings of hybridity and promoting multicultural exoticism.

For example, when South Asian, East Asian, or Southeast Asian students outperform white students on standardized test scores, the sociopolitical and cultural realities of "model minority" students are often obscured in favor of positive test scores (McGowan & Lindgren, 2003), and systems of colonization and white supremacy that maintain their subordinate status go unnamed and unexamined. Instead of achievement standards changing to make space for multiple academic realities and aspirations, whiteness as the norm ensures that model minority students are all constructed as overly obsessed with grades and achievement to the detriment of other aspects of their growth and development (Wing, 2007). This is especially problematic in light of the fact that the successful model minority stereotype was developed in the mid-1960s when Black Americans were asserting demands for racial equity (Wing, 2007), an example of interest convergence in CRT.

Furthermore, IBD processes that intend to identify gaps have not made and cannot make visible the ways in which new forms of consciousness, connections, experiences, communities, and identities emerge from occupying multiple and hybrid spaces, nor do they capture students' linguistic and cultural resources. In effect, it is not simply that hybrid identities are viewed as deficits (see Preface,

The Case Against Exoticism **107**

this volume): the possibilities that emerge from hybrid identities that cannot be conceived of from the dominant gaze will not be measured, quantified, or valued.

Third, identity operates along multiple and intersecting axes, for example, race, gender, gender identity, sexual orientation, social class, ability, faith, ethnicity, and so on (Ghosh & Abdi, 2013), and IBD processes can account for this complexity to some degree. For example, one study in the TDSB explores the intersections of race, class, and gender in gifted identification (Parekh, Brown, & Robson, 2018). Another study explores the intersection of race, sex, and poverty in determining transitions to postsecondary education (Robson, Anisef, Brown, & Nagaoka, 2019). These studies are important not simply because they identify large-scale gaps in policies and programming that hold districts accountable to critical reforms but also because they challenge how white supremacy, capitalism, and other intersecting forms of oppression maintain achievement and opportunity gaps for historically marginalized students. Despite a focus on critical perspectives, it is beyond the scope of a quantitative IBD collection to explore the historical, contextual, and temporal complexity of multiple marginalities (Vigil, 2002; Vigil & Yun, 2002) or multiple jeopardy (King, 1988), which speak to the additive effects of being discriminated against across multiple identities. Quantitative IBD processes alone may flatten and essentialize identity in ways that discount experiences of multiple, intersecting marginalities.

Fourth, IBD often fails to account for the role of power in constructing identity; instead of focusing on how systems of oppression create marginal and racialized identities in reference to and in support of the white subject, the focus is on marginalized and racialized identities themselves. If identity is not understood to be inherently political, IBD processes will fail to account for the politics of recognition. Power relations inevitably create oppressive circumstances in which those who do not identify with dominant identities become the "other." The power afforded to those in dominant groups allows them to be the definers of reality since they remain outside the hierarchy of social relations and notions of difference (Ghosh & Abdi, 2013).

In his groundbreaking essay "The Politics of Recognition," Charles Taylor (1994) notes that how one defines oneself is partly dependent on the recognition, misrecognition, or absence of recognition by others and that nonrecognition or misrecognition "can inflict harm and literally constitute a form of oppression that incarcerates people in a false, deformed and existentially reduced mode of being" (p. 25). Therefore, without an intentional and critical focus on how systems, structures, and ideologies recognize, misrecognize, or fail to recognize students, IBD processes can erase student experiences, promote deficit narratives, and normalize low achievement for English language learners and students who are racialized or marginalized by low income (Darder & Torres, 2002; Portelli & Vilbert, 2002).

For example, decades of focus on the racial achievement gap in the United States has constructed Black students as deficient and incapable, whereas a growing focus on Black brilliance or excellence recognizes the impacts of the

108 Vidya Shah

education debt (Ladson-Billings, 2006) on Black student success and provides counternarratives of successful Black students (James, 2012b; Leonard & Martin, 2013). Similarly, a noncritical read of the gifted data in the TDSB may lead one to conclude that white, wealthy males have greater intellectual capacities. However, a critical read of these same data, as evidenced in Parekh et al. (2018), demonstrates how intersecting systems and ideologies can construct ability to maintain eugenic ideologies.

In 2018, over 225 community members, educators, researchers, district leaders, and policy-makers gathered at the annual two-day York University Faculty of Education Summer Institute to explore the pedagogical and political challenges and opportunities of collecting, integrating, and reporting IBD (York University, 2018). Findings, based on observation notes from workshops and participant feedback, indicate two significant ways that IBD processes were positioned to support in/equity in education: data as narrative (pedagogical contributions) and data as a political tool (political contributions). I address each of these themes below.

Data as Narrative: Pedagogical Contributions of IBD Processes

A major contribution of IBD processes is the learning they provide educators about how power shapes conceptions of identity and how these constructions influence teaching and learning. As with any critical read of narrative, it is important to consider who authors the text, who the characters are, how they are being characterized, and how the problem and solution are being defined.

Who Tells the Narrative?

The author of the narrative has tremendous power in determining which story is told and how it is told. Who are the authors of narratives derived from IBD processes? What are the implications if those who author the narratives see these numbers as "neutral" and fail to account for the impact of these numbers on student achievement, engagement, and well-being? How might white authors construct narratives about race that further racialization or maintain whiteness as the norm? Are there processes in place to involve racialized and other marginalized students, families, and community members to co-generate and co-author these narratives?

Discursive Characterizations

In IBD narratives, white, middle-upper class, heterosexual, temporarily abled students become the norm against which excellence and success are defined. From this vantage point, students "in the gap" are often constructed as unintelligent, incapable, deficient, deviant, lacking school readiness, poor, pitied, helpless, and disposable. These are iterations of deficit thinking (García & Guerra, 2004) and

The Case Against Exoticism **109**

damage-centered narratives (Tuck, 2009), in which oppression singularly defines the community. How might IBD processes be organized if we (un)consciously viewed students "in the gap" through these disempowering lenses rather than as agentic beings with complex lives and identities that greatly transcend their perceived deficit or damage? For example, analysis of large-scale data sets may falsely conclude that factors affecting between-group differences (e.g., differences in achievement between Black and white students) are the same as factors causing within-group differences (experiences of Black students in different contexts), with analysis of between-group differences locating success/failure in individual, naturalized differences and analysis of within-group differences exploring inequitable sociopolitical and economic factors affecting schooling.

Narratives that locate the cause of and solution to achievement/opportunity gaps with students, families, and communities will look to gap-closing strategies that "fix" or "reform," such as positive-parenting workshops, remedial supports, or oppressive discipline policies and practices. These "solutions" fail to account for larger structural inequities that influence student learning and engagement and tend to highlight the grit and resilience of racialized and marginalized students who "made it," absolving systems of their responsibility in changing the conditions for all students to succeed (Gorski, 2019). Similarly, narratives that locate the cause of and solution to achievement/opportunity gaps with individual teachers, leaders, or schools tend to focus on professional development and training to change behaviors and mindsets and highlight the maverick educator who is able to create the conditions for success despite the larger educational and sociopolitical environment. Conversely, narratives that identify the cause of and solutions to achievement in school systems and the larger society focus on structural changes in school and district policies and practices and the societal contexts that give rise to equity or inequity.

Numbers alone can create the impression that complex and ambiguous experiences are "simple, countable, and precisely defined" (Stone, 2012, p. 196). Qualitative data can be used alongside quantitative data to explore the complexity in IBD processes, to humanize data specifically about students "in the gap," and to challenge the systemic structures that give rise to these realities in the first place. IBD processes can explore more than discrete categories in quantitative surveys by also offering qualitative data collection methods that explore history and context. For example, instead of asking students "What is your ethnoracial identity?" IBD collection processes may ask "How is your ethnoracial identity relevant to you and how has it changed over time?" (Phillips, 2010). Or students may be asked how understandings and experiences of their ethnic identity change between school, home, and other contexts (Phillips, 2010).

What Narratives are Not Being Told?

As data can confirm or challenge bias, people package data to tell the narrative they want to tell (Stone, 2012). In the same vein, we might ask questions such as:

110 Vidya Shah

What gets counted and who gets counted? How might our politics erase, silence, negate, or disregard the realities and unjust experiences of particular groups of students? For example, despite numerous observations, there are few data on the experiences of Black male students in French immersion classes being streamed into designated special education classes. This, in part, is because of colonized linguistic legacies of what constitutes "French language" and "French culture," as many students (and teachers) from French-speaking African countries are not considered "real francophones."

The absence of particular types of data also tells a different narrative, as evident in processes of student and parent/caregiver self-identification. Self-identification requires trust in the person/organization collecting the data and a sense of safety that they will not endure harm now or in the future by sharing this information. Processes of self-identification need to be attended to with care. This is especially true when inviting Indigenous students and families to self-identify given the historical use of processes like data collection in Canada and elsewhere to dispossess, disenfranchise, and dehumanize, as John Hupfield notes in the documentary *This is Not a Resilience Story* (El-Husseini, 2019). This situation speaks to the importance of *Indigenous data sovereignty*. We have much to learn from the ethical principles of utility, self-voicing, access, and inter-relationality that guide research of the Ontario Federation of Indigenous Friendship Centres and its partners (Ontario Federation of Indigenous Friendship Centres, 2016). Participatory action research with Indigenous communities is often guided by a different but related set of ethical principles of ownership, control, access, and possession in the collection, protection, use, and sharing of data with First Nations (First Nations Information Governance Centre, 2014). Creating public trust and working to ensure the safety of students and families is integral to authoring more accurate stories. With a critical, antiracist theoretical grounding, IBD processes can be used as a pedagogical tool to trouble our collective understanding of identities and power by considering the ways in which different variables interact with one another to generate more complex theories and better understand the contexts that create the greatest opportunities for student learning and the conditions required to close racial and other achievement/opportunity gaps.

Data as a Political Tool

Data are not neutral; therefore, IBD processes have material effects on people's lives. In her book *Policy Paradox*, Deborah Stone (2012) outlines several ways in which both counting and measuring are political acts. For example, numbers can be very powerful when they are used as (white) norms, even if there is no efficacy behind them. Also, by seeming to be so precise, numbers give power and authority to those who count and additional power to those who own the data and serve as their (white) gatekeepers. Stone (2018) notes that counting entails cultural

The Case Against Exoticism   **111**

coercion because we force things into categories and those categories have consequences. She invites us to consider how we know that the rights of those being counted are upheld and what processes we have in place when they are not.

Legitimizing the Voices and Expertise of Community Partners in IBD Processes

Community members are often invited into IBD processes when school districts need access to particular groups of students or when they want to ensure that their survey questions are culturally sensitive. This engagement with a few community members in a respectful manner is a shallow approach to equity. Deeper approaches include community members at every stage of the IBD process. This includes engaging their expertise in crafting the initial survey/census questions, supporting school district staff with data analysis and reporting back to communities, and co-constructing ideas for interventions and other systemic changes. It may also include developmental evaluations conducted by communities and greater opportunities for participatory action research alongside the community. Even more equitable approaches to IBD processes are as follows: legitimizing community-based research/data alongside IBD collected by school districts and other educational institutions; inviting community members to engage with the school districts at every stage of the IBD process *as paid consultants*; and expecting and encouraging community partners and organizations to hold the board accountable for changing student outcomes for those most impacted by inequitable schooling practices.

Intentionally Sustaining Gaps

As alluded to previously, student-led and community-led research is often invalidated because it is not deemed to have the same "academic rigor" as research conducted by school districts, policy-makers, and academics. Dismissing these data becomes even more problematic when the findings from student-led and community-led research differ from those of academics and school district researchers. For example, when some Muslim students, families, or educators raise concerns about Islamophobia, they are often deemed overly sensitive, and their complaints are framed as a misunderstanding of the offender's intention. Hence, there are almost no data on the subtle Islamophobia experienced by Muslim students (such as microaggressions, the assumption and portrayal of Muslim women as oppressed, and the framing of Muslim students through the lens of terrorism), and only marginal data on overt forms of Islamophobia (such as students being told they are terrorists, women's hijabs being pulled off, and public debates about human rights in relation to Muslim identity) (Hindy & Chowdhury, 2018). This silencing of experiences reinforces the idea that since Muslim students are not "in the gap," Islamophobia can be ignored.

112 Vidya Shah

Achievement and opportunity gaps are also intentionally created and sustained when critical, evidence-based data and research are dismissed because they identify patterns of injustice operating at various levels and create potential challenges from parents and communities with greater social capital. In her study of the TDSB, Parekh (2020) notes that when recommendations were made to remodel traditional self-contained special education practices, change approaches to academic streaming, and open access to more elite ability-based programs, there was significant backlash from more privileged parent communities. Even though the goals of these communities came into conflict with evidence-based research, they ultimately influenced the district's response. Attempts to close gaps are often met with requests to "raise the bar" for all students. In a study on the effects of educational policy changes on racial achievement gaps, Gillborn, Demack, Rollock, and Warmington (2017) note that new policy efforts to "raise the bar" have widened racial achievement gaps, restoring historic levels of racial inequity.

(Un)Intentional Inaction

Intentional gaps are closely connected to intentional and unintentional action, both of which have the same impact on students "in the gap." What data are not being acted on *at the expense of students and families* because they are deemed "too political"? How might IBD processes be used to stall action or create the illusion of action to maintain the status quo and perpetuate domination?

Similar to gap talk (Gillborn, 2008) and gap fetishizing (Gutiérrez, 2008), school districts, policy-makers, and other educational institutions continue to gather and overanalyze data about students "in the gap," with little to no actual change in student access and opportunities to learning. What are the political and pedagogical consequences of not acting? Greater accountability at the district, provincial, and federal levels is necessary to close achievement/opportunity gaps. For example, in recognition of the impacts of opportunity gaps on educational outcomes for racialized and marginalized students, the Ontario Ministry of Education has been providing the Learning Opportunity Grant to districts since 1998 to help close opportunity gaps by supporting initiatives such as breakfast programs, after-school programs, and homework programs. The Learning Opportunity Grant is provided in addition to regular per-pupil funding and the extra allocation for students designated with special education exceptionalities and English language learners (Johnston, Queiser, & Clanfield, 2013). However, administrators and school districts are not required to account for how funds are spent and may use the money to make up budget shortfalls in other areas unrelated to equity and inclusivity.

Thus, IBD processes alone are not enough to effect changes in student outcomes. However, they can be important tools in identifying the ways in which power and politics are used to maintain hegemonic structures such as white supremacy, heteropatriarchy, and capitalism. This increased awareness has the potential to generate political will and mobilize political action among multiple members of school communities to effect change (Henig, Hula, Orr, & Pedescleaux, 1999; Shah, 2016).

Pedagogical and Political Possibilities

Deep Critical Learning

The collection, analysis, and reporting of identity-based data can support governments and school districts in learning about the realities faced by students and their families and provide insight into the historical and present-day barriers to access and opportunity for students overrepresented in achievement and opportunity gaps. These processes can also broaden understandings of learning, success, and curriculum. Collecting multiple measures of student success disaggregated by IBD supports more complex understandings of the relationships between student achievement, opportunity, engagement, well-being, and experience, thus guarding against equity initiatives that only address gaps in student achievement. They can also highlight the racist, heterosexist, ableist, and classist practices inherent in the one-size-fits-all approach of standardized testing that serve to "push out" students from schooling processes (Dei, Holmes, Mazzuca, McIsaac, & Campbell, 1995; James, 2012a). Instead, IBD processes can support multiple purposes of schooling, beyond neoliberal ideals of preparing students for the workforce (Portelli, Shields, & Vilbert, 2007), and also invite us to grapple with the relationship between equity and excellence, two concepts that are often positioned as contradictory and independent in education. Ghosh and Abdi (2013) emphasize that if quality and excellence signify a comparison using assessments based on the universal application of the cultures, values, and norms of the dominant group despite the diversity of students, then equity and excellence are at odds. However, "if quality and excellence are viewed as self-actualization and self-improvement, then equity and quality converge into equality" (p. 50).

Finally, IBD processes can support deep, critical reflection of the ways in which schooling institutions are complicit in oppression even as they are working to end it. Governments and school districts are encouraged to think about how structures created to reduce inequities are causing and perpetuating the very problems they seek to address. For example, how might school districts measure the extent of white supremacy and other systems of oppression in their policies and structures and subsequent reductions of that extent over time? Supports for un/learning such as a network of district leaders, researchers, and policy-makers committed to exploring the ethics of IBD would be beneficial in working through challenges to equitable and antiracist accountability.

114 Vidya Shah

Democratizing Education

Critical approaches to IBD processes include students, families, and communities whose realities illuminate the data in meaningful and authentic ways at every stage of IBD processes. This is a structure that can serve to create the conditions for a more critical democratic approach to public education, in which "difference and disagreements are not hidden or silenced; they are taken seriously and form the basis of dialogue and change" (Shah, 2016). Critical, democratic approaches to education allow for a broader understanding of whose voices and knowledge(s) are valued in schooling processes. They include: centering the expertise of community-based researchers and the experiences captured in community-based research; meaningfully involving students and parents/guardians in the process of determining the questions to be asked and definitions of success; centering the expertise of critical academic scholars who both conduct empirical research and theorize about antiracism and other critical approaches to schooling; and valuing the tremendous contribution of critical, antiracist educators in understanding the complexities of IBD processes (especially those who are Indigenous, Black, racialized, or marginalized). While racialized educators often face professional repercussions if they are seen as challenging the status quo (Kohli, 2018), they are often the people most trusted by the community and most capable of co-leading IBD processes alongside the community.

IBD processes can lead to systemic changes such as a revisioning of the mission and goals; policy changes that center identities and differences in student realities; hiring and promotion practices that promote antiracist pedagogies and practices; changes to student programming that challenge exclusive streaming and desegregation practices; curriculum changes that identify and challenge inequitable sociopolitical contexts and provide positive representations of students' identities; resource redistribution that accounts for differences in access and opportunity; authentic and accountable relationships with families and communities; opportunities for students' ideas and voices to inform decision-making; and targeted interventions for specific populations of students "in the gap" (powell, Menendian, & Ake, 2019). Changes to systemic practice then inform the types of IBD collected, the purpose of collecting it, and the ways in which it is analyzed and reported. This form of praxis (Freire, 1998) allows schools and school districts to monitor whether equity initiatives are effective by measuring their influence on multiple and intersecting student outcomes over time, while also supporting deep, critical learning.

IBD processes alone will not necessarily change student outcomes; and ahistorical, atheoretical, acontextual, and apolitical approaches to IBD will perpetuate and exacerbate racial and other gaps in student achievement, opportunity, engagement, and well-being. However, not engaging IBD processes will *ensure* sustained educational inequities for racialized and marginalized students.

References

Arora, A. (2019). *Toronto—A data story on ethnocultural diversity and inclusion in Canada.* Ottawa, ON: Statistics Canada. Retrieved from https://www150.statcan.gc.ca/n1/pub/11-631-x/11-631-x2019002-eng.htm

Ashcroft, B., Griffiths, G., & Tiffin, H. (Eds.). (1995). *The post-colonial studies reader.* London, UK: Routledge.

Bell, D. (1980). *Brown v. Board of Education* and the interest convergence dilemma. *Harvard Law Review, 93,* 518–533.

Bell, D. (1995). *Brown v. Board of Education* and the interest convergence dilemma. In K. Crenshaw, N. Gotanda, G. Peller, & K. Thomas (Eds.), *Critical Race Theory: The key writings that formed the movement* (pp. 20–45). New York: New Press.

Bhabha, H. (1994). *The location of culture.* New York: Routledge.

Bonilla-Silva, E. (2009). *Racism without racists: Color-blind racism and the persistence of racial inequality in the United States* (4th ed.). Lanham, MD: Rowman & Littlefield.

City of Toronto. (2018). *2018 Indigenous peoples.* Retrieved from https://www.toronto.ca/city-government/council/2018-council-issue-notes/indigenous-peoples/

Darder, A., & Torres, R. D. (2002). Shattering the "race" lens: Toward a critical theory of racism. In A. Darder, M. Baltodano, & R. D. Torres (Eds.), *The critical pedagogy reader* (pp. 245–261). New York: Routledge.

Darling-Hammond, L. (2004). Standards, accountability, and school reform. *Teachers College Record, 106*(6), 1047–1085.

DeCuir, J. T., & Dixson, A. D. (2004). "So when it comes out, they aren't that surprised that it is there": Using Critical Race Theory as a tool of analysis of race and racism in education. *Educational Researcher, 33*(5), 26–31.

Dei, G. J. S., Holmes, L., Mazzuca, J., McIsaac, E., & Campbell, R. (1995). *Drop out or push out: The dynamics of Black students' disengagement from school.* Toronto, ON: Ontario Institute for Studies in Education.

Delgado, R., & Stefancic, J. (2001). *Critical Race Theory: An introduction.* New York: New York University Press.

El-Husseini, N. (Producer & Director). (2019). *This is not a resilience story* [video]. Retrieved from https://youtu.be/7wkh1sxKGxI

First Nations Information Governance Centre. (2014). *Ownership, control, access and possession (OCAP™): The path to First Nations information governance.* Ottawa, ON: Author. Retrieved from https://fnigc.ca/sites/default/files/docs/ocap_path_to_fn_information_governance_en_final.pdf

Freire, P. (1998). *Pedagogy of freedom: Ethics, democracy and civic courage.* Lanham, MD: Rowman & Littlefield.

García, S., & Guerra, P. (2004). Deconstructing deficit thinking: Working with educators to create more equitable learning environments. *Education and Urban Society, 36*(2), 150–168.

Ghosh, R., & Abdi, A. A. (2013). *Education and the politics of difference: Select Canadian perspectives* (2nd ed.). Toronto, ON: Canadian Scholars' Press.

Gillborn, D. (2008). Coincidence or conspiracy? Whiteness, policy and the persistence of the Black/White achievement gap. *Educational Review, 60*(3), 229–248.

Gillborn, D. (2015). Intersectionality, Critical Race Theory, and the primacy of racism: Race, class, gender, and disability in education. *Qualitative Inquiry, 21*(3), 277–287.

Gillborn, D., Demack, S., Rollock, N., & Warmington, P. (2017), Moving the goalposts: Education policy and 25 years of the Black/White achievement gap. *British Educational Research Journal, 43,* 848–874. doi: 10.1002/berj.3297

116 Vidya Shah

Giroux, H. (2003). Spectacles of race and pedagogies of denial: Anti-Black racist pedagogy under the reign of neoliberalism. *Communication Education, 52*(3–4), 191–211.

Gorski, P. (2019). Avoiding racial equity detours. *Educational Leadership, 76*(7), 56–61.

Grande, S. M. A. (2009). American Indian geographies of identity and power: At the crossroads of indigena and mestizaje. In A. Darder, M. P. Baltodano, & R. D. Torres (Eds.), *The critical pedagogy reader* (pp. 183–208). New York: Routledge.

Gutiérrez, R. (2008). A "gap-gazing" fetish in mathematics education? Problematizing research on the achievement gap. *Journal of Research on Mathematics Education, 39*(4), 357–364.

Henig, J., Hula, R., Orr, M., & Pedescleaux, D. (1999). *The colour reform: Race, politics and the challenge of urban education.* Princeton, NJ: Princeton University Press.

Hindy, N., & Chowdhury, S. (2018, June). *Silenced narratives—The erasure of the Muslim students' experiences from the Canadian school narrative.* Presentation at the 2018 Faculty of Education Summer Institute, York University, Toronto, ON, Canada.

hooks, b. (2000). *Where we stand: Class matters.* New York: Routledge.

James, C. E. (2012a). *Life at the intersection: Community, class and schooling.* Halifax, NS: Fernwood.

James, C. E. (2012b). Students "at risk": Stereotypes and the schooling of Black boys. *Urban Education, 47*(2), 464–494.

Johnson-Ahorlu, R. (2012). The academic opportunity gap: How racism and stereotypes disrupt the education of African American undergraduates. *Race, Ethnicity and Education, 15*(5), 633–652.

Johnston, L., Queiser, S., & Clanfield, D. (2013). *A triple threat to equity: Changing priorities for Toronto schools.* Toronto, ON: Social Planning Council. Retrieved from https://www.socialplanningtoronto.org/a_triple_threat_to_equity_changing_priorities_for_toronto_schools

Kincheloe, J. L., and Steinberg, S. R. (1997). *Changing multiculturalism.* Buckingham, UK: Open University Press.

King, D. K. (1988). Multiple jeopardy, multiple consciousness: The context of a Black feminist ideology. *Signs, 14*(1), 42–72.

Kohli, R. (2018). Behind school doors: The impact of hostile racial climates on urban teachers of color. *Urban Education, 53*(3), 307–333.

Kubota, R., & Lin, A. (2009). *Race, culture, and identities in second language education: Exploring critically engaged practice.* New York: Routledge.

Kumashiro, K. K. (2004). Preparing teachers for healing: A conversation with Buddhism. In K. K. Kumashiro (Ed.), *Against common sense: Teaching and learning toward social justice* (pp. 45–50). New York: Routledge.

Ladson-Billings, G. (2006). From the achievement gap to the education debt: Understanding achievement in U.S. schools. *Educational Researcher, 35*(7), 3–12.

Ladson-Billings, G., & Tate, W. F., IV. (1995). Toward a Critical Race Theory of education. *Teachers College Record, 97*(1), 47–68.

Ladson-Billings, G., & Tate, W. F., IV. (2017). Toward a Critical Race Theory of education. In A. D. Dixson, C. K. Rousseau Anderson, & J. K. Donnor (Eds.), *Critical Race Theory in Education: All God's children got a song* (2nd ed., pp. 10–31). New York: Routledge.

Leonard, J., & Martin, D. B. (2013). *The brilliance of Black children in mathematics: Beyond the numbers and toward new discourse.* Charlotte, NC: Information Age Publishing.

Leonardo, Z. (2004). The color of supremacy: Beyond the discourse of "White privilege." *Educational Philosophy and Theory, 36*(2), 137–152.

Lynn, M., Yosso, T. J., Solórzano, D. G., & Parker, L. (2002). Critical Race Theory and education: Qualitative research in the new millennium. *Qualitative Inquiry, 8*(1), 3–6.

Mahtani, M. (2002). Interrogating the hyphen-nation: Canadian multicultural policy and "mixed race" identities. *Social Identities, 8*(1), 67–90.

McGowan, M. H., & Lindgren, J. T. (2003). *Untangling the myth of the model minority* (Minnesota Public Law Research Paper No. 03-8; Northwestern Public Law Research Paper No. 03-10). Retrieved from SSRN: https://ssrn.com/abstract=420600. doi: 10.2139/ssrn.420600

Milner, R. (2012). But what is urban education? *Urban Education, 47*(3), 556–561.

Ontario Federation of Indigenous Friendship Centres. (2016). *USAI research framework: Utility, self-voicing, access, inter-relationality* (2nd ed.). Toronto, ON: Author. Retrieved from https://ofifc.org/wp-content/uploads/2020/03/USAI-Research-Framework-Second-Edition.pdf

Ontario Ministry of Education. (2017). *Ontario's education equity action plan.* Toronto, ON: Author. Retrieved from http://www.edu.gov.on.ca/eng/about/education_equity_plan_en.pdf

Organisation for Economic Co-operation and Development. (2018a). *Equity in education: Breaking down barriers to social mobility.* Retrieved from http://www.oecd.org/education/equity-in-education-9789264073234-en.htm

Organisation for Economic Co-operation and Development. (2018b). *PISA 2018 results.* Retrieved from https://www.oecd.org/pisa/publications/pisa-2018-results.htm

Parkekh, G. (2020). How inclusive do we really want to be? A critical exploration of the Toronto District School Board's special and inclusive education policies and outcomes. In S. Winton & G. Parekh (Eds.), *Critical perspectives on education policy and schools, families and communities* (pp. 123–140). Charlotte, NC: Information Age Publishing.

Parekh, G., Brown, R. S., & Robson, K. (2018). The social construction of giftedness: The intersectional relationship between Whiteness, economic privilege, and the identification of gifted. *Canadian Journal of Disability Studies, 7*(2), 1–32. doi: 10.15353/cjds.v7i2.421

Phillips, C. (2010). White, like who? Temporality, contextuality and anti-racist social work education and practice. *Critical Social Work, 11*(2), 71–88. Retrieved from https://ojs.uwindsor.ca/index.php/csw/article/view/5825/4781

Picower, B. (2009). The unexamined Whiteness of teaching: How White teachers maintain and enact dominant racial ideologies. *Race, Ethnicity and Education, 12*(2), 197–215.

Portelli, J., Shields, C., & Vilbert, A. (2007). *Toward an equitable education: Poverty, diversity and students at risk.* Toronto, ON: Ontario Institute for Studies in Education/University of Toronto. Retrieved from http://utoronto.academia.edu/JohnPPortelli/Books/373536/Toward_an_Equitable_Educat ion_Poverty_Diversity_and_Students_at_Risk

Portelli, J., & Vilbert, A. (2002). Standards, equity, and the curriculum of life. *Analytic Teaching, 22*(1), 4–19.

powell, j. a., Memendan, S., & Ake, W. (2019). *Targeted universalism: Policy and practice.* Berkeley, CA: University of California, Haas Institute for a Fair and Inclusive Society. Retrieved from https://belonging.berkeley.edu/targeteduniversalism

Robson, K., Anisef, P., Brown, R. S., & Nagaoka, J. (2019). A comparison of factors determining the transition to postsecondary education in Toronto and Chicago. *Research in Comparative and International Education, 14*(3), 338–356. doi: 10.1177/1745499919865140

Said, E. (1978). *Orientalism.* New York: Pantheon.

Schecter, S. R. (2015). Language, culture, and identity. In F. Sharifian (Ed.), *The Routledge handbook of language and culture* (pp. 196–208). New York: Routledge.

Shah, V. (2016). *Urban district reform for equity: The case of the Model Schools for Inner Cities Program in the Toronto District School Board* (Unpublished doctoral dissertation). Ontario Institute for Studies in Education/University of Toronto, Toronto, ON, Canada.

Shah, V. (2018). Different numbers, different stories: Problematizing "gaps" in Ontario and the TDSB. *Canadian Journal of Educational Administration and Policy*, *187*, 31–47.

Sleeter, C. E. (2001). Preparing teachers for culturally diverse schools: Research and the overwhelming presence of Whiteness. *Journal of Teacher Education*, *52*, 94–106.

Stone, D. (2012). *Policy paradox: The art of political decision making* (3rd ed.). New York: W. W. Norton.

Stone, D. (2018). *Keynote address at the Walter Gordon Symposium*. Toronto, ON: Munk School of Global Affairs and Public Policy.

Taylor, C. (1994). The politics of recognition. In C. Taylor (Ed.), *Multiculturalism* (pp. 25–72). Princeton, NJ: Princeton University Press.

Taylor, E. (2006). A critical race analysis of the achievement gap in the United States: Politics, reality, and hope. *Leadership and Policy in Schools*, *5*(1), 71–87.

Tuck, E. (2009). Suspending damage: A letter to communities. *Harvard Educational Review*, *79*(3), 409–427.

UNESCO, Global Education Monitoring Report Team. (2016). *Educating for people and planet: Creating sustainable futures for all*. Paris: United Nations Educational, Scientific and Cultural Organization. Retrieved from https://unesdoc.unesco.org/ark:/48223/pf0000245752

United Nations. (2015, September 25). *Transforming our world: The 2030 agenda for sustainable development*. Resolution adopted by the General Assembly. Retrieved from https://www.un.org/ga/search/view:doc.asp?symbol=A/RES/70/1&Lang=E

Vigil, J. D. (2002). Community dynamics and the rise of street gangs. In M. M. Suárez-Orozco & M. M. Páez (Eds.), *Latinos: Remaking America* (pp. 97–109). Berkeley, CA: University of California Press.

Vigil, J. D., & Yun, S. C. (2002). A cross-cultural framework to understand gangs: Multiple marginality and Los Angeles. In C. R. Huff (Ed.), *Gangs in America* (3rd ed., pp. 161–174). Thousand Oaks, CA: SAGE.

Wing, J. Y. (2007). Beyond Black and White: The model minority myth and the invisibility of Asian American students. *Urban Review*, *39*, 455–487.

York University. (2018). *2018 Faculty of Education Summer Institute*. Retrieved from http://fesi.blog.yorku.ca/2018-2/

PART 3

Forging Cosmopolitan Pedagogies

8

TRANSLATING GLOBAL MEMORY ACROSS COLONIAL DIVIDES

Critically Contextualizing the Intimacies of Learning from Oral Histories of Colonial Violence

Lisa K. Taylor

Contemporary challenges for equity and social justice education include global processes that foster both plurality and exclusion, greater but also more segregated arenas of communication and community within persistent inequality and violence.[1] While youth social identities are experienced and performed in more explicitly multifaceted and fluid ways, racial hierarchies and grammars continue to circulate and structure youth opportunity and precariousness within the colonial matrix of power.[2] How, then, do students in contexts of diversity and complexity experience and make sense of social difference and disparity in their lived experience? How can educators support them in analyzing the forces and patterns structuring this experience in a historical and global context? What are the pedagogical models and implications for equity, antiracism, and social justice education (see also Schroeter, this volume) that pertain to multicultural and multilingual *superdiverse* contexts (Vertovec, 2016), contexts in which students perform transnational, transcultural, and intersectional identities that affiliate in unpredictable ways (Vertovec, 2016), even as their lives are shaped by ongoing histories of imperialism and settler colonialism?

These questions have implications for history and civic education in particular, as schools are challenged to respond to growing movements that are democratizing the ways we remember the past: the "ourstories" we tell as the basis of guiding how we live in a shared present and imagine shared futures. Social histories and oral histories are proliferating in the public sphere and educational settings, and communities of countermemory are challenging institutional hierarchies of voice and authority, claiming space to set the terms on which "history" is written and studied. Digital and multimedia memory cultures pluralize the voices young people engage with, personalizing, inviting empathy, and demanding historical context and critical structural analysis. When articulated from the underside of

DOI: 10.4324/9780429327780-8

122 Lisa K. Taylor

coloniality, social and oral histories and communities of memory make truth claims that hold the potential to unravel the totalizing universalism of Eurocentric and settler colonial histories in a country like Canada. They can open listeners to the complexity and contingency of historical processes that are shaping the very conditions of students' everyday lives, the very ground beneath our feet.

These "history wars" extend older "culture wars" in education with direct implications for curriculum and pedagogy. This is particularly the case in a global city like Toronto, striated and layered as a crossroads of empire and informed by decades of leadership by equity-seeking communities locally. Toronto classrooms are also shaped by a national movement initiated by the 2009–2014 Truth and Reconciliation Commission of Canada that challenges teachers to critically deconstruct white settler national narratives of liberal multicultural Canadian exceptionalism (Regan, 2010; Taylor, 2018; Truth and Reconciliation Commission of Canada, 2015) and to honor Indigenous land-centered ways of knowing and remembering (Donald, Glanfield, & Sterenberg, 2012; Marker, 2011; McGregor, 2017; Ontario Ministry of Education, 2018).

This chapter takes up these questions of how students in superdiverse contexts make sense of historical accounts articulated by survivor communities of mass atrocity, what tensions can arise between students' critical structural analysis and their imaginatively engaged deep listening when studying contemporary world history, and the implications for antiracist and anticolonial education.

Curriculum Research in a Context of Urban Superdiversity

This chapter draws from a community-led participatory research project aimed at expanding the sources and pedagogical approaches used in the study of the 1994 Rwandan genocide against the Tutsis in the context of a unique Canadian and World Studies course titled "Genocide and Crimes Against Humanity: Historical and Contemporary Implications" (CHG38).[3] The project focused on the implications of centering antiracism and anticolonial frameworks and introducing memory studies and methods of oral history in studying histories of mass violence from the perspectives of "survivor-historians" (see below). Community-led in-service workshops with partner teachers generated curriculum to support the inclusion of community-produced oral history resources and guest speaker classroom visits. This collaboration generated a series of qualitative classroom case studies with individual teachers piloting the curriculum.[4] This chapter reports on the findings of one case study.

In citing this study, it is essential to clarify the collective nature of the planning and implementation, including research questions, conceptualization, theorization, and resource development, within an explicitly antiracist feminist commitment to situated critical reflexivity, reciprocity, and dialogic analysis of the politics of knowledge production in educational research and institutional practices (Taylor, Rwigema, & Sollange, 2012, 2014; Taylor, Rwigema, Sollange, & Kyte, 2017). Umwali Sollange and Marie-Jolie Rwigema, members of the Rwandan community in Toronto, have

Global Memory across Colonial Divides **123**

been active as equity educators and organizers in community processes of healing and commemoration. They are also cocreators in *The Rwandan Genocide as Told by its Historian-Survivors* (Rwigema, Karera, Nsabimana, Sharangabo, & Sollange, 2009), a collectively produced documentary that explicitly challenges the hegemony of Eurocentric discourses dominating scholastic and popular accounts of the genocide by centering the critical anticolonial perspectives of survivors (Rwigema, 2018). This collaboration in community knowledge production was extended to encompass a community-school partnership with myself, a white settler scholar, and Shelley Kyte, a curriculum lead teacher for Canadian and World Studies and for this course. The Rwandan Canadian members of the research team prioritized goals of decolonizing relations of power, voice, and authority in the research process and the curriculum design and implementation. Shelley brought research questions focused on addressing the need for Rwandan-authored resources and oral histories. This chapter aims to extend this collective knowledge production through my analysis of data from one case study.

The case study collected data from a Grade 11 class of students of mixed grade level, ethnoracial identity, and socioeconomic status during the four-week course section focused on the 1994 genocide.[5] The teaching materials and activities included: an introductory teacher-led "KWL" discussion on what students Know, Want to know, and Learned about Rwanda; the teacher's introductory PowerPoint and a student-led class discussion of an abbreviated historical overview of the genocide; two graphic novels dramatizing the genocide (Bazambamba, 2009; Woolley, 2009) used in an individual response journal and group critical literacy exercise comparing Rwandan and non-Rwandan perspectives on the genocide to produce timelines of short- and long-term factors; a one-page definition of racism; a "power triangle" exercise in structural analysis of different forms of individual and systemic discrimination (Toronto District School Board, 2005, 2006); individual structured response prompts for the guest speaker presentation and documentary screening by Marie-Jolie Rwigema (responses are cited below as "R2S"); and individual expository essays.

Samples of student learning from Shelley's classroom included participant observation of teacher-led introductory lectures and guided reading, large-group discussions, student group activities (a group poster exercise creating a "power triangle" on different forms of discrimination involved in the 1994 genocide; a whole-class placemat response to poetry), student presentations, and the guest speaker-led class discussion after the documentary screening (Rwigema et al., 2009); and copies of two individual writing assignments (a structured response to the guest speaker and documentary [R2S], and a final expository essay).

"When is it Over?": Mobilizing Critical Frameworks to Address Charged Responses to Testimony

The introductory KWL class discussion surfaced a key tension in the intersectional social justice lens of the course, reflecting Shelley's research goals of (a)

124 Lisa K. Taylor

integrating intersectional antiracism into the curriculum and (b) contextualizing students' everyday experiential understandings of racism within a longer history of European imperialism and modernity/coloniality (Mignolo, 2011). This can be thought of as the tension between, on the one hand, popular notions of racism that circulate in students' diverse discourse communities and, on the other, a structural analysis of the ways racial grammars and categories play out in the particular imperial and postcolonial history of Rwanda.

The 1994 genocide against the Tutsi cannot be understood outside the context of Belgian and French imperial governance and postindependence interference and the racial ideologies underpinning these (including racial ideologies introduced under Belgian rule but then deployed by Hutu postcolonial regimes against Tutsi). In the full-class discussion, this distinction between different historical expressions of racism manifested, for example, in the reactions of many students to the scale, speed, and methods of the genocide: many students responded emotionally to accounts of interpersonal brutality, speculating on the psychology and racial ideologies motivating the violence. Reminding students that racism had been invented neither by the Hutu nor even Nazi Germany in the Holocaust, Shelley reviewed the development of racial thinking from Social Darwinism to colonial ideology in the European imperial project of conquest and exploitation (Class Observation, May 1).

The challenge of discerning the distinctions, interdependence, and shared racial grammars of imperial and postcolonial ideologies and policies emerged as a theme throughout student learning in the class. The word *discrimination* became a catchall term in classroom discussions for a range of practices including the racial classification system of identity cards under Belgian colonial rule, interethnic political rivalries and tensions, the explicit targeting of Tutsi by Hutu schoolteachers and state media in postcolonial pregenocide Rwanda, and the international community's complicity, apathy, and failure to intervene to end the genocide (Class Observation, May 5, 8, 17). Several students were able to identify these as examples of institutional discrimination in particular; one group of students identified the media and school scapegoating of Tutsis within Stanton's (2009) stages of genocide (a previously studied framework; Class Observation, May 8).

In general, however, the class struggled to explain how these scapegoating practices constituted examples of racism. One variously racialized group of female students articulated this understanding in their power triangle that identified several examples of institutional discrimination (Belgian race-based identity cards, Hutu teacher-led persecution of Tutsi students, and the international media's portrayal of the genocide as "tribal conflict"). The group contextualized these within the longer history of imperialism: "Tutsis are superior to Hutus, then Hutus are superior to Tutsis but Europeans are always superior to Tutsis and Hutus" (Class Observation, May 8; Group 2, Power Triangle, May 9).

A significant pattern emerges with longitudinal analysis of classroom observation and individual student writing samples. In initial classes (May 5, 8), large

Global Memory across Colonial Divides **125**

group discussion of the introductory reading (a historical overview) focuses on the interpersonal violence of the 1994 genocide: there is, for example, a discussion of cannibalism (a trope that gestures to the visual repertoire of European imperialism and anti-Black racism). Students focus on examples of individual brutality, contrasting these with what they had learned of the systemic and seemingly impersonal mass violence in the Holocaust; there is an oblique reference by one student linking the methods of the Rwandan genocide to economic and technological poverty (Class Observation, May 5).

Of note is the tone of student reflections after Marie-Jolie Rwigema's class visit to screen the documentary *Historian-Survivors* (May 17). Marie-Jolie brings a clear anticolonial analysis to leading the class discussion of the film (cf. Rwigema, 2018), highlighting moments when the film refuses the Eurocentric gaze that is common to non-Rwandan accounts of the genocide. Marie-Jolie explicitly asks students to observe their own expectations as listeners and to pay attention to the influence of racially coded imaginaries of continental Africans in general and victims of violence in particular. In the film, Axelle Karera points out the ways survivors are relegated to the nonacademic realm of emotion. She argues that this constitutes a "colonial continuity" in which "Africans have never been considered historians, intellectuals, politicians" or individuals with any type of agency (Karera in Rwigema et al., 2009). Marie-Jolie prompts students to consider what they learn from the documentary subjects as survivor-historians (rather than as suffering victims; cf. Razack, 2007) and how this reframes their analysis of the genocide with implications for their own lives.

After the screening and discussion, students write journal responses structured by a series of teacher-written prompts (see Appendix). The writing prompts invite students to record their emotional or imaginative responses to the film and then to extend these into critical and reflexive questions.

The shift in tone between the two class discussions is reflected in this journal exercise. What is notable across the set of student journal responses is the way the emotional content of student writing is organized around repeated references to particularly vivid images from survivor testimony. These images figure in students' attempts to empathize with or imagine the experience recounted by a survivor. This trait is particularly marked in the case of four pupils: below, I trace the writing of each student longitudinally across a series of assignments and discussions.

There is a series of questions that stand out in the response entry of Jill, a female, white-identified student. This was a structured response exercise completed while the guest speaker, Marie-Jolie, led the class in a discussion of the long-term consequences of trauma and the ways it is transmitted intergenerationally, but also the ways it is amplified by inequality, racism, and the continuing global coloniality of power. Jill writes, "How is trauma passed down from one generation to the next?"; she continues, "How would you heal? When is it over? How are Africans still represented? Has this changed?" (R2S, May 17). The shift from third- to second-person address that occurs between the first ("How is trauma passed

126 Lisa K. Taylor

down from one generation to the next?") and second ("How would you heal?") questions suggests a shift in Jill's engagement from distance to personal empathetic imagination. The following question, "When is it over?" wavers between these two stances, carrying undertones of the pain of intergenerational trauma. The shift to questions of media representation leaves open the subjective experience of being represented as racialized other or outsider.

Jill goes on to cite Marie-Jolie's post-screening discussion that linked the racism of Canadian media representations of the genocide to hegemonic settler colonial constructions of Euro-Canadian identity. Quoting Marie-Jolie, she writes, "Do I belong in Canada? Which Canada?" (R2S, May 17). Her *"big ethical questions"* for further exploration[6] extend this attention to the politics of representation raised by Marie-Jolie: "Does it matter whos [sic] story it is? What gets passed down? Other peoples [sic] story? I wouldn't be comfortable talking about this yet" (R2S, May 17).

It is noteworthy that in the subsequent power triangle activity, Jill's group was unique in identifying examples of institutional discrimination that include not only "international media called it 'tribal conflict'" but also "Outsider perspective telling the history" (Group #2, May 9). The first example names the politics of media representation in 1994; the second uses the gerund ("telling"), encompassing the entire project of historiography and history education, including academic and curricular constructions of this history: this could include the selection of the very sources the students are studying, and the kinds of attention they themselves bring to listening and reading these sources. That this group includes these historiographic questions of voice, authority, and power among their examples of institutional injustice in the triangle exercise suggests that they may be developing an understanding of the genocide's historical significance extending far beyond the immediate physical brutality (the focus of the first class discussion), beyond the structural violence of a postcolonial genocide inspired by European imperial racial ideologies. Categorizing "outsider perspective telling the history" as institutional discrimination suggests they are also thinking about the global and contemporary salience of this violence and its implications for their own learning and responsibilities as they attend to differently positioned accounts of the genocide.

Pearl, a female Chinese Canadian student, writes extensively in her structured response with a particular focus on the image of hiding:

> *This makes me wonder* ... Hiding seemed to be the only way to survive. A lot of people would hide in schools and churches for days, up to 20+ days. *I feel that* ... A lot of younger children survived this way. *I can connect this to* ... the 12-year old hider (Girl) we watched in class ... 12 year old girl in hiding pretended to be dead.
>
> *(R2S, May 17; prompts in italics)*

This repetition ("hiding"/"hider") suggests a particular imaginative intensity to her engagement with the image of concealment and entrapment: It appears she

Global Memory across Colonial Divides **127**

"wondered" about this experience of violence, violence so extensive as to preclude escape.

Her wondering was clearly scaffolded by Marie-Jolie's discussion of the postcolonial geopolitics abetting the genocide: to the prompt, "*What big ethical questions are raised in this section? (e.g. Questions of justice, responsibility)*," she writes:

> How do we make sense of this?? How and Why would it get to that point of genocide? How do you organize the mass killing of people? Where'd the arms come from? How was it planned? How come nobody did anything from the international community? Was there resistance?—standup and speakout/protest. Need Primary source.
>
> *(R2S, May 17)*

There is an ethical demand to her question of how to make sense of the genocide, linked as it is to the stages of genocide preparation, the role of institutional organizational power, and the collective international responsibility to stop genocide. Her ending by signaling a "need" to seek out accounts by Rwandans of resistance and her reference to these accounts as "primary sources" suggests that her subjective response to survivors' testimony of individual hiding was channeled into a sense of urgency to make sense and learn from the genocide and a sense of responsibility to critically analyze the perspective taken in writing this history: "Who should be the people telling this story?" (R2S, May 17).

In her response, Sarah, a female, white-identified student, writes that this testimony was "hard to watch":

> *This makes me realize/wonder … **who you can trust*** because somebody betrayed Jean-Paul's family … nobody should have to find their mother shot and dead. I would never forget this—having to constantly run away; I would give up eventually/lose all hope; I would feel there is no reason to live—I would not be able to talk about my experiences because I would want to forget about it.
>
> *(R2S, May 17; emphasis in original)*

The length of the response suggests a deeply subjective engagement but a difficult one, torn between the desire to forget and the very impossibility of it. In his landmark elaboration of an educational model of historical memory and pedagogies of remembrance, Roger Simon explored the potential workings of testimonial accounts of historic atrocity. Beyond the provision of evidence, he argues, testimony *acts* on listeners, placing a moral claim or demand upon them to make some sort of emotional, imaginative, or ethical significance out of difficult learning, significance that might be brought to bear in their lived lives. For Simon, the address of testimony is "transitive" and performative, constituting students not simply as historians but also as witnesses who carry a responsibility for and to both the past and the future (Simon, 2013).

128 Lisa K. Taylor

In Sarah's response, the tension between the phrases "I would never forget this" and "I would want to forget about it" suggests a deeply imaginative—and deeply conflicted—emotional engagement with the survivor testimony. There are several potential sources of difficulty underlying this conflict: these include the particular horror of the victimization of children (including the psychic wounds and primal fears this can awaken). It also includes the demands of witnessing—the inescapable persistence of memory and the way testimony commands witnesses not to look away in horror but to remember and retell, to carry these stories into their lived worlds (Britzman, 1998; Simon, 2013; Taylor, 2015).

Sarah begins her response by asking, "Who can you trust?" (R2S, May 17). Her response signals the individual and societal erosion of social trust effected by the breakdown of the shared collective community that happens through dehumanization, the expulsion of one segment of a population from the status of shared humanity and political membership. Theories of colonial racial ideology and Stanton's (2009) stages of genocide are essential frameworks arguing for an understanding of the historical uniqueness and significance of this scale of existential and political violence, a historic violence that demands historic forms of repair.

Sarah lists a series of urgent "*big ethical questions*" to the fifth writing prompt:

> Who is responsible for the genocide? (the Europeans ie. Belgians for creating the initial divisions and racism) How did this turn into hatred? Why would somebody do something like this on such a big scale? How was the genocide so well planned? How come the people from the international community do something? [sic] Should Europeans (because of colonialism) be held responsible? Why didn't Rwanda get any reparations?
>
> *(R2S, May 17)*

This series of questions, filling the allotted journal space and spilling onto the next page, brings several interpretive frameworks to bear on the task of historical analysis and witnessing historic atrocity. Several of these frameworks had been introduced in previous classes. For example, when responding to her students' focus on the spectacular violence recounted in introductory readings, Shelley had contextualized the role of colonial racial ideologies of Social Darwinism in sowing divisions to facilitate imperial governance, referring to Stanton's (2009) stages of genocide to trace the hierarchies of (in)humanity and logics of extermination within these ideologies that amplify interethnic competition and scale up racialized resentment into genocidal hatred (Class Observation, May 8). Sarah's final two questions take up the documentary's explicit critiques of not only European conquest but also the continued coloniality of power (international indifference, France's interference, complicity, and abetment in 1994). This is suggested in the apparent slip in her sentence: "How come the people from the international community do something? [sic]" (R2S, May 17).

Global Memory across Colonial Divides   129

In her final essay, Sarah focuses on questions of immediate and long-term international responsibility, contrasting the Rwandan genocide to the Holocaust in ways that take up the questions she articulated in her earlier response: "Why is the Holocaust the most 'memorable' genocide? Why isn't the Rwandan genocide more important?" (R2S, May 17). In her final essay, she documents the refusal to intervene by the United Nations and the United States and the subsequent debates concerning the international legal responsibility to protect and ends with a focus on the *gacaca* courts as an institutional mechanism to rebuild social trust within Rwandan society at local and interpersonal levels (Final Essay, May 31).

In another response to the documentary, Latisha, a female, Black-identified student, writes that "*What this makes me realize/wonder*" was "how much they were determined to make sure no one survived (they first used machete to kill then cut the ankles of the victim to track them if they escape)" (R2S, May 17). The image of machetes, of repeated blows, is powerful and has been used extensively in media coverage of the genocide; these are tropes from the visual archive of anti-Black racism that animate racist fascination with the degradation of the Black body and fears of the violent racialized other. Latisha's focus signals a different interest guiding her attention: her focus is on understanding the underlying collective determination motivating the act, and the ways this collective commitment was organized into a project of greater historical proportions than the immediate actions themselves. Her response to the prompt "*What big ethical questions are raised*" suggests her interest is focused on the ideological and institutional infrastructure of the genocide. This infrastructure is a point Marie-Jolie stressed in her post-screening discussion of the visual repertoire of anti-Black racism, including representations of Africa and Afrodiasporic peoples through the imagery of savagery, inhumanity, and irrational tribal enmity (Class Observation, May 17). In this discussion, Marie-Jolie traced the way these tropes continue to be reinforced by Western media accounts and secondary historical sources that focus solely on the 100 days in 1994, decontextualized from the longer history of imperialism, colonial ideologies, and contemporary geopolitics (Class Observation, May 17). In her response, Latisha questions "how this just didn't happen suddenly, it was caused by racism that came from Imperialism ideals. Children schools were taught about it to hate (institutionalized) … the perpetrators didn't just wake up and decide to kill" (R2S, May 17).

Latisha makes clear use of the frameworks of antiracism, anticolonial structural analysis of systemic discrimination (Power Triangles), and genocide studies (Stanton's stages) to articulate a critical stance that refuses to spectacularize or essentialize interpersonal violence in racial terms but instead focuses on collective responsibility, institutional obligations, and historical legacies. This emphasis on structural analysis had emerged in the class discussion Shelley led after Marie-Jolie's visit. Reviewing the long and complex history of forces coming to a head in 1994 Rwanda and pointing to course readings on the legal norm of the "responsibility to protect," Shelley asked the class if the international community

130 Lisa K. Taylor

had/has a moral obligation to get involved in this and similar events. What ensued was a wide-ranging and at times emotional discussion in which students experimented with a range of course frameworks, taking up myriad positions and mobilizing different moral, economic, and psychological arguments.

Latisha was among the few students who referred back to Marie-Jolie's postscreening discussion to explicitly contextualize the genocide within imperial and postcolonial histories. In response to one student arguing against international intervention, "But what if everyone asks for help? What if there's just too much to do it all?" (Min Yeong, Class Observation, May 23), Latisha countered, "But Rwanda wasn't just everyone. Like, for the Belgians and the French. I mean, no one's even talking reparations" (Class Observation, May 23). Contextualizing the discussion of human rights and international legal conventions and institutions in the continuing coloniality of power, Latisha's reference to Belgium and France mobilizes the critical analyses from Rwandan survivor-historians in the documentary. Her response focuses the class discussion on the continuities of colonial and postcolonial violence, on the persisting Eurocentrism in the ways the genocide is framed, represented, and narrated, and on the particular political complicities, beneficiaries, and interests that need to inform any discussion of contemporary projects of international justice. No other course resource raised the issue of reparations: it is Axelle in the final scene of the documentary who speaks directly to the audience, demanding reparations for the history of colonial conquest and terror, transatlantic slavery, and the postcolonial history of political and economic exploitation not only of Rwanda but of the entire African continent.

Discussion: Making Critical Sense of the Affective Intensity and Complex Address of Testimony

These excerpts offer insight into the myriad dimensions of subjective and critical learning and the ways these are shaped by teacher and student intersectional positionality, curricular and popular discourse communities, competing belongings, and the discursive horizons of what is imaginable and thinkable. The analysis of student engagement and written texts points to a relation between students' subjective responses to the testimony of the guest speaker and documentary (personal emotion, imaginative roleplaying, curiosity, speculation) and the compelling questions that these responses generated for each pupil, questions that point to their mobilizing course frameworks (historical thinking skills; Stanton's stages of genocide; power triangles) in the pursuit of answers.

Put differently, what students learn—what draws their attention, what is raised in classroom questions and discussion, what finds its way into their note-taking, circulates in their engagement of different sources and activities, and potentially finds its way into their final assignments and "takeaways" from curriculum—appears to be shaped by the dynamics of identification, imaginative empathy, and

Global Memory across Colonial Divides **131**

imaginative curiosity and speculation: what is colloquially and commonly captured in the curious term *relatability*.

Analysis of student writing in this study points to the importance of offering spaces for young people to articulate the emotional and imaginative intensity that listening to oral history inspires in them. It highlights pedagogical designs within which students can bring their responses into dialogue with analytic and interpretive frameworks and other sources that provide a historical and critical context for articulating the significance to be made of their engagement. The analyses of anti-Black racism, colonial discourse, and white settler colonial constructions of Canadian identity offered by Marie-Jolie allowed Jill to comprehend not only the traumatic consequences and legacies of genocide for survivors and their families, but also the ways the psychological ripples of trauma are amplified by postcolonial injustice and impunity, white supremacy, and the racial terms of belonging within her own society.

Sarah's struggles in witnessing accounts of inescapable violence seem to revolve around the impossibility of forgetting. The writing prompts in the film response activity offered her a space to channel this experience into conversation with genocide studies and anticolonial frameworks. In this way, she could understand the historical significance of genocidal violence and discourses of extermination, and their continuity with the dehumanization of anti-Black racism. The anticolonial analysis by Rwandan survivor-historians that contextualized this violence within the European imperial project offered her the critical framework of reparations to understand the historic challenge facing the world today, the challenge of not only (re)building but decolonizing the international order and international human rights law.

For Latisha, understanding the spectacular brutality of killing within an analysis of the colonial ideological and material infrastructure developed in preparation and extension of the genocide was a critical insight that helped her frame her own argument for the application of international legal conventions within the particular legacies and obligations that bear on former imperial powers.

These dynamics of student imaginative, emotional, and critical attention are not in any way straightforward. Young people's affiliations, identifications, and cultural expressions reflect intersectional tensions, intergenerational family and community memory and silences, fracture lines and cleavages, and hegemonic models and affective structures of inclusion. Young people identify in highly complex ways that are shaped by the discourse communities and collective memory formations to which they do and do not have access. This is illustrated in the class discussion Marie-Jolie led after the screening. She offered a brief analysis of the myriad ways European imperialism, racism, and the continuing coloniality of power have shaped the history of her family and the Rwandan Canadian community in terms of structures of opportunity, choices, conditions, and challenges, in terms of intergenerational trauma and healing, and in terms of access, resistance, and political action in Canada. She then asked students how they and their families may have

132 Lisa K. Taylor

been affected by European imperialism. Students volunteered very little knowledge of their family histories and the colonial histories of countries of origin; differently racialized students framed their family histories of migration within a liberal pluralist discourse of Canadian multiculturalism.

Analysis of student responses suggests the resiliency of white settler colonial discourses that pose a further challenge to antiracism education. The degree to which settler models of citizenship circulate within diverse communities that have been and continue to be targeted by racism reflects the dynamics of what Jafri (2012) theorizes as "settlerhood": a field of operations within the larger settler-colonial project that differently positions, privileges, and implicates all non-Indigenous Canadians in relation to Indigenous people and to Land. This finding does not imply a critique of this course and classroom in particular: a final course section turns to an examination of Canadian settler colonialism, and more recent iterations of the course can include the findings of cultural genocide by the Truth and Reconciliation Commission of Canada (2015) and of outright genocide by Canada's National Inquiry on Missing and Murdered Indigenous Women and Girls (2019), findings that have subsequently informed provincial curriculum reform (Ontario Ministry of Education, 2016, 2018[7]).

Of particular salience to critical educators is the complexity of student subjective responses—the different ways they self-position and identify in their listening practices and their struggles to make sense of emotionally charged narratives and powerful images using concepts and frameworks from the highly mediated social worlds of their lives as well as from the course. The complexity of student responses raises the question of what we mean by "culture" and what we are focusing on when we practice "culturally responsive pedagogy" or other community-referenced approaches (cf. Ladson-Billings, 1995; Moll, Amanti, Neff, & Gonzalez, 1992).

We might also ask what we mean by "community," as well as how different community members self-position and set the terms for community partnerships (Schecter, & Cummins, 2003; Pease-Alvarez & Schecter, 2005). For Shelley, building relationships with diverse Rwandan community members is crucial to bringing diverse voices into her classroom (Taylor et al., 2017). This commitment had important implications for her approach to teaching the course. In this project, Rwandan Canadian partners made it clear that their participation depended on the commitment of teachers to practice critical and anti-oppression pedagogies. They articulated a clear expectation that their testimonies of survival would be received not solely with sympathy or interest but more importantly with critical reflexivity and historical knowledge contextualizing the testimonies within long and ongoing histories of imperialism. The "community perspective" they bring is grounded in a rigorous critique of colonial representations of the genocide within Eurocentric discourses of African violence, helplessness, victimhood, and voicelessness, especially as these play out in educational spheres.[8]

Finally, the analysis of student writing above underlines the value of oral history frameworks within which speakers and sources can address learners in a relationship that opens onto the complexity of lived experience, identifications, and meanings: "culture" and "community" are dynamic figurations of lives lived within and against historical forces and the sense people make of them. This conclusion is supported by extensive research in integrative antiracism education (Dei, 2017; Dei & Kempf, 2006; James, 2004; Yon, 2000) that foregrounds and centers the complex, diverse cultural expressions, knowledge formations, and political concerns of communities targeted by racism.

Challenges for Critical Cosmopolitanism: The Dynamic Resilience of Racial Grammars, the Coloniality of Power, and Settler Colonial Projects

I return to the overview I sketched in the introduction, gesturing to the cultural, sociolinguistic, socioeconomic, geopolitical, and technological complexity that characterizes today's classrooms in global cities. This complexity exceeds the scope of any single theoretical or methodological framework we may bring to bear as educators and researchers committed to curriculum development that is both responsive to and supportive of the always-emergent identifications and resources that youth bring to their experiences of living and learning within persistently stratified glocal contexts and global designs (Mignolo, 2000). The critically reflexive research concerns and analysis emerging from the project reported here recommend that cosmopolitan spaces of superdiversity need to be understood as complex but clearly not as horizontal. As explored in this collection, critical cosmopolitanism offers many insights and tools but must always prioritize the knowledge generated by communities in the face of colonial and postcolonial violence, knowledge that breaks the silencing of colonial/modernity's "abyssal line" (Mignolo, 2011; Santos, 2007). In a historical era of liquid modernity, of hypermobile, coconstructed and intersectional subjectivities, students need tools to make sense of the structural forces shaping the "colonial intimacies" (Lowe, 2015) of daily life.

One aspect of these intimacies consists of the subjective dimensions of learning through modes and knowledge forms that personalize the apparently distant experiences of global events and developments and trace our interconnected, implicated relationships within coloniality/modernity. The teaching of Rwandan survivor-historians in this project invited diverse youth into intimate forms of listening that opened up the intensity and immediacy of difficult knowledge (Britzman, 1998) and refused the paternalism of liberal empathy, instead calling them into the noninnocent, self-implicated responsibilities of witnessing (Simon, 2013).

Critically framed, then, oral counterhistories offer tremendous possibilities for critical and emotional literacies, expanding questions of "What happened?" to those of "Why does it matter? To whom? For what social projects?" (Llewellyn, 2015).

134 Lisa K. Taylor

They invite further questions: Which people's memories are important to listen to and how is one's access to them filtered through relations of power? How does the meaning of this event change as each generation re-members it differently through the lens of their historical consciousness? How is forgetting organized? What is at stake in remembering? How are collective identities defined and redefined through contemporary practices of remembering the past through oral history? And finally, what kinds of futures do and can our remembrance practices build?

Appendix

During and after the in-class screening of *Historian-Survivors*, students are given time to write freely in response to a series of writing prompts, including:

> "Today you will view MJ Rwigema's documentary on the Rwandan Genocide … Remember to be specific and try to make connections to class concepts. If you have questions write them down and ask them during discussions.
>
> **Part I—Survivor Testimonies.** Respond to prompts written below. You may do so while viewing; however, you will be given time to write before watching Part II.
>
> *This makes me realize/wonder …*
> *I feel that …*
> *I can connect this to …*
>
> **Part II—Answer the questions below**
> 1. *What big ethical questions are raised in this section? (e.g. questions of justice, responsibility …)*
> 2. *Compare and contrast this documentary to other sources that you have studied on genocide. Use the back of the sheet if you need more space."*
>
> (Kyte, n.d.)

Notes

1 This chapter extends the work of the research collective: Umwali Sollange, Marie-Jolie Rwigema, and Shelley Kyte (Taylor, Rwigema, & Sollange, 2012, 2014; Taylor, Rwigema, Sollange, & Kyte, 2017).
2 The colonial matrix of power comprises enduring structures of colonial domination founded on modern/colonial geopolitics of knowledge underpinning heteropatriarchal racial capitalism (Grosfoguel, 2007; Mignolo, 2011).
3 The co-researchers and co-authors in this project (see Taylor, Rwigema, & Sollange, 2012, 2014; Taylor, Rwigema, Sollange, & Kyte, 2017) give primacy to the designation "The Rwandan genocide against Tutsi" given the reality of discourses of denial and revisionism. This is done alongside the recognition that those targeted for massacre

Global Memory across Colonial Divides **135**

extended beyond ethnic lines to include those identified as sympathizers, traitors, or internal threats. Following this practice, a range of terms appear in this chapter, including "1994 Rwandan genocide" and "Rwandan genocide."

4 Activities included community-led in-service workshops, curriculum development and piloting using community-produced oral history resources, and guest speaker classroom visits, as well as qualitative analysis of student work and participant observation.

5 To ensure confidentiality of student data, the year of data collection will not be cited.

6 See Appendix, fifth writing prompt; all writing prompts from the handout are transcribed in this chapter in italicized text.

7 The 2018 secondary history curriculum announces, "The revisions in the 2018 curriculum support Ontario's commitment to respond to the Truth and Reconciliation Commission's Calls to Action. These revisions were made in collaboration with Indigenous teachers, Elders, Knowledge Keepers, Senators, Indigenous community representatives, and residential school survivors. The revisions focus on strengthening students' knowledge and understanding of Indigenous histories, cultures, perspectives, contributions, and ways of knowing, as well as of the history of the residential school system, treaties, and the Indian Act" (Ontario Ministry of Education, 2018).

8 See Marie-Jolie Rwigema and Umwali Sollange in Taylor, Rwigema, & Sollange, 2012, 2014; Taylor, Rwigema, Sollange, & Kyte, 2017.

References

Bazambamba, R. (2009). *Smile through the tears*. Sutton, ON: Soul Asylum Poetry.

Britzman, D. (1998). *Lost subjects, contested objects: Towards a psychoanalytic inquiry of learning*. Albany, NY: State University of New York Press.

Canada, National Inquiry into Missing and Murdered Indigenous Women and Girls. (2019). *Reclaiming power and place: The final report* (Vol. 1a). Retrieved from https://www.mmiwg-ffada.ca/wp-content/uploads/2019/06/Final_Report_Vol_1a.pdf

Dei, G. J. S. (2017). *Reframing Blackness and Black solidarities through anti-colonial and decolonial prisms* (Vol. 4). New York: Springer.

Dei, G. J. S., & Kempf, A. (Eds.). (2006). *Anti-colonialism and education: The politics of resistance*, Rotterdam, The Netherlands: Sense Publishers.

Donald, D., Glanfield, F., & Sterenberg, G. (2012). Living ethically within conflicts of colonial authority and relationality. *Journal of the Canadian Association for Curriculum Studies, 10*(1), 53–77.

Grosfoguel, R. (2007). The epistemic decolonial turn: Beyond political-economy paradigms. *Cultural Studies, 21*(2–3), 211–223.

Jafri, B. (2012). Privilege vs. complicity: People of colour and settler colonialism. *Equity Matters* [Blog]. Ottawa, ON: Federation of Humanities and Social Sciences. Retrieved from http://www.ideas-idees.ca/blog/privilege-vs-complicity-people-colour-and-settler-colonialism

James, C. E. (2004). Urban education: An approach to community-based education. *Intercultural Education, 15*(1), 15–32.

Kyte, S. (n.d.). *Responding to survivors*. Unpublished curriculum resource. Toronto, ON, Canada.

Ladson-Billings, G. (1995). Toward a theory of culturally relevant pedagogy. *American Educational Research Journal, 32*(3), 465–491.

Llewellyn, K. (2015, May 24). *Oral history as peacebuilding pedagogy*. Unpublished conference paper. Ottawa, ON: University of Ottawa.

136 Lisa K. Taylor

Lowe, L. (2015). *The intimacies of four continents*. Durham, NC: Duke University Press.

Marker, M. (2011). Teaching history from an Indigenous perspective: Four winding paths up the mountain. In P. Clark (Ed.), *New possibilities for the past: Shaping history education in Canada* (pp. 97–112). Vancouver, BC: UBC Press.

McGregor, H. E. (2017). One classroom, two teachers? Historical thinking and Indigenous education in Canada. *Critical Education, 8*(14), 1–18.

Mignolo, W. D. (2000). *Local histories/global designs: Coloniality, subaltern knowledges, and border thinking*. Princeton, NJ: Princeton University Press.

Mignolo, W. D. (2011). *The darker side of Western modernity: Global futures, decolonial options*. Durham, NC: Duke University Press.

Moll, L. C., Amanti, C., Neff, D., & Gonzalez, N. (1992). Funds of knowledge for teaching: Using a qualitative approach to connect homes and classrooms. *Theory Into Practice, 31*(2), 132–141.

Ontario Ministry of Education. (2016). *The journey together: Ontario's commitment to reconciliation with Indigenous peoples*. Toronto, ON: Author. Retrieved from https://www.ontario.ca/page/journey-together-ontarios-commitment-reconciliation-indigenous-peoples

Ontario Ministry of Education. (2018). *Secondary history curriculum document*. Toronto, ON: Author. Retrieved from http://www.edu.gov.on.ca/eng/curriculum/secondary/canworld.html

Pease-Alvarez, L., & Schecter, S. R. (Eds.). (2005). *Learning, teaching, and community: Contributions of situated and participatory approaches to educational innovation*. New York: Routledge.

Razack, S. (2007). Stealing the pain of others: Reflections on Canadian humanitarian responses. *Review of Education, Pedagogy, and Cultural Studies, 29*, 375–394.

Regan, P. (2010). *Unsettling the settler within: Indian residential schools, truth telling, and reconciliation in Canada*. Vancouver, BC: UBC Press.

Rwigema, M.-J. (2018). *Fragments, webs and weavings: Rwandan-Canadian perspectives on the 1994 genocide against Tutsi* (Unpublished doctoral dissertation). University of Toronto, Toronto, ON, Canada.

Rwigema, M.-J., Karera, A., Nsabimana, N., Sharangabo, N., & Sollange, U. (Producers). (2009). *The Rwandan genocide as told by its historian-survivors* [videotape]. Toronto, ON: Kabazaire Productions.

Santos, B. D. S. (2007). Beyond abyssal thinking: From global lines to ecologies of knowledges. *Binghamton University Review, 30*(1), 45–89.

Schecter, S. R., & Cummins, J. (Eds.). (2003). *Multilingual education in practice: Using diversity as a resource*. Portsmouth, NH: Heinemann.

Simon, R. I. (2013). *A pedagogy of witnessing: Curatorial practice and the pursuit of social justice*. Albany, NY: State University of New York Press.

Stanton, G. H. (2009). The Rwandan genocide: Why early warning failed. *Journal of African Conflicts and Peace Studies, 1, 2, 3*.

Taylor, L. K. (2015). Curation as public pedagogy: Roger Simon, *A Pedagogy of Witnessing*. *Journal of the Canadian Association for Curriculum Studies, 12*(3), 175–196.

Taylor, L. K. (2018). Pedagogies of remembrance and "doing critical heritage" in the teaching of history: Counter-memorializing Canada 150 with future teachers. *Journal of Canadian Studies, 52*(1), 217–248. doi: 10.3138/jcs.2017-0056.r2

Taylor, L. K., Rwigema, M.-J., & Sollange, U. (2012). What you see depends where you stand: Critical anticolonial perspectives on genocide education addressing the Rwandan genocide. In P. P. Trifonas & B. Wright. (Eds.), *Critical peace education: Difficult dialogues* (pp. 115–134). New York: Springer.

Taylor, L. K., Rwigema, M.-J., & Sollange, U. (2014). The ethics of learning from Rwandan survivor communities: The politics of knowledge production and shared authority within community-school collaboration in genocide and critical global citizenship education. In S. High & Concordia University Centre for Oral History and Digital Storytelling (Eds.), *Beyond testimony and trauma: Oral history in the aftermath of mass violence* (pp. 88–118). Vancouver, BC: UBC Press.

Taylor, L. K., Rwigema, M. J., Sollange, U., & Kyte, S. (2017). Learning with and from Rwandan survivor-historians: Testimonial oral history as relationship building in schools. In N. Ng-a-Fook & K. Llewellyn (Eds.), *Oral history and education: Theories, dilemmas, and practices* (pp. 337–359). New York: Palgrave Macmillan.

Toronto District School Board. (2005). *Challenging class bias.* Toronto, ON: Author.

Toronto District School Board. (2006). *Tools for equity: A resource for best practices (Grades 7–12).* Toronto, ON: Author.

Truth and Reconciliation Commission of Canada. (2015). *Canada's residential schools: The final report of the Truth and Reconciliation Commission of Canada* (Vols. 1–7). Toronto, ON: James Lorimer & Company. Retrieved from http://nctr.ca/reports.php

Vertovec, S. (2016, April 4). *Super-diversity as concept and approach: Whence it came, where it's at, and whither it's going.* Opening address to Workshop on Super-Diversity: A Transatlantic Conversation, CUNY Graduate Center, New York. Retrieved from https://vimeo.com /161619990

Woolley, N. (2009). *Rescue in Rwanda.* Boston, MA: Houghton Mifflin School.

Yon, D. A. (2000). *Elusive culture: Schooling, race, and identity in global times.* Albany, NY: State University of New York Press.

9

TRILINGUAL INSTRUCTION IN AN INDIGENOUS COMMUNITY IN NORTHWESTERN MEXICO

A Case for Cosmopolitanism from Below in Intercultural Education

María Rebeca Gutiérrez Estrada and Sandra R. Schecter

This chapter contextualizes the findings of an ethnographic study conducted in the state of Sonora, in northwestern Mexico, within a framework that privileges a critical cosmopolitan perspective, applicable to nonurban as well as urban contexts. For the original research project, the first author followed a trilingual teacher and other key participants who navigated the demands of a complex educational system, that of Intercultural Bilingual Education (IBE) in Mexico, while seeking to be responsive to stakeholders' goals and commitments to maintaining the minority language in a rural, Indigenous community. The study's findings focused partly on the agency of three key educators who acted *in* and *on* that setting from 2008 to 2010, the period in which the fieldwork was conducted, and partly on the relational configurations among the three languages taught in the community school: Spanish, the societal language and *de facto* language of communication; Mayo, the heritage language[1]; and English, the recognized global language (Gutiérrez Estrada, 2015). These findings revealed a counternarrative to one that could be anticipated given the historicity of second language acquisition and learning research since the mid-1960s, posing a challenge to the prevalent disciplinary construct of *additive/subtractive bilingualism* (Gutiérrez Estrada & Schecter, 2018). This essay represents our best effort to explain why we found what we found. In the course of reinterpreting our findings, we were drawn to ideas and concepts associated with critical, dialogic cosmopolitanism (Canagarajah, 2012), while resisting the homogenizing derivations that issue from more simplistic framings of cosmopolitanism that underscore shared values and connections beyond the here and now.

We begin this chapter with a discussion of the sociolinguistic landscape and infrastructural context related to language and language of education policies in Mexico, elaborating on the macro context for multilingual education within

DOI: 10.4324/9780429327780-9

Indigenous communities that lay the groundwork for the original study. We next elaborate on the theoretical frameworks that we are working with in this chapter. We then situate in time and texture the community that was the focus of the ethnographic inquiry, and go on to introduce the perspectives of the study's key participants toward the three languages in relation in this study. Finally, we revisit the original findings in light of the ideas taken up here and elsewhere in this volume, perspectives that have impelled us to reconsider the theoretical and applied implications of our work.

Situating Educational Policies in Mexico

Like other modern societies, in recent years Mexico has undergone a series of changes in its language and educational policies. These changes have had a direct impact on the way teacher practices are expected to accommodate a series of mandates established through the influence of international standards. Mexico's political history is complex and paradoxical: briefly, before the current left-wing government, only two major parties had ascended to power—the Partido Revolucionario Institucional (PRI) and the Partido Acción Nacional (PAN). Both PRI and PAN have been associated with violence, corruption, and fraudulent elections.

Nonetheless, these two major political parties, under Enrique Peña Nieto's presidency (2012–2018), supported the New Educational Reform, a set of policies that follow the United Nations Sustainable Development Goals. These policies endorse the Global Education Agenda 2030, promoted worldwide by both the UN and UNESCO, which sees its major goal to "ensure inclusive and equitable quality education and promote lifelong learning opportunities for all." This said, these goals were already being promoted through two major institutions in Mexico: a federal program known as Programa Nacional de Inglés (National Program of English), or PRONI, which began in 2009; and the Coordinación General de Educación Intercultural Bilingüe (CGEIB), or General Office of Intercultural Education. The PRONI seeks to promote the teaching of English as an additional language beginning in the last year of preschool through junior high. It follows a series of international guidelines—those established by the Common European Framework of Reference for Languages: Learning, Teaching, Assessment (CEFR)—and national standards.

Established in 2001, the CGEIB was put in place as a branch of the National Ministry of Education (SEP) with an ambitious objective of delivering intercultural education to the entire population of Mexico, and not exclusively minority Indigenous populations. Such a policy approach was the first of its kind in Mexico. The CGEIB is also tasked with providing culturally relevant education to Indigenous communities at all levels of education. Thus, the CGEIB oversees the creation and design of courses, textbooks, and materials for the many Indigenous languages and communities of the country or certifies extant resources as culturally

140 Gutiérrez Estrada and Schecter

appropriate. The CGEIB also focuses on the promotion, training, material design, and evaluation of teacher education and preparation of programs for Intercultural Bilingual Education (IBE).

Given the policy imperatives of both IBE and the PRONI at the national level and under the mandates of UNESCO, one would expect that these offices would work in collaboration, informing each other of recent developments and transferring expertise across the two programs; however, this has not been the case (Gutiérrez Estrada, 2015). Despite the progressive rhetoric undergirding such premises, the execution of related mandates has more often than not proved paradoxical, inconsistent, and conflict-ridden. Findings from Gutiérrez Estrada's (2015) study show that the motto "intercultural education for all" put forward by the CGEIB is far from an accurate description of the status quo of pedagogic practices in elementary schools throughout Mexico. Nor is this situation the result solely of poor organization, for at the heart of this incongruity lies an unresolved contradiction. The sociolinguistic conditions embedded in Mexico's language policy reflect a dichotomous mainstream persona: on the one hand, Mexico as a Mestizo nation, reflecting the multicultural, plurilingual influences of a mixed-heritage people, and on the other hand, a homogenizing and assimilating Spanish-speaking Mexico. Evidence of this unresolved identity dilemma is reflected in pages from textbooks used in elementary schools that portray contradictory cultural and historical "facts" about the country's history, especially in relation to Indigenous cultures and languages.

With regard to education for Indigenous groups, inclusion remains a pressing issue. At the center of the dilemma for educators, policy-makers, and informed, progressively minded citizens is the question: *What kind and combination of language education policies and practices at the local, state, and national levels would most beneficially facilitate the preservation of heritage languages and cultures while at the same time promoting a multilingual agenda that affords Indigenous peoples the same life choices and opportunities as are available to other citizens of Mexico?* And if, as appears to be the case, Mexican citizens are receptive to a worldview that acknowledges the status and role of English as a global language, a *lingua franca* as it were, how then should English intersect with the societal and minority languages in the education of subaltern, Indigenous peoples that have undergone centuries of colonial violence, entailing linguistic and cultural repression (Go, 2013; Mignolo, 2000)?

Conceptual Frameworks

The findings presented in this chapter illustrate a successful trilingual education program in an Indigenous community in rural northwestern Mexico, where curricular and practical decisions taken by the teacher, key administrators, parents, and other community stakeholders reveal a scenario in which a powerful language such as English did not, in fact, marginalize a minority language, but instead served as a catalyst for nurturing a favorable language learning environment. At the same time, these findings shed light on the tensions between macro- and micro-level language policy and planning in the context of Mexico's Intercultural Bilingual Education Program and the National Program for English Language Teaching.

In fact, we would argue that these positive outcomes were achieved *in spite of* the many actual and potential obstacles that the community faced in implementing such a desired program. These obstacles—canceled classes, official textbooks from Mexico City that did not arrive, labor disputes, and inconsistencies between interpretations of the language of education policies at the macro, meso, and micro levels—could have acted as major deterrents to pedagogic delivery and reception. This felicitous scenario was possible because the different key actors were able to balance a strong commitment to the maintenance and revitalization of their cultural and linguistic heritage with a realistic understanding of the entrenched status of the societal variety, Spanish, as a first language for the large majority of community members, as well as a prescient vision of the role that English had the capacity to play in their children's future life trajectories. We characterize this perspective as consistent with a dialogic cosmopolitan stance (Canagarajah, 2012).

In this section, we elucidate the theoretical basis that makes the case for critical cosmopolitanism at the heart of language policy and planning decision-making in this rural, Indigenous setting. Cosmopolitanism, as it has been commonly presented, puts forward the idea of a "worldly" citizen, attuned to global developments and committed to negotiation of a shared universal perspective. Some authors elucidate the limitations of this view by asserting that such an implied liberal agenda lacks a critical understanding that recognizes power and multiplicity and foregrounds the role of local, everyday decisions and actions (Stornaiuolo & Nichols, 2019; see also Preface, this volume). Vertovec and Cohen (2002) articulate one of the more persistent attacks on cosmopolitanism as an essentializing force: that it is "only available to an elite—those who have the resources necessary to travel, learn other languages and absorb other cultures" (p. 5).

While we view this critique as one with historical validity, at the same time we take the position that in today's world, cultural and linguistic diversity is the norm, not the exception, and the opportunity to be influenced by cross-cultural currents is available to many (Vertovec & Cohen, 2002, p. 4). This said, we are not seeking to advance an argument that privileges inter- or multi-culturalism as a normative ideal; rather we are navigating a stance for a "cosmopolitanism from below" (Kurasawa, 2004), or "locally rooted forms of cosmopolitanism [that] take into descriptive account people's lived histories and everyday realities of negotiating multiple commitments, particularly in circumstances of forced migration, state-sponsored violence, and diaspora" (Stornaiuolo & Nichols, 2019, p. 2). We do so with the intention of bringing to light alternative ways of approaching the philosophical and ethical dilemmas of issues of language revitalization and maintenance in the 21st century. Thus, we don't view cosmopolitanism as a notion that competes with that of sociocultural diversity. Rather, we maintain that cosmopolitanism, or

142 Gutiérrez Estrada and Schecter

at least "rooted cosmopolitanism" (Appiah, 2006), must be understood *from the departure point* of sociocultural diversity: that is, from an approach that has an eye on the notion of a world community while being grounded in "border thinking" (Mignolo, 2000) that recognizes heterogeneity and the plural composition of local realities (Beck, 2012).

Into this conceptual mix, we want to integrate a second framework represented by an *engaged policy and practices perspective* (Davis, 2014; Low & Merry, 2010; Schecter, Parejo, Ambadiang, & James, 2014). While our project proceeds from the understanding that schools are places where state ideologies relative to language and teaching are converted into practice (Lewis, Jenson, & Smith, 2003), as socially engaged researchers we also want to examine how evolving politically situated perspectives result in the negotiation of new educational practices, or the adaptation or mutation of extant ones, both locally and on a broader, societal level (Lin, Wang, Akamatsu, & Riazi, 2002; Norton, 2000). Within an engaged educational policy perspective, school-based administrators and classroom practitioners are positioned not as unwitting reproducers but rather as being at the heart of educational policy, given their strategic ability to transform institutional settings and bring about educational change. Moreover, as we have demonstrated (Gutiérrez Estrada & Schecter, 2018; Schecter et al., 2014), research within an engaged policy and practices perspective presents an opportunity to involve professional educators at the macro, meso, and local infrastructural levels in dialogic processes that identify pockets of agency for interrupting extant schooling practices and influencing the outcomes of social processes that affect the lives of at-risk language minority students.

Additionally, the concept of *teacher agency* proves significant in relation to this study's findings in that it highlights the importance of language teachers' choices and dispositions when interpreting and (re)articulating language policy and planning in actual classrooms at the local level. The notion of teacher agency that we work with in this chapter by necessity links up with our understandings of the issues involved in language policy and planning in minority language contexts and is therefore influenced by the works of Baldauf (2006), Canagarajah (1999, 2005), Handsfield (2002), Menken and García (2010), Paris (1993), Ricento and Hornberger (1996), Schecter et al. (2014), and Sichra (2006), among others. As we began to weave these perspectives together in the original study, we took notice of how committed teachers can embody (or not embody) language maintenance through ways of taking up policy and transforming it. It is at this juncture that local changes have the potential to ignite a *cosmopolitanism from below* that may inform policies at a macro level and provoke important discussions about policy and pedagogy that impact minority language and ELT classrooms.

According to Todd (2007), agency also involves *judgments*, made in particular situations and embodied in specific actions that take place in the language classroom. This agency is further described by Le Page and Tabouret-Keller (1985) and Todd (2007) as visible, ongoing decision-making processes that are enacted in linguistic and cultural practices. Todd (2007) asserts:

> Judgments are moments that fix thinking in time, that implicate teachers in the here and now of their work. For judgment is, ultimately, about implication: it is a definite decision that breaks with the duration of thought. And it reveals precisely the point where teachers feel the pull between the professional and the personal most profoundly: judgment commits "me" to something.
>
> *(p. 35)*

As we will see with respect to this project, the crucial manifestations of educators' decisions are located in the "here and now" (Todd, 2007) of language instruction that reveal commitments to linguistic and cultural maintenance and survival. This notion resonates with Canagarajah's (2014) reference to *dispositions*, through which he invokes the way in which cultural capital is bound up in how we take up and respond to "new modes of negotiating language diversity" (p. 783).

Both judgments and dispositions are also represented in the ethical issues that language teachers encounter in their day-to-day professional practice. Indeed, the agency of teachers working with or on behalf of minority language students implicates them in questions of choice. Handsfield (2002) poses an intriguing question: "Is it utopian … to suggest that teachers in practice can take on the role of transformative intellectuals and agents of change?" (p. 552). Her answer, with others (e.g., Canagarajah, 1999; Freire & Macedo, 1987), suggests that changes can be made when teachers are able to "invent and create methods in which they can maximize the limited space for possible change that is available to them" (Freire & Macedo, 1987, p. 127). What characteristics might we expect from an agentive teacher? With regard to the subject at hand, an agentive teacher will perceive "a need to recognize the agency of subaltern communities to negotiate language politics in creative and critical ways that go beyond the limited constructs of language rights" (as cited in Baldauf, 2006, p. 166). This said, we are not so naïve as to ignore the possibility that this concept can be taken up in counterproductive ways, co-opted such that being agentive is associated with some "educational reform" agenda connected to an externally imposed instructional or accountability framework (Lasky, 2005). Ramanathan and Morgan (2007) emphasize the need for a shift in paradigm so that teachers, rather than succumbing to policies that restrict and bind their decision-making, will "interpret the ambiguities and gaps in critical ways that open up moments and spaces for transformative interventions" (p. 448).

Research Context: The Mayo People and Language

The Mayo region is located in the northwest of Mexico, spanning the states of Sonora and Sinaloa, in elevations that extend from sea level to up to 100 meters

144 Gutiérrez Estrada and Schecter

corresponding to the Pacific coastal zone. It includes valleys that extend to the foothills of the Sierra Madre Occidental that rise up to 2000 meters above sea level (Aguilar Zéleny, 1995). Regarding the Mayo population, *Ethnologue* (18th edition) cites the census of 1995, indicating a population of 40,000 people of whom only 113 are referred to as monolingual Mayo (Mayo, 2015). However, Terborg, García Landa, and Moore (2006) cite a 2000 census which postulates that "the population of the Mayo is considerably lower, at 31,513" (p. 434). The Mayo language is classified broadly in the Uto-Aztecan family, which comprises 61 languages. Specifically, Mayo is categorized as Southern Uto-Aztecan, Sonoran, Cahita (Mayo, 2015).

The Mayo, as both community and language, are divided mainly into two major groups: the Mayo from Sonora and those from Sinaloa. Based on Aguilar Zéleny (1995):

> The Mayo people self-identify as *Yoremes* (those who respect tradition) in counterpoint to the *Yori* (those who do not respect tradition, that is, the white man). There is also another label, used emically—the *Torocoyori*, those who betray, referring to those indigenous Mayo who deny their roots and community commitments, pretending to pose as *Yoris*.
>
> *(p. 83, translation ours)*

The Mayo choose to live in their communities that are distributed in the current ceremonial centers. Some of these have been extended and turned into huge urban centers. This process, according to Aguilar Zéleny (1995), "has led to the displacement/replacement of the *Yoreme* by the *Yori*" (p. 85), assimilation to Mestizo culture, and language loss (Fishman, 1989, 1991).

In connection with language revitalization, *Ethnologue* reports that there are government scholarships offered to young people who demonstrate proficiency in Mayo (Mayo, 2015). Benito Juárez Intercultural School, the field site for this ethnographic study, was a clear example of government efforts to promote education in Mayo. At the time of the study, it held the status of "escuela de calidad" (quality school), receiving funding from several sources because of the high scores obtained by students in national standardized tests.[2] This said, in this Indigenous community, the Mayo language is used mainly by the elderly; and researchers working for *Ethnologue* (Mayo, 2015), in addition to data obtained for the original study, show that the majority of Mayo-descent individuals are reticent to self-identify as Mayo.

Trilingual Education in the Town of Seagulls

Site, Participants, Method

The original ethnographic study conducted by Gutiérrez Estrada (2015) over a span of two years presented the case of a trilingual primary level classroom where an Indigenous language (Mayo of northwestern Mexico) and a global language (English) were taught simultaneously in a Spanish-speaking context. The field site for the study was Benito Juárez Intercultural School, a federally funded bilingual school located in the town of Seagulls (pseudonym) by the Sea of Cortez in the southwestern part of the state of Sonora. The population of Seagulls is approximately 8000 people, who are predominantly Indigenous Mayo. The major economic activity of the townspeople is fishing. The school offers Grades 1 through 6 plus a year of preschool. The structure also serves as a boarding school for children who live outside the town of Seagulls and attend the school. At the time that the study took place, between 2008 and 2010, there were approximately 144 students attending the school, 50 of whom were boarders. As for instructors, there were eight, three of whom self-reported as fully bilingual Spanish-Mayo. The remaining instructors self-reported as having "some" knowledge of the Mayo language.

For the purpose of this chapter, we will focus mainly on three participants: Juan, the trilingual teacher at Benito Juárez Intercultural School whose classes were observed; Rosa, the regional coordinator of the Program for English in Elementary schools, or PIP, from 2004 to 2009; and María, principal of Benito Juárez School. We would identify Juan as our major key informant since he was *the* vehicle for Intercultural Bilingual Education in Seagulls throughout 2008–2010. Rebeca observed Juan's classes over a two-year period and interviewed him on three separate occasions.

Data collection methods for the original study included interviews, participant observation in Juan's class and the community at large, survey questionnaires, and textual analysis of both policy documents and instructional resources. For the purposes of this chapter, we focus on data obtained from interviews with the three primary participants, and from fieldnotes taken in the course of participant observation in Juan's class. The interviews, which were audiotaped, followed a semi-structured, conversational format (Mishler, 1986) and engaged a variety of topics, including: the community's attitudes toward cultural maintenance and the Mayo language; views/values concerning the importance of English, Mayo, and Spanish in the school and community, and in relation to future life opportunities beyond (Codó, 2008); and participants' views regarding current language and educational policies.

Before continuing, we should provide a snapshot of Juan's background, given his status as the study's key informant. Juan was born in a house on a dirt road around a 30-minute drive from Seagulls. In Rebeca's first conversations with Juan, dating back to 2008, he told her about the time he had immigrated to the United States for a few years and his family (wife and children) still resided in Tijuana— one of the biggest cities on the Mexico–United States border. Juan explained that he learned English as an undocumented worker in California while also attending night classes in San Diego. It was during his time living in the United States that Juan began to recognize the value of speaking more than one language. After returning to Tijuana, Juan decided he wanted to become a teacher and work near

146 Gutiérrez Estrada and Schecter

his place of birth, where he could foster linguistic and cultural diversity while cultivating his heritage as a Mayo speaker. Rebeca asked whether his children spoke Mayo; he answered that they did not, but were able to understand most of the conversations he carried out with them in Mayo (interview, March 2009). Throughout our interviews and informal conversations, Juan was sensitive to the linguistic and cultural complexities entailed in meeting the educational needs of Indigenous communities as well as to the tenuous nature of government policies attending to cultural diversity.

Stakeholders' Perspectives on Minority Language Maintenance and Learning English

In this section, we use excerpts from interviews with Juan, Rosa, and María to reveal themes that connect to stakeholders' dispositions toward the revitalization and maintenance of Mayo in relation to the teaching and learning of English as a global language. In the first interview with Rosa, the regional coordinator of the Program for English in Elementary Schools (PIP), she recounted how members of two Indigenous communities, both located in rural areas, had approached her office to request English language classes for children in their communities. One of these cohorts comprised primarily Mayo children residing in the town of Seagulls. Rosa explained that the PIP had also been approached by the director of Indigenous education in Sonora, who had made a compelling case that support for English language classes was in these communities' interests and would prove beneficial to the children's educational futures and expand their vocational opportunities.

One persuasive argument was that in the town of Seagulls, students in junior high school were failing their English subject matter class, delivered via *telesecundarias* (see UNESCO, n.d.). Created in the 1960s, *telesecundarias* is a program of instruction via satellite devised to reach students in rural areas throughout Mexico where the placement of teachers has proven to be a challenge. Seagulls community members were most concerned that their children who were registered in the *telesecundarias* program were not passing their English tests and consequently were being denied admission to high schools elsewhere, forcing them to remain in Seagulls.

At the time that English classes were put in place at Benito Juárez Intercultural School, there was a clear *investment* (Norton, 2000, 2015) on the part of the Seagulls community in learning English. This investment is represented in the thoughts that Rosa expressed at the start of the study (2008) with regard to the community's strong interest in and proactive stance on behalf of learning English:

Rosa: The people in the Mayo community were always concerned with having English in the school. … When we paid them a visit, the community was really happy. Children and people of the community were in the classroom

looking through the windows … we [people from the PIP] were not prepared for this, we thought we would only observe their classes … but we
noticed there were a lot of elderly who are obviously the ones that make
the decisions.

Throughout the interview, Rosa revealed that in this particular situation, English
was viewed as a symbolic and material resource (Bourdieu, 1977) that ideally
provided children with access to future opportunities such as gainful employment, better education, and upward social mobility. However, Rosa also stressed
that according to a mandate established by her and the director of the PIP, Mayo
would be the primary language of instruction, even in the English classroom, in
this manner reinforcing heritage language maintenance. The perception of the
interrelationship of the two language varieties, Mayo and English, is made clear
in the following points included in the minutes of an initial discussion between
Rosa and the director of the PIP that took place on April 27, 2005:

> It is important to consider the degree of proficiency in the Mayo language
> of the students participating in the English program.
>
> The educational materials utilized for these courses should be used in
> both Mayo and English in order to reinforce the learning of the children's
> second language [in this case Mayo is considered the second language and
> Spanish the first].
>
> If after initiating English classes, children prefer English to Mayo, the
> English classes will be stopped.
>
> *(our translation)*

We note in Rosa's pronouncements at the time of the creation of the English
program of study a dedication on the part of members of the Seagulls community
to minority language maintenance, but also an effort on the part of stakeholders
to place Mayo at the center of the decision-making process. This commitment
on the part of key stakeholders that the heritage language would be privileged in
pedagogical planning was reinforced in subsequent interviews with study participants and throughout the fieldwork experience.

These stated community commitments to English language instruction in tandem with revitalization and maintenance of the heritage variety placed the consideration of finding a teacher who would enable a curriculum in both languages
as a priority in staffing decisions. Here again is Rosa, regional coordinator of the
PIP:

Rosa: After meeting the parents and community of Seagulls, we came back [the
director of the PIP and Rosa] and discussed the importance of hiring a
teacher with the "sensibility" of the three languages, being able to use them,
a teacher who would need to have the "disposition" to only be paid [a small

amount of money] a month per group and manage all of these factors. The teacher would go to work by commuting three times a week and teaching a class of 50 minutes each. We also had to think of creating a program, so we asked the surrounding schools and other indigenous schools to give us their thematic outlines.

And so it was that Juan was hired as the teacher of the dual-language classes at Benito Juárez Intercultural School. Throughout our interviews and observations, we witnessed multiple examples of instances that showed the metalinguistic awareness that the teacl.er and his colleagues had about both the importance of multilingualism to the life opportunities of students in this Indigenous community and the relationality among the language varieties in play. In the following excerpt, Juan explains how he adapted content to fit both Mayo and English and also reveals indirectly his conviction that learning the world language, English, would reinforce the learning of the heritage variety:

Juan: I think that a language that is not used disappears, right? So that is not what we want, that our traditions or practices get lost … that is why I consider that is important to educate children on these issues. For instance, on the Day of the Dead, we carried out several activities with the kids, we don't celebrate Halloween, we celebrated the Day of the Dead explaining things to children in Mayo … then I would teach them things in English, vocabulary, such as flowers, etc. … The principal told me, "Let's do this activity [the Day of the Dead] so that kids become accustomed to our traditions," and in the end it was quite pretty.

Another illustration of Juan's proactive disposition toward the coexistence and fostering of both Mayo and English is represented by a one-hour demo class (April 2009) that he conducted for the parents (mostly mothers) of his Grade 5 and Grade 6 students. Bolstered by his principal's support, Juan went to considerable effort to prepare for this event—producing materials in Spanish, Mayo, and English and procuring refreshments that were served to both parents and students. In the background of the illustration (Figure 9.1), one notes a banner welcoming parents as well as displays of different materials in the three languages.

The demo class consisted of Juan modeling his teaching techniques and eliciting parents' participation in several of the scenarios he would normally carry out with his Grade 5 and 6 students. The class started with an introduction to the class schedule for that day, followed by an activity that included greetings in both Mayo and English. This activity began with a child carrying out a sign with the greeting in Mayo on one side and the greeting in English on the other. Next, a parent volunteer did the same. Juan then asked participants to repeat this scenario. The overall tone of this event was lively and positive; and parents stayed afterward to exchange with the teacher. Moreover, the children seemed eager to have their

FIGURE 9.1 Juan's demo class for parents.

parents acknowledge their performances in the demo class. At the end of the class, Juan conveyed his pleasure with the high level of parent attendance at the school event.

We feel obliged to introduce several caveats into this encouraging portrait. First, we should point out that although the Mayo language was an integral part of the IBE curriculum in Seagulls, at the time of the study there was no formal instruction in reading and writing in Mayo. This was a result partly of time limitations, but mostly of the fact that curricular materials forthcoming from the central office failed to arrive. In our first interview with principal María, she noted the difficulties and challenges she encountered obtaining materials for the school. Below she is discussing an argument that she had with the head of Indigenous Education where she conveyed her frustration about not obtaining the official textbooks from the National Ministry of Education, which are free materials provided by the government. With regard to macro policy on Indigenous Education, she points out a lack of logistical organization and stakeholders at the ministry level who are not genuinely invested in advancing an intercultural agenda:

María: In connection to the official textbooks, which are free, we are [Indigenous Schools] the last ones to get them … I have told the director of Indigenous Education, "I am not telling you how to do your job," but I tell him, "I am not trying to do this to impress anyone, I defend my school, you are in a higher position to defend us too. If you see that we are left behind as indigenous schools, that we receive materials later than in other schools, you are here to defend us." I am always photocopying material until January. Photocopying books because children did not have the textbooks. How is that possible?

Indeed, there can be no doubt that discrepancies, inconsistencies, and contradictions in educational policies between the macro, meso, and micro levels complicated community members' efforts to maintain the minority language. For example, although the PRONI curriculum document cited the CEFR extensively, there were no references in the curriculum documents to multilingualism as a resource when programs for the teaching and learning of Indigenous/minority languages were discussed. This predicament became especially apparent during Rebeca's last interview with Juan in the summer of 2010 when she was made aware that PRONI government officials not schooled in the tenets of language policy and planning had omitted certain elements in their workshops and documents that supported the teaching of Indigenous languages, instead placing the emphasis on English-only classrooms.

Juan himself picked up on this theme in an interview with Rebeca:

Juan: [Referring to the PRONI content and workshop] In the first level it was suggested that we create an environment in the school and classroom of 100% English. From the time when the child enters the school, for instance, the principal should greet the child in English. This is obviously funny.

This said, throughout the fieldwork carried out over the period of 2008–2010 in Seagulls, the two languages were distributed and honored equally in Juan's classes and there were no instances where English displaced Mayo in the language classroom. Juan and other stakeholders had a prescient awareness of the possible loss of culture and identity in Indigenous communities and the need to be proactive in counteracting these potential losses both strategically and pedagogically. In this case, and in this matter, the judgments and dispositions by stakeholders at both the local PIP and school levels enabled and promoted the teaching and learning of the heritage language.

Discussion

In the case of the teaching and learning of Mayo in the town of Seagulls, we observed that key stakeholders—Juan, the Mayo-English teacher, María, the school principal, and Rosa, the regional coordinator, as well as other community members—were proactive in shaping and impacting local language of/in education policy. Mayo and English were taught simultaneously at Benito Juarez Intercultural School, and materials were developed despite the lack of infrastructural funding and the absence of consistency in the delivery of curricular materials, including textbooks.

The curricular and practical decisions made by the classroom teacher, educational administrators, parents, and other stakeholders in this community revealed a scenario where a globally powerful language such as English did not marginalize the minority language. In fact, we found the opposite: the various stakeholder discussions around issues of language instruction and language *of* instruction in the local school served to foster community members' commitment to their cultural and linguistic heritage and propelled on-the-ground decisions in support of revitalization of the native variety. In this scenario, the role of the language teacher was as an agent of change to promote both minority language maintenance and the learning of English. This involved devising a symbiotic strategy whereby a global and a local language could coexist for mutual benefit, not one at the expense of the other (Kamwangamalu, 2005).

The excerpts reproduced in this chapter that show the efforts of key actors involved in this Indigenous community school to privilege heritage language maintenance within a trilingual instructional setting illustrate a case of "cosmopolitanism from below." These excerpts, in combination with Juan's and colleagues' numerous other accounts of their experiences in adapting their teaching situation and resources, show how educational policy was interpreted, negotiated, and realigned through dynamic conversation (Canagarajah, 2012) among members of the Seagulls community. It is important to underscore that while the study focused mostly on Juan's work on behalf of minority language revitalization and maintenance, the administrative platform of educators such as Rosa, the coordinator of the PIP, and María, principal of Benito Juárez Intercultural School, also supported and facilitated changes toward the maintenance of Mayo. On the whole, stakeholders'—i.e., professional educators' and parents'—judgments and actions toward their children learning an additional language, English, promoted and enabled the revitalization and maintenance of the community's Indigenous language. The fact that these scenarios were realized in a rural setting testifies additionally to the reach of global trends far beyond urban centers, and to local educators' and other stakeholders' commitments to build connections that acknowledge the historical and sociomaterial conditions that link their communities with other worlds, and hence to cosmopolitanism as a simultaneously rooted and relational practice.

Notwithstanding these encouraging findings, IBE still faces a series of challenges at many levels in Latin America, and certainly in Mexico. According to Gutiérrez Estrada (2015), "*IBE* lacks a framework of citizenship education and intercultural competence that would create awareness in the mainstream population of the country" (p. 108). Similarly, current educational reforms in Mexico that follow the UNESCO 2030 agenda reveal that intercultural competencies need to be put in place and developed such that learners of all ages become aware of the cultural and linguistic diversity within their local contexts and are able to

152 Gutiérrez Estrada and Schecter

engage in discussions about the importance of linguistic and cultural maintenance in relation to the perceived power of global languages such as English (Clemente, 2009). Del Val and Sánchez (2019) link many of these challenges to a need for affirmative action policies at all levels of education—including policies at the university level that are proactive on behalf of inclusion of Indigenous peoples and the teaching of minority languages—and beyond.

While we support such proactive stances, from our vantage as critical ethnographers we want to privilege our perspective that socio- and ethno-linguistic equity of the kind we advocate cannot be achieved solely through enacting policies from above. Rather, such needed policies are embodied in the deliberative actions of key subjects at local levels who are prepared to construct alternative pedagogies that are inclusive and support multilingualism as both a resource and a right (Ruiz, 1998). In our vision, existing language and educational policies in Mexico will be reworked and reorganized from below by agentive individuals so that critical cosmopolitan thinking is integrally intertwined with social justice advocacy in the service of the public good.

Notes

1 For a discussion on the distinction of heritage language in the context of the study, see Gutiérrez Estrada (2015).
2 This information was obtained from María, the principal of the school, in our first interview.

References

Aguilar Zéleny, A. S. (1995). Los Mayos. In Instituto Nacional Indigenista (Ed.), *Etnografía contemporánea de los pueblos indígenas de México: Región noroeste* (pp. 83–130). México, D.F.: Instituto Nacional Indigenista, Secretaría de Desarrollo Social.

Appiah, K. A. (2006). *Cosmopolitanism: Ethics in a world of strangers.* New York: W. W. Norton.

Baldauf, R. B., Jr. (2006). Rearticulating the case for micro language planning in a language ecology context. *Current Issues in Language Planning,* 7(2), 147–170. doi: 10.2167/cilp092.0

Beck, U. (2012). Redefining the sociological project: The cosmopolitan challenge. *Sociology,* 46(1), 7–12.

Bourdieu, P. (1977). Cultural reproduction and social reproduction. In I. Karabel & A. H. Halsey (Eds.), *Power and ideology in education* (pp. 487–510). Oxford, UK: Oxford University Press.

Canagarajah, A. S. (1999). *Resisting linguistic imperialism in English teaching.* Oxford, UK: Oxford University Press.

Canagarajah, A. S. (Ed.). (2005). *Reclaiming the local in language policy and practice.* Philadelphia, PA: John Benjamins.

Canagarajah, A. S. (2012). *Translingual practice: Global Englishes and cosmopolitan relations.* London, UK: Routledge.

Canagarajah, A. S. (2014). In search of a new paradigm for teaching English as an international language. *TESOL Journal,* 5(4), 767–785. doi: 10.1002/tesj.166

Clemente, A. (2009). Pedagogía crítica en el aprendizaje de lenguas en México. *Imaginales: Revista de investigación social, 8*, 11–32.

Codó, E. (2008). Interviews and questionnaires. In L. Wei & M. Moyer (Eds.), *The Blackwell guide to research methods in bilingualism and multilingualism* (pp. 158–176). Malden, MA: Blackwell.

Davis, K. A. (2014). Engaged language policy and practices. *Language Policy, 13*(2), 83–100. doi: 10.1007/s10993-013-9296-5

Del Val, J., & Sánchez, C. (2019). La diversidad cultural en México ayer y hoy. In J. E. González (Ed.), *Multiculturalismo e interculturalidad en las américas: Canadá, México, Guatemala, Colombia, Bolivia, Brasil, Uruguay* (pp. 102–123). Bogotá: Universidad Nacional de Colombia, Cátedra UNESCO.

Fishman, J. (1989). *Language and ethnicity in minority sociolinguistic perspective*. Clevedon, UK: Multilingual Matters. (Original work published 1977)

Fishman, J. (1991). *Reversing language shift: Theory and practice of assistance to threatened languages*. Clevedon, UK: Multilingual Matters.

Freire, P., & Macedo, D. (1987). *Literacy: Reading the word and the world*. Westport, CT: Bergin & Garvey.

Go, J. (2013). Fanon's postcolonial cosmopolitanism. *European Journal of Social Theory, 16*(2), 208–225.

Gutiérrez Estrada, M. R. (2015). *Emergent identities and representations in ELT in minority language contexts in northern Mexico* (Unpublished doctoral dissertation). York University, Toronto, ON, Canada.

Gutiérrez Estrada, M. R., & Schecter, S. R. (2018). English as a "killer language"? Multilingual education in an indigenous primary classroom in northwestern Mexico. *Journal of Educational Issues, 4*(1), 122–147.

Handsfield, L. J. (2002). Teacher agency and double agents: Reconceptualizing linguistic genocide in education. *Harvard Educational Review, 72*(4), 542–560.

Lewis, B., Jenson, J., & Smith, R. (2003). The global and the local: Policy and policy processes for education. *International Electronic Journal for Leadership in Learning, 7*, Article 10.

Kamwangamalu, N. M. (2005). Mother tongues and language planning in Africa. *TESOL Quarterly, 39*(4), 734–738. doi: 10.2307/3588533

Kurasawa, F. (2004). A cosmopolitanism from below: Alternative globalization and the creation of a solidarity without bounds. *European Journal of Sociology, 45*, 233–255.

Lasky, S. (2005). A sociocultural approach to understanding teacher identity, agency and professional vulnerability in a context of secondary school reform. *Teaching and Teacher Education, 21*(8), 899–916.

Le Page, R. B., & Tabouret-Keller, A. (1985). *Acts of identity: Creole-based approaches to language and ethnicity*. Cambridge, UK: Cambridge University Press.

Lin, A. M. Y., Wang, W., Akamatsu, A., & Riazi, M. (2002). Appropriating English, expanding identities, and re-visioning the field: From TESOL to teaching English for glocalized communication (TEGCOM). *Journal of Language, Identity, and Education, 1*(4), 295–316.

Low, S., & Merry, S. (2010). Engaged anthropology: Diversity and dilemmas. *Current Anthropology, 51*(2), S203–S226.

Mayo. (2015). In M. P. Lewis, G. F. Simons, & C. D. Fennig (Eds.), *Ethnologue: Languages of the world* (18th ed.). Dallas, TX: SIL International. Retrieved from http://www.ethnologue.com/show:language.asp?code=mfy

Menken, K., & García, O. (2010). *Negotiating language policies in schools: Educators as policymakers*. New York: Routledge.

154 Gutiérrez Estrada and Schecter

Mignolo, W. D. (2000). The many faces of the cosmo-polis: Border thinking and critical cosmopolitanism. *Public Culture, 12*(3), 721–748.

Mishler, E. G. (1986). *Research interviewing: Context and narrative.* Cambridge, MA: Harvard University Press.

Norton, B. (2000). *Identity and language learning.* London, UK: Longman.

Norton, B. (2015). Identity, investment, and faces of English internationally. *Chinese Journal of Applied Linguistics, 38*(4), 375–391.

Paris, C. L. (1993). *Teacher agency and curriculum making in classrooms.* New York: Teachers College Press.

Ramanathan, V., & Morgan, B. (2007). TESOL and policy enactments: Perspectives from practice. *TESOL Quarterly, 41*(3), 447–463.

Ricento, T., & Hornberger, N. (1996). Unpeeling the onion: Language planning and policy in the ELT profession. *TESOL Quarterly, 30*(3), 401–427.

Ruiz, R. (1998). Orientations in language planning. In S. McKay and S. Wong (Eds.), *Language diversity: Problem or resource?* (pp. 3–25). New York: Newbury House.

Schecter, S. R., Parejo, I., Ambadiang, T., & James, C. (2014). Schooling transnational speakers of the societal language: Language variation policy in Madrid and Toronto. *Language Policy, 13*, 121–144.

Sichra, I. (2006). *Entre la realidad y el deseo: Enseñanza de la lengua indígena e interculturalidad. Investigación sobre la enseñanza del quechua en colegios particulares en Cochabamba, Bolivia.* Paper presented at the 52nd International Congress of Americanists, Seville, Spain.

Stornaiuolo, A., & Nichols, T. P. (2019, March). Cosmopolitanism and education. *Oxford Research Encyclopedia of Education.* doi: 10.1093/acrefore/9780190264093.013.252

Terborg, R., García Landa, L., & Moore, P. (2006). The language situation in Mexico. *Current Issues in Language Planning, 7*(4), 415–518.

Todd, S. (2007). Teachers judging without scripts, or thinking cosmopolitan. *Ethics and Education, 2*(1), 25–38. doi: 10.1080/17449640701302750

UNESCO. (n.d.). *Abstract 8: Telesecundaria, Mexico (lower secondary school learning with television support).* Retrieved from http://www.unesco.org/education/educprog/lwf/doc/portfolio/abstract8.htm

Vertovec, S., & Cohen, R. (2002). Introduction: Conceiving cosmopolitanism. In S. Vertovec & R. Cohen (Eds.), *Conceiving cosmopolitanism: Theory, context and practice* (pp. 32–41). Oxford, UK: Oxford University Press.

10

RACE IN LIMINAL SPACE

Youth Discourse in a Francophone School

Sara Schroeter

Theater offers endless possibilities for representing people, objects, and ideas in complex ways by bringing diverse artistic conventions into conversation with current events and making creative use of metaphor, symbolism, and ambiguity. Theater's innovative potential has led many artists, educators, activists, and researchers to turn to it in search of solutions to some of the most pressing issues of our times—often searching for ways to help people from diverse communities get along and communicate in spite of their differences. Yet, while thoughtful and provocative representations of difference can be found on some stages, this is not always the case. Nor is it the case when theater techniques are used in schools in the form of drama-in-education (DiE) (Gallagher, 2010; Rivière, 2008). In classroom performances, both in drama or theater classes and in content area classrooms where DiE is used, students often resort to easily recognizable tropes and stereotypes in their representations. The reiteration of reductive and negative signifying practices can be detrimental for students in classrooms characterized by ethnic, racial, cultural, linguistic, religious, and gender diversity, as is increasingly the case in most metropolitan centers in North America. The slippery terrain between thoughtful artistic representations and avoiding reductive tropes when working with embodied art forms in superdiverse settings is the subject of this chapter about a DiE research project in a francophone school in British Columbia.

This chapter presents youth discourses of race as they emerged in liminal spaces during a teacher-researcher collaboration wherein DiE was used to teach Grade 9 social studies for a year at a francophone minority language school. Drama was used to teach the curriculum and unpack categories of difference present in it. Drawing on critical race and whiteness studies, this chapter analyzes how the students' representational practices in drama activities and decisions by the teacher-researcher team may have reinforced social stigmas and strengthened logics of

DOI: 10.4324/9780429327780-10

156 Sara Schroeter

white supremacy in the classroom. As such, this chapter troubles oft-repeated claims about the radical possibilities of DiE and its ability to foster empathy by drawing attention to the limitations encountered in a school characterized by superdiversity. Elsewhere (Schroeter, 2017), I have examined the youth's awareness of the changes to their race talk as they moved through different educational spaces in greater detail.

Theoretical and Pedagogical Orientations

The Production of Race

Hall (1996) writes that race can be understood as a "floating signifier," one of many discursive categories that emerged during the period of European imperialism and colonial expansion and was used to classify people according to a system of difference that placed white Europeans on top. Yon (2000) adds that the "modernist obsessions with classification and ordering [were] a strategy for control" (p. 10), one that worked to justify dominance and privilege (Battiste, 2013). While race is understood as an unstable, historically constructed category, its establishment was an exercise in what Foucault (1976/1990) calls "positive power." It created ideas about racial differences that were internalized by European colonial subjects and used to justify the use of negative, disciplinary power against the people and lands they colonized.

The meaning of race emerges through the evolving historically and culturally laden meaning-making functions of language (Hall, 1997), which is why an examination of discursive productions is important. At the same time, the concept of race inscribes sociopolitical conflicts and interests onto characteristics of human bodies (Winant, 2004). Race is thus a social construct that produces ideas about difference cued by arbitrarily selected visible signs (skin tone, hair color or texture, eye color, etc.). This process, widely understood as "racialization," is brought about by the interplay between discursive practices and established material structures (Omi & Winant, 1994). On the individual level, racial identities change as individuals construct and reconstruct their identifications in shifting cultural and structural circumstances (James, 2007). Acknowledging this instability does not deny the persistence of racial thinking or the material impact of these ideas on individual lives (Hall in Jhally, 1997). In fact, the construction and maintenance of differences are important to the ways people identify and how societies organize and are deeply ingrained in public institutions like schools.

Discourses of difference, such as those of nation, language, race, class, gender, and sexuality, are always present in the classroom (Schick & St. Denis, 2005). Leonardo (2002) writes that "'whiteness' is a racial discourse" (p. 31), one that is perpetuated in and by schools. This discourse involves an unwillingness to name racism and the participation of white people in racism; when white people avoid naming their belonging to racial groups, whiteness is constructed as a neutral norm that minimizes racist legacies (Frankenberg, 1993; Gillborn, 2009; Leonardo,

2002). Therefore, while "whiteness" should not be confused with the constructed category of "white people," white folks do participate in the circulation of this discourse (Leonardo, 2002).

Multimodality and Embodiment

Focusing on the communicative function of art aligns with how literacy has been theorized in recent decades as a socially situated practice involving more than the development of independent skills to decode and encode neutral texts (New London Group, 1996). What is perceived as "text" has expanded from a focus on written script to a range of works including paintings, musical scores, dance phrases, architecture, and so on. Responding to this change and the increasing popularity of digital, image-based modalities, as well as to classrooms that are increasingly composed of multilingual learners and students from different ethnic, racial, and cultural backgrounds, the New London Group's multiliteracies project sought to make literacy instruction more inclusive by recognizing the validity of nondominant languages and modes of expression. The concept of multimodality explains how meaning is made through the interaction between multiple semiotic modes (Jewitt & Kress, 2008; Kalantzis, Cope, Chan, & Dalley-Trim, 2016). The integration of multiple modalities into teaching and evaluation practices is now widely promoted as a valid way to have students demonstrate learning.

Theater makes use of multiple modes (spatial, gestural, aural, linguistic, textual, etc.) to create rich aesthetic texts that tell stories about human and nonhuman experiences and events. Through the layering of different modalities, artists craft stories that contain many possible interpretations, enabling audiences to engage in complex meaning-making experiences of their own. As understandings of literacy have expanded, DiE has sometimes been theorized as a multimodal literacy practice (Booth, 1994; Gallagher & Ntelioglou, 2011; Medina, 2004; Rowsell & McQueen-Fuentes, 2017; Schroeter & Wager, 2017; Winters, Rogers, & Schofield, 2006) and has a longstanding connection to critical pedagogies (Fleming, 2017). While these are significant ways of understanding the affordances and wider applications of DiE, it is important to note that theater is an aesthetic form that transcends literacy practices.

A powerful element of DiE is the constant activation of the physical body, reminding students and teachers that learning occurs in the sensate body. DiE encourages educators to attend to the ways that the body's movement through time and space impacts what things are learned and how they are learned. Ellsworth (2005) highlights the significance of architectural design in meaning-making and the indivisible link between mind, body, and knowledge. In other words, the presence of the body and its engagement in different spaces impacts what can be learned. Similarly, the subjectivities encompassed within different bodies will learn differently in various settings. This is in no small part linked to the ways in which bodies are represented in particular spaces of learning

158 Sara Schroeter

(Hall, 1997; Rogers, 2014) and, conversely, how different forms of knowledge and experiences of power are scripted onto the body (Boal, 1974/1979). These aspects of embodied learning serve as a reminder of the constant interplay between being and not being, movement in time and space, and the affective and embodied significance of these dynamics.

Working in Liminal Spaces

Theorizing performance as "a paradigm of liminality" (Schechner, 1985, p. 123), Schechner writes that a performer "no longer has a 'me' but has a 'not not me'" (p. 112). The double negative is important because it is this space that performers occupy. Students participating in DiE also work in a liminal space. Rather than exploring what it is like *to be* other people or take on another person's (or an other's) identity, students engage in role-play neither completely as themselves nor completely as another person. Schechner (1985) explains: "It isn't that a performer stops being himself or herself when he or she becomes another—multiple selves coexist in an unresolved dialectical tension" (p. 6). Nevertheless, DiE is often perceived as a way of enabling students to gain empathy for others. This is likely because some approaches to actor training emphasize learning what it feels like to be characters in order to find their truths and portray them authentically.

Turner (1969, 1982) argues that liminal spaces disrupt social order and that the passage from one state of being to another is often marked by liminal rituals. He further theorizes that during liminal activities cultural codes can be questioned, making way for subversion and discovery (Turner, 1969). Similarly, Sutton-Smith (1997) proposes that play represents a break from governed orderliness, necessarily involving ambiguity and disorder. Conceptualizing DiE as a liminal space of play draws on this work, as well as that of theater theorists and drama educators (Finneran & Freebody, 2016; Gallagher, 2007; Nicholson, 2005; Perry & Rogers, 2013; Schechner, 1985). However, as this chapter demonstrates, DiE is not the only way liminal spaces are created in schools.

(Post)critical Pedagogy

Ellsworth's (1989) critique of critical pedagogies draws on her experiences of times when patriarchal and/or racist power structures have been problematically reasserted in the classroom. Specifically, Ellsworth cites instances when members of dominant groups speak of desires to engage in "dialogue across difference" but end up "consuming" the stories of others, thus intensifying preexisting unequal power relations. Building on this seminal feminist critique, Lather (1998) posits that critical pedagogies are impossible to implement in schools and proposes (post)critical pedagogy, an approach that engages impossibility by examining the "stuck places" of critical pedagogies. Lather's *post* is not a rejection of the goals of democratizing educational practices, grounding curriculum in students' experiences, and creating equitable power relations in the classroom. Rather, it signals an awareness of some shortcomings of critical educational practices, moving educators toward an engagement with our failures. Such critical engagement can enrich understandings of what socially just education is and looks like (Lather, 1992), particularly for educators belonging to dominant groups. Ellsworth (1989) and Lather (1992, 1998) encourage troubling the ways that dominance is rooted in underlying ideas about rationality, dialogue, and empowerment held within many critical pedagogical approaches.

In consultation with Rose, the teacher I collaborated with, my analysis of our work focuses primarily on analyzing moments of failure: times when our objective of deconstructing difference and creating classroom experiences that were engaging and affirming for all Rose's students fell short. This is done deliberately following Lather's (1998) call to attend to "stuck places." While this process often feels uncomfortable, it is necessary to learn more about the circulation of racial discourses in the classroom and how, as white educators, our teaching practices and beliefs make us complicit in the maintenance of white supremacy. In particular, it is necessary for improving the educational experiences of differently racialized students in superdiverse francophone minority schools where most teachers remain white.

Superdiversity in Francophone Minority Language Schools

This study was conducted at École secondaire Gustave-Flaubert, a francophone minority language school in British Columbia (BC) that provides Grade 7–12 education in French. Born from the paradoxical marriage between ethnonational privilege and linguistic marginalization, francophone schools in Canada outside Quebec exist as the result of concerted activism and legal challenges by francophone communities across the country. Initially conceived for communities that were imagined as homogeneous, composed of children whose ancestry could be traced to France and Quebec, francophone minority language public schools now serve largely multiethnic, multiracial, multifaith, multicultural, and plurilingual populations (Heller, 2003; Levasseur, 2012; Madibbo, 2007; Prasad, 2012). Francophone schools are in fact *superdiverse* (Vertovec, 2007) sites, representative of colonialism and transnational movements of people and capital within and between locations around the world, especially between large cosmopolitan cities.

Nevertheless, in light of continued and sometimes accelerated transnational migration and shifting trends in school choice among newly settled migrants, tensions have emerged between the priorities of francophone minority school boards and the superdiverse communities they now serve (Madibbo, 2007). The historical objective of these schools to maintain the francophone communities in these provinces rests uncomfortably with the needs of students and parents from diverse linguistic, ethnic, and racial backgrounds. In many francophone school policy documents, the various Frenches and diverse francophone communities

160 Sara Schroeter

that compose the world *Francophonie* are problematically articulated as "*the* French language" and "*the* francophone community."

An Ethnography of Discourse and Difference

This ethnography (Buch & Staller, 2007; Gallagher, 2007) that was carried out during a school year follows the findings of a previous study in which students expressed feeling racialized and excluded at school (Schroeter, 2009), as well as research suggesting that race is rarely taken up in francophone minority language schools (Carlson Berg, 2011; Jacquet, 2009; Madibbo, 2007). The research questions reflect feminist interests in "the ways difference is organized across lines of gender, race, class, and sexuality" (Buch & Staller, 2007, p. 194), the circulation of power, and intersections between race, gender, ethnicity, indigeneity, and class. BC's Grade 9 social studies curriculum provided fertile ground for examining discourses of differences circulating in the school because it stipulates that students learn how identities are formed based on multiple factors such as family, gender, belief systems, ethnic origin, and nationality (British Columbia Ministry of Education, Skills and Training, 1997). Participant observation, fieldnotes, video footage, artifacts, individual interviews, and focus groups were used to document our work together and develop an understanding of the ways in which discourses of difference circulated in Rose's classroom and their significance for participating youth.

I was introduced to Rose, a social studies teacher at Gustave-Flaubert responsible for supporting the school's First Nations, Métis, and Inuit (FNMI) students, while negotiating access to the school. Rose agreed to participate in this study because she believed that her students benefited from the use of different modalities yet felt ill-equipped to use drama in her classroom. She was also intrigued by my teaching practice in which ideas about difference, race, representation, and colonization are addressed through activities like process dramas, wherein students and teachers create imaginary worlds through improvisation. In this way, they make connections to students' lived experiences by studying how different people interact, how events unfold, and how imaginary societies organize.

When presenting the project to Rose's students and their parents and guardians, I explained that the purpose of the study was to see what happened when drama was used to teach social studies and to have conversations about difference and identity with youth from different backgrounds in francophone schools. The ethnographic nature of the project made it difficult to pinpoint what themes would become most relevant or salient throughout the year; however, I clearly stated that we would explore difference and colonization in class and that I would be looking at the affordances and limitations of drama for having these conversations. As the year progressed, there were several opportunities for me to re-present the research project to the youths and talk to them about my emerging curiosities. The first was during individual or pair interviews that I conducted with all participating students in January and February. At that point, my questions were primarily about what the students were learning about the curriculum, themselves, and one another as we used drama in their social studies classes.

In March and April, as the curriculum moved to an exploration of the first contact between First Nations peoples of North America and European colonizers, we talked about anthropology and I explained that my study was anthropological in nature because I was studying the students, their teacher, and their classroom culture. At that point, I observed more conversations between the students about the nature of my observations and recordings. This drove home some of the ethical conundrums caused by conducting and participating in ethnographic research; from my perspective, these tensions remain unresolved.

By May, when I was conducting focus group interviews, I had specific questions about race, race talk, and the different discourses the youth used in different school spaces. These questions and reciting the youth's words back to them as I posed my questions led to rich conversations about race and ethnicity, but also about my research and work as a researcher. I believe that some of the youths understood and observed the evolution of my project and questions as it was occurring, whereas others remained unsure of the purpose of my project, even after its conclusion. Whenever I saw the youths in the years following our work together, we would revisit my project and its purpose, and I would tell them what I was writing about.

Rose's Grade 9 students were between 13 and 16 years of age and of FNMI, Canadian, immigrant, and refugee backgrounds. Those who participated in this study came from the provinces of British Columbia, Quebec, and Ontario, as well as Algeria, Brazil, the Democratic Republic of Congo, Kenya, Mauritius, Saudi Arabia, South Africa, and Tahiti. The youths spoke a minimum of two languages each, though several were plurilingual. In each class, the students had a range of racial, ethnic, linguistic, national, and religious origins. Nine youths claimed "Canadian" heritage, and three declared FNMI heritage.

I attended both sections of Rose's Grade 9 social studies class and we shared some teaching responsibilities throughout the year. Rose taught standard course content and evaluated the students' work, while I planned and facilitated drama activities, and documented classes for my research. The pedagogical approach we adopted made use of multimodal drama strategies: tableau, improvisation, roleplay, spatial analyses, reenactments, interviewing, writing-in-role, drawing, reading, and watching videos. We typically planned a large drama activity each month and integrated drama strategies into two of three social studies classes each week.

Race in Liminal Spaces: Changing Rules of Engagement

During the year, it became apparent that the students spoke differently about race in different school spaces. In "informal school spaces," like hallways between classes and during lunch hour, the students made frequent, explicit reference to race in their conversations; they often joked with one another by using and/ or mocking common stereotypes. In "formal educational spaces," such as Rose's

162 Sara Schroeter

classroom when class was in session, race was rarely mentioned and the students explained that it was deliberately avoided (for more detail, see Schroeter, 2017). Many students explained that it was okay to talk about race in formal educational spaces "as long as you're not insulting people" (Jamie, Focus group interview, June 10, 2014). This section illustrates how the rules for talking about race changed in "liminal" educational spaces; that is, spaces between formal and informal, created by drama activities, moments in class when Rose's attention was directed elsewhere, field trips, and focus group interviews.

Working on a unit about contact between First Nations peoples and European colonizers, the students were asked to dramatically present biographies they had written about historical figures. It took a long time to get through the activities planned on that day, and the students' performances, such as the one depicted in Table 10.1, were rushed at the end of class.

The group's decision to fall back on a stereotypical representation of Indigenous peoples illustrates a significant limitation to the use of DiE in core subjects. De Saussure's theory of language posits that "language is a system of signs" (Culler, 1986, p. 19). As an aesthetic art form, theater relies heavily on easily identifiable material and auditory cues, or signs, to signify and portray various concepts and ideas (Elam, 2002). However, as the skit in Table 10.1 illustrates and Hall's (1997) work attests, the use of signs and symbols to stand in for concepts or groups of people can easily lead to stereotyping by flattening the diversity that exists within each constructed category. By tapping on their mouths and chanting as they ran in, the girls used a visual, auditory, and material shorthand to signify Indigenous peoples, even though this representation may not have accurately portrayed Haudenosaunee people. Mia also used the wrong name, referring to Chief Donnacona as Stadaconé, and then incorrectly implied that he was the Chief of the Stadaconé people when Stadaconé was in fact the name of his village (as rendered in French).

This group's performance could be seen as making fun of First Nations, rendering it inappropriate for the classroom, according to the students' own rules for talking about race. This would have been an important moment to unpack with the students to probe what effects such representations might have on Indigenous peoples. However, as the transcript indicates, the bell rang and the students fled once they had guessed which historical figure the girls had portrayed. My fieldnotes reveal concern about this skit:

> They stage an entrance of Donacona [sic] in a way that is very theatrical and thus great for getting across the intended point of having them do a theatrical representation, but they also represent First Nations people in a way that is quite stereotypical and that I really want to unpack with them. The bell rings while they are performing their biography and I don't get a chance to do this. This would be something to bring up with the students next class, if we have time.
>
> *(Fieldnote, April 29, 2014)*

Race in Liminal Space **163**

TABLE 10.1 Class video recording, April 29, 2014

Paroles mot à mot	*Verbatim speech*	*Actions and gestures*
Sara: OK!	Sara: OK!	Genevieve runs past the camera. Mia directs Kelsey to go stand somewhere else.
Mia, Kelsey, et X: Oh-woo-woo-woo-woo-woo-woo!	Mia, Kelsey, and X: Oh-woo-woo-woo-woo-woo-woo!	The girls run toward the performance area from different directions with their arms held over their heads as though they are holding something. They tap their mouths with their hands, mimicking the "Indian" sounds from antiquated childhood games of "Cowboys and Indians." They come together and stop.
Mia: Un, deux, trois.	Mia: One, two, three.	The girls all stomp one foot and simultaneously plant the object that they mime holding in their hands—I interpret this as a spear—into the ground.
Mia: Je suis le chef de Stadaconé, un des peuples de l'Amérique du Nord. J'ai rencontré Jacques Cartier pour la première fois à Québec, quand il faisait un voyage par bateau et nous faisons la pêche.	Mia: I am the chief of Stadacona, one of the peoples of North America. I met Jacques Cartier for the first time at Quebec when he was making a trip by boat and we were fishing.	The girls mime fishing.
Mia: Sur son retour, il m'a kidnappé pour montrer aux gens ce qu'il avait trouvé. Ils m'ont très bien traité.	Mia: On Jacques Cartier's return, he kidnapped me to show people what they had found. They treated me very well.	Genevieve runs in, places her arms around Mia, and pulls her away from the other girls. Genevieve pats Mia on the head.
Mia: Mais je me sentais toujours très inconfortable.	Mia: But still, I felt very uncomfortable.	Mia slowly moves away from Genevieve toward Kelsey and another student. (*Bell rings announcing the end of class.*)
Mia: Plus tard j'ai mourru en 1539.	Mia: Later, I died in 1539.	Mia laughs.

164 Sara Schroeter

My use of the conditional "if we have time" indicates how constrained I felt by a 60-minute period, and that I anticipated not returning to this moment. Normally, my practice focuses less on content and more on unpacking representational practices; however, late in the school year, I felt the same pressures teachers express about the necessity to cover course content. In this instance, unpacking the group's choices would have been critical for starting a formal class discussion about representational practices, pervasive stereotypes, and how we, the teachers and students, contributed to their circulation. It also would have created space for students who had questions about how their racial, ethnic, or cultural groups are misrepresented (see Schroeter, 2019). The fact that we did not return to this moment as a class reinforced whiteness, as we did not question how skits like the one in Table 10.1 might reinforce contemporary racism experienced by FNMI peoples.

Time constraints are a limitation in DiE, and it can be hard to gauge the amount of time necessary for unpacking issues that arise from students' skits and improvisations. Ideally, DiE lessons provide ample time for debriefings. Though this was part of our established practice, on this day our timing was off. While such occurrences are common in teaching, I believe we should have made time to reflect on this skit in spite of the constraints we faced. Not only did we fail to provide an opportunity for the students to raise questions, but by not correcting Mia's mistake and insisting on accuracy, we also participated in reinforcing white supremacy because inaccurate naming is one factor that enabled the unjust theft of Indigenous lands, precipitating settler colonialism.

Drama educators and applied theater practitioners often claim that DiE enables people to know others (Diamond, 2007; Yassa, 1999). In fact, it is the liminal space between self and other that DiE capitalizes on to create rich learning experiences for students (Gallagher & Ntelioglou, 2011; Heathcote & Bolton, 1995; O'Neill, 1995). This is why debriefings are essential. Unpacking moments like the one above is important for helping students make distinctions between performing as an Other and *knowing* the life experiences of Others. Debriefings might help students resist making claims like:

> I think it's good that we do these things [drama activities] because we can really be in a person's place and understand how life was.
>
> *(Anna interview, February 6, 2014)*

In my experience, students often report gaining empathy for others through role play, but this is not always or necessarily the case.

Thinking with Schechner (1985), I argue that learning through drama is more complex than gaining an understanding of another person's perspective. Students interact in the "as if" world of DiE by taking on roles informed by their outlooks, biases, and social locations. Although students may gain appreciation for a perspective they have not previously considered, they remain ignorant of what it is like to be someone else. Responding to the empathic and transformative claims made about applied theater, Nicholson (2005) writes that in DiE participants are transported into another world rather than transformed by it. The "gifts" students receive from this experience can take the form of new insights that challenge their previously held assumptions or the normative structures of their social context; however, as the previous skit illustrates, drama can also reify stigmatized representations.

Focus groups with students at the end of the year created another liminal space, what Ellsworth (2005) refers to as "pedagogical encounters." Taking up Winnicott's (1989) notion of "transitional space," Ellsworth calls these encounters "pedagogical pivot points ... times and places of putting self in relation to self, others and the world" (2005, p. 57). These relationships occurred when the youths answered and discussed my questions together, sometimes discovering that they had different and contradictory experiences in school. The focus groups also provided the youths with a rare opportunity to discuss and theorize their ways of talking about race with an adult. As I analyzed video of the focus groups, I was struck by the richness of these conversations, how several students had seriously contemplated categories of difference, and the ways we used the youths' theories as opportunities to discuss the social construction of race and the complexities of identification.

In the brief interaction recorded in Table 10.2, Genevieve's gaze and gestures relate that she may have never thought about race as a category that might have multiple definitions, or one that is socially constructed. Her actions, looking up and gesturing with her hands, suggested that her mind had been opened by the possibility of multiple definitions of race. As she spoke, Genevieve's eyes were opened wide and animated, as though she was running through the possibilities that multiple definitions of race could create for her identification and relations.

TABLE 10.2 Video, focus group, June 9, 2014

Verbal	Gestures and gaze
Sara: I mean, it depends on how you're defining race.	[Off camera.]
Genevieve: Hunh.	Exhales and looks away from Sara.
Sara: What is race?	
Genevieve: Wow! That brings out, like, a whole new field.	Smiles, looks up to ceiling, and makes circular motions with hands in front of her face. Then looks down.
Sara: Yeah. I mean, like, what is race?	[Off camera.]
Genevieve: I always base it on, like, skin tone.	Looks at Sara.

166 Sara Schroeter

Although several of the Grade 9 students found racial categories inadequate for capturing their identifications, their discussions suggest that they sought to understand the limitations of boundaries and control when one could or could not belong.

In the liminal space recorded in Table 10.3, R. K. discussed his understanding of race as an empty or limiting social category. Simultaneously, he and Théo started unpacking their use of racial categories and pop culture tropes to tease others. My observations of the boys' interactions throughout the year suggest that

TABLE 10.3 Video, focus group, May 29, 2014

Verbal	Gestures and gaze
R. K.: Yeah, I don't know, like, race is basically, nothing. You know, like, everyone is really…	Looking at Sara
Théo: Whoa, deep.	Looking at R. K. Théo, R. K., and Sherlock laugh.
Sara: No, you know what? That really *is* deep. And it's also, really the way, at the university, how we theorize and talk about race as being a floating signifier. It can mean one—it can mean many, many things.	Looking at R. K. and reaching a hand out to him. Gesturing up with hands. Looking at all five youth and making a circular motion with hands.
R. K.: Yeah. Just because you have that color or you have that culture doesn't mean you couldn't be something else.	Looking at Nico, George, and Théo. [Blocked from view.]
Théo: [Inaudible.]	Looking at R. K. Nico and Georges are listening and watching R. K. and Théo.
R. K.: Wow, wow!	Everyone laughs.
Sara: Uh-hunh.	Laughing.
R. K.: Except for Carlton	Looking at Théo.
Sara: Except for Carlton… Are you talking about *Fresh Prince* now?	Laughing. All youth start laughing.
Georges: It's Roger.	Laughing and looking at Sara.
R. K.: We call Roger, Carlton.	Looking down at fingers.
Théo: No we don't.	Looking down and then up at R. K. Tilts head to side.
R. K.: Oh we do… It's a joke, but we start playing the music (the Tom Jones song "It's not unusual to be loved"), but then he gets mad at me!	Looking back at Théo. Does the *Fresh Prince of Bel-Air* Carlton dance, snapping fingers. Laughs hard.
Théo: But you can't really tell if he's mad or not.	Looking at R. K.
R. K.: No, he is, that's the thing. He gets really mad.	Looking down at lap.

it is likely that Théo and R. K.'s joke did upset Roger. Théo's behavior during this focus group appeared guarded. While he would laugh with the others, he also tried to present himself in a positive light when he addressed me directly, or when R. K. said things that could implicate him in "bad" behavior. Théo seemed intent on showing that his jokes were not mean. However, during focus groups, several youths said that Théo and R. K. often excluded others and made jokes at other people's expense.

Significantly, Roger self-identified as Black and white and believed that race was an important factor in a person's identity. Théo shared these racial affiliations with Roger, but did not identify in these terms, as they showed by calling Roger "Carlton," a character from the 1990s sitcom *The Fresh Prince of Bel-Air* mocked for not being "Black enough" or for identifying with white culture. In this way, Théo and R. K.'s gaze took on a disciplinary power (Foucault, 1975/1995) that served to determine which identifications were possible for Roger. This gaze suggested that Roger should not identify as Black because he was mixed. Embedded in this thinking are defunct, yet discursively persistent, ideas about racial purity (Tizard & Phoenix, 2002), which place Black and white categories in binary opposition. By this logic, to be mixed was to be neither Black nor white, but something in-between. Ironically, in the same conversation, R. K. highlighted the fallacy of fixed racial categories.

It is possible that Théo disidentified with Blackness by siding with R. K., who held social power and race privilege (his appearance was racially ambiguous, though he had Laotian and Croatian heritage). However, since Théo identified with Blackness in his music preferences—he liked Old-School Hip Hop—and cultural references, it is also possible that he was making his own claims to Blackness by distancing Roger. Together, Théo and R. K. performatively iterated a form of heteronormative masculinity that is steeped in whiteness by telling others how they should or should not name themselves or identify. In the liminal space of the focus group, the rules governing race talk were loosened, and R. K. and Théo had a metacognitive conversation about race that could trouble the way they addressed Roger or highlight the contradictory ways they perceived race. This interaction suggests that, whereas classifying and labeling were projects of colonialism that produced ideas about race (Leonardo, 2002; Yon, 2000), enduring cultural practices of jokingly labeling people is a performative of whiteness that anyone can participate in. In a context where transnational movements produce radically mixed racial, ethnic, and cultural affiliations, access to power becomes tied to one's ability to navigate shifting discursive categories of difference and to participate in their naming.

Concluding Thoughts: Seizing Liminal Moments

Students working through DiE must navigate the tensions of casting and portraying scenarios or characters from their situated positionalities while creating

168 Sara Schroeter

dramatic interest and finding authenticity in representation. This is no different from the questions that contemporary theater companies grapple with: When does cross-racial or cross-gender casting work, and when does it fail? When does cross-casting provoke new insight that can help answer pressing questions of our time? When does the use of particular artistic devices result in cultural appropriation?

Yet, while these tensions exist in DiE, they are often overlooked in practice and in the literature. Teachers must consider many factors when managing their classrooms and are often so concerned about having students participate in DiE that these questions get pushed aside. However, creating space for these discussions is critical, particularly in superdiverse contexts like École Gustave-Flaubert where students grapple with questions about representation. Furthermore, like Roger and others in this study (see Schroeter, 2019), they find themselves positioned at the intersection of multiple discourses of race, ethnicity, culture, gender, and nationality.

Teachers mediate the liminal spaces created by DiE, which can enable educators to gain access to the students' informal discourses of race, creating the possibility for deconstructing stereotypes and categories of difference in the classroom. However, moving to deconstruction is a complicated process. The focus group interviews presented in this chapter demonstrate that the liminal spaces created by drama are not necessarily ideal for deconstruction, given the time constraints of the classroom and external curricular mandates. In fact, research practices like setting up informal focus group interviews wherein students gathered in friendship groups and food was provided created liminal spaces that were more conducive to unpacking categories of difference. These interviews also provided the students with a rare opportunity to talk openly about race at school with an adult. These findings suggest that the adults working in informal school spaces, like lunchrooms and hallways, have access to students' informal discourses of race and could play an important role in helping students to deconstruct stereotypes, national and cultural mythologies, and racial categories. However, for these rich conversations to happen, their training would have to be grounded in understandings of racial discourse and colonization and reinforced by classroom teachers who also ground their practice in antiracist and decolonizing pedagogies.

References

Battiste, M. (2013). *Decolonizing education: Nourishing the learning spirit.* Saskatoon, SK: Purich Publishing.

British Columbia Ministry of Education, Skills and Training. (1997). *Social studies 8 to 10. Integrated resource package 1997.* Victoria, BC: Author.

Boal, A. (1979). *Theatre of the oppressed* (C. A. Leal McBride & M. Leal McBride, Trans.). London, UK: Pluto Press. (Original work published 1974)

Booth, D. (1994). *Story drama: Reading, writing, roleplaying across the curriculum.* Markham, ON: Pembroke Publishers.

Buch, E. D., & Staller, K. M. (2007). The feminist practice of ethnography. In S. N. Hesse-Biber & P. L. Leavy (Eds.), *Feminist research practice: A primer* (pp. 187–222). Thousand Oaks, CA: SAGE.

Carlson Berg, L. (2011). Un regard critique sur les initiatives d'éducation inclusive des élèves immigrants en milieu scolaire fransaskois. *Francophonies d'Amérique, 32*, 65–86.

Culler, J. D. (1986). *Ferdinand de Saussure*. Ithaca, NY: Cornell University Press.

Diamond, D. (2007). *Theatre for living: The art and science of community-based dialogue*. Victoria, BC: Trafford.

Elam, K. (2002). *The semiotics of theatre and drama* (2nd ed.) London, UK: Routledge.

Ellsworth, E. (1989). Why doesn't this feel empowering? Working through the repressive myths of critical pedagogy. *Harvard Educational Review, 59*(3), 297–324.

Ellsworth, E. (2005). *Places of learning: Media, architecture, pedagogy*. New York: Routledge Falmer.

Finneran, M., & Freebody, K. (2016). Tensions and mythologies in the liminal space between drama and social justice. In K. Freebody & M. Finneran (Eds.), *Drama and social justice: Theory, research and practice in international contexts* (pp. 15–29). London, UK: Routledge.

Fleming, M. (2017). *Starting drama teaching* (4th ed.). Abingdon, UK: Routledge.

Foucault, M. (1990). *The history of sexuality* (Vol. 1) (R. Hurley, Trans.). New York: Vintage Books. (Original work published 1976)

Foucault, M. (1995). *Discipline and punish: The birth of the prison* (A. Sheridan, Trans.). New York: Vintage Books. (Original work published 1975)

Frankenberg, R. (1993). *White women, race matters: The social construction of Whiteness*. Minneapolis, MN: University of Minnesota Press.

Gallagher, K. (2007). *The theatre of urban: Youth and schooling in dangerous times*. Toronto, ON: University of Toronto Press.

Gallagher, K. (2010). Improvisation and education: Learning through? *Canadian Theatre Review, 143*, 42–46.

Gallagher, K., & Ntelioglou, B. Y. (2011). Which new literacies? Dialogue and performance in youth writing. *Journal of Adolescent and Adult Literacy, 54*(5), 322–330.

Gillborn, D. (2009). Education policy as an act of White supremacy: Whiteness, Critical Race Theory, and education reform. In E. Taylor, D. Gillborn, & G. Ladson-Billings (Eds.), *Foundations of Critical Race Theory in education* (pp. 51–69). London, UK: Routledge.

Hall, S. (1996). New ethnicities. In D. Morley & K. Chen (Eds.), *Stuart Hall: Critical dialogues in cultural studies* (pp. 441–449). New York: Routledge.

Hall, S. (1997). *Representation: Cultural representations and signifying practices*. London, UK: SAGE.

Heathcote, D., & Bolton, G. (1995). *Drama for learning: Dorothy Heathcote's mantle of the expert approach to education*. Portsmouth, NH: Heinemann.

Heller, M. (2003). *Crosswords: Language, education and ethnicity in French Ontario*. Berlin, Germany: Mouton de Gruyter.

Jacquet, M. (2009). La dimension marginale de l'inclusion de la diversité ethnique à l'école: l'exemple de la Colombie-Britannique. *Canadian Ethnic Studies, 41*(1–2), 95–113.

James, C. E. (2007). Who can/should do this work? The colour of critique. In P. R. Carr & D. E. Lund (Eds.), *The Great White North: Exploring Whiteness, privilege, and identity in education* (pp. 119–131). Rotterdam, The Netherlands: Sense Publishers.

Jewitt, C., & Kress, G. R. (2008). *Multimodal literacy*. New York: Peter Lang Publishing.

Jhally, S. (Producer & Director). (1997). *Race: The floating signifier* [Film]. United States: Hillside Studios.

170 Sara Schroeter

Kalantzis, M., Cope, B., Chan, E., & Dalley-Trim, L. (2016). *Literacies*. Cambridge, UK: Cambridge University Press.

Lather, P. (1992). Postcritical pedagogies: A feminist reading. In C. Luke & J. Gore (Eds), *Feminisms and critical pedagogy* (pp. 120–137). New York: Routledge.

Lather, P. (1998). Critical pedagogy and its complicities: A praxis of stuck places. *Educational Theory, 48*(4), 487–496.

Leonardo, Z. (2002). The souls of White folk: Critical pedagogy, Whiteness studies, and globalization discourse. *Race, Ethnicity & Education, 5*(1), 29–50.

Levasseur, C. (2012). "Moi je ne suis pas francophone!": Paroles d'élèves de francisation à Vancouver. *Québec Français, 167*, 55–57.

Madibbo, A. (2007). Race, language and la Francophonie: Black francophones caught between racism and linguicism. In N. Massaquoi & N. N. Wane (Eds.), *Theorizing empowerment: Canadian perspectives on Black feminist thought* (pp. 199–227). Toronto, ON: Inanna.

Medina, C. (2004). The construction of drama worlds as literary interpretation of Latina feminist literature. *Research in Drama Education, 9*(2), 143–160.

New London Group. (1996). A pedagogy of multiliteracies: Designing social futures. *Harvard Educational Review, 66*(1), 60–92.

Nicholson, H. (2005). *Applied drama: The gift of theatre*. Basingstoke, UK: Palgrave Macmillan.

Omi, M., & Winant, H. (1994). *Racial formations in the United States: From the 1960s to the 1990s* (2nd ed.) New York: Routledge.

O'Neill, C. (1995). *Drama worlds: A framework for process drama*. Portsmouth, NH: Heinemann.

Perry, M., & Rogers, T. (2013). Meddling with "drama class," muddling "urban": Imagining aspects of the feminine self through an experimental theatre process with youth. In K. Gallagher & J. Neelands (Eds.), *Drama and theatre in urban contexts* (pp. 47–54). London, UK: Routledge.

Prasad, G. (2012). Multiple minorities or culturally and linguistically diverse (CLDD) plurilingual learners? Re-envisioning allophone immigrant children and their inclusion in French-language schools in Ontario. *Canadian Modern Language Review, 68*(2), 190–215.

Rivière, D. (2008). Whiteness in/and education. *Race, Ethnicity and Education, 11*(4), 355–368.

Rogers, P. (2014). Flagging dominance: Social geographies of colonial violence in a Canadian classroom. *Critical Literacy: Theories and Practice, 8*(1), 36–49.

Rowsell, J., & McQueen-Fuentes, G. (2017). Moving parts in imagined spaces: Community Arts Zone's movement project. *Pedagogies, 12*(1), 74–89.

Schechner, R. (1985). *Between theater and anthropology*. Philadelphia, PA: University of Pennsylvania Press.

Schick, C., & St. Denis, V. (2005). Troubling national discourses in anti-racist curricular planning. *Canadian Journal of Education, 28*(3), 295–317.

Schroeter, S. (2009). *Theatre in my toolbox: Using Forum Theatre to explore notions of identity, belonging and culture with francophone secondary students in a context of diversity* (Unpublished master's thesis). York University, Toronto, ON, Canada.

Schroeter, S. (2017). *Difference at play: An ethnography of discourse and drama in multiracial classrooms in a francophone minority language school* (Unpublished doctoral dissertation). University of British Columbia, Vancouver, BC, Canada.

Schroeter, S. (2019). Embodying difference: A case for anti-racist and decolonizing approaches to multiliteracies. *Studies in Social Justice, 13*(1), 142–158.

Schroeter, S., & Wager, A. (2017). Blurring boundaries: Drama as a critical multimodal literacy for examining 17th-century witch-hunts. *Journal of Adolescent and Adult Literacy*, *60*(4), 405–413. doi: 10.1002/jaal.585

Sutton-Smith, B. (1997). *The ambiguities of play*. Cambridge, MA: Harvard University Press.

Tizard, B., & Phoenix, A. (2002). *Black, White or mixed race? Race and racism in the lives of young people with mixed heritage*. London, UK: Routledge.

Turner, V. W. (1969). *The ritual process: Structure and anti-structure*. New Brunswick, NJ: Aldine Transaction.

Turner, V. W. (1982). *From ritual to theatre: The human seriousness of play*. Cambridge, MA: PAJ Publications.

Vertovec, S. (2007). Super-diversity and its implications. *Ethnic and Racial Studies*, *30*(6), 1024–1054.

Winant, H. (2004). *The new politics of race: Globalism, difference, justice*. Minneapolis, MN: University of Minnesota Press.

Winnicott, D. W. (1989). *Playing and reality*. New York: Routledge.

Winters, K. L., Rogers, T., & Schofield, A. (2006). The *Antigone* project: Using drama and multiple literacies to support print literacy among youth. In J. Jasinski Schneider, T. P. Crumpler, & T. Rogers (Eds.), *Process drama and multiple literacies: Addressing social, cultural, and ethical issues* (pp. 35–51). Portsmouth, NH: Heinemann.

Yassa, N. (1999). High school involvement in creative drama. *Research in Drama Education*, *4*(1), 37–49.

Yon, D. A. (2000). *Elusive culture: Schooling, race, and identity in global times*. Albany, NY: State University of New York Press.

11

GLOBAL JINZAI AND SHORT-TERM STUDY ABROAD

Expectations, Readiness, and Realities

Martin Guardado and Rika Tsushima

Summer abroad programs with a focus on English as a second language (ESL) have become increasingly popular in many English-speaking countries, and they tend to attract students from all over the world (Conroy, 2016; Serrano, Llanes, & Tragant, 2016). In general, such short-term study abroad (STSA) programs aim to provide authentic and meaningful interactive settings for learners, based on the common understanding among educators and language learners that the best way to learn a language is to live in a country where learners can be fully immersed in the target language, even for a short period of time (Tanaka & Ellis, 2003). The current evidence from STSA program research suggests that such learning experiences impact not only students' linguistic skills but also their knowledge about language, the host culture, and their intercultural awareness.

Indeed, this latter aspect of the students' learning experiences (in this chapter also understood as developing global competence), has been reported positively, whereas a concrete understanding of their linguistic development has been more challenging to measure. Study abroad research has shown that students' cross-cultural skills and awareness of global issues tend to improve through their experiences abroad (Kitsantas, 2004). Yet, what is missing in the literature is a comprehensive understanding of STSA students' readiness for the study abroad experience in terms of global competence (GC). For instance, what are students' dispositions to participate in an STSA program? To what extent are they open, if at all, to challenging and questioning their behaviors, practices, and worldviews, and to learning new ways of thinking?

The cultivation of *global jinzai* (global human resources) has been a pressing agenda for tertiary level education across Japan. This government-initiated movement calls for Japanese "human resources who can positively meet the challenges and succeed in the global field" (Japan, Ministry of Education, Culture, Sports,

DOI: 10.4324/9780429327780-11

Science, and Technology, n.d., para. 1). We designed a mixed-methods study to understand what a particular STSA program could do to produce a long-lasting impact on Japanese students' capacity to think and act as global citizens and professionals. With the premise that study abroad programs can be a great opportunity for students to develop open-minded dispositions toward cultural difference, and given the goals of the students' home universities, this study explored the state of students' readiness to undergo an intensive cultural immersion over a period of four weeks.[1] This chapter draws on the qualitative component of the first part of the project, which investigated the readiness of Japanese university students who were preparing for an STSA program offered in the English-language center at a major university in western Canada.

Literature Review

The practice of studying outside of one's home country ranging from short summer sojourns to degree-length programs is well established in higher education. Study abroad programs are often billed as serving to promote intercultural awareness and language learning, in addition to offering a "rite of passage" into adulthood (Grabowski, Wearing, Lyons, Tarrant, & Landon, 2017). A growing number of (largely) survey-based studies have demonstrated the numerous benefits of study abroad, including: enhanced opportunities for language learning and professional networking (Isabelli-García, Bown, Plews, & Dewey, 2018); increased intercultural sensitivity (Jackson, 2009; Martinsen, 2011); personal identity transformation and validation (Bright, 2018); and a sense of global responsibility (Long, 2013; cf. Woolf, 2011).

The reasons students choose to study abroad are not uniform, however, and vary according to socioeconomic status and along cultural lines. As Beerkens, Souto-Otero, de Wit, and Huisman (2016) have observed, most study abroad researchers only "survey students who have participated in a study abroad program" (p. 188), and even among those who have studied abroad, motivations tend to differ. Research in the UK found that study abroad students at one university treated study abroad as a "gap year," using it more for pleasure, whereas non-Western students tend to use their time abroad more strategically, in a career sense, studying in areas like business, engineering, and the physical sciences (Waters & Brooks, 2011; cf. Trower & Lehmann, 2017). Other research has shown that the transformative effects of study abroad in terms of identity seem to depend on students' previous travel experiences (Kuhn, 2012). Regardless of students' motivations and abilities to study abroad, however, much of the literature focuses on students' perceived benefits of their sojourns.

Short-Term Study Abroad

Despite the increasing popularity of STSA sojourns, our understanding of their capacity to enhance language learning outcomes or intercultural understanding (and related concepts) is in the early stages—particularly in programs under five to six weeks in duration (cf. Lumkes, Hallett, & Vallade, 2012). Nevertheless, at least one large-scale survey study concluded that programs "even as short as one month, are worthwhile educational endeavors that have significant self-perceived impacts on students' intellectual and personal lives" (Chieffo & Griffiths, 2004, p. 174; cf. Bloom & Miranda, 2015; Cubillos & Ilvento, 2018). Chieffo and Griffiths (2004) surveyed 2300 students from the United States over a period of two years and concluded that students who spent as little as one month abroad experienced greater intercultural awareness, personal growth, and global-mindedness than students who remained on campus.

Short-Term vs. Long-Term Study Abroad: Comparing Learning Gains

While the gains of STSA are still being established in the literature, researchers in this area seem to agree that the benefits of STSA relative to long-term study abroad (LTSA)—particularly in the area of intercultural sensitivity—depend to a great extent on multiple factors: the length of stay; student personalities, attitudes, goals, and previous experiences; and the quality of preparation/programming they receive at all stages (during their time abroad as well as pre- and post-departure) (e.g., Anderson, Lawton, Rexeisen, & Hubbard, 2006; Dwyer, 2004; Jackson, 2009; Kehl & Morris, 2008; Martinsen, 2011; Nagengast, 2017). For instance, regarding length of stay specifically, from her data set comprising 3723 study abroad participants over a period of 50 years at her institution, Dwyer (2004) concluded that "the age-old premise that 'more is better' holds true when it comes to the duration of a study abroad experience"—a finding that Medina-López-Portillo's (2004) smaller-scale study ($N = 18$) supported. However, Dwyer (2004) was optimistic about the potential for STSA programs to achieve similar results to LTSA programs: "The results of this study would suggest that programs of at least 6 weeks duration can be enormously successful in achieving important academic, personal, career and intercultural development outcomes" (p. 162) provided that they benefit from "very careful educational planning, expert implementation, and significant resources" (p. 161; see also Jackson, 2009).

One critique that might be made of current STSA research is that it tends to assess student gains in relation to LTSA students. It is not clear that such a comparison is warranted or even desirable. What a student gains in terms of perspective over the course of a year versus what they gain on a two-week sojourn is arguably incomparable, as Dwyer's (2004) data seem to suggest. Do LTSA and STSA students have the same goals and expectations of their programs in terms of GC and/or language learning? Is it realistic for them or for the programs that host them to desire or promise the same outcomes? The *de facto* point of comparison between LTSA and STSA programs is fertile ground for further investigation.

Despite Dwyer's (2004) compelling findings and analysis, the results of at least one study that compared a long-term program and a short-term program to examine the participants' GC present a different perspective on the issue. Kehl and Morris (2008) examined the differences in global-mindedness in students who studied abroad for a semester, students who participated in a short-term program, and those on the home campus who were planning to study abroad in the future. They found that there was no statistically significant difference between students who participated in a short-term program and those who were planning to study abroad in the future in terms of their global-mindedness. Based on the finding that only the long-term program participants made significant progress in that area of development, Kehl and Morris suggested that "if colleges and universities have as an objective student growth in global-mindedness, they should promote semester-long programs" (p. 76).

Relatedly, the concept of *readiness* has been studied since the middle of the 20th century, particularly in educational psychology research (Smith, 1950). More recently, readiness has attracted study abroad researchers' attention (Chang, 2012). However, Medina-López-Portillo (2004) has cautioned against sending students abroad "with inflated ideas about their own intercultural sensitivity in comparison with their compatriots at home" (p. 196), as this can lead to a false sense of readiness and unrealistic expectations about their capacity to achieve the intended learning outcomes. Perhaps the greater risk, she points out, is the potential to assume "a comprehensive understanding of the foreign culture, rather than a slice of the culture within a very specific context" (p. 196).

The Japanese Context: "Global Jinzai"

The term グローバル化 (globalization) entered the Japanese language in the context of global economic activities in the 1990s (Yoshida, 2017). Owing to challenging issues related to economic and various domestic phenomena in Japan (e.g., the quickly aging population), the Japanese government has emphasized the importance of cultivating global jinzai (global human resources) since the early 2000s. Global jinzai is defined by the government as follows (original in English): "1) Fundamental competencies for working persons usually required for an adult, 2) communication ability in [a] foreign language, and 3) ability to understand and take advantage of different cultures" (Global Human Resource Development Committee of Industry-Academia, 2010, p. 7).

Yoshida (2017) argues that the promotion of global jinzai has been led by the economic context of the job market in Japan, and that such needs were translated into higher education policies as a national project to help enable Japanese businesses to become globally competitive. The Ministry of Economy, Trade and Industry has been leading the global jinzai discussion and has stated that the "whole industry and academia should collaboratively engage in the cultivation of human resources" (Industry-Academia Collaborative Roundtable Conference

176 Martin Guardado and Rika Tsushima

on Human Resources Development, 2012, p. 1). Consequently, the Ministry of Education, Culture, Sports, Science, and Technology (MEXT) moved to align higher education policies with the economy-driven agenda by making changes in various aspects of university administration, such as increasing the number of international students (Yonezawa, 2014).

Furthermore, in 2014, MEXT announced the multimillion-dollar Top Global University Project, with the goal to "enhance the international compatibility and competitiveness of higher education in Japan" (Japan, Ministry of Education, Culture, Sports, Science, and Technology, 2014, para. 1). Notably, the funding for this project aims to internationalize education at Japanese universities, which includes promoting study abroad programs. MEXT also launched a campaign, "トビタテ！留学JAPAN (Tobitate! Ryugaku Japan)" ("Leap for Tomorrow! Study-Abroad Japan"), to promote study abroad among Japanese students, including a website and a series of promotional events featuring prominent business personalities, artists, and athletes who have previously studied abroad.

Considering the complex social, economic, and political context detailed previously, the main goal of this chapter is to understand what an STSA program can do to make a long-lasting impact on students' dispositions toward otherness and to think and act as global citizens and professionals. With this goal in mind, we investigated students' stated expectations and sense of readiness about their upcoming study abroad experience.

Methodology

This chapter draws only on the qualitative component of the first part of the mixed-methods project, which involved semi-structured interviews conducted at three universities in Japan. This component addresses the following questions:

1. What are the characteristics of a cohort of Japanese university students who joined a short-term study abroad program at a Canadian university?
2. What is their level of readiness in relation to their participation in the short-term study abroad program?
3. What are their views regarding global competence?

The STSA program, housed in the English-language unit of a top-ranked Canadian university with institutional partners around the world, offers programs of study that combine language study with touristic and cultural experiences.

Data collection took place at three institutional sites in Japan, based on access and their disposition to collaborate. Twenty-four students participated in the semi-structured interviews, and they were given the choice to be interviewed in either English or Japanese, as they felt comfortable. All the interviews were audio-recorded, transcribed, and coded using the Dedoose mixed-methods analysis software package. For the GC analysis, we employed the OECD PISA

Global Competence Framework (Organisation for Economic Co-operation and Development, 2018). This framework includes a set of core competencies (knowledge, skills, abilities, and values) that guided the analysis and interpretation process.

Findings

Overall, there were no salient differences in the findings based on the students' choice of interview language, home university, gender identity, or study major. Rather, we found there were some individual differences in the students' degree of commitment to their upcoming STSA experience. Another general observation is that, despite the goals of many universities in the Japanese context in relation to fostering global jinzai, there was a lack of GC education to support the students' aspirations for a transformative learning experience.

Overall Characteristics of This Cohort

The first question addressed the general background characteristics of the participants. Participant ages ranged from 18 to 21. They were in their first, second, or third year of study at the Japanese universities and had diverse majors (e.g., computing science, biology, engineering, education, law). All of the participants spoke Japanese as their first language, but in terms of English competency, the cohort was quite mixed, with IELTS (International English Language Testing System) scores ranging between approximately 3.0 and 5.0. None of the students had previously participated in a structured study abroad program.

Expectations for the Short-Term Study Abroad Program

The second research question concerned the experiences the participants would like to have while in the program, and what they were doing to maximize their learning prior to departure. All interviewees stated that they were very excited about their first STSA experience, expecting to make significant gains in English speaking and intercultural communication skills, which are two characteristics of global jinzai. For instance, Toshi (all names are pseudonyms) described his motivation for learning English as being to get himself ready for globalization in Japan:

> As we hear often, everything will be globalized eventually, right? In fact, more and more companies in which English became the official language of business are accepting foreign people. When I think of such a situation, the must-have skill is English. So, this [STSA] experience will be helpful for me to be an English speaker.

One quote from Yuka, a student who chose to be interviewed in English, is a good example of the way students described how they envisioned their learning in the one-month program (I2 = Interviewer 2):

I2: What do you think you will get from the program in Canada?

Yuka: Communication skills, um English skills ... Speaking with others,

I2: How do you think you will learn things in Canada? In the school and outside?

Yuka: School and at host family,

Although their expectations for language skill development through the program were very high, there seemed to be a gap between their aspirations and the pre-departure actions that they took (or did not take) to support those aspirations.

Commitment to the Program

Regarding commitment to the program, there were marked differences at the individual level. Some students, especially those who were planning to have a longer experience in the future, had been taking English courses, joining English conversation clubs, and even taking private lessons with English language tutors. Many of the students, on the other hand, seemed to equate "preparing" with "packing" and nothing else. For example, one interviewee justified his lack of preparation as follows (I3 = Interviewer 3):

Naoto: I am currently too busy to do these things [i.e., English learning or information gathering].

I3: So, maybe you will start just before your departure?

Naoto: Well, actually, I don't think I will. 'Cause I will learn in Canada, right?

This attitude, "I will learn things automatically once I am in Canada," was common among interviewees who were not putting effort into their preparation. Furthermore, this tendency was even more salient in their perception of intercultural communication learning. Indeed, many interviewees had adopted the perspective that their GC skills would be and should be developed naturally through the STSA experience, not in their home country, Japan. Interestingly, only those interviewees who had a close friend or a family member who had previously participated in the STSA program reported that they had had access to information beyond the official information sessions at their university.

Global Competence

Although their home universities offered either a series of seminars or a course designed to help students prepare for their sojourn abroad, the content of the preparation materials seemed to vary widely from institution to institution. Moreover, we found that their knowledge of Canada and Canadian culture was rather limited at the time of the interviews. Unsurprisingly, Canada's multiculturalism was an obscure concept for participants. In the following quote, Maki acknowledged that she knew little about Canada in the pre-departure stage, but that learning about Canadian culture was very useful:

I3: What do you know about Canada now?
Maki: Nothing, really. Well, their maple syrup has a good reputation. That's probably all I know.
I3: Anything you know about Canadian culture?
Maki: (long pause)
I3: In the program, you will take a course that focuses on Canadian culture. How do you feel?
Maki: Oh, I think that is fantastic. You know, by living in a culture that is different from Japan, we can examine our own culture from a different angle and expand our worldviews. I am sure this program will help me broaden my horizon.

Maki did not receive any pre-departure preparation at her university, except for an information session that simply focused on the logistical aspects of the sojourn. Motoki, who chose to be interviewed in English, shared his thoughts on the experience in a preparation course at his university as follows:

I2: Now I'm going to be asking you about Canadian culture. What do you know about Canada?
Motoki: I've been to Canada only once. I've been to Toronto and I saw Niagara Falls, but I don't feel like [there were any] cultural differences, and I don't feel any challenges. And I asked teachers in this university, teachers from Canada, and I asked the teachers what are the cultural differences between Japan and Canada. And they said, the differences are only mother tongue, English and Japanese. And so, and other points, there are few. There are no differences. No different cultures.

Even having had a previous experience of visiting Canada, coupled with his curiosity about the cultural differences between the countries, Motoki's comment implied that it might require explicit and deliberate teaching for students to develop an awareness around recognizing differences across cultures.

Even though the concept of multiculturalism remained obscure, elusive, and intangible, some interviewees, in fact, referred to the multicultural and multiethnic nature of Canadian society, as such information seemed to be given in their preparation seminars. For example, describing her pre-departure knowledge of Canada, Unana shared her struggle to reconcile Canada's multiethnic composition with its singular nation-state status:

> Canadian culture? Hmmm … nothing comes to mind. Well, when asked to think about what makes Canada "Canada," I am not sure what it might be.

I wonder if it is because of the multiethnicity, or, hmmm, but now I am not sure if I know what Canada is.

The concept of multicu.turalism was challenging for interviewees to grasp, indicating that they had not been exposed to deep discussions on the topic—a finding that is congruent with a recent report that found that Japanese youths generally abstain from discussions on global or social issues (Nippon Foundation, 2019). This absence of GC education was also apparent in the interviewees' attitudes toward and values about cultural coexistence, even in their own country.

Global Citizen = Proficient English Speaker

One dimension of GC is the capacity to examine local, global, and intercultural issues and to understand and appreciate different perspectives and worldviews (Organisation for Economic Co-operation and Development, 2018). This dimension parallels the third component of global jinzai: intercultural understanding. In our interviews, however, the dearth of sociocultural awareness of their own country emerged as a salient theme across the participants' reflections. Students failed to acknowledge the existence of non-Japanese groups living in Japan unless they were obviously of Western origin (English or European-language speakers). Rather, they referred to Japan as a homogeneous society, a notion that is not culturally, ethnically, or even linguistically accurate (Douglass & Roberts, 2015). The statement below, by a student who was interviewed in Japanese, captures this sentiment:

I3: In your future job, do you think you will interact with non-Japanese people [in Japan]?
Ayana: Well, no. I don't think so

In response to its declining labor force, Japan has been accepting large numbers of foreign workers, but this reality seemed surreal to Ayana and other interviewees. This issue is reminiscent of the discussion by Laniel-Tremblay and Low (this volume) regarding the lack of acceptance often experienced by minorities. Although all interviewees in the current study likely had interactions with non-Japanese people in their everyday lives, they did not seem to consider this a sign of globalization in Japan. The excerpt below is one of many examples that indicate ethnic diversity was largely invisible to the interviewees:

I3: Do you have any interactions with non-Japanese people?
Kei: Not currently. In my high school, we had a foreign student and sometimes I talked to her in English. But that's it.
I3: You don't see non-Japanese people, like in your part-time workplace?
Kei: Yeah, actually, we have a Vietnamese colleague, but we speak in Japanese because his Japanese is excellent. His Japanese is almost perfect.

In these cases, regardless of the Japanese language skills of the individuals they interacted with, interviewees did not refer to such interactions as instances of intercultural communication. The lack of awareness of their own country's diversity might be related to their difficulty in understanding Canadian multiculturalism. In addition, in their view, GC was solely and dominantly associated with English speaking skills.

According to the OECD's PISA, "Global competence embodies and is propelled by key dispositions or attitudes" (Organisation for Economic Co-operation and Development, 2018, p. 17). To further investigate the degree of GC of the Japanese STSA students in this study, we explored how they described what globally competent individuals were able to do when they interacted with people from different cultures. We asked participants to explain what they saw as obstacles to establishing positive interactions with people of different backgrounds, other than language. This abstract question turned out to be quite difficult for them to elaborate on. Several students, in fact, could not think of any barriers that might hinder their effective communication with others. Here is an example:

Hisa: Communication barriers? Hmm … probably nothing. I think.
I3: So, if your English is good enough, do you think your communication with Canadian people will always be smooth?
Hisa: Well, I suppose so. I can't think of any reasons. Hum, why not?

As in this excerpt, some students appeared to be clearly puzzled by the question itself and could not think of any concrete answers other than the obvious language barrier.

Data from the pre-STSA interviews indicated that the students' level of readiness was quite low overall, suggesting that structured GC-focused learning might be missing in their home university programs. In addition, they had unrealistic expectations for the amount of progress they would be able to make in terms of their English language skills, as well as in terms of the skills to successfully engage in intercultural interactions, within the space of only a month.

Discussion: A Paradigm Change in Study Abroad Programs?

With the premise that study abroad programs can be a great opportunity for students to develop an openness to new ideas, this section discusses how education can foster and enhance the students' readiness for undertaking an intensive cultural immersion program of study.

The Gap between Students' Expectations and Reality

The findings point to the existence of profound chasms between the students' expectations and the reality of their readiness both in English and in their openness to otherness, which indicates a more careful and informed approach might be required to promote STSA programs. We found that students' dedication at the preparation stage varied between individuals in terms of learning English and seeking information about the destination and the program. In fact, some students seemed to solely rely on the one-month program to equip them with advanced English and intercultural communication skills. The tendency to have unrealistically high expectations of a study abroad program is reported in the language education literature (e.g., Tanaka, 2007). The issue here seems to stem from the profound lack of realistic information regarding STSA programs in higher education, and also from the industry-driven promotion of study abroad programs in Japan.

Regarding language development, for instance, the extant research literature on the language gains generated by STSA programs is limited. Most studies to date suggest that students cannot improve their language skills significantly through STSA experiences alone. Likewise, in terms of GC, the Japanese student participants considered the STSA program a life-changing opportunity to be global citizens by immersing themselves in an unfamiliar culture. Certainly, it is often argued that study abroad can be a substantial educational activity that will help students obtain skills to actively engage with pressing issues as global citizens (Lewin, 2009). Yet, study abroad researchers have argued that STSA is less likely to benefit students compared with long-term programs (Kehl & Morris, 2008). A solid pedagogical framework is required to "reinforce the value of short-term programming of at least 6 weeks duration" (Dwyer, 2004, p. 161), but how often and to what extent is such information circulated among stakeholders of STSA programs, and especially among students?

In fact, the website of the Japanese government–initiated SA campaign states:

> Short-term study abroad: It does not require much preparation compared to long-term because in many cases there is no English or academic requirement for the program. The biggest advantage for you is to be part of it casually whenever you feel the urge.[2]
>
> *(Tobitate! [Leap for Tomorrow] Study Abroad Initiative, n.d.)*

This is the quintessential example of how STSA programs have been characterized in promotional campaigns, and consequently, students do not see the need to engage in serious preparation beforehand.

Elitism in STSA Program Promotion

The strong association between English speakers and global jinzai came up repeatedly in the interviews. The study abroad experience was highly fetishized in an elitist manner, in relation to the idea of English as a global language (see Reid, this volume; see also Delanty, 2009; Guardado, 2018; Werbner, 2006). Moreover, from

Global Jinzai and Short-Term Study Abroad **183**

how the students described their understanding of their local environment and the diversity, or lack thereof, in their own society, it was apparent that foundational GC education was missing in that context.

As defined by PISA, students with GC can investigate the world, consider a variety of perspectives, communicate ideas, and take meaningful action. The definition also challenges students to understand their local environment and the diversity within their own communities. The findings show, however, that when asked for their opinions on globalization and intercultural communication, the interviewees only referred to interaction with English speakers, even in hypothetical future situations in their native Japan. The invisibility of non-Japanese people in their environment emerged as a main theme in this research. In fact, according to the Organisation for Economic Co-operation and Development (2019), compared with the world average of 13.1%, the ratio of foreign-born people in the total population of Japan was much lower at 1.9%. However, the number of foreign workers in Japan has been rapidly increasing in the last 20 years, and the government has just submitted an amendment to the immigration control law to the Imperial Diet ("National Assembly"), which will further attract foreigners to work in Japan.

In this research, the students' strong motivation for learning English was described as a type of prestige, in line with previous study abroad research (e.g., Coleman, 2006; Pennycook, 1994), as well as reflecting scholarship with other foci (see, e.g., Reid, this volume). Furthermore, echoing Campion and Joseph-Salisbury (this volume) and extending their argument, Eurocentric ways of seeing the world should not be reinforced by study abroad programs. Fostering young Japanese people's efforts to become global citizens should start with supporting them in "appreciating the differences in the communities to which they belong— the nation, the region, the city, the neighborhood, the school" (Organisation for Economic Co-operation and Development, 2018, p. 5).

We argue that recognizing, respecting, and valuing diversity in their own community should be the primary agenda for cosmopolitan education. Time and commitment are required to nurture GC, and it is questionable whether students would be able to develop the necessary skills by simply participating in a month-long program in a foreign country, especially without any psychological preparation. On the contrary, intercultural education literature has repeatedly shown that students with poor intercultural competence skills who study abroad can find themselves in—or initiate—conflict due to stereotypical and racist attitudes (Trede, Bowles, & Bridges, 2013). Thus, without adequately preparing or supporting STSA participants—simply sending or receiving them and exposing them to international experiences—can result in negative learning outcomes.

The study findings strongly suggest the need to exercise caution when promoting STSA programs as simple solutions for developing global-mindedness and conveying the elitist and simplistic message that study abroad participation turns people into global jinzai. Learning English and GC skills may take place

184 Martin Guardado and Rika Tsushima

concurrently and synergistically, but English language development should not be treated as a pre- or co-requisite for the development of GC. Study abroad students should arrive in the host country with foundational GC skills so that they can actually exercise skills in any setting, including their own country, and not just in what they might see as authentic settings for intercultural encounters, such as the host country. Arguably, anywhere—even their own country—can be an authentic context in which to develop the dispositions and skills for global citizenship.

Conclusion

This study set out to investigate the expectations and readiness of a group of 24 Japanese students from three universities before they traveled to a short study abroad destination in western Canada. The findings show that there was a mismatch between their expectations and the reality of their readiness in terms of gains in both their English language skills and GC, which suggests that a more informed and informative approach is required to promote STSA programs. In addition, based on how the respondents described their understanding of their local environment and the diversity of their own society, it was apparent that foundational intercultural education might be missing in the Japanese higher education context. Consequently, the study abroad experience was fetishized in a rather elitist manner, in relation to the idea of English as *the* global language. These findings lead us to argue for a paradigm shift in STSA programming from an idealized one-size-fits-all event to a customized educational package that promises concrete and attainable learning outcomes.

To date, the body of knowledge in this area has largely advanced the longer-is-better argument. However, as Dwyer (2004) pointed out, very short-term programs like the one described in this chapter have the potential for positive long-term impacts on student growth in a range of important areas. High-quality programming, as other researchers have also suggested, is clearly critical with shorter programs (e.g., Anderson et al., 2006; Nagengast, 2017). Cultural immersion is clearly not, on its own, an assurance of intercultural learning. Providing international experiences without a meaningful pedagogical framework that helps students to reflect on themselves and others can reinforce stereotypical thinking and racist attitudes, which are paradoxically some of the very phenomena that study abroad purports to help eliminate.

The elephant in the STSA room appears to be the fact that English language teaching and learning has become a profitable industry, and it is often a key revenue-generating stream in postsecondary institutions (Tsushima & Guardado, 2015). Thus, STSA students are seen as low-maintenance guests who come for a brief stay. Furthermore, international student recruitment in general (including STSA programs) is portrayed as an initiative that enriches the cultural fabric of university campuses, enhances the learning experience of the entire student

Global Jinzai and Short-Term Study Abroad **185**

population, and benefits society at large, but the financial benefits that drive these programs are not frequently highlighted. Indeed, in 2018 alone, international students in Canada spent an estimated $21.6 billion (CAD) on tuition and other expenses. Clearly, in the words of Matthews and Sidhu (2005), "marketized expressions of international education are ultimately disengaged from notions of a global public good" (p. 63). In this way, STSA programs are in effect monetizing a highly fantasized cosmopolitanism.

It is crucial to note that the neoliberal ideologies that drive the burgeoning commodification of international education today are the same forces motivating top-down initiatives like the Japanese global jinzai agenda. This is a seemingly benevolent notion that seeks to foster a workforce with the ability to function across cultures in an interconnected global arena. A globally oriented mindset can be understood as a sense of openness toward other people, places, cultures, and ways of thinking (Beck, 2006; Guardado, 2018; Mignolo, 2000). Arguably, it is unrealistic to expect STSA students to develop these orientations during such a short sojourn. This unreasonable expectation sets them up for a failure that they would likely see as their own.

Like global jinzai, the higher education institutions in mostly English-speaking countries that attract these students are strongly driven by market economics. As a result of rapidly declining public funding, Canadian universities are increasingly looking to international students to fill their financial shortfalls. Indeed, the government of Canada has explicitly identified international education as "an important source of revenue and human capital for Canada" (Government of Canada, 2019, para 34). Thus, evidently, both the sending country of our student participants, Japan, and the receiving institutions in Canada are economically motivated. Even when Canadian higher education institutions attempt to mask their rationales with goals related to cultural enrichment and global understanding, in practice, the primary motivators are clearly financial. Otherwise, rather than barely scraping by to sustain their academic operations, study abroad programs would have the freedom to invest in the development of educational programming of the highest quality, which might actually help STSA students develop dispositions of openness toward difference. While most academic programs are held accountable for measuring student-learning outcomes, STSA programs tend to be exempt from this responsibility. Such an approach is not only unsustainable for the field of education but also a pedagogically unethical practice in which the academic units offering these programs are complicit.

Notes

1 For the purposes of our argument, we use the definition of global competence provided by the Programme for International Student Assessment (PISA) 2018 assessment produced by the OECD, which states, "Global competence is the capacity to examine local, global and intercultural issues, to understand and appreciate the perspectives and

186 Martin Guardado and Rika Tsushima

worldviews of others, to engage in open, appropriate and effective interactions with people from different cultures, and to act for collective well-being and sustainable development" (Organisation for Economic Co-operation and Development, 2018, p. 7).

2 英語力や成績が参加の条件となっていないことが多く、長期留学ほど準備を必要としない。思い立ったら気軽に参加できるのが最大のメリット。(our translation).

References

Anderson, P. H., Lawton, L., Rexeisen, R. J., & Hubbard, A. C. (2006). Short-term study abroad and intercultural sensitivity: A pilot study. *International Journal of Intercultural Relations, 30*(4), 457–469.

Beck, U. (2006). *Cosmopolitan vision*. Cambridge, UK: Polity Press.

Beerkens, M., Souto-Otero, M., de Wit, H., & Huisman, J. (2016). Similar students and different countries? An analysis of the barriers and drivers for Erasmus participation in seven countries. *Journal of Studies in International Education, 20*(2), 184–204.

Bloom, M., & Miranda, A. (2015). Intercultural sensitivity through short-term study abroad. *Language and Intercultural Communication, 15*(4), 567–580.

Bright, D. (2018). *Post post-trip follow-up with postsecondary students after short-term study abroad: Transformational learning and international experiential education* (Unpublished Master's thesis). Brock University, St. Catharines, ON, Canada.

Chang, D.-F. (2012). College students' perceptions of studying abroad and their readiness. *Asia Pacific Education Review, 13*, 583–591.

Chieffo, L., & Griffiths, L. (2004). Large-scale assessment of student attitudes after a short-term study abroad program. *Frontiers: The Interdisciplinary Journal of Study Abroad, 10*, 165–177.

Coleman, J. A. (2006). English-medium teaching in European higher education. *Language Teaching, 39*(1), 1–14.

Conroy, M. A. (2016). Contextual factors in second language learning in a short-term study abroad programme in Australia. *Language Learning Journal, 44*(1), 1–21.

Cubillos, J., & Ilvento, T. (2018). Intercultural contact in short-term study abroad programs. *Hispania, 101*(2), 249–266. doi: 10.1353/hpn.2018.0117

Delanty, G. (2009). *The cosmopolitan imagination: The renewal of critical social theory*. Cambridge, UK: Cambridge University Press.

Douglass, M., & Roberts, G. (2015). *Japan and global migration: Foreign workers and the advent of a multicultural society*. London, UK: Routledge.

Dwyer, M. M. (2004). More is better: The impact of study abroad program duration. *Frontiers: The Interdisciplinary Journal of Study Abroad, 10*, 151–164.

Global Human Resource Development Committee of Industry-Academia. (2010). *Report: Develop global human resources through industry-academia-government collaborations*. Retrieved from http://www.meti.go.jp/english/press/data/pdf/Human_Resource.pdf

Government of Canada. (2019). *The international education report*. Retrieved from https://www.international.gc.ca/education/strategy-2019-2024-strategie.aspx?lang=eng

Grabowski, S., Wearing, S., Lyons, K., Tarrant, M., & Landon, A. (2017). A rite of passage? Exploring youth transformation and global citizenry in the study abroad experience. *Tourism Recreation Research, 42*(2), 139–149. doi: 10.1080/02508281.2017.1292177

Guardado, M. (2018). *Discourse, ideology and heritage language socialization: Micro and macro perspectives*. New York: De Gruyter Mouton.

Industry-Academia Collaborative Roundtable Conference on Human Resources Development. (2012). *San-Gaku Kyodo Jinzai Ikusei Entaku Kaigi Akushon Plan no Gaiyo*

[Summary of an action plan industry-academia collaborative roundtable conference on human resources development]. Retrieved from http://meti.go.jp/policy/economy/jinzai/san_gaku_kyodo/entaku2/1320909_6.pdf

Isabelli-García, C., Bown, J., Plews, J. L., & Dewey, D. P. (2018). Language learning and study abroad. *Language Teaching, 51*(4), 439–484.

Jackson, J. (2009). Intercultural learning on short-term sojourns. *Intercultural Education, 20*(sup. l), 59–71.

Japan, Ministry of Education, Culture, Sports, Science, and Technology. (2014). *Selection for the FY2014 top global university project.* Retrieved from http://docplayer.net/16379288-Selection-for-the-fy-2014-top-global-university-project-we-hereby-announce-the-s election-of-universities-for-the-top-global-university-project.html

Japan, Ministry of Education, Culture, Sports, Science, and Technology. (n.d.). *Project for promotion of global human resources.* Retrieved from https://www.mext.go.jp/en/policy/education/highered/title02/detail02/sdetail02/1373895.htm

Kehl, K., & Morris, J. (2008). Differences in global-mindedness between short-term and semester-long study abroad participants at selected private universities. *Frontiers: The Interdisciplinary Journal of Study Abroad, 15*, 67–79.

Kitsantas, A. (2004). Studying abroad: The role of college students' goals on the development of cross-cultural skills and global understanding. *College Student Journal, 38*, 441–452.

Kuhn, T. (2012). Why educational exchange programmes miss their mark: Cross-border mobility, education and European identity. *JCMS: Journal of Common Market Studies, 50*(6), 994–1010. doi: 10.1111/j.1468-5965.2012.02286.x

Lewin, R. (2009). *The handbook of practice and research in study abroad: Higher education and the quest for global citizenship.* New York: Routledge.

Long, T. E. (2013). From study abroad to global studies: Reconstructing international education for a globalized world. *Frontiers: The Interdisciplinary Journal of Study Abroad, 22*, 25–36.

Lumkes, J. H., Jr., Hallett, S., & Vallade, L. (2012). Hearing versus experiencing: The impact of a short-term study abroad experience in China on students' perceptions regarding globalization and cultural awareness. *International Journal of Intercultural Relations, 36*(1), 151–159.

Martinsen, R. (2011). Predicting changes in cultural sensitivity among students of Spanish during short-term study abroad. *Hispania, 94*(1), 121–141.

Matthews, J., & Sidhu, R. (2005). Desperately seeking the global subject: International education, citizenship and cosmopolitanism. *Globalisation, Societies and Education, 3*(1), 49–66. doi: 10.1080/14767720500046179

Medina-López-Portillo, A. (2004). Intercultural learning assessment: The link between program duration and the development of intercultural sensitivity. *Frontiers: The Interdisciplinary Journal of Study Abroad, 10*, 179–199.

Mignolo, W. D. (2000). The many faces of cosmo-polis: Border thinking and critical cosmopolitanism. *Public Culture, 12*, 721–748.

Nagengast, E. (2017). An assessment of learning outcomes in short-term study abroad and human rights education. *International Research and Review, 7*(1), 77–92.

Nippon Foundation. (2019). *18-sai Ishiki Cyousa* [Awareness survey of 18-year-olds] (Report No. 20). Retrieved from https://www.nippon-foundation.or.jp/app/uploads/2019/11/wha_pro_eig_97.pdf

Organisation for Economic Co-operation and Development. (2018). *Preparing our youth for an inclusive and sustainable world: The OECD PISA global competence framework.* Retrieved from http://www.oecd.org/pisa/Handbook-PISA-2018-Global-Competence.pdf

Organisation for Economic Co-operation and Development. (2019). *OECD economic surveys—Japan 2017.* Paris: OECD Publishing. doi: 10.1787/eco_surveys-jpn-2017-en

Pennycook, A. (1994). *The cultural politics of English as an international language.* Harlow, UK: Longman.

Serrano, R., Llanes, À., & Tragant, E. (2016). Examining L2 development in two short-term intensive programs for teenagers: Study abroad vs. "at home." *System, 57,* 43–54.

Smith, N. (1950). Readiness for reading. In National Conference on Research in English, National Council of Teachers of English (Eds.), *Readiness for reading and related language arts: A digest of current research* (pp. 3–33). Urbana, IL: National Conference on Research in English.

Tanaka, K. (2007). Japanese students' contact with English outside the classroom during study abroad. *New Zealand Studies in Applied Linguistics, 13*(1), 36–54.

Tanaka, K., & Ellis, R. (2003). Study-abroad, language proficiency, and learner beliefs about language learning. *JALT Journal, 25*(1), 63–84.

Tobitate! (Leap for Tomorrow) Study Abroad Initiative. (n.d.). [website]. Retrieved from https://www.tobitate.mext.go.jp/univ/

Trede, F., Bowles, W., & Bridges, D. (2013). Developing intercultural competence and global citizenship through international experiences: Academics' perceptions. *Intercultural Education, 24,* 442–455.

Trower, H., & Lehmann, W. (2017). Strategic escapes: Negotiating motivations of personal growth and instrumental benefits in the decision to study abroad. *British Educational Research Journal, 43*(2), 275–289.

Tsushima, R., & Guardado, M. (2015). English language "education" or "industry"? Bridging parallel discourses in Canada. In L.T.Wong & A. Dubey-Jhaveri (Eds.), *English language education in a global world: Practices, issues and challenges* (pp. 239–250). Hauppauge, NY: Nova Science.

Waters, J., & Brooks, R. (2011). "Vive la différence?": The "international" experiences of UK students overseas. *Population, Space and Place, 17*(5), 567–578. doi: 10.1002/psp.613

Werbner, P. (2006).Vernacular cosmopolitanism. *Theory, Culture & Society, 23*(2–3), 496–498.

Woolf, M. (2011). "Study abroad changed my life" and other problems. *International Educator, 20*(6), 52–55.

Yonezawa, A. (2014). Japan's challenge of fostering "global human resources": Policy debates and practices. *Japan Labor Review, 11*(2), 37–52.

Yoshida, A. (2017). Global human resource development and Japanese university education: "Localism" in actor discussions. *Educational Studies in Japan, 11,* 83–99.

12
PLAYING AND MAKING
Re-Fusing the Digital Divide

Jennifer Jenson

Digital games are a global entertainment industry, and millions of adults and children play games and increasingly watch others playing games through streaming platforms like Twitch and YouTube. Video games are, for many adults and children in Canada and elsewhere, a top leisure activity, and the Entertainment Software Association of Canada reports in its annual poll that 80% of Canadians consider video games a "mainstream entertainment" medium. Far more people than ever before are reporting that they play games on their mobile devices at all age levels, and men and boys report playing on a PC or console more often than women and girls (Entertainment Software Association of Canada, 2018). Outside of school, digital games are for many a valued part of socialization and communication, and they can be valuable assets for learning, especially for those who are on the margins. As Schecter and James ask in the Preface to this book, "What materiality (artifacts and objects, including technologically enabled resources) is produced in the service of cosmopolitan users … and how can these artifacts be pressed into service for purposes of teaching and learning?" This chapter demonstrates the ways in which playing and making digital games helps inner-city students in the Greater Toronto Area (GTA) engage with, learn about, and more skillfully understand this global, cultural, social, and economic medium of the 21st century.

Digital games have not just captivated the leisure time of adults and children, but are increasingly played to generate revenue, whether online through streaming on Twitch or YouTube or through e-sports tournaments. Reaching players not just through PCs and consoles (such as XBOX, Playstation, or a Nintendo Switch) but also through mobile devices such as cellphones and tablets, digital games have been designed and developed explicitly for educational/learning contexts, while commercial games have been adopted for use in classrooms worldwide.

DOI: 10.4324/9780429327780-12

Since the early part of the 21st century, digital-game-based learning (DGBL) has captured the attention of researchers, educators, and policy-makers. Digital games, whether students play or make them, are held up as exemplary tools for supporting the acquisition of "21st-century skills and competencies," especially those related to science, technology, engineering, arts, and mathematics (STEAM).

Early theorists such as James Paul Gee (2003) and Mark Prensky (2006) argued that digital games model good learning environments and can be sites where deep learning can take place. While that early theoretical work was certainly enthusiastic, the empirical studies that have followed report mixed results, with the primary problem being how to understand and assess what is learned through play (Linderoth, 2012; Tobias & Fletcher, 2012; Young, Slota, Cutter, & Jaletter, 2012). In terms of making games, connections to the acquisition of STEAM and/or computational competencies are clearer, but the assessment of learning from making games remains an open research question (Kafai & Burke, 2015). Much like the literature on makerspaces (see, for example, Daley & Child, 2015; Hughes, Laffler, Mamolo, Morrison, & Petrarca, 2016; Kafai, Fields, & Searle, 2014), research on digital game-making typically examines the ways in which students are able to "tinker," create, and engage in design-based thinking.

Building on critically framed earlier work from computing, Alan J. Perlis, the first recipient of the now prestigious ACM A. M. Turing Award[1] in 1966, argued that learning programming should be integral to a liberal education, as important today as teaching undergraduates how to write in first-year courses has been (Perlis, 1964). Similarly, Alan Kay and Adele Goldberg argued in the 1970s that computers were a new medium for expression that should be accessible to everyone (Kay & Goldberg, 1977). Not much later, in 1980, Seymour Papert proposed that children could use their programming skills to "recast powerful ideas in computational form" (p. 183) and that "learning by making" was the preferred method because children learn best when they have an "object-to-think-with" (p. 182).

Two decades on, Andrea diSessa extended and elaborated on these (and other) earlier discussions in his book *Changing Minds* (2000), arguing for "computational literacy" that "will allow civilization to think and do things that will be new to us in the same way that modern literate society would be almost incomprehensible to pre-literate cultures" (pp. 4–5). DiSessa (2018) updated this notion significantly in a more recent article, stating, "I view computation as, potentially, providing a new, deep, and profoundly influential literacy—computational literacy—that will impact all STEM [science, technology, engineering, and mathematics] disciplines at their very core, but most especially in terms of learning" (p. 4). In other words, diSessa argues strongly for thinking about computation and its attendant forms, meanings, and ways of knowing and learning as a literacy for the 21st century and beyond.

Related to diSessa's definition of "computational literacy" is a concept that has had quite a lot of academic and lay attention, "computational thinking." One influential scholar in this area has been Jeannette Wing (2006), who argues that computational thinking "represents a universally applicable attitude and skill set everyone, not just computer scientists, would be eager to learn and use" (p. 33). So why thinking rather than literacy? According to Wing (2006), "computational thinking involves solving problems, designing systems, and understanding human behavior by drawing on the concepts fundamental to computer science" (p. 33). She further elaborates in 2011 that "computational thinking is the thought processes involved in formulating problems and their solutions so that the solutions are represented in a form that can be effectively carried out by an information-processing agent" (n.p.).

Reviewing the distinction between computational literacy (diSessa, 2000) and computational thinking (National Science Foundation, 2011; Wing, 2006, 2011), Grover and Pea (2013) argue that "computational literacy," unlike "computational thinking," is too easily confused with other, earlier forms of "digital literacies." They state, "The term *computational literacy* is perhaps susceptible to confusion with earlier ones like *computer literacy, information literacy,* and *digital literacy* that have assumed various meanings over the years" (emphasis in original, p. 39). They follow up by stating that the preference now is for the "phrase and notion of *computational thinking*" (p. 39).

That said, in his 2018 article, diSessa reclaims computational literacy as important and distinct from computational thinking, situating the promotion of computational thinking by Wing and others as too narrowly focused on one subject area: computer science. I would argue that diSessa (2018) misses an important distinction between *literacy* and *thinking* in his critique of Wing: that *computational thinking* embeds what is educationally significant about computation as something to think about and/or know. *Computational literacy*, on the other hand, embeds what is significant about "computation"—that is, those broad understandings it entails (such as mathematics, computer science, engineering, coding, philosophy), including new ways of "reading the world" that are not available without computational understandings. Computational thinking, in other words, is necessary, but not sufficient, for computational literacy. Understanding this relationship between thinking and doing is especially important in supporting the acquisition of STEAM-based know-how through the design of digital games. This chapter sets out a "production pedagogies" approach (see de Castell, 2016) that focuses on the kind of knowing that comes from making and doing.

Orientation to the Chapter

This chapter sets out, through a series of "lessons learned," some of the highs and lows of game-making and play in schools, connecting these where possible to contexts and know-how outside of schools. These lessons are compiled from a five-year collaboration with two inner-city schools in the Greater Toronto Area. One is considered a "high needs" school with a large immigrant, and therefore also English Language Learner (ELL), population. The other is in an increasingly

192 Jennifer Jenson

gentrified neighborhood with a high population of students on Individual Education Plans (IEPs)—"special needs" students.

In both settings, participation by students was entirely voluntary, whether they took part in a during- or after-school club focusing on game design or game play or participated in a whole-class intervention. Oversight by participating teachers, whether in clubs or in the classroom, was also voluntary, and depended on teachers who were willing to lend their time and energy to the clubs or during a class intervention. Overall, the teachers' ethnicity did not reflect the ethnic, linguistic, or cultural diversity of the students in the schools in which they taught, as they were overwhelmingly monolingual, white, Canadian, and from southern Ontario (only one teacher identified as Asian-Canadian).

The methodological approach in each of these studies was a mixed-methods study design, with quantitative and qualitative data collected from participants in during-school and after-school clubs and/or whole-classroom groups (where most if not all students had opted into the study). A mixed-methods approach to data collection (Creswell & Plano Clark, 2011) allowed me and my research team to triangulate the data collected: pre- and post-surveys of game play and prior coding experience, a pre- and post-test of computational concepts, daily fieldnotes, images and short video recordings, and post-interviews with teachers. This mixed-methods approach created a more complete picture of the studies' results.

I hope to show, through these lessons learned, the social, cultural, and technological gaps that are present even in a highly networked, racially and culturally diverse, large Canadian city like Toronto. Presentation of the compiled cases is preceded by a brief overview of related literature on the exclusionary cultures of game making and play, and on game making and game playing as pathways to learning.

Global Reach, Local Impacts: Digital-Game-Based Learning

Much of the research—theoretical and empirical—on games for learning in classroom settings has focused on two themes: (a) *playing* games to develop subject-matter skills and/or competencies (see, for example, Annetta, Cheng, & Holmes, 2010; Corredor, Gaydos, & Squire, 2014; Divjak & Tomic, 2011; Muehrer, Jenson, Friedberg, & Husain, 2012; Salen, 2007; Yong, Gates, & Harrison, 2016), and (b) *creating* games to support, specifically, the acquisition of STEM-related competences, such as computational thinking (see, for example, Denner, Werner, & Ortiz, 2012; Jenson & Droumeva, 2016; Kafai & Peppler, 2012; Koh, Repenning, Nickerson, Endo, & Motter, 2013; Robertson, 2013; Salen, 2013). Play-focused research tends to employ games as a substitute for other media such as books or films in language or media curricula with the underlying assumption that the novel and interactive medium of games increases motivation and engagement. The games used in these studies are of two varieties: off-the-shelf triple-A titles or proprietary games developed for specific learning outcomes. However, both approaches have been troubled for a lack of scaffolding and assumptions that learning will occur simply through the act of play (see Young et al., 2012).

An example of using a commercial off-the-shelf game for subject-matter learning are studies that use games to bridge linguistic barriers, focused on the use of massively multiplayer online games (MMOGs) as environments that support second-language (L2) learning. A review of literature in the area by Nasser Jabbari and Zohreh Eslami (2019) argues that MMOGs are "low language anxiety" spaces that promote communication and socialization through the games' affordance. For example, an MMOG such as World of Warcraft (WoW) has opportunities for players to interact through text chat and/or via voice chat, and game play is supported by paratexts (WoW lore and background, forums, and fan fiction) and other resources such as game walkthroughs and live streaming of game play. The review concludes that "MMOGs encourage learners to get actively involved in L2 socialization and collaborative interactions with other PCs [player characters] to perform a variety of goal-oriented tasks within and beyond game contexts" (Jabbari & Eslami, 2019, p. 106). For the purposes of this chapter, the point is that WoW is being used in educational contexts globally—studies took place in Turkey (Alp & Patat, 2015), South Korea (Y. J. Lee & Gerber, 2013), Spain (Rama, Black, van Es, & Warschauer, 2012), and the United States (Newgarden, Zheng, & Liu, 2015), for example, and in a variety of languages—to support learning.

Digital Game Design

Game-making studies are largely rooted in constructionist principles that hands-on learning allows students to personally situate knowledge (Kafai & Burke, 2016) or make use of increasingly accessible game development tools as a means of introducing programming logic and paradigms (Denner, Campe, & Werner, 2019). Some studies have shown that programming games increase familiarity with computational concepts (Hsu & Wang, 2018; Kazimoglu, Kiernan, Bacon, & Mackinnon, 2012; T. K. Lee, Mauriello, Ahn, & Bederson, 2013; Leonard et al., 2016) and enhance problem-solving abilities as students learn to debug their code (Akcaoglu, 2014; Allsop, 2016; Hamlen, 2018).

Looked at in the context of international critique, global citizenship, and sustainability, however, there remain hurdles, very much predictable and by no means "rapidly changing," that are still not being addressed. For example, the push for coding, i.e., coming to understand computer programming functions and concepts (see Wing, 2006, for an exhaustive list), and STEAM-related competencies create a deficit model for women and other minorities in which they are always prepositioned as "lacking" the requisite skills (Jenson, Fisher, & de Castell, 2011; Lewis et al., 2017). Further, these programs tend to leave code-based curriculum abstracted—a longstanding critique of computer science education at all levels (Konecki, 2014)—and thus devoid of context, and, as Andrea diSessa (2018) argues, inducing an impoverished understanding of what constitutes

194 Jennifer Jenson

computational literacies today. In the next section, I take up the literature to date that persuasively demonstrates that game making and playing can be inhospitable spaces, for girls and women in particular.

Problematics with Game Making and Play Cultures

Games, whether students make or play them, can allow learners to "tap in" to a cultural form that has both global reach and local impacts. That said, the game industry and its surrounding player culture have long been exclusionary spaces for girls, women, and others on the margins. Heavy policing occurs around what constitutes a "real game" and "legitimate gamers," while the industry remains risk-, politics-, and diversity-adverse. One example of policing what makes a "real" gamer went viral on Twitter. In mid-August 2014, Twitter, Reddit, YouTube, gaming websites, and 4chan exploded with allegations of corruption in games journalism, naming the phenomenon "Gamergate" (see Twitter hashtag #Gamergate). At that time, nearly every major English news outlet and game-related journalistic website reported on "Gamergate" (Collins, 2014; Dockterman, 2014; Farokhmanesh, 2014). Women in all capacities within the games industry, including critics, game players, game makers, and journalists, were at the center of the controversy, and many received threats that, as games journalist David Auerbach (2014a, 2014b) put it, were "so egregious" that a prominent female journalist (Jenn Frank) publicly announced that she would no longer be writing on games.

This situation further escalated into a public threat of a "massacre," forcing games critic Anita Sarkeesian (Executive Director, Feminist Frequency) to cancel a public address (Farokhmanesh, 2014).[2] As caustic and hostile as game culture has become for women, exposed so publicly over the past decade (Jenson & de Castell, 2013), as the largest entertainment industry worldwide (Entertainment Software Association, 2018) it represents vital opportunities for economic growth, cultural participation, and future jobs.

However, the industry (and wider gamer culture) is perpetually awash in news of harassment of women and other marginalized people. In August 2019, attention was once again focused on sexual harassment and assaults that women in the industry have endured. First, Riot Games settled a class-action discrimination lawsuit filed by female employees who accused their employer of "endemic" gender-based discrimination and sexual harassment (Dean, 2019). Next, people in the industry bravely started sharing stories of the abuse they faced, primarily by men, on Twitter (Webster, 2019). Games industry professionals were outing not just sexual predators but emotionally abusive bosses as well: the outing of sexual harassment and the outing of labor violations were working hand in hand.

So why would we want to introduce this often toxic and certainly harassment-prone medium into schools and ask our students to play there? There are two primary reasons: (a) if videogames are the creative medium of the 21st century, then not understanding them or not being able to play them is a kind of illiteracy;

and (b) videogames and their surrounding industries and cultures are growing exponentially and opportunities for cultural and economic participation are also growing. For example, exceptional players can win scholarships to top US schools to play in a fast-growing collegiate e-sports league. Public education has always aimed to provide opportunities for learning that would not otherwise be available to children and youth, and the longitudinal research project I report on here strove for just that: to put game making and playing opportunities in the hands of those who might not already have those opportunities.

Takeaway 1: Notions of Progress are Incorrect

Over the nearly two decades that my colleagues and I have run game-play and game-design programs in under-resourced schools in the GTA, the one consistent finding across all contexts and studies is that girls (and young women) do not have the same access either to computers in general or game-play technologies more specifically, nor do they volunteer as often as boys (and young men) to participate in coding activities. For example, girls in our questionnaires and in face-to-face settings reported playing games less often than boys, if at all, and when they did report playing games it was often for one or more of three reasons: (a) there were no male siblings, and girls therefore played with their fathers; (b) an older brother or male cousin played, and girls watched them play or were sometimes handed the controller when their male relative left the room; and (c) their game play was regulated/overseen by their parents, and in contrast with their male siblings, "girl-appropriate" games like "pinkified" games about babysitting, horseback riding, and cooking or educational games about geography and math were purchased for them. When given the opportunity to play games, however, girls invariably "leveled up" and skilled up and, if they were able to play long enough, played very much like the boys.

To accomplish that upskilling, in both game-play and game-making sessions I constructed girls-only and boys-only groups. Part of the reason for this is that boys had prior experience playing games, and even if that experience was limited, they still acted as if they played games a lot. Another reason is that the boys, in part because they had prior experience playing, understood that they were the audience cultivated by game companies (as one 12-year-old boy participant put it, "they make the games for us, not for you [girls]"), and literally took up more space (they would move around more, take controllers out of girls' hands, talk during play, and generally act as if that space was exclusively theirs). To intervene in that male-dominated space and interrupt the hegemonic order of play, all-girls groups were necessary.

That is not to say we did not try mixed-gender groups over nearly two decades, but those invariably led to the very thing we were trying to avoid: boys and young men taking over, and girls and young women retreating. One example was a game-making project that involved three Grade 6 classes (65 students, with

196 Jennifer Jenson

integrated support for ESL students). All of the students were from immigrant families (South and Southeast Asia), some recently arrived, some having been in Canada between one and five years. The game-making project involved seven in-class sessions where students worked in pairs of their choosing (only two pairs across all three classes were mixed-sex) with near-peer mentors hired as research assistants to teach the sessions. The final session involved a full-day field trip to a nearby university where students mostly completed a workable game.

During the three full-class iterations of the game-making project, one thing that stood out was that when we asked questions on the fly, in nearly every case over the six weeks boys raised their hands to answer the question, even when they gave incorrect answers. The girls, on the other hand, seemed to prefer one-on-one, just-in-time help, and did not want the whole class to observe them being incorrect. The teacher who championed our research in the school, and who also oversaw the game-play sessions (voluntary, during lunch) one day remarked to me that she had noticed how differently one of the boys behaved when in the boys' group playing games in his free time, versus in class making games under much more supervision. In particular, she observed that in the boys' group he was less disruptive and more collaborative, while in the mixed-sex group he seemed to need to "show off." When we moved to single-gender groups in the same school the following year, the research assistant who had observed both years commented in a fieldnote at the beginning of the program:

> This surprised me it is so different. The behavioral issues with the boys are nearly gone, the girls speak more, if at a lower volume, and in the boys' group there is always a nice volume of chatter and interaction going on. Last year it seemed like all we did is try to get the girls to speak up and participate, but we don't have to do that this year.
>
> *(MA, January 17, 2017)*

In both configurations, both boys and girls improved their computational understanding and acquired vocabulary related to game-making and coding, and most made a playable game that they could share with their peers, teachers, and families. In most cases, the technological and coding abilities of the boys started at a higher point, especially if they participated in "hour of code" at the school or in after-school coding or robotics clubs. For many girls, our programming during class or lunch or after school represented their first try at making games or coding. In an increasingly algorithmically dominated world, where our social lives, our politics and political decisions, and even our personal choices are driven by algorithms created and deployed by big data advertising firms like Facebook and Google, it seems increasingly important that students have school-based opportunities to know and do with code. From an equity standpoint, this is especially important— even in a megacity like Toronto, technological know-how is unevenly distributed and girls especially are being left behind.

Takeaway 2: Games Can Disrupt Classroom Hierarchies

> Yeah, I think it was nice to see some of the special ed kids succeed and do well and become leaders, so that was nice. Like when we first played, one of the kids was walking around and helping the other kids out and providing advice and it was nice to see him be able to take that kind of leadership and feel good about himself because it was like an equalizer in terms of creating a more equal playing field than otherwise.
>
> —*Ivana,[3] Grade 6 Teacher*

Two examples are worth highlighting here to support this assertion. Rather than individual cases, they are composites of many individual encounters over many years of fieldnotes and observations. As composites, I hope they are recognizable not necessarily as a "universal" but as weightier cases, given their repetition. The first example that demonstrates how playing games can, literally, level the playing field is a learner who seems always to be referred to euphemistically as "That Kid" (TK)—someone who has a difficult time making it through the school day, is off task more than on, is often disruptive, and is often scolded or in trouble. These are the students who sometimes have learning difficulties, are on IEPs to help support their learning, and who can be isolated (behaviorally, socially, and emotionally) from their peers. TK is sometimes asked to sit off to the side or right next to the teacher's desk or is even moved outside the classroom context because they are too often interrupting the concentrated efforts of teachers and students.

When games are part of an integrated learning program, however, time and again we heard how "on task" TK is—how focused, engaged, excited, and able to participate in the classroom activities. Playing a digital game at times allowed TK to take the lead and show others how the game worked or how to move along in a level. Playing the game was also when teachers would come up to us in whispers to report that TK "hadn't sat still for 20 minutes the entire year" or "TK has rarely seemed so engaged" or "TK is thrilled to show off their skills" or "it is great that they finally get to share their expertise." In these cases, playing a game, even for a limited time, over a few days or a few weeks, gave TK the opportunity to participate in the classroom in ways they rarely were able to, and in that way acted as a legitimizing scaffold for them as well. Importantly, digital games were a bridge for these students, allowing them (and certainly not all of them, of course) to enter into the practices and discourses of the classroom meaningfully and differently than at other times.

The second example is the ELL. Ontario, and especially the schools I worked in most closely, is home to a diverse immigrant community, and therefore to many students who have little to no spoken or written English. Depending on school board policies, the ELL is integrated into regular classroom activities either part-time or full-time with additional supports provided. Because videogames are

198 Jennifer Jenson

multimodal and not primarily language-dependent, in the studies conducted, the ELL was integrated into all the research activities.

For the ELL (and not all of course), playing videogames had two outcomes: (a) it allowed them to take up the role of an "expert," a role not necessarily available to them otherwise; and (b) it scaffolded peer interaction and socialization that was centered around playing the game. Hence, the interaction was not necessarily about being correct or even being linguistically understood—the ELL could still be "in the game." Since games are a popular entertainment medium, the ELL would often have played them at home or at a friend's or cousin's house. That meant they already knew how to participate fully in game play, usually without support, sometimes taking on the role of the expert in the class and showing others how to move on in the game or strategizing with their peers on how to best move a character through a level. Teachers commented on the "equalizing" effect this had for some students (though, of course, for others, and often girls, DGBL could be a disadvantage). For other ELLs, playing a game with a peer meant that they were communicating and socializing in ways that they could not otherwise. The digital game acted as the intermediary object around which discussion and conversation could take place, and without necessarily invoking classroom discourse. Indeed, digital games have given rise to significant discourses, paratexts, and thriving, creative fan communities outside the classroom.

These two composites highlight ways that digital games can "level the playing field" for some students—and also show that not all students are "hailed" by game making or play. As a tool for differentiated instruction, digital games provide opportunities for participation by students who might not otherwise excel or even display the expertise they have. This should not be taken to suggest that games are a universal draw: they are decidedly not, especially for girls. But they can, with attentive pedagogical support, become a valuable resource for learning and engaging in the curriculum in a different medium.

Takeaway 3: Research Can (and Should) Have Surprising Impacts

> Nobody really did badly through the unit, everybody was pretty engaged, and there were no real surprises. I'd say over all they all enjoyed it, they liked it. The spec ed kids, it was an equalizer for them. It did allow them to kind of feel up to par and do well, so yeah it was good from that perspective.
>
> —*Tom, Grade 7 Teacher*

What is surprising about this statement is that it *should* be surprising that "over all" students were engaged and that things were "equalized." How often can we say that as teachers we have succeeded in reaching all if not most of our students during any given learning activity? That game playing and making can open up those opportunities for quite a large number of students (and as previously stated,

Playing and Making **199**

for many different types of learners, and especially boys) is and has been surprising for us.

The Ontario curriculum has no mandate at any level to teach students to code, nor does it have any kind of "computational civics" curriculum that would examine the impact of codes and algorithms on our everyday lives. Giving students the opportunity to engage with coding as an integrative part of making digital games entails, in addition to coding, creating their own artwork and sound for their games and, if narratively driven, their own stories. Game-making gave students the opportunity to participate in an activity that they could also pursue as a career in the real world, a connection that is not made as clearly when coding is abstracted and taught as a stand-alone piece.

Through the many game-making projects we ran with over 400 students in different locations in the GTA, there were two other outstanding and surprising impacts. First, game-making was not confined to the classroom or the school: it spilled into leisure time at home, becoming the subject of conversations with family, friends, and teachers. At the end of each game-making session, for example, when most students had made a complete and shareable game, we held a "game showcase" either in a local university space or at the school where the project took place. On these evenings, we set up the students' games, ordered pizza, provided snacks and drinks, and invited parents, guardians, siblings, and friends to come together and play the games that participants had made. Again and again, we heard from parents who said this was the "best thing their son or daughter had done all year" or that "we bought a laptop just to support their game making" or "they couldn't stop talking about the game they were making and would look up code online at home" or "this [program] changed my child's life." While that may come across as an exaggeration, we heard comments like that, unsolicited, at each and every event we held. The uptake by students and the support from the parents/guardians and the value they placed on the students' participation in the research were very much surprise outcomes of this work.

Second, these kinds of research projects are incredibly resource intensive. For example, because we decided to use Game Maker, which is game-making software that runs on PCs and is not free, it meant we had to bring in our own equipment. That also meant that we had to purchase and run our own internet network so students could use the computers, as they were not set up to access school board Wi-Fi. Next, to support just ten students in a club setting, it took at least two facilitators and a research assistant, and for a full class (of around 25–28 students), three or four facilitators, plus the classroom teacher and a researcher. Just to get ready for the games showcase at the end of many of the sessions, it took two people working for at least 15–20 hours just to prepare the laptops and games. Then there was scheduling, contingency plans in case of illness or snow days, team meetings, troubleshooting the curriculum, and meeting with supporting teachers. The labor intensity of doing this kind of research in schools is something that is rarely, if ever, written about. Couple that with the fact that working in schools

Takeaway 4: Digital and Other Divides

It shouldn't be that surprising that it takes so much support to carry out these projects in these superdiverse contexts, particularly when a "digital divide" persists, and not everyone has the technological skills that teachers, schools, policymakers, and the wider public assume they do. In fact, we observed that very few students, boys or girls, had technical skills that could be considered "advanced." Having basic skills meant almost all of them could call up a browser and search for information with some success and navigate around an operating system and access files and applications. They understood the basics of using word processing programs and presentation programs like Word, Google Docs, Google Slides, and PowerPoint. But we observed very few students who could use formulas in spreadsheets or who knew more advanced features of word processing or presentation programs. Nor did many indicate that they knew other software, though some had used the drag-and-drop game-making program "Scratch" and others had participated in "hour of code" activities during and after school. Crosscutting linguistic, social, and cultural diversity are chasms of inequity that remain unbridged by public schooling. Those inequities were most apparent in this project in relation to technological and programming skills, as that was our focus, but there are always already other divides—skill and gender divides, divides related to abilities and disabilities, linguistic and cultural divides, and social and political divides, and all of these are barriers to participation.

Conclusion: Re-Fusing Digital Divides

This collection of projects sought to level up local participating students and bring them into the global technocultures of game making and playing. It is not the case, at least in the schools that we were present in, that "superdiverse" students—by immigrant status, culturally, ethnically, linguistically, neurologically, and physically—are digitally savvy. On the contrary, such diversity calls for many more, and more diverse, opportunities to upskill when it comes to technology and coding, and a recognition that girls, more than boys, lack time and experience with 21st-century technologies, whether those are computer skills, game-playing skills, or coding skills. In our current, global, technologically and algorithmically saturated lives in North America, we do not expect to find a technological skill gap among school-aged children; and yet, again and again, we've documented the extent of this chasm that could, with reasonable time and resources, be bridged.

What is needed? Increasing resources for schools with superdiverse students—not just technological resources, but professional development for teachers so they

Playing and Making **201**

can also become more technologically savvy and support their students to do the same. Our work has shown that learning through making and playing games is an access point for moving from the local to the global. Many students who participated in these projects (and their parents) were able to connect to the larger cultures of game making and play, be that through YouTube tutorials, Let's Play videos, walkthroughs of games, and other surrounding paratexts including online fan communities and forums.

While this chapter has demonstrated ways in which an overarching program of research supported the acquisition of digital skills and competencies in inner-city contexts, it also concludes that there is a digital divide present for marginalized youth. For many of the students who participated in this study, those marginal identities are attributed to economic class, immigrant status, and gender. When I examine the findings in relation to the goals of this volume, it seems as though the hope that theories of cosmopolitanisms hold out for transforming the transnational spaces of schools in urban centers into global equalizers, as it were, are brought into question, as gender, ethnic, and racially nonconforming youths vie for access to scarce resources.

Re-fusing the "digital divide" means identifying and working to undo the multiple and intersecting oppressions that marginalized urban youth are subjected to. At the writing of this chapter, we are experiencing an unprecedented educational shift—the moving of K–12 and postsecondary education online during the global COVID-19 pandemic—which is revealing deep digital literacy divides at all levels of education, not to mention gaps in sheer physical access to technologies. And although public institutions and private corporations will continue to scramble to bridge those divides, many are being not just "left behind," but are being completely cut off from public education's inexorable online migration.

Notes

1 The ACM A.M. Turing award has a long history, some of it debated, but it remains a significant, collegially awarded accomplishment for what has become known as "the Nobel Prize in Computing." See Association for Computing Machinery (2019).
2 Using Montreal Massacre shooter Marc Lepine's name, as well as his words, the warning read "Feminists have ruined my life and I will have my revenge"—chilling reminders of the obstacles still very much in play for women.
3 All participant names have been changed. And while we quote a teacher here, and certainly they were important to this work, it is beyond the scope of this chapter to meaningfully integrate their voices.

References

Akcaoglu, M. (2014). Learning problem-solving through making games at the game design & learning summer program. *Education Technology Research and Development*, *62*(5), 583–600.

Allsop, Y. (2016). A reflective study into children's cognition when making computer plans. *British Journal of Educational Technology, 47*(4), 665–679.

Alp, P., & Patat, E. (2015). Gameplay in Italian: The impacts of World of Warcraft on second language learners in Turkey. *International Journal of Technologies in Learning, 22*(3), 1–9.

Annetta, L., Cheng, M., & Holmes, S. (2010). Assessing twenty-first century skills through a teacher created video game for high school biology students. *Research in Science & Technological Education, 28*(2), 101–114.

Association for Computing Machinery. (2019). *Pioneers of modern computer graphics recognized with ACM A.M. Turing Award.* Retrieved from https://amturing.acm.org/

Auerbach, D. (2014a, August 27). Letter to a young male gamer: Some ground rules to keep in mind in the wake of an ugly, sexist scandal. *Slate.* Retrieved from http://www.slate.com/articles/technology/bitwise/2014/08/zoe_quinn_harassment_a_letter_to_a_young_male_gamer.html

Auerbach, D. (2014b, October 7). Twitter is broken. *Slate.* Retrieved from http://www.slate.com/articles/technology/technology/2014/10/twitter_is_broken_gamergate_proves_it.html

Collins, S. T. (2014, October 17). Anita Sarkeesian on GamerGate: "We have a problem and we are going to fix this." *RollingStone.* Retrieved from https://www.rollingstone.com/politics/politics-news/anita-sarkeesian-on-gamergate-we-have-a-problem-and-were-going-to-fix-this-241766/

Corredor, J., Gaydos, M., & Squire, K. (2014). Seeing change in time: Video games to teach about temporal change in scientific phenomena. *Journal of Science Education and Technology, 23*(3), 324–343.

Creswell, J. W., & Plano Clark, V. L. (2011). *Designing and conducting mixed methods research* (2nd ed.). London, UK: SAGE.

Daley, M., & Child, J. (2015). Makerspaces in the school library environment. *Access, 29*(1), 42–49.

de Castell, S. (2016). The pedagogy of production: A media modules introduction [Video]. *New Media Modules.* Retrieved from https://vimeo.com/181978126

Dean, S. (2019, August 22). Riot Games settles class-action suit by female employees who alleged harassment and discrimination. *Los Angeles Times.* Retrieved from https://www.latimes.com/business/story/2019-08-22/riot-games-settles-class-action-suit-women-employees-harassment

Denner, J., Campe, S., & Werner, L. (2019). Does computer game design and programming benefit children? A meta-synthesis of research. *ACM Transactions on Computing Education, 19*(3), Article 19. doi: 10.1145/3277565

Denner, J., Werner, L., & Ortiz, E. (2012). Computer games created by middle school girls: Can they be used to measure understanding of computer science concepts? *Computers & Education, 58*, 240–249.

diSessa, A. A. (2000). *Changing minds: Computers, learning & literacy.* Cambridge, MA: MIT Press.

diSessa, A. A. (2018). Computational literacy and the "big picture" concerning computers in mathematics education. *Mathematical Thinking and Learning, 20*(1), 3–31.

Divjak, B., & Tomic, D. (2011). The impact of game-based learning on the achievement of learning goals and motivation for learning mathematics—Literature review. *Journal of Information and Organizational Sciences, 35*(1), 15–30.

Dockterman, E. (2014, October 16). What is #GamerGate and why are women being threatened about video games? *Time.* Retrieved from http://time.com/3510381/gamergate-faq/

Entertainment Software Association (ESA). (2018). *2018 essential facts about the computer and video game industry*. Retrieved from https://www.theesa.com/wp-content/uploads/2019/03/ESA_EssentialFacts_2018.pdf

Entertainment Software Association of Canada (ESAC). (2018). *Essential facts about the Canadian video game industry, 2018*. Retrieved from http://theesa.ca/wp-content/uploads/2018/10/ESAC18_BookletEN.pdf

Farokhmanesh, M. (2014, October 14). Utah State University threatened with school shooting over Sarkeesian appearance. *Polygon*. Retrieved from http://www.polygon.com/2014/10/14/6979071/utah-state-university-anita-sarkeesian-threats

Gee, J. P. (2003). *What video games have to teach us about learning and literacy*. New York: Palgrave Macmillan.

Grover, S., & Pea, R. (2013). Computational thinking in K–12: A review of the state of the field. *Educational Researcher, 42*(1), 38–43.

Hamlen, K. R. (2018). General problem-solving styles and problem-solving approaches in video games. *Journal of Educational Computing Research, 56*(4), 467–484.

Hsu, C.-C., & Wang, T.-I. (2018). Applying game mechanics and student generated questions to an online puzzle-based game learning system to promote algorithmic thinking skills. *Computers & Education, 121*, 73–88.

Hughes, J., Laffler, J., Mamolo, A., Morrison, L., & Petrarca, D. (2016). *Full STEAM ahead: Building preservice teacher's capacity in makerspace pedagogies*. Paper presented at the Higher Education in Transition Symposium, Oshawa, ON, Canada.

Jabbari, N., & Eslami, Z. R. (2019). Second language learning in the context of massively multiplayer online games: A scoping review. *ReCALL, 31*(1), 92–113.

Jenson, J., & de Castell, S. (2013). Tipping points: Marginality, misogyny and videogames. *Journal of Curriculum Theorizing, 29*(2). Retrieved from https://journal.jctonline.org/index.php/jct/article/view/474

Jenson, J., & Droumeva, M. (2016). Exploring media literacy and computational thinking: A game maker curriculum study. *Electronic Journal of e-Learning, 15*(2), 111–121. Retrieved from http://www.ejel.org

Jenson, J., Fisher, S., & de Castell, S. (2011). Disrupting the gender order: Leveling up and claiming space in an after-school video game club. *International Journal of Gender, Science & Technology, 3*(1), 148–169. Retrieved from http://genderandset.open.ac.uk/index.php/genderandset/article/view/129

Kafai, Y. B., & Burke, Q. (2015). Constructionist gaming: Understanding the benefits of making games for learning. *Educational Psychologist, 50*, 313–334. doi: 10.1080/00461520.2015.1124022.

Kafai, Y. B., & Burke, Q. (2016). *What making video games can teach us about learning and literacy*. Cambridge, MA: MIT Press.

Kafai, Y. B., Fields, D., & Searle, K. (2014). Electronic textiles as disruptive designs: Supporting and challenging maker activities in schools. *Harvard Educational Review, 84*(4), 532–556.

Kafai, Y. B., & Peppler, K. A. (2012). Developing gaming fluencies with Scratch: Realizing game design as an artistic process. In C. Steinkuehler, K. Squire, & S. Barab (Eds.), *Games, learning, and society: Learning and meaning in the digital age* (pp. 355–380). New York: Cambridge University Press.

Kay, A., & Goldberg, A. (1977, March). Personal dynamic media. *Computer, 10*(3), 31–41. doi: 10.1109/CM.1977.217672

Kazimoglu, C., Kiernan, M., Bacon, L., & Mackinnon, L. (2012). A serious game for developing computational thinking and learning introductory computer programming. *Procedia—Social and Behavioral Sciences, 47*, 1991–1999.

Koh, A., Repenning, A., Nickerson, H., Endo, Y., & Motter, P. (2013). Will it stick? Exploring the sustainability of computational thinking education through game design. In *Proceedings of the 44th ACM Technical Symposium on Computer Science Education* (pp. 597–602). New York: Association for Computing Machinery.

Konecki, M. (2014). Problems in programming education and means of their improvement. In B. Katalinic (Ed.), *DAAAM international scientific book 2014* (pp. 459–470). Vienna, Austria: DAAAM International.

Lee, T. K., Mauriello, M. L., Ahn, J., & Bederson, B. B. (2013). CTArcade: Computational thinking with games in school age children. *International Journal of Child-Computer Interaction, 2*(1), 26–33.

Lee, Y. J., & Gerber, H. (2013). It's a WoW world: Second language acquisition and massively multiplayer online gaming. *Multimedia-Assisted Language Learning, 16*(2), 53–70.

Leonard, J., Buss, A., Gamboa, R., Mitchell, M., Fashloa, O. S., Hubert, T., & Almughyirah, S. (2016). Using robotics and game design to enhance children's self-efficacy, STEM attitudes, and computational thinking skills. *Journal of Science Education and Technology, 25*, 860–876.

Lewis, K. L., Stout, J. G., Finkelstein, N. D., Pollock, S. J., Miyake, A., Cohen, G. L., & Ito, T. A. (2017). Fitting in to move forward: Belonging, gender and persistence in the physical sciences, technology, engineering and mathematics (pSTEM). *Psychology of Women Quarterly, 41*(4), 420–436.

Linderoth, J. (2012). Why gamers don't learn more: An ecological approach to games as learning. *Journal of Gaming and Virtual Worlds, 4*(1), 45–62.

Muehrer, R., Jenson, J., Friedberg, J., & Husain, N. (2012). Challenges and opportunities: Using a science-based video game in secondary school settings. *Cultural Studies of Science Education, 7*(4), 783–805. Retrieved from http://link.springer.com/10.1007/s1 1422-012-9409-z

National Science Foundation. (2011). *Women, minorities, and persons with disabilities in science and engineering 2011.* Arlington, VA: Author.

Newgarden, K., Zheng, D., & Liu, M. (2015). An eco-dialogical study of second language learners' World of Warcraft (WoW) gameplay. *Language Sciences, 48*, 22–41. doi: 10.1016/j.langsci.2014.10.004

Papert, S. (1980). *Mindstorms: Children, computers, and powerful ideas.* New York: Basic Books.

Perlis, A. J. (1964). The computer and the university. In M. Greenberger (Ed.), *Computers and the world of the future.* Cambridge, MA: MIT Press.

Prensky, M. (2006). *Don't bother me mom. I'm learning!* St Paul, MN: Paragon House.

Rama, P. S., Black, R. W., van Es, E., & Warschauer, M. (2012). Affordances for second language learning in World of Warcraft. *ReCALL, 24*(3), 322–338. doi: 10.1017/ S0958344012000171

Robertson, J. (2013). The influence of a game making project on male and female learners' attitudes to computing. *Computer Science Education, 23*, 58–83.

Salen, K. (Ed.). (2007). *The ecology of video games: Connecting youth, games and learning.* Cambridge, MA: MIT Press.

Salen, K. (2013, March). *Agile development meets evidence-centered design: Glasslab and the design of game-based assessments.* Paper presented at the Digital Media & Learning Conference, Chicago, IL.

Tobias, S., & Fletcher, D. (2012). Learning from computer games: A research review. In S. De Wannemacker, S. Vandercruysse, & G. Clarebout (Eds.), *Serious games: The challenge* (pp. 6–17). Berlin, Germany: Springer.

Webster, A. (2019, August 27). Several high-profile game developers publicly accused of sexual assault. *The Verge*. Retrieved from https://www.theverge.com/2019/8/27/20835249/game-developers-sexual-assault-publicly-accused-allegations-metoo

Wing, J. M. (2006). Computational thinking. *Communications of the ACM*, *49*(3), 33–35. doi: 10.1145/1118178.1118215

Wing, J. M. (2011). Research notebook: Computational thinking—what and why? *Link*. Retrieved from https://www.cs.cmu.edu/link/research-notebook-computational-thinking-what-and-why

Yong, S. T., Gates, P., & Harrison, I. (2016). Digital games and learning mathematics: Student, teacher and parent perspectives. *International Journal of Serious Games*, *3*(4), 55–68.

Young, M. F., Slota, S. T., Cutter, A., & Jaletter, G. C. (2012). Our princess is in another castle: A review of trends in serious gaming for education. *Review of Educational Research*, *82*(1), 61–89. doi: 10.3102/0034654312436980

PART 4

Challenges for Cosmopolitan Education

13
STUDENTS' INTERCULTURAL EXPERIENCES IN AN INTERNATIONALIZING UNIVERSITY IN CHINA

A Critical Discursive Perspective

Yang Song and Angel M. Y. Lin

Cultivating global citizenship with the cosmopolitan vision has become one of the leading agendas of the internationalization of higher education (IHE) (Streitwieser & Light, 2018). The cosmopolitan vision, commonly enlisted and celebrated in university policies, leads to the institutional desire to foster intercultural awareness and competence among international and local students with diverse sociocultural backgrounds. Nevertheless, recent studies on critical cosmopolitanism and decolonial perspectives on IHE have called for critically examining the rosy depiction of cosmopolitanism by drawing explicit attention to intersectional inequalities across social, economic, political, and racial factors (Mignolo, 2010). The present chapter is aimed at contributing to critical studies on the students' lived experiences of interculturality and their effects on the cultivation of cosmopolitan mindsets in China.

According to the Institute of International Education (2018), the total number of inbound international students in China has reached 489,200 in 2018, ranking China the first destination in Asia and the third in the world for international students. Recent studies have identified the future career prospects promised by the rapid growth of the Chinese economy together with the abundance of scholarship opportunities as a major driver for the increase in the number of international students in China (Jiani, 2017; Ma & Zhao, 2018; Yang, 2014). The efforts to attract international students by the Chinese government and universities are partly aimed at fulfilling the diplomatic mission of cultivating "international personnel who are well-versed in Chinese and friendly towards China" (Tian & Lu, 2018, p. 59) and partly oriented toward creating world-class, internationalized universities in China (J. Song, 2018). As a major strategy of internationalization, Chinese universities have increasingly launched English-medium-instruction

DOI: 10.4324/9780429327780-13

(EMI) master's degree programs to attract international students, while the dominant medium of instruction on campus is Chinese. Nevertheless, it remains largely unknown how international and home students perceive and understand their intercultural experiences, particularly in international EMI degree programs in internationalizing Chinese universities (Kuroda, 2014).

Intercultural communication among international and home students is a desired and yet hard-to-achieve outcome. The recent studies in the field are aimed at addressing the interplay among the macro, meso, and micro dimensions of IHE as relevant to students' intercultural relationships (Kudo, Volet, & Whitsed, 2019). Kudo, Volet, and Whitsed (2019) identified three major limitations of previous empirical studies on students' intercultural experiences in the IHE context, including "a vague or loose operationalization of key concepts (e.g., intercultural interactions, contact, relations, relationship, friendship)," "the dominance of studies with a narrow focus on the individual," and a lack of attention to "intercultural relationship development ... located in a particular environment" (p. 101). Within the field of intercultural communication and discourse analysis, recent studies (Collins, 2018; Kudo, 2016) have examined how the notions of *culture*, *intercultural*, and *international* have been mobilized in institutional policies and perceived by academic staff and students in the UK and Japan. Their analysis highlighted the persistent paradigmatic tension between the essentialist view of nation-bound cultural stereotypes and the dynamic, hybrid, and performative view of intercultural student identity formation at the interface between the institutional (in particular, the neoliberal university system) and interpersonal dimensions that are involved in shaping students' intercultural experiences.

Relevant research on IHE in China has examined the historical evolution of policies and rationales concerning the reception of international students (Haugen, 2013; Ma & Zhao, 2018) and international students' studying and living experiences in internationalizing universities in China. While they shared a similar implication that intercultural communication between international and home students should be fostered through both formal and informal curricula, there are two major research limitations: (a) a definition of *intercultural* and *cross-cultural* in the existing literature that hinges predominantly on a nation-bound conception of culture; and (b) a lack of attention to the interface between the institutional and the interpersonal dimensions where relevant policies, curricula, and students' agency co-work in shaping their intercultural experiences.

This chapter reports on an ethnographic study of how *intercultural* and *culture* have been discursively constructed by institutional discourses of varied kinds as well as by international and home students co-enrolled in a top-rated internationalizing comprehensive university in Shanghai. It also examines the implications of this construction for intercultural education and IHE policy-making. The notion of *discourse* in "discursive construction" here shares Gee's (2012) conception of Discourses (big *D*) as referring to "ways of behaving, interacting, valuing, thinking, believing, speaking, and often reading and writing, that are accepted

Student Experiences in China **211**

as instantiations of particular identities by specific groups" (Gee, 2012, p. 3). The notion of *intercultural* is used to highlight empirical emphasis on the lived-experience dimension of culture-related encounters that involve the enactment, hybridization, conflict, and negotiations among multiple discourses concerning culture at multiple dimensions and sites of investigation.

(Neo-)Essentialist Cultural Dichotomies, Othering, and Critical Cosmopolitanism

The present study draws on the three key theoretical concepts in the field of intercultural communication—(neo-)essentialist cultural dichotomies, othering, and critical cosmopolitanism—to analyze different discourses on culture and intercultural experiences. Essentialism refers to assigning generalized, stereotypical attributes to (imagined) cultural communities while ignoring their internal diversity. In the depiction of intercultural encounters, the essentialist discourse tends to use binary oppositions to establish cultural dichotomies based on stereotypical attributes (e.g., collectivism vs. individualism, patriarchy vs. gender egalitarianism) to establish moral hierarchies between different cultural groups (e.g., inferior vs. superior). Although opposing the hierarchical moral judgments built into essentialism, neo-essentialism maintains the emphasis on cultural stereotyping of seemingly stable, clear-cut social groups with reference to nationality, ethnicity, and racial backgrounds. Neo-essentialism regards the relevant cultural descriptions as ideology-free and equally appreciable. Holliday (2011) argues that neo-essentialism is a simplistic hybrid that combines the liberal intention to pursue fairness and diversity among different cultural communities with the chauvinist momentum of essentialism that turns a blind eye to the diversity within a cultural community.

The cultural dichotomies entail a politics of difference indispensable for boundary-setting between the self and the other (Dervin, 2016, p. 46). Deeply rooted in Orientalism, the dominating Western *self* defines itself by positioning the East as the culturally inferior other on the basis of morally hierarchical, essentialized cultural dichotomies, such as civilized vs. barbarian and industrialized vs. agricultural (Said, 1978). Postcolonial studies generally define othering as "the process of representing an individual or a social group TO RENDER THEM distant, alien or deviant" (emphasis in original) (Coupland, 1999, p. 5). Researchers have analyzed processes of othering at the conjuncture where "multiple axes of differentiation—economic, political, cultural, psychic, subjective and experiential—intersect in historically specific contexts" (Dhamoon, 2010, p. 61). A multisectional analysis can help reveal the constructed nature of cultural dichotomies together with the underlying power relations and relevant sociohistorical mechanisms (Bakhtin, 1982; Dhamoon, 2010; Fairclough, 1992).

Critical cosmopolitanism defines culture as experience-based, emergent, and socially constituted, while also shaped by unequal power relations in the era of globalization. Delanty (2006, p. 35) posits that "cosmopolitan culture is one of self-problematization and while diversity will, by the pluralizing nature of cosmopolitanism, be inevitable the reflexive and critical self-understanding of cosmopolitanism cannot be neglected." This resonates with Beck and Sznaider's (2010) conception of divergent modernity by rejecting a single Western model of modernity and attending to a diversity of (emergent) forms of modernity in response to globalization around the world. At the level of interpersonal encounters, a critical cosmopolitan mindset features (a) openness toward and care about global others, (b) critical, self-reflexive inquiry about one's own epistemic assumptions and the development of epistemic virtues that help understand and appreciate divergent cultural experiences, and (c) constant exploration and imagination about alternative discourses when articulating those experiences (Appiah, 2005; Hannerz, 2009; Hawkins, 2018).

Research Context and Methodology

The data collected investigated the intercultural experiences of students enrolled in EMI degree programs in a top-rated comprehensive university in Shanghai. As one of the first universities to receive international students in China, the university has over 2100 full-time international degree students, according to 2020 university statistics. According to the International Students Office brochure for 2020 student admission, the university has 24 two-year EMI master's degree programs and 14 four-year doctoral degree programs. One-fifth of the international EMI master's degree programs admit both home and international students (referred to as "mixed programs" below), whereas the majority of EMI degree programs in Chinese universities are exclusive to international students (Kuroda, 2014). With a specific focus on intercultural experiences, the present study further sampled seven out of the 24 EMI programs, which are all from the Department of Political Sciences and whose curricula overlap substantially.

A multidimensional, multisite approach was used for data collection (Saarinen, 2017). Written and multimodal sources include (a) national and institutional regulations on international student admissions and management, (b) the institutional promotional video for international student admissions, and (c) curricula and syllabi for sampled EMI master's degree programs.

Student interviews were combined with classroom observation in order to understand intercultural communication enacted in both formal and informal curricula. From September 2017 to June 2018, the first author conducted ethnographic observation and took fieldnotes in four of the disciplinary courses (two courses for each semester with a total of 68 international and Chinese students). Interviews were conducted with both Chinese and international students, with interviewees selected on the basis of maximum diversity of students' nationality, educational background, program subtype, and year of study.

Two rounds of semi-structured interviews were conducted with a total of 23 student informants during the period of classroom observation. The interview data were audio-recorded with consent from the students and transcribed by the author. All the interviews with international students were conducted in English while those with Chinese students were in Chinese.

Inductive coding was used to identify emerging themes in transcribed interviews and written and audio-visual sources (Strauss & Corbin, 2005). The coding process is recursive and generative as different types of data were juxtaposed to reveal the intertextual relations among a diversity of discourses and construct students' intercultural experiences in multiple dimensions (i.e., national, municipal, institutional, and interpersonal). Intertextuality refers to processes where texts "draw upon and transform other contemporary and historically prior texts" (Fairclough, 1992, pp. 39–40). Categories and themes were abstracted from the coded data with reference to existing literature while being facilitated by the three theoretical concepts introduced previously, including (a) three types of (cultural) dichotomies shaped by multiple discourses at the institutional level, (b) students' interpersonal othering based on varied sociocultural and linguistic factors, and (c) students' self-cultivated critical cosmopolitan mindset.

The Discursive Construction of the Intercultural Experience

Cultural Dichotomies Constructed in Institutional Promotional Discourses

In March 2018, the International Students Office released a promotional video, aiming at attracting international students to study at the university. With five international students studying at the university as first-person narrators, the promotional video takes the city of Shanghai as a salient selling point (see excerpt below). The image of Shanghai comprises three cultural dichotomies. The first is the Western vs. the traditional. Corresponding to S1's account, Shanghai as a very "Western" city is illustrated by the Western-style buildings of the semicolonial era in the early 20th century along the Bund on the Huangpu River. Meanwhile, Shanghai's Chinese heritage is anchored in visual shots of a locally well-known Buddhist temple and the traditional heritage tourism area known as Yuyuan Garden. In S3's account, the stereotypical female image of a Chinese lady features a paper-oil umbrella, a traditional Chinese-style fan, and a Chinese silk gown and/or scarf.

Promotional video transcript excerpt:

S1: I was so surprised that a city can be so **Western [visual cue: the Bund]**, and at the same time hold so much of **the Chinese heritage [visual cue: Yuyuan Garden and Jing'an Temple]**. Shanghai works **cashless**, so everyone **pays on WeChat or on Alipay. [visual cue: the student talking to the camera]**

S2: When I first came up here, I heard about **the four inventions of China [visual cue: the student talking to the camera]**. But these like the four

new inventions. Just the other day I was riding **my Ofo bike,** which is **a public used bike.** And I was using my headphones that I got from Taobao. **[visual cue: actuality footage of S2 bicycle riding on campus]** And when I got to ★★★ [a shopping center], I used my phone to pay for some hotpot. I love hotpot. **[visual cue: the student talking to the camera]**
S3: When my girlfriend is here, I'm gonna spoil her with all those presents to **decorate her into a proper Chinese lady, like umbrella, with the fan, and silk scarf on her neck. [visual cue: the student talking to the camera]**

The interview footage with S1 and S3 resonates with the city-branding discourse of the Shanghai municipal government. To make Shanghai a global city like New York and London, the local government stressed its cultural capital as grounded on its historical heritage of being a major cosmopolitan city in the 1920s. The imperialist history has been depoliticized and reinvented as "Shanghai nostalgia" for its prosperity in an era when "Eastern and Western influences merge [中西合璧]" (Pan, 2005). The aspects that have been handpicked by urban planners, historians, and architects include: (a) the Bund, where foreign banks established in the 1920s line one side of the Huangpu River while its opposite side is a forest of skyscrapers symbolic of modernized Shanghai after the Reform and Opening Up in 1978; (b) the lilong (local residential alleys together with schools, churches/temples, and factories, which serve as a full-fledged community of residence); and (c) Jiangnan culture (江南文化) as represented by the historically documented and contemporarily appropriated lifestyle of ancient literati living in the Jiangnan region (i.e., Jiangsu Province and Zhejiang Province adjacent to Shanghai). As part of the branding of Jiangnan culture, the typical image of a lady born and raised in the Jiangnan region is normalized into the one described by S3 in the video transcript excerpt.

The second cultural dichotomy is the international vs. the local. In S2's account, the trademark of Shanghai's modernized lifestyle is the "four new great inventions." Yet in the student interview, S2 said that in referring to these inventions he was quoting a report in *People's Daily*, the official newspaper of the central government of China, that referred to dockless shared bicycles, high-speed rail, Alipay, and e-commerce as "the four great new inventions" (Xinhua, 2017). The fact that he was quoting a newspaper report was edited out in the final version of the promotional video. When asked about whether he agrees with the newspaper report, S2 replied, "I wouldn't say they are Chinese inventions. I would say they are so ingrained in everyday life. I think they are like a Chinese version of international inventions." Instead of characterizing the technology-saturated urban lifestyle as a nation-state model unique to China, S2 asserted a critical cosmopolitan stance that highlights the modernized way of life in cities as an inherent aspect of globalization and allows for variations in form and degree in local manifestations of modernization.

In the very few instances of co-organized activities among international and home students, the cultural dichotomies of Chinese vs. non-Chinese and East vs.

FIGURE 13.1 Snapshot of a promotional board for a talent competition on campus.

West were adopted as major rhetorical resources to frame intercultural student activities. During the International Cultural Festival, international student representatives from each country other than China shared nation-bound cultures typified by food, artifacts, and popular culture in temporary stalls arranged in an outdoor space on campus. Another major intercultural activity is the annual talent contest for both Chinese and international students. A large promotional board was erected on campus on December 26, 2017 (see Figure 13.1). The poster is divided into two parts by color and language. The English title of the event refers to "international" students as "foreign students," corresponding to "外" in the Chinese title and implicitly setting a conceptual division between the insider and the outsider based on national boundaries. The division is further complicated by the symbolic integration between the West and the East signaled by the acronym *WE* at the center of the promotional board. Nevertheless, in contrast with the symbolic integration, the actual talent contest was operationalized in two independent subcontests, one for home students and one for international students.

Cultural Dichotomies Embedded in the Formal Curricula

Cultural dichotomies were also embedded in the formal curriculum design and enactment of the international EMI master's degree programs under study.

Among the four disciplinary courses under observation, the two courses that focus respectively on comparative Asian politics and Chinese government policies have embedded cross-cultural comparison as one approach to political research. The basis of the culture-based comparison is the dichotomy between Confucian Heritage/Asian and Western cultures. For instance, the course on Chinese government policies seeks to explain why China resorted to incremental economic reform, while the Soviet Union resorted to comprehensive methods. In addition to comparative analysis that addresses historical contingencies and sociopolitical specificities, the instructor uses a pictograph by Yang Liu, a Chinese artist and visual designer living in Germany, which compares Eastern and Western cultures. Two international students in the after-class discussion called into question the essentialist comparison between Eastern and Western cultures by asking whether it is appropriate to categorize the Soviet Union as a representative of Western countries and whether incremental reform is exclusive to China's economic reform as determined by nation-bound cultural differences. In comparison, a more dynamic and fluid stance toward culture could be found in an elective course on cross-cultural communication in the curriculum, where in-group diversity and multifactor (e.g., economic, social-class, and ethnic backgrounds) analysis have been stressed in both course content and in-class discussion.

Cultural Dichotomies Reinforced by Institutional Student Management

The most salient construction of the local/international dichotomy by institutional management has been the segregation between international and home student dormitories. Not unlike other universities in China, the international dormitory occupies a specialized area segregated from dormitory buildings for Chinese students. The international dormitory is equipped with single dorm rooms and individual bathroom facilities, whereas four to six Chinese students commonly share a standard dormitory room.

The segregation between international and home student dormitories together with the inequality in dormitory resource allocation per student is historically tied to and influenced by the diplomatic agenda behind the reception of international students since the 1950s. As part of the national agenda of modernization and strengthening alliances with Third World countries in Asia, Latin America, and Africa, international students were received at that time in accordance with similar standards for foreign delegations and experts regarding dining and residential arrangements (Yang, 2018).

The segregated dormitory arrangements have reinforced the institutional positioning of international students as exclusive experiencers of Chinese culture and/or learners about China as framed by cultural activities and a lecture series entitled "Feel and know China [感知中国]" organized by the International Students Office. Cultural activities include dumpling making, dragon-boat races, knowledge contests on ancient Chinese civilization, traditional Chinese craft workshops on paper cutting and pottery, and historical heritage tourist excursions in and around Shanghai. Those cultural activities resonate with the dominant discourse in Chinese culture textbooks for international students studying in China that tend to fix Chinese culture as ritualistic in practice and historically remote from the modern way of life. W. Qu (2013, p. 151) has argued that such framing of Chinese culture is self-imposed othering, as if the only way for Chinese people to exert a legitimate cultural identity is "to trace [the] way to the time of a hypothetical virginity" without being able to "tolerate at all the evidence of foreignness."

On the other hand, the lecture series on China is co-organized with a research institute specializing in China studies at the university and is aimed at introducing "China Discourse" with regard to the political and social systems of contemporary China. "China Discourse" is a political term that came into being after the Third Plenary Session of the 18th Central Committee of the Communist Party of China in 2013. The emphasis on the international discourse system later turned into a major national agenda to develop and publicize governmental discourse on China, including China Practices, China Paths, China Stories, Chinese Voices, and China Discourse [中国实践、中国道路、中国故事、中国声音、中国话语]. Han (2014) has pointed out that the fundamental objective of developing the China Discourse system is to address the ideological conflicts and tensions between socialism with Chinese characteristics and Western neoliberalism and to counter Western discursive hegemony in the era of globalization (pp. 47–48). Hence, it is hard to ignore the West–East ideological dichotomy built into the national policy underlying the lecture series.

To sum up, the institutional discourse on intercultural experiences for international students involves intertwined dichotomies, including local vs. international, East/China vs. West, us vs. them, traditional vs. modern, and one-sided experiencers vs. two-way communicators. Those dichotomous discourses are constructed through multiple means and presented in multiple forms and yet risk shaping and reinforcing othering in intercultural communication among university students on campus.

Multisectional Interpersonal Othering

Politico-ideological Othering

The most prominent type of interpersonal othering reported by Chinese student informants is related to the perceived evaluation of China's politico-ideological status by international students, particularly those from North America and Europe. Dan is a Chinese student who actively engages in in-class discussions with international students of varied backgrounds. When asked about whether he also interacted with international students after class, Dan said:

218 Yang Song and Angel M. Y. Lin

> Almost never. To be frank, Chinese students directly admitted into our EMI Master's programs are outstanding on average. They [the international students] went through simple procedures of application and got admitted without meeting similar high academic standards. I understand that's because our university wants to increase its level of internationalization … But when they came here, they made me feel that "we arrived at China, a developing country, a place where access to the internet is restricted. We who came from the free world will show you how we live, what our world looks like, you know?" That's the impression they gave me … Such a sense of privilege is ingrained.

As explicated by Dan, the diplomatic strategy of internationalization typified by well-equipped dormitories, abundant scholarships for international students, and relatively low criteria for admission creates a structural inequality on top of individual students' perceived hierarchy among countries with politico-economic-ideological differences (e.g., the developed vs. the developing, the Western democratic vs. the Eastern socialist).

Linguistic/Academic Othering

The cultural politics of English as an international language also serves as a catalyst of othering among Chinese and international students. Joseph, a student from Thailand, talked about how the perception of (academic) English proficiency hinders his interaction with his Chinese classmates:

> They speak good English and they go abroad very often. I don't know, they are more eager to get Western friends than Asian friends. They seem to want to improve English and talk to mother-tongue English speakers. I don't know, if I talk about Thailand in Shanghai, they will think about TV drama and tourism. Just that.

Joseph's comment enacts a self-perceived linguistic hierarchy that positions native English speakers at the very top, Chinese and other students who are proficient nonnative English speakers in the middle, and those who are less proficient nonnative English speakers at the bottom. Although Joseph's perception is not borne out by the fact that the majority of Chinese students rarely interact with international students in general outside the classroom, his comment highlights the privileged role of the English language as valued symbolic capital in the local job market and the craze for English language learning among students of all levels in Shanghai (Y. Song, 2019).

The linguistic othering is further complicated by the stereotypical impression of Thailand mentioned by the Chinese student he talked to. Although the national stereotype itself would not directly result in interpersonal othering, the underlying inequality of politico-economic status between Thailand and China has intermingled with the self-perceived hierarchy based on English-language proficiency. Being self-positioned at the lower end of the scale deters Joseph from taking initiatives to interact more with his Chinese classmates.

Experiential Othering

Experiential othering hinges on lifestyle differences, identified by both Chinese and international student informants as a global phenomenon, as put by David:

> International students have their own "bubble." It happens everywhere. If you share more cultural commonality, you will naturally form a clique very quickly … And the structure does not encourage such interaction [between international and local Chinese students]. It's not organic. You have to pursue it yourself. We differ in terms of lifestyle and teaching style.

According to accounts of both international and Chinese student informants, the "international" lifestyle features clubbing and partying, sports, and food preferences commonly shared among those from Europe and North and Latin America, whereas most Chinese and other Asian student informants are more inclined to socialize in cafés and libraries. The gentrified area around the campus and the places frequented by non-Chinese-speaking expatriates around the former French Concession and the Bund in Shanghai have enabled those international students who are not highly motivated to interact with local people to sustain an English-mediated lifestyle in line with cosmopolitan aesthetic and consumption tastes not unlike those in other metropolitan cities around the world.

Self-Cultivated Orientation Toward Critical Cosmopolitanism

Despite the multisectional othering analyzed previously, some international students have developed a cosmopolitan mindset as manifested in reflexive articulation about intercultural differences. Daniel has spent one year studying Chinese in another top-tier comprehensive university in Shanghai before joining the EMI master's program on comparative Chinese politics. When asked about his intercultural experiences in China, he stressed that even though he did not have much interaction with Chinese students, he was exposed to China by living and studying in Shanghai and refrained from a quick judgment based on a fixed set of rules from his hometown in the United States on what everyday life should look like:

> I think a lot of issues here are just people applying their own country's or their hometown's set of rules onto a completely new place. They think these rules are the right rules because these are the only rules they've ever

experienced. I think the very simple example is the traffic rules. It's very different here from where I came from in the US Maybe I would have expected people to stop and let people go before turning right, but now I would just stop and let them turn right. It's just adjusting to a new set of rules . . . It's not wrong but it's just different.

Daniel's comment shows "an openness toward divergent cultural experiences, a search for contrasts rather than uniformity, but not simply as a matter of appreciation" (Hannerz, 2009, p. 70). Venturing beyond aesthetic or conceptual appreciation of diversity in societal norms, his reflexive articulation on differences in traffic rules between his hometown and Shanghai is grounded on embodied everyday practice that he consciously socialized himself into.

Qiping is one of the Chinese students who actively interact with both international students and teaching and research fellows at the university. When asked about why he would like to interact with international students, he answered:

They [international students] brought us some new visions of life. Like in China, most people need to complete certain missions at certain ages, such as when to find a job, to buy an apartment, to get married, and to have children. To enter the university and successfully graduate is to pave your way for completing those missions. If you do not follow the expected trajectory, your life seems to be a disaster. With my Chinese classmates, they often talk about doing [an] internship in leading enterprises or getting job offers with high payment. I'm not interested in that. International students showed me alternative ways of life and eased my anxiety about being "different."

While Daniel and Qiping align with the cultural orientation of cosmopolitanism, David from the United States regards self-cultivation of knowledge on cultural diversity and adaptation to the local way of life in Shanghai as "symbolic capital in competitive elite games of distinction" (Hannerz, 2009, p. 74). When asked about why he is so committed to learning the Chinese language and interacting with Chinese students, he answered, "That's how I distinguish myself. That's how I create value for myself. That's how I can be successful economically, culturally and socially." The cosmopolitan orientation motivates David to actively organize entrepreneurial experience-sharing events as a member of the Postgraduate International Student Association at the university to establish social networks with Chinese and international elites in Shanghai. Having learned Chinese for half a year at Peking University as an undergraduate exchange student, David also maintained a close relationship with his alma mater in Beijing in preparation for his prospective career development in China after graduation.

Conclusion

As we have shown, the institutional discourses on students' intercultural experiences are structured by multiple pairs of (neo-)essentialist cultural dichotomies rather than critical, interpretive conceptions of culture. Distinct from concerns about the alignment of institutional discourses on intercultural communication with neoliberal discourse in previous studies situated in universities in English-speaking countries (Collins, 2018), the institutional discourses on culture and intercultural communication at the university under study resonate intertextually with a range of national and municipal discourses specific to IHE in China. In the present case, the national agenda of strengthening China's soft power together with the institution-level centralized model of international student management have partly supported the adoption of discourses of cultural dichotomy to structure students' intercultural experiences (Ma & Zhao, 2018; Yang, 2014). Nevertheless, there is some evidence in the present study that a few student informants have cultivated critical cosmopolitan ideas and practices, though the institutional curricula have not provided them with sufficient structural support. The analysis echoes with previous studies on transnational students' agency that acknowledge students' agentive roles in negotiating and contesting institutional and curricular constraints or norms to develop and construct intercultural domains of self-transformation (Marginson, 2014; M. Qu, 2018).

The multidimensional, ethnographic perspective on students' intercultural experiences as highlighted by Kudo et al. (2019) provides an insightful lens for examining "the temporally and spatially fluctuating networked contacts between different actors (human or institutional), and the dynamics between those contacts" (Saarinen, 2017, p. 556). In the present study, the institutional discourses on intercultural communication have been mediated by and distributed through: (a) multisite, multisemiotic resources in the form of student promotional videos, online/offline linguistic landscapes for extracurricular student activities, and written and enacted formal curricular; and (b) infrastructural design and allocation for both student residences and teaching venues as influenced by discrepancies between old and new regulations on international student management. These multisectional factors are in turn intertwined with politico-ideological, linguistic-academic, and experiential factors, which hinder the formation and enactment of cosmopolitan mindsets. The coexistence of oppositional and nonnegotiable tensions that center on those factors needs to be critically examined, reflected, and reimagined through the theoretical lenses in intercultural studies. Alternative paths could then be explored with efforts made by agents across multiple scales of IHE.

References

Appiah, K. A. (2005). *The ethics of identity*. Princeton, NJ: Princeton University Press.
Bakhtin, M. M. (1982). *The dialogic imagination*. Austin, TX: University of Texas Press.

Beck, U., & Sznaider, N. (2010). Unpacking cosmopolitanism for the social sciences: A research agenda. *British Journal of Sociology, 57*(1), 381–403.

Collins, H. (2018). Interculturality from above and below: Navigating uneven discourses in a neoliberal university system. *Language and Intercultural Communication, 18*(2), 167–183.

Coupland, N. (1999). "Other" representation. In J.Verschueren, J.-O. Ostman, J. Bloomaert, & C. Bulcaen (Eds.), *Handbook of pragmatics* (pp. 1–24). London, UK: John Benjamins.

Delanty, G. (2006). The cosmopolitan imagination: Critical cosmopolitanism and social theory. *British Journal of Sociology, 57*(1), 25–47.

Dervin, F. (2016). *Interculturality in education: A theoretical and methodological toolbox*. London, UK: Palgrave Macmillan.

Dhamoon, R. (2010). *Identity/difference politics: How difference is produced, and why it matters.* Vancouver, BC: UBC Press.

Fairclough, N. (1992). *Language and social change*. Cambridge, UK: Polity.

Gee, J. P. (2012). *Social linguistics and literacies: Ideology in discourses* (4th ed.). London, UK: Routledge.

Han, Q. (2014).The construction of "China discourse system" and "China's discursive power" in the era of globalization [国际化背景下"中国话语体系"建设与"中国话语权"]. *Journal of the Party School of the Central Committee of the C.P.C.* [中共中央党校学报], *18*(5), 47–50.

Hannerz, U. (2009). Cosmopolitanism. In D. Nugent & J.Vincent (Eds.), *A companion to the anthropology of politics* (pp. 69–85). London, UK: Blackwell.

Haugen, H. Ø. (2013). China's recruitment of African university students: Policy efficacy and unintended outcomes. *Globalisation, Societies and Education, 11*(3), 315–334.

Hawkins, M. R. (2018). Transmodalities and transnational encounters: Fostering critical cosmopolitan relations. *Applied Linguistics, 39*(1), 55–77.

Holliday, A. (2011). *Intercultural communication and ideology*. London, UK: SAGE.

Institute of International Education. (2018). *Project Atlas: Trends and global data*. Retrieved from https://www.iie.org/en/Research-and-Insights/Project-Atlas/Tools/Current-Infographics.

Jiani, M.A. (2017).Why and how international students choose Mainland China as a higher education study abroad destination. *Higher Education, 74*, 563–579.

Kudo, K. (2016). Social representation of intercultural exchange in an international university. *Discourse: Studies in the Cultural Politics of Education, 37*(2), 256–268.

Kudo, K.,Volet, S., & Whitsed, C. (2019). Development of intercultural relationships at university: A three-stage ecological and person-in-context conceptual framework. *Higher Education, 77*, 473–489.

Kuroda, C. (2014).The new sphere of international student education in Chinese higher education: A focus on English-medium degree programs. *Journal of Studies in International Education, 18*(5), 445–462.

Ma, J., & Zhao, K. (2018). International student education in China: Characteristics, challenges, and future trends. *Higher Education, 76*(4), 735–751.

Marginson, S. (2014). Student self-formation in international education. *Journal of Studies in International Education, 18*(1), 6–22.

Mignolo, W. (2010). Cosmopolitanism and the de-colonial option. *Studies in Philosophy and Education, 29*(2), 117–127.

Pan, T. (2005). Historical memory, community-building and place-making in neighborhood Shanghai. In L. J. C. Ma & F. Wu (Eds.), *Restructuring the Chinese city: Changing society, economy, and space* (pp. 122–137). London, UK: Routledge.

Qu, M. (2018). The idea of an international university shaped by students: An ethnographic study in a Chinese university. *Frontiers of Education in China, 13*(3), 375–400.

Qu, W. (2013). Dehistoricized cultural identity and cultural othering. *Language and Intercultural Communication, 13*(2), 148–164.

Saarinen, T. (2017). Policy is what happens while you're busy doing something else: Introduction to special issue on "language" indexing higher education policy. *Higher Education, 73*, 553–560.

Said, E. (1978). *Orientalism*. London, UK: Penguin.

Song, J. (2018). Creating world-class universities in China: Strategies and impacts at a renowned research university. *Higher Education, 75*, 729–742.

Song, Y. (2019). English language ideologies and students' perception of international English-Medium-Instruction (EMI) master's programmes: A Chinese case study. *English Today, 35*(3), 22–28.

Strauss, A., & Corbin, J. (2005). *Basics of qualitative research: Procedures and techniques for developing grounded theory*. London, UK: SAGE.

Streitwieser, B. T., & Light, G. J. (2018). Student conceptions of international experience in the study abroad context. *Higher Education, 75*, 471–487.

Tian, M., & Lu, G. (2018). Intercultural learning, adaptation, and personal growth: A longitudinal investigation of international student experiences in China. *Frontiers of Education in China, 13*, 56–92.

Xinhua. (2017, August 8). China's "four great new inventions" in modern times. *China Daily*. Retrieved from http://www.chinadaily.com.cn/bizchina/tech/2017-08/08/content_30370096_2.htm

Yang, R. (2014). China's strategy for the internationalization of higher education: An overview. *Frontiers of Education in China, 9*(2), 151–162.

Yang, R. (2018). *The third delight: The internationalization of higher education in China*. London, UK: Routledge.

14

THE RESISTANCE TO GETTING USED TO ONE ANOTHER

Ninni Wahlström

In this chapter, I take my point of departure from Mary's story, which was published in Sweden's largest daily newspaper (the name of the student has been changed in this text). The story affected me because it illustrates, in all its mundanity, how difficult it can be to be open to the values and traditions of others, even if you have lived in the same country as the "others" for a long time. The narrative revolves around a very Swedish tradition that affects almost all young people living in Sweden: Swedish high school graduation. In Sweden, a student attends high school for three years, ending the year the student turns 19. Students have to apply to a high school and a specific program. Although high school is not mandatory, almost all Swedish youth go there, partly because there is no labor market available as an alternative. Traditionally, the students wear formal suits and white dresses on their graduation day. A key detail in the dress code is the graduation cap (*studentmössa*). It is white with a black ribbon at the bottom. At the front of the black area of the cap, they usually have their name written in gold and a mark symbolizing the school or program from which they are graduating. The typical colors used for the students' graduation celebration are the Swedish national colors of blue and yellow; they appear everywhere during the celebration day, on flags, balloons, ribbons, cards, flowers, and the like.

The purpose of this study is to reach a deeper understanding of the complex webs of relationships that have the potential to promote or constrain a cosmopolitan attitude in everyday life. The theoretical framework for understanding the story of Mary's struggle with issues of identity, rejection, and belonging, all coming to the surface through the purchasing of a graduation cap, includes both philosophical and sociological perspectives. My research questions are formulated as follows: How can moments of cosmopolitan expression as well as cosmopolitan resistance be traced and analyzed? How can the relationship between

DOI: 10.4324/9780429327780-14

cosmopolitanism and communicative action be understood, and what is characteristic for contexts where transactional cosmopolitan situations appear?

In the next section, the theoretical framework for the analysis is outlined, based on cosmopolitanism and transactional realism. The theoretical framework is followed by a methodological approach to critical cosmopolitanism aimed at empirical studies. The third section describes Mary's story, which constitutes the data for the analysis. The fourth section comprises the analysis of the story, followed by a discussion in light of the analysis of differences at the philosophical level of a cosmopolitan attitude and a sociological level of "reality," causing cosmopolitan resistance. The article concludes with some reflections on the relationships needed for self-transformation and self-reflection to occur in relation to the unfamiliar.

A Theoretical Framework of Cosmopolitanism and Transactional Realism

The sociologist Ulrich Beck (2006) notes that "the important fact now is that the human condition has itself become cosmopolitan" (p. 2). By that, he means that global risks implicate the shaping of global publics. Beck argues for a cosmopolitan outlook, a sense of boundarylessness, to be able to grasp social and political realities in our time. He makes a distinction between cosmopolitanism, as a philosophical concept, and cosmopolitanization, at the level of practice. Cosmopolitanization is a dialectical process where the similar and the dissimilar, the global and the local, need to be conceived as interconnected principles. The term draws attention to the idea that being cosmopolitan is often an unwilling choice, a coerced side-effect of living in a globalized world.

From an ethical philosophical perspective, Appiah (2007) views a cosmopolitan approach as the challenge rather than the solution. From a rather modest goal of cosmopolitanism as primarily about getting "used to one another" (p. 85), Appiah suggests that conversations across boundaries of identities are the opportunity we have to meet over differences. Conversations can be either oral or through engaging in literature, film, media, and the like. The crucial point is that the ordinary conversation is placed at the center—conversations that speak from a perspective other than your own. Cosmopolitanism can be understood as the idea that we also have obligations to others outside our own family, relatives, and country. In addition, the attitude of cosmopolitanism includes the idea that we are interested in the particular beliefs and practices that are of significance for different people. The central point in cosmopolitanism, according to Appiah (2007), is that "everybody matters" (p. 144), which means that the basic principles are pluralism and fallibilism; that is, there are many ways we can live our lives, and there is always the possibility that you can learn something from listening to others and their perspectives on life. This viewpoint is in contrast to that of the "counter-cosmopolitans" (Appiah, 2007, p. 137) who advocate universalism based on uniformity, thus opposing the tolerance of differences embedded in the principle of pluralism.

226 Ninni Wahlström

While Dewey (1929/1958) emphasizes communication as the basis of our understanding of the world and the way we find something in common, Appiah (2007) suggests that conversations start from curiosity when encountering other ways of living and believing that differ from your own. These conversations often start from details in the environment that are common as ways of engaging with other people. A communicative understanding of cosmopolitanism emphasizes a relational stance toward the other and the world as a potentiality (Wahlström, 2016), in line with a provisional understanding of the world in the transactional realism outlined by John Dewey.

Transactional Realism

Today, there is renewed interest within pragmatism in examining how realism can be understood from a transactional perspective (Biesta, 2014; Rosiek, 2013). John Dewey's version of pragmatism is an example of a philosophy going beyond a dualism of subject and object. The core concept in this integrated view of subject and object is *experience*. A prerequisite for human experiences to be conscious for individuals is that they include thinking. A reflective form of thinking "transforms confusion, ambiguity and discrepancy into illumination, definiteness and consistency" (Dewey, 1929/1958, p. 67). However, reflective thinking, or reflective inquiry, also points to the context where the problem that gave rise to the experience occurred. "At no point or place is there any jump outside empirical, natural objects and their relations" (Dewey, 1929/1958, p. 67). The way we can reach an understanding of the natural world is through communication. The assumptions and knowledge of things and objects in the environment are established by social cooperation and exchange through human encounters with a material world. As Putnam (1995) notes, to have access to a common reality does not "require access to something *preconceptual*"; it rather enables us to "form *shared* concepts" (p. 21).

> If we had not talked with others and they with us, we should never talk to and with ourselves. Because of converse, social give and take, various organic attitudes become an assemblage of persons engaged in converse, conferring with one another, exchanging distinctive experiences, listening to one another, over-hearing unwelcome remarks, accusing and excusing.
> *(Dewey, 1929/1958, p. 170)*

As Dewey saw it, all scientific or reflective inquiry represents a process where natural existences are engaged, including human beings. For Dewey, experiences are the way that humans interact with their environment and social interactions represent the source of meaning. Dewey's notion of an interest in "learning from all the contacts of life" (Dewey, 1916/2008, p. 370), not only those that are familiar and confirming, demonstrates "the very possibility of meaningful contact across and within differences" (Hansen, 2011, p. 100).

According to Sleeper (1986/2001), knowledge, in Dewey's philosophy, is something to be sought for the sake of action. Action itself becomes instrumental, as a means to change conditions as they are. Sleeper (1986/2001) argues that Dewey's pragmatism is "a radical form of realism—a transactional realism" where "thinking entails active involvement with independent reality" (p. 3). The conception of experience involves both inquiry and continuity, referring to the piecemeal and situational in transactional realism, where "knowing is … regarded as a transaction that takes place between an organism and its environment, and its occurrence denotes changes in relationships as existential events, actual changes in the real world" (Sleeper, 1986/2001, p. 92).

Drawing on Dewey (1940/1991), there is no fixed gap between inanimate and animate individuals, even if there are differences. What all individuals, human and nonhuman, have in common is a temporal dimension; "the principle of a developing career applies to all things in nature, as well as to human beings" (Dewey, 1940/1991, p. 108). Potentialities for change are neither internal to individuals nor external forces, but "a matter of an indefinite range of interactions in which an individual may engage" (Dewey, 1940/1991, p. 110). Thus, change and temporality are inherent in Dewey's philosophy of individuals and relationships. Things exist, they are real, but they are contingently real in two ways. First, temporality is built into all inanimate and animate "individuals" in terms of "life career." Second, things become "temporal real" through interactions with other human and nonhuman individuals as well as through human inquiry. Things as well as humans act upon one another, thereby shaping and changing one another through transactions.

As Sundström Sjödin and Wahlström (2017) argue, temporality and potentiality constitute an intersection between transactional realism and actor–network theory (ANT), developed by Latour (2007). Another affinity between transactional realism and ANT is constituted by the recognition of the influence of nonhuman factors. In Dewey's words, material phenomena "express the ways in which things act upon another and upon us; the ways in which, when objects act together, they reinforce and interfere" (Dewey 1934/1980, pp. 100–101). According to Latour (2007), mediators are actors transporting meaning, while at the same time transforming and modifying it.

The third resemblance between Latour and Dewey is in what matters. Dewey suggests that "the things with which a man *varies* are his genuine environment" (Dewey, 1916/2008, p. 15). Dewey makes a distinction between "surroundings" and "environment." While surroundings contain all sorts of things in the world, "environment" denotes the continuity of objects in the environment that the organisms are actually interacting with. Latour (2007) suggests, in similar terms, that reality could best be understood if we shift our understanding from "matters of fact" to "matters of concern" (p. 114). Matters of concern are real and objective, not directly as objects but rather as "gatherings." Latour (2007) argues against an idea of "the social" as being a fixed predefined dimension. Instead, Latour redefines

228 Ninni Wahlström

the social as being the assemblages of humans and things that are of concern. When the focus is on tracing associations, the social is no longer a "thing" among other things "but *a type of connection* between things that are not themselves social" (Latour, 2007, p. 5). When the common world has to be collected and composed by matters of concern, both "world" and "reality" need to be expressed in plural as "worlds" and "realities." We do not know what the world might become, provided it is collected, assembled, and mediated. The assemblages of matters of concern constitute the core of potentiality and plurality in ANT, which bridge ANT and transactional realism, where transactions between an organism and its environment represent a contingency of different actions, relationships, and influences.

In analyzing the situation in which Mary finds herself, I will trace the matters of concern shaping the situation to explore what transactions are taking place and with what implications. While Dewey's concept of transactions is helpful for understanding reality in terms of the actions and transformations of human beings and things in their environment, Latour's concept of the social as the assemblages of matters of concern is conducive to understanding the actual situation.

A Methodological Approach

Cosmopolitanism may also be considered a methodological approach for social science, developed as a response to the challenge of globalization (Delanty, 2009). In this sense, cosmopolitanism responds to the insight that the cosmopolitan condition permeates social relations and institutions more generally. Cosmopolitanism, as a methodological approach, includes a critical attitude, in contrast to merely describing social actions and relationships. Although influenced by postcolonial theories, cosmopolitanism, as a methodological approach, is located within modernity and the conditions of the individuals in a time of globalization. Cosmopolitanism has been fostered as an approach in social science by two different phenomena: a change in social reality in terms of conflicting social relations and a view of the human condition that emphasizes its interactive and multifaceted character. Critical cosmopolitanism is a way to "theorize the transformation of subjectivity in terms of relations of self, other and world" (Delanty, 2009, p. 6). This means that the cosmopolitan approach is always contextual and, in its particularity, opposed to universalism. The cosmopolitan perspective focuses on the transformative moments of self-understanding and self-problematization of the self and society, implying that the cosmopolitan perspective is a relational approach.

Thus, a methodological critical cosmopolitanism is interested in the "moral and political shifts in self-understanding that occur as a result of the impact of global tensions" (Delanty, 2009, p. 67). These analyses can be performed on both micro and macro levels. Global tensions can be exemplified as tensions between the global and the local and between the universal and the particular. Since the cosmopolitan approach is a relational approach of self-transformation, the communicative dimension is central. In a broad sense, critical cosmopolitanism is understood in terms of deliberative democracy, albeit without the traditional national boundaries that usually frame the terms of democracy (Delanty, 2009).

The transformative and communicative approach of cosmopolitanism forms the basis for the understanding of the term in this chapter. It is an analysis at the micro level where Mary's story is the central situation. The analysis concerns the social, relational, and communicative aspects of the situation.

Mary's Story

The following story is from an article published in Sweden's largest daily newspaper. The text is in the form of a report under the byline of the journalist Niklas Orrenius (2018).

The journalist had a cup of coffee with Mary, a high school student who would soon graduate. Mary talked about her graduation cap. It turns out that in 2018, a graduation cap is not just a cap. It is also a manifestation of your identity, with many individual choices concerning the details of the cap. In Mary's case, it was the design of the rain cover for the cap that became central, because the design of the rain cover gave rise to a dispute with Mary's mother. Mary wanted to have one of the most common varieties of rain cover, in the shape of a Swedish flag in blue and yellow, to protect the graduation cap in case of rain. The student celebration includes a part where the students travel through the town in procession, and the weather is not very reliable. However, Mary's mother disagreed. Since Mary's family background is Iraqi, Mary's mother argued that Mary should have an Iraqi flag as the rain cover for her cap, not a Swedish one. Mary, who has lived her entire life in Sweden, told her mother that she wanted a Swedish flag because she felt Swedish. Mary's mother, also a Swedish citizen, said that if Mary bought a rain cover for her graduation cap with an Iraqi flag, she would pay for it, but if Mary chose a Swedish flag for the rain cover, she had to pay for it herself.

However, what troubled Mary was not the expense. Mary was sad because the dispute about the rain cover made her realize that even though her parents had lived in Sweden for decades, they do not consider themselves Swedes. They also transmitted this attitude to Mary. Mary's mother said, "Why do you see yourself as Swedish? Swedes do not see you as Swedish!" Mary reflected on the issue of identities. She thought that her parents' identities were primarily as Muslims and secondarily as Iraqis. Being Swedish is not even conceivable for them, Mary pondered, because Sweden is only a place where they live. In contrast to her mother, Mary did not see the Swedish flag as a betrayal of her old homeland and against her family's identity. Mary thought that she could be both Iraqi and Swedish. She liked to think of herself as being Swedish with Swedish values, while simultaneously being an Iraqi with her darker skin. Mary noticed that almost none of her mates from immigrant families in her neighborhood wanted a Swedish flag on their graduation celebration cap, which is the tradition in Sweden. In Mary's

230 Ninni Wahlström

residential area, "Swedishness" is perceived as diffuse and distant. Many students from the neighborhood would instead wave their families' old homeland flags on their graduation day.

Mary understood her mother's and her neighbors' rejection of the Swedes and Swedish identity as a kind of defense mechanism. If you feel unwanted, it may be easier to say that you do not want to be a part of this country, Mary reflected. However, when they go back to the countries that they regard as their home countries, they will not feel entirely at home because they will notice that they have nevertheless become "Swedish" in many ways, Mary concluded (Orrenius, 2018).

The Cosmopolitan Situation

The first step in the analysis is to establish what constitutes "the social" (or "the environment") in Mary's story. In ANT, the social "is the name of a type of momentary association which is characterized by the way it gathers together into new shapes" (Latour, 2007, p. 65). The means to produce the social consists of mediators, which "transform, translate, distort, and modify the meaning or the elements they are supposed to carry" (Latour, 2007, p. 39). The dominant mediator in Mary's story is the graduation cap. With a history in the two oldest Swedish universities from the middle of the 19th century onward, and soon thereafter as a symbol of graduation from high school, the graduation cap in the social situation in which Mary saw herself becomes a powerful mediator of national identity. Strictly speaking, it was not the graduation cap in itself but its rain cover, which, despite our not knowing if it was ever used, transformed the graduation cap from a historical symbol of education to a burning symbol of potential belongings. The graduation cap as a mediator causes uncertainty and hesitation in the social situation. It functions as a driver of the contingency and the momentary in the assemblages of the social.

The Assemblages of the Social

In Mary's story, there are several actors forming the social dimension of the situation. In addition to Mary and her mother, the graduation cap, the rain cover, the flags from two different countries, the yellow and blue colors, the classmates, and the neighbors are all actors who contribute to the formation of social relations. Mary and her graduation cap are at the center. For Mary, her graduation from Swedish high school is an important occasion. With this, it follows that all the rituals that accompany a Swedish high school graduation become important to Mary, including the cap and its details. Thus, the graduation cap becomes an important actor in forming the scene of the social, creating uncertainty and estrangement. Another important aspect of the graduation celebration is the presence of family and relatives. Family and relatives are expected to participate in the celebration by coming to the schoolyard and celebrating with the students. The family holds up a placard with the name and picture of "their" student, and they hang flowers and balloons around the necks of the students. Accordingly, the mother, as a representative of the family's participation in the graduation celebration, is also a significant actor in the forming of the social in Mary's preparation for her graduation. As a mediator, the mother transforms the Swedish symbol of the cap from being a symbol of a completed education to being a core symbol of national identity.

The Communicative Aspects of the Social

As a second step in the analysis, the communicative competence (Delanty, 2009), or formulated differently, the different communicative attitudes that can be distinguished in the current situation are put to the fore. In accordance with transactional realism (Sleeper, 1986/2001), the transformative aspects of the actor as well as of the object are the focus of interest in understanding "real" events in an environment where people and objects are in active interaction with one another. Through communication, events become subject to reflections and reconsiderations. "Events turn into objects, things with a meaning" (Dewey, 1929/1958, p. 166).

In a conversation with her mother regarding the upcoming graduation celebrations, Mary shared her plans for how she would like to design the different details associated with her graduation cap. This part of the conversation can be characterized as a routine dialogue between a daughter and her mother that goes on in thousands of homes during the preparations for the celebration of a high school graduation. It was only when the conversation turned to the design of the rain cover that there was a shift in the character of the conversation, turning it into an event of transactions affecting the actors' identities. A rain cover is usually a neutral object. However, when the rain cover includes the design of a national flag, it suddenly becomes part of a statement of the owner's identity. By communicating her plan of buying a rain cover designed with a Swedish flag, Mary transformed the rain cover into a main actor in identity formation in the conversation with her mother. The protests from Mary's mother on the matter transformed Mary from being a daughter to acting as a representative of Swedish school traditions and Swedish society.

When Mary's mother argued that Mary should have an Iraqi flag on the rain cover instead, she transformed from primarily being a mother taking an interest in her daughter's affairs to being a representative for the country of Iraq and the Iraqi family. The transaction of roles and identities heightened when the mother questioned Mary's identity as Swedish. With the direct question "Why do you see yourself as Swedish?", the mother tried to transform Mary's dual identity into a perception of herself as first and foremost Iraqi. As reinforcement of her questioning of her daughter's choice of identity and as argument that her daughter had

232 Ninni Wahlström

perceived her role incorrectly, the mother included the entire Swedish society in her response, by claiming that "Swedes do not see you as Swedish!" With this claim, the mother acted as an interpreter for Swedish society. In this dialogue, the initially so important upcoming high school graduation suddenly appeared as distant and subordinate, while national identity emerged as the core issue. As indirect communication, the choice of their national flags by the other students in the neighborhood informed Mary about what the "right" choice should be. The graduation cap was transformed and modified from being an inoffensive part of a Swedish school tradition to becoming a personal position, expressing an Iraqi identity.

The Relationships of the Transactional Event

In the third step of the analysis, the relationships included in the situation are explored. The starting point for the communication was a conversation between a young girl approaching her high school graduation and her mother. Thus, the environment consists of a mother and her daughter with the daughter's outfit for the graduation celebration at the fore and the Swedish school system in the background. The relationship to the Swedish school system, although as a background factor in the formation of the environment, places Mary as a Swedish school student and her mother as a parent of a Swedish school student, with certain implied expectations of both of them. These relationships are consequences of the school system and the graduation traditions and are the same for all high school students in the country.

When the routine conversation turns into a transactional event, the relationships with the two countries of Iraq and Sweden appear as the most significant factor. In that specific moment, the mother situated herself as exclusively having an Iraqi identity, albeit living in Sweden, thereby rejecting her Swedish citizenship and the potentiality of being a Swede. From her point of view, the mother's relationship with her daughter is built on the assumption that her daughter also identifies herself as only being Iraqi. This leads to the further assumption, from the mother's perspective, that Mary has opportunities to develop relationships with people in the neighborhood, since according to Mary it is common to maintain one's original identity in the residential area where they live.

For Mary, the relationships are more complex. From her position, she is primarily a Swedish student. She has lived in Sweden all her life and has attended the Swedish school system for 12 years. Moreover, in this situation, a school event functioned as the instigator of relationship transactions. Mary's relationships with her classmates are important. She wanted to take part in the school class community and be perceived as a member of this particular class. This desire placed her in a position where she became loyal to Swedish experiences, values, and opinions in general. Through her schooling, she has acquired deep knowledge of the Swedish language and society. Because of her daily contact with Swedish teachers and schoolmates, she has developed an identity of being a Swedish school student. However, this identity is not exclusive. Mary is very aware of her family's origin and sees herself as an Iraqi as well. Since she grew up in Sweden, her knowledge and experiences of her parents' homeland are perhaps indirect, conveyed through the stories of her parents and relatives.

The difference between first-hand and second-hand access to experiences does not prevent Mary from developing her identity in relation to both countries. It is clear from her story that it is important for her to include both the Swedish and the Iraqi belongings in her identity. Mary's relationships with young people of her own age in the residential area appear to be more complex. While the schoolmates in the neighborhood usually show their solidarity with their original country by choosing that country's flag in the school context, Mary chose the new country's flag, thereby distancing herself from her peers in the neighborhood.

From Mary's story in the newspaper, we know very little about the mother's experiences in Sweden and of Swedish society. We only know that the mother draws the conclusion that Swedes do not think of Mary as being a Swede. It is reasonable to believe that Mary's mother has felt such an exclusion from Swedish society herself and therefore tries to protect her daughter from having similar experiences of being excluded. From such a viewpoint, it might appear a better strategy to remain "outside" to protect oneself from being rejected.

There are at least two possible structural factors that potentially could have an impact on the mother's encounters with Swedish society. The first factor relates to residential areas. In larger cities, what the politicians call "areas of alienation" have been formed. This concept lacks a clear definition but can be understood as areas where a majority of residents have their roots in countries other than Sweden, where unemployment is high, and where contacts with the majority community are few. The second factor is access to the labor market, an acknowledged path to integration. According to Sweden's labor force surveys, unemployment among foreign-born persons was 15.4% in 2018. Among the native-born, the corresponding figure was 3.8% (Confederation of Swedish Enterprise, 2019). Taken together, the residential and labor market situations for foreign-born persons make it difficult for migrants to feel involved in Swedish society. Moreover, a rather large proportion of the Swedish population feels that immigrants with low levels of education and different religions threaten their jobs and culture.

Thus, it is reasonable to believe that Mary's mother has experienced difficulties reaching into Swedish society and that encounters with Swedish institutions, like school, may have been characterized by language difficulties and mutual feelings of distance. Nor is it self-evident that meetings with Swedes in everyday life—at the bus stop, in the shop, and elsewhere—have led to the kinds of mundane conversations based on the situation in which they find themselves that can create a sense of fellowship in the moment.

234 Ninni Wahlström

Transactional Moments of Cosmopolitanism and Resistance

In Mary's story, the cosmopolitan situation is complex. The cosmopolitan perspective is present, but it is at the same time challenged by what Beck (2006) terms *cosmopolitanization*. Beck (2006) argues that the distinction between cosmopolitanism and cosmopolitanization is a distinction between the level of philosophy and that of practice. The term *cosmopolitanization* designates a "forced" cosmopolitanism that transforms society through transactional encounters with cosmopolitanism from within the nation. These encounters are the side-effects of global phenomena such as migration, international interdependence, and everyday influences of foreign countries' culture through media, film, food, and the like. In reality, becoming cosmopolitan is primarily a function of coerced choices and a side-effect of unconscious decisions, according to Beck (2006): "Cosmopolitanization is a compulsory re-education program in openness to the world" (p. 102). Like all forced learning, it is often met by resistance and stubborn claims of what is right with "my country" and what is wrong with "your country."

Mary's mother migrated to Sweden from Iraq decades ago. However, it was probably a coerced decision, of which she could not foresee the consequences at the moment she arrived in the new country. As a side-effect of globalization and internationalized conflicts, she was forced to move from her native country and learn all the fundamental elements of a new society and culture. Through the transactions between her "old" habits and way of thinking and "new" everyday experiences and unfamiliar viewpoints, she has likely changed a lot of her actions, ways of communicating, and ways of thinking about the world. However, she has not chosen for her daughter to attend a Swedish school. Her daughter's schooling is a side-effect of the primary choice of not staying in Iraq. When Mary's mother realizes that her daughter has become "Swedish" as a result of the daughter's upbringing in Sweden and her Swedish schooling, she demonstrates a strong resistance to this consequence of her own migration. She does not want her daughter to be "a stranger" in relation to herself. Instead, the mother wants to bridge the gap between herself and her daughter by claiming that mother and daughter are "the same": that they are both "non-Swedes."

The mother's reaction is played out on a practical level. The situation is about the design of a rain cover for a graduation cap. The resistance occurs when it turns out that Mary has chosen a Swedish flag as the decoration for the rain cover. In the transaction between the mother and the Swedish flag on the rain cover, the mother becomes a representative of Iraqi society and culture rather than merely a mother. Simultaneously, the rain cover becomes a symbol for Swedish society rather than a piece of plastic to protect the cap in case of rainy weather.

In contrast, Mary's perspective can be understood on a philosophical level. She has developed a cosmopolitan attitude by living with two cultures all her life. She has reflected on the possibility of having a dual belonging to two different cultures, and she finds the idea appealing. It is this attitude that Mary strives for: to be able to feel at home in two cultures and to see the values in both. Following Appiah (2007, p. 57), the cosmopolitan idea is that "all cultures have enough overlap in their vocabulary of values to begin a conversation." With a shared language of value, people can coordinate their lives with one another because they can guide one another to shared responses. Even when people do not agree, the shared vocabulary of values makes it easier to agree to disagree (Appiah, 2007). The conversations across borders are mundane dialogues, taking place at the workplace, at school, at the bus stop, or the like. The aim of people's everyday conversations is to make contact, rather than to agree on values.

Mary has experienced countless everyday conversations at home and in school. Through these conversations, she has become familiar with two cultures, or in Appiah's (2007) view, she has been used to encountering and acting within different cultures without disrespecting or resisting either of them. In the transaction between Mary and the graduation cap, Mary becomes a Swedish student rather than a daughter to an immigrant mother. The graduation cap becomes a context-dependent piece of one's graduation outfit rather than a positioning of one's nationality.

It is precisely in the differences in the transactions in relation to the graduation cap that it becomes analytically clear why Mary and her mother cannot reach out to each other in the current situation. While the mother, in this situation, positions herself exclusively as a representative of her original homeland, Mary defines herself, at this moment, exclusively as a Swedish student. Moreover, while Mary's mother perceives the cap as a national symbol, Mary perceives it as a graduation symbol. The cap is primarily a symbol that Mary shares with her schoolmates, independent of their different backgrounds. In the situation being analyzed, the language of values does not sufficiently overlap, which leads to a gap regarding the meaning of the graduation cap. Mary and her mother fail to understand each other and each other's motives.

In this story, Mary seems to have access to broader experiences of encounters with different groups of people with different backgrounds. This helps her to develop a cosmopolitan outlook, without necessarily embracing all aspects of those encounters. To develop a cosmopolitan attitude, an important factor seems to be the environment within which we are interacting. In Latour's (2007) terms, the elements forming our social assemblages will be of significance. The school is a place where routine as well as learning conversations take place and where people get to know one another and can listen to one another's stories. According to Appiah (2007), "evaluating stories together is one of the central human ways of learning to align our responses to the world" (p. 29). Thus, the school as an institution has a valuable "side-effect" in the "assemblages" of students from different backgrounds telling their stories in daily conversations in relation to the

236 Ninni Wahlström

school's knowledge content as well as to everyday events. It is through these daily conversations that the students have the opportunity to "get used" to one another (Wahlström, 2016). As Appiah (2007) notes, what actually moves people is often "just a gradually acquired new way of seeing things" (p. 73).

Some Concluding Reflections

A methodological cosmopolitan approach has an empirical–analytical focus that combines empirical and normative dimensions. The transformation in self-understanding and the tracing of self-transformative moments are central to cosmopolitanism (Delanty, 2009). By taking Dewey's view of transactional realism as a starting point, it becomes possible to explore moments of transactional events that transform the meaning and identity of actors, both human and nonhuman. Through analysis of three categories—(a) the elements that constitute the environment, (b) the communicative actions in the situation, and (c) the relationships that are in play between different actors—it is possible to explore the cosmopolitan orientation or its contrast, the cosmopolitan resistance.

The critical cosmopolitan moments occur in the interplay between the individual, the unfamiliar, and the world (Delanty, 2009). For moments of cosmopolitan self-understanding and self-transformation, all three categories need to be present in one way or another. However, you do not know beforehand if being in a particular environment leads to cosmopolitan understanding. The relationships in the triad presuppose communication. It is the meaning arising through conversation, as well as how the different participants interpret the conversation, that becomes crucial for the possibilities of self-transformation and changing views by the actors involved. The cosmopolitan process is a process of listening and learning through direct and indirect conversations (Appiah, 2007). What we can learn from Mary's story is that the cosmopolitan reality takes place in transactional moments of conflicting orientations and belongings.

References

Appiah, K. A. (2007). *Cosmopolitanism: Ethics in a world of strangers*. London, UK: Norton.
Beck, U. (2006). *The cosmopolitan vision*. Cambridge, UK: Polity.
Biesta, G. (2014). Pragmatising the curriculum: Bringing knowledge back into the curriculum conversation, but via pragmatism. *Curriculum Journal, 25*(1), 29–49.
Confederation of Swedish Enterprise. (2019). *Ekonomifakta*. Retrieved from https://www.ekonomifakta.se/fakta
Delanty, G. (2009). *The cosmopolitan imagination*. Cambridge, UK: Cambridge University Press.
Dewey, J. (1958). *Experience and nature*. New York: Dover. (Original work published 1929)
Dewey, J. (1980). *Art as experience*. New York: Perigee. (Original work published 1934)
Dewey, J. (1991). Time and individuality. In J. A. Boydston (Ed.), *John Dewey: The later works, 1925–1953: Vol. 14. 1940* (pp. 98–114). Carbondale, IL: Southern Illinois University Press. (Original work published 1940)

Dewey, J. (2008). Democracy and education. In J. A. Boydston (Ed.), *John Dewey: The middle works, 1899–1924: Vol. 9. 1916* (pp. 3–370). Carbondale, IL: Southern Illinois University Press. (Original work published 1916)

Hansen, D. T. (2011). *The teacher and the world*. New York: Routledge.

Latour, B. (2007). *Reassembling the social: An introduction to action-network-theory*. Oxford, UK: Oxford University Press.

Orrenius, N. (2018, May 11). Du är inte svensk, sa … mamma till sin dotter [You are not Swedish, … mother said to her daughter]. *Dagens Nyheter*. Retrieved from https://www.dn.se/nyheter/sverige/niklas-orrenius-du-ar-inte-svensk-sa-saras-mamma-till-sin-dotter/

Putnam, H. (1995). *Pragmatism*. Malden, MA: Blackwell.

Rosiek, J. L. (2013). Pragmatism and post-qualitative futures. *International Journal of Qualitative Studies in Education, 26*(6), 692–705.

Sleeper, R. W. (2001). *The necessity of pragmatism: John Dewey's conception of philosophy*. Urbana, IL: University of Illinois Press. (Original work published 1986)

Sundström Sjödin, E., & Wahlström, N. (2017). Enacted realities in teachers' experiences: Bringing materialism into pragmatism. *Journal of Curriculum Studies, 49*(1), 96–110.

Wahlström, N. (2016). Cosmopolitanism as communication? On conditions for educational conversations in a globalized society. *Scandinavian Journal of Educational Research, 60*(1), 32–47.

15

THE IMPACT OF FORECLOSURES ON THE HOME ENVIRONMENTS AND EDUCATION OF BLACK YOUTH IN THE UNITED STATES

Nemoy Lewis

In this chapter, I explore the burden of homeownership on Black families and children when foreclosure occurs. Specifically, I seek to understand the ways in which foreclosure affects Black families' attempts to live meaningful and productive lives for themselves and contribute to their children's education. In what follows, I first discuss the theoretical approaches that might help shed light on the economic conditions that play a role in the lives of Black people as they reside in diverse spaces. While cosmopolitanisms engage questions of how people from various backgrounds live with and manage their differences, there are also particular differences for which we need to account if we are to fully understand the social and economic situations of racial groups such as Black people. I go on to explore the significance of homeownership and the social and economic possibilities it could offer Black families and their children. Finally, I analyze the impact of foreclosures on Black households and their children, giving attention to how the environments in which they live affect students' successful engagement at school. I reference the contribution of the risk of foreclosure to "family tensions" that in turn affect the parents' ability to support their children at school and negatively impact the children's education. While owning a home might improve children's life chances, there also lurks the possibility of its having a detrimental effect on their lives.

The information presented in this chapter is from a larger qualitative study that examined the effects of foreclosure on the experiences of Black families in Jacksonville, Florida, families who either had lost their homes to foreclosure or had received notices for having defaulted on their mortgages (that is, having missed at least one mortgage payment). I draw on data from 14 semi-structured interviews with parents detailing their own and their children's unsettling experiences during the foreclosure process. The audio-recorded interviews and

DOI: 10.4324/9780429327780-15

observational fieldnotes of the various communities that were studied during the summer of 2014 provide valuable insights into the parents' attempts not only to share their lived experiences but also to demonstrate that they were not irresponsible borrowers or parents.

The interviews explored the parents' motivations for purchasing a home, some of the factors that cause Black families to default on their mortgage payments, and how parents and children coped with foreclosures. Pseudonyms are used to safeguard the identity of individuals and places referenced in this chapter. In expressing concerns about their children's welfare and education, the parents talked of grappling with the following: whether to discuss the foreclosure or pending repossession with their children; the impact that moving from their home would have on their children's education; the possible changes in family lifestyle and parenting; and what it means to provide adequate shelter for one's children.

Theoretical Framework

As societies become increasingly diverse with the accelerated flow of people and capital, social scientists have provided us with insights into the spatial, social, and capital implications of this process for people who seek to create conditions for meaningful and productive lives for themselves and their children. Theorists on cosmopolitanisms have discussed how differences among diverse groups of people are managed as they co-inhabit the same urban or suburban spaces (e.g., Appiah, 2006; Beck, 2006; Harvey, 2009). Recent formulations have moved away from idealized scenarios of cultural openness and acceptance of the "other," while retaining endorsements for principles of democracy, inclusivity, and equity among peoples. Beck (2006) points out that cosmopolitanism, in reality, "is also, and even primarily, a function of coerced choice or a side effect of unconscious decision" (p. 19; see also Vertovec & Cohen, 2002) regarding residence and mobility. In diverse societies, one finds people from different racial, social, economic, and cultural backgrounds for whom the context presents profound challenges for themselves and their families—their children in particular. In the case of Black people, their social and economic situations present important concerns that warrant particular investigation. Specifically, how and where they reside, the economic burdens that must be endured to live in today's urban environments, and the social and educational conditions that their children experience growing up in these newly adopted communities are factors relevant to our understanding of how this particular racial group engages with, or is able to escape, economic oppression.

In this chapter, I draw on the theoretical perspectives of critical cosmopolitanism, neoliberalism, and financialization, as they offer a constructive framework that helps us to understand the economic conditions shaping the lived experiences of Black people as they seek to establish productive lives for themselves and their children through the American dream of homeownership. I treat neoliberalism as the key to understanding the regulatory reforms that introduced subprime mortgages that led Black people to lose their homes to foreclosure. Neoliberal theory contends that an unregulated market is essential for economies to operate at their optimal capacity to produce and will lead to "efficiency, income distribution, economic growth, technological progress—as well as securing individual liberties" (Kotz, 2015, p.12). Deregulation, a bedrock of the neoliberal economy (Springer, Birch, & MacLeavy, 2016), combined with state responsibilities that were reconfigured or, as Wendy Brown (2017) explains, "economized" to facilitate economic growth and individual prosperity, contributed to a situation where families were not protected from the insecurities of the housing market. This situation empowered the economic market to become the sole arbiter of individual worth, and the only viable option to resolving longstanding social inequalities, so that all people could obtain the economic resources needed to receive the benefits of the market—choice and freedom. Put differently, individuals were now responsible for social provisions such as housing, healthcare, education, and other social needs (D.-A. Davis, 2007).

Financialization provides a useful frame of reference for this story in that it allows for an understanding of the impacts of the collapse of the housing market on everyday family life. Manuel Aalbers (2016) defines financialization "as the increasing dominance of financial actors, markets, practices, measurements, and narratives, at various scales, resulting in a structural transformation of economies, firms (including financial institutions), states, and households" (p. 3). Sociologist Randy Martin (2002) uses the term *financialization* to reference the penetration of financial logics and concepts into all domains of everyday life. He describes financialization as a process that calls upon individuals to "accept a great deal of risk into their homes that was hitherto the province of professionals" (p. 12) and argues that financial markets place great demands on individuals and households. People of little financial means are expected to behave like capitalists, and in so doing citizens become transformed into investors who manage their own risk by leveraging their human capital to build wealth and accumulate assets. In this context, homes become investment assets that are closely tied to the global financial market through the securitization of mortgages.

In addition, home values are generated on the basis of their potential to create additional wealth through the speculative appreciation of the home. Economic geographer Paul Langley (2008) submits that technological advancement in finance, along with the pursuit of a neoliberal agenda by the state, have assisted in the formation of self-disciplined subjects for a highly financialized society. Through this economic process, the home became the central investment vehicle not only for amassing household wealth but also for accessing higher-quality schools to afford children early life advantages.

Neoliberalism and financialization are useful concepts for understanding the practices and policies that shape Black people's access and outcome in potentially cosmopolitan spaces. However, it is necessary to take into account how capitalist systems operate, especially the structural racial logic undergirding the economic

The Impact of Foreclosures **241**

principles that produce racial inequalities. In this regard, racial capitalism helps us to understand how racial differences are operationalized to prevent Black people from realizing the benefits of homeownership. Leong (2013) defines racial capitalism "as the process of deriving social and economic value from the racial identity of another person" (p. 2153). And Robinson (1983) argues that racism is the organizing principle of capitalism, asserting that "capitalism and racism ... did not break from the old [feudal] order but rather evolved from it to produce a modern world system of 'racial capitalism' dependent on slavery, violence, imperialism, and genocide" (p. xiii). Therefore, racial capitalism demands that we focus our attention on these continued histories to understand how contemporary racial inequalities are manifested for capitalism to sustain itself.

In the context of homeownership, economic racism operates in targeting Black borrowers and hence subjecting them to what Ruth Wilson Gilmore (2007) describes as "premature death." The financial crisis contributes to pernicious conditions for Black people that further exacerbate the uneven distribution of wealth and resources (A. Y. Davis, 2012; Gilmore, 2017; Osuna, 2017). The inequities Black families experience are even more insidious since they produce forms of dehumanization and dispossession that subject Black people to extreme strains of racism and racialization, which are often attributed to individual aberration rather than being seen as systemic features of a broader political and economic system.

Significance of Homeownership in American Culture

Homeownership has long been the primary means for households to accumulate wealth within American society. Owning a home carries tremendous cultural weight and is often associated with achieving the American Dream. Becoming a homeowner is said to allow first-time buyers to embrace the values of freedom and individualism. Homeowners are graced with a higher social status, which usually translates into a mark of success within American culture. Since the establishment of the Federal Housing Administration in 1934, homeownership has been touted as low-risk and inexpensive as compared to renting, and it is perceived as the ideal way to increase household wealth in America (Dickerson, 2014). Homeownership provides property owners with greater security and the freedom to choose how to live. In American society, renting has long been characterized as an un-American way of life or as a failure to optimize one's true potential to become a homeowner (van Ham, 2012). Another benefit of owning a home is the ability to use the home as collateral to secure bank loans to pay the tuition of postsecondary education for their children or acquire capital to start up a business. A common theme promoted through neoliberal thought is that homeownership develops responsible agents who invest in the market to enhance their quality of life.

Property ownership has also been conceived by the government as a viable measure of assessing one's political value and commitment to the country (Rohe

& Linblad, 2014). Owning a home has been seen as not just social practice but also a political activity (Rothstein, 2017). For example, out of fear of the Russian Revolution of 1917, President Woodrow Wilson promoted homeownership as a means to defeat and discredit Communist ideology (Rothstein, 2017). The idea was that citizens who owned their homes would become invested in the capitalist system and reject Communist beliefs. US housing policies have supported this notion with its implicit biases toward homeowners while stigmatizing renting (Goetz, 2007).

For some Black families, homeownership offered a sense of hope in achieving the American Dream. The home served as a social navigation tool that figuratively liberated Black people from their racial identity and allowed them to gain access to better amenities, jobs, and schools for their children. In American society, homeownership served as the optimal path for most families to accumulate wealth and lift themselves out of poverty and toward a better life. For some first-generation homeowners, the home represents triumph, especially considering the history of discrimination and segregation their parents and grandparents endured in attempting to cement their own legacy and build wealth. For decades, homeownership has constituted an important symbolic marker of inclusion in the middle class, especially for Black middle-class households, which have few wealth markers available to them (Lacy, 2007). Once regulatory restrictions were relaxed, members of the Black middle class sought new distinctions to further sever their ties to working-class Black households. Lacy (2007) found that Black middle-class households were continuously drawing boundaries to distance themselves from other classes of Black people. More specifically, Lacy found that Black middle-class families used their choice of residence, the subdivision, and the cost of their home to communicate their symbolic differences and erect social boundaries.

Homeownership also enabled working-class Black families to escape a life of poverty and provided them with opportunities to give their children the best chances at life. Black parents in this study were convinced that suburban communities with a large share of owner-occupied dwellings were safer and more stable than those populated with renter-occupied housing units. Parents held suburban spaces in high regard because they offered more space, greater privacy, and, most importantly, better educational and social opportunities for their children. Black parents held these beliefs largely because of devalorized narratives that characterized their lived space in urban areas as violent and having high levels of poverty and a failing education system. As a result, some Black parents aspire to abandon these spaces out of fear that their children will not obtain the adequate educational training necessary to secure their upward social and economic mobility. This was, in part, because of the abundance of resources poured into suburban school districts, which could help to catapult the life chances of the children in these areas (Lewis-McCoy, 2014) and provide them with an early life advantage over those residing in economically disadvantaged spaces.

Researchers (Lacy, 2007; Oliver & Shapiro, 2013; Shapiro, 2004) indicate that members of the Black community were excited about the social and material benefits that accompanied homeownership, especially the opportunity for intergenerational transmission of wealth to their children. The home was something that essentially became a part of a family's legacy and was later passed down to future generations. For this reason, the home ascended to what Paul Langley (2008) describes as "good debt" and not "bad debt," when compared with other financial instruments such as credit cards. The withdrawal of social welfare policies, coupled with the rise of precarious employment, led Black people to become increasingly dependent on debt for survival in this neoliberal environment (Mahmud, 2012). As a result, lenders persuaded Black borrowers to acquire costly subprime loans with excessive fees and exorbitant interest rates so that they could own their home and begin building equity. However, accumulation of wealth by way of equity for Black households through homeownership was not as straightforward as simply owning a home in any neighborhood. In fact, the location of the home has been central to the wealth accumulation process, as modalities of difference such as race continue to dictate one's level of prosperity and mobility (Shapiro, 2017). According to Thomas Shapiro (2017), "desirable, resource-rich neighborhoods allowed families to build housing wealth, which by far accounts for the largest wealth reservoir for middle- and lower-middle-class families" (p. 76). Black parents worked profusely to obtain the necessary resources to give their children the opportunities they needed to be successful during their formative and adult years.

The Impact of Foreclosure on Black Family Life and Children

Foreclosures have a substantial impact on households. They can create tensions between partners leading to divorce or separation—which could result in one parent left with the responsibility of making the monthly mortgage payments based on their single income (Lewis, 2018; McCormack & Mazar, 2015). The psychological and emotional stresses of a pending foreclosure along with a divorce led some parents to engage in less supportive parenting strategies, resulting in children feeling afraid to make mistakes (Lewis, 2018). Schneider, Waldfogel, and Brooks-Gunn (2016) found that parents experiencing high levels of stress due to financial hardships tended to apply more hostile and pugnacious parenting styles toward their children, which can have a concomitant effect on a child's self-esteem and self-confidence.

The threat of foreclosures created a high-stress environment for some households at risk of losing their home. Once the interest rates on mortgages sharply increased, coupled with the precarious nature of incomes, some households struggled to remain current on their monthly financial obligations. Vanessa, a 45-year-old divorced single mother of four children in Jacksonville, said that all her troubles began soon after her employer downsized and began laying off workers. Vanessa remained employed with the company, although in a different capacity and at barely half of her previous salary. The reduction in her pay further exacerbated her difficulty in remaining afloat and current on her mortgage. The decrease in Vanessa's salary, compounded by her recent divorce, created a considerable challenge for her because the burden of all the household expenses now fell squarely on her shoulders. Furthermore, the impending foreclosure also caused Vanessa's health to deteriorate. The stress and anxiety from the foreclosure process led Vanessa to suffer severe panic attacks, loss of appetite, and sleep deprivation. In turn, this left Vanessa feeling as if she had failed as a mother in not being able to provide a stable and secure home for her daughters. In fact, studies have linked the stress of an impending foreclosure to reduced confidence in the parenting ability of troubled homeowners (Kingsley, Smith, & Price, 2009). Vanessa recalls:

> I had a lot of panic attacks and anxiety to the point I believed I was going through depression. My appetite was gone and I couldn't sleep. My hair was falling out due to the stress. I went to my primary care provider and he said to me, "You're not depressed, you just have a lot of anxiety because of what you're currently experiencing" [foreclosure], and told me not to worry about things out of my control. He prescribed some medication to help me sleep, which essentially shut my brain down.

Vanessa's recollection indicates how the thought of losing the home induced a great deal of anxiety in some homeowners. Additionally, with the growing number of completed foreclosures, this concern was becoming a reality for some distressed homeowners. For example, studies revealed that such insecurities and uncertainties surrounding one's housing outcome increased the chances of anxiety and depression (Ford, Burrows, & Nettleton, 2001; Ross & Squires, 2011), which as some scholars warn could have a long-term effect on a child's scholastic abilities and mental well-being (Collins & Berg, 2019).

In a study on mortgage foreclosures in the UK, Nettleton (2001) found that it was common for parents to minimize the impact of foreclosures on their children. The study found that in relation to their children, parents were most concerned about the following: whether or not to tell their children about the repossession; their own parenting; the schooling experience; their children's friends; changes to their lifestyle; behavioral, health, and space concerns (Nettleton, 2001). These issues raised in Nettleton's study correspond with concerns identified by parents in this study. Some parents communicated details of their financial situation to their children with great caution, thinking that it was important to inform their children about their financial struggles in an effort to maintain a transparent relationship with them. Some parents did not wish to burden their children with details of their financial hardship because they did not want them to worry or be distracted from their learning. Most parents in this study used their discretion when determining the amount and type of information that was shared; and

The Impact of Foreclosures **245**

factors that determined what information was communicated were based on the age of their children or whether they were still in school (Lewis, 2018).

James, a 49-year-old married father and homeowner in Jacksonville, said, "We never not [inform] them [children] about what was going on. It was a lesson in faith for them too … they needed to know how to deal with stressful situations and know who ultimately supplies their needs." For some parents, deciding whether to inform the children about their financial hardship and pending foreclosure was extremely difficult. As in other studies, the parents in this study deployed one of two approaches with regard to informing their children. Some parents believed it was imperative not to leave their children in the dark with respect to their pending foreclosure and did their best to remain honest about their financial hardship and imminent foreclosure. James explained that the children took the news really well and recalled, "They were fine with it, as long as they knew that they had a roof over their heads and that we were able to provide for them." Learning to live with their needs and not wants was an important life lesson, one James had learned during childhood and now suggested he was passing on to his children. Reflecting on the past, James commented:

> They [children] needed to understand needs and wants. So, the need was to have shelter within your means. That was a lesson we were taught, and that's a lesson we are teaching our kids: to live within their means and to save for the future.

Other parents used a more subtle approach to their disclosure by providing their children with a small glimpse into their financial hardship. The subtle approach appeared to be linked to the age of the children, particularly in cases where the parents felt their children were too young to learn about their pending foreclosure and eviction. Vanessa represented this approach when she said:

> For my younger daughters it wasn't something that I was going to involve them. They knew that Mommy was stressed out. They knew I no longer have a job with the same salary. I think it was important for me to let them know to a certain extent why we were not able to do some of the things that we used to be able to do. So, certain activities that we were accustomed to like recreational sports—we can no longer do because other things needed that money.

Communication was key for parents like Vanessa because it offered her children a brief snapshot of her financial hardships, which enabled her children to remain realistic about things she could provide for them. As Vanessa puts it:

> I did not sit them down to say this is what Mom's paystub looks like. They were too young for that. I wanted them to have realistic expectations of

different things. I didn't want to crush them, but I wanted them to know opportunities existed based on what I now make.

Some parents chose not to disclose their economic hardship to their college-aged children because they wanted them to focus on school and not worry or stress about their pending foreclosure. Recounting her decision on informing her two older daughters about her pending foreclosure, Vanessa explained, "They're at college and with them being away from home that was too much stress." Eventually, Vanessa's daughters learned about the foreclosure after she lost the home. And on reflecting on the situation Vanessa said, "It was very challenging! Just having something what you knew to be a part of your life without a thought. The thought was going back home after completing college." Frank and Sandra, a married couple with three children, followed a similar approach in not informing their college-aged children. "We didn't want to stress them out … we had two daughters who were both in college. It would've probably been too much for them," Sandra said, "They don't need to know because they're not paying any bills." Although their home was saved, Sandra later explained she would have advised her kids if the home was foreclosed.

Food insecurity was also problematic for some homeowners during the foreclosure crisis. Heads of households made tremendous sacrifices, such as not dining out at restaurants, to shield their children from the fallout of an impending foreclosure. Participants in this study indicated that it was a shared duty to ensure that their children's needs were met and they were not affected by their financial hardship. Interestingly, however, the study found that mothers frequently took leadership in preventing their children from going hungry in food-insecure households. A recurring trend in the data provided by the mothers in this study was that they deliberately abstained from eating certain meals during the day to ensure that their children had something to eat for each mealtime. Feminist sociologist Marjorie L. DeVault (1991) notes, "Women seem to be expressing a heightened sense of the more widespread notion that women's own food is less important than that prepared for others" (p.199).

More than half of the homeowners interviewed in this study reported food security (assessed as skipping or delaying meals as a result of cost) as a significant issue during their fight to avoid foreclosure. The rationing of food in the home followed a logical ordering that was primarily based on age, which exemplified the sacrifices mothers were willing to make by putting the children's needs before their own. Roxanne recounted:

> I make sure that my kids eat—that's my number one priority. There are times I would come home if I cooked a meal and it's enough for two days and if there's just enough for them [kids] then they would eat. I wouldn't eat. That's just what a mother does and that's what I did.

While such deeds are highly commendable, some scholars argue these selfless acts pose a significant health risk for women. One study revealed that mothers residing in food-insecure households are at a higher risk of suffering from nutrient deficiencies in vitamin A, iron, and magnesium, which are vitally necessary for health (Tarasuk & Beaton, 1999).

Some distressed homeowners even struggled to keep up payments on their household utility bills. In this study, three homeowners reported that their household utilities were disconnected on several occasions. Vanessa describes this ordeal as one of the most gut-wrenching experiences in her life, particularly when her daughter returned home from school to find the home in darkness. Vanessa's daughter waited inside the sweltering house during a hot summer day in Jacksonville until her mother returned from work to sort things out. Vanessa was forced to neglect all other bills, including her electricity bill, just to pay her mortgage. Her strategy was to try to make partial payments on all her utility bills each month until the next billing cycle, hoping that there would not be any service disruptions.

Despite her best efforts to maintain this strategy, Vanessa's worst fear came to fruition when her young daughter was unable to enter the home through the garage after the electricity was disconnected because of lack of payment. Although her daughter had a key to the house, Vanessa preferred that she enter the home using the garage door opener. This was a daily routine for Vanessa's daughter, who had been removed from her after-school program to reduce household expenses. Unable to enter the house, Vanessa's daughter went over to the neighbor's house to phone her mother and inform her that the garage door opener was not working. Vanessa reported that her heart dropped because she knew right away that the electricity was disconnected. Vanessa tried to console her daughter by letting her know that everything was okay. The lack of thermal comfort in the home and the disconnection were the direct sources of Vanessa's ongoing stress and anxiety during foreclosure. Vanessa felt as if she failed as a parent and was no longer able to shield her daughters from the fallout from the foreclosure process. Vanessa expressed her frustrations over her financial hardship, saying:

> I felt like I failed as a mother. Juggling the electrical bill to then make my car payment because I need to have transportation and fuel to get to work to make more money to try to pay bills and have that cycle continue. I want to say my electricity was disconnected probably about four times.

The cycle of juggling bills left many homeowners frustrated because as they became current on one bill, they knew there were other bills they were unable to pay. Frank and Sandra, who also experienced several utility disconnections, spoke candidly about this predicament. Frank noted:

> Every now and then we would fall behind on the utilities bill and we would call and make arrangements. We would rob Peter to pay Paul. We know that

248 Nemoy Lewis

> merry-go-round story … We tried to focus on the bills that were going to affect our credit score. That was the mortgage and the car note.

However, Sandra and Frank were not indifferent to how the service interruptions made them feel, especially when their children were present. Sandra noted she felt embarrassed and recalled one occasion during the summer when it was 90° Fahrenheit (32° Celsius) in the home after the electricity was disconnected. She indicated that in a casual voice she alerted one of her children who was present at the time, saying, "Lights are out. Go to someone's house and cool off." She felt especially embarrassed when her daughter said, "Mom, we don't have no lights," to which Sandra indicated that she replied in a sharp tone, "I know!" Frank, on the other hand, reported that he was quite composed during the disconnection. "It happened; it's done," Frank recalled saying. "What's the worst thing that could happen? You pay it and it comes back on and you keep moving."

The foreclosure crisis also had many parents stressed about the possibility of their children changing schools. All the parents in this study were determined to keep their children enrolled in the same school. The imminent threat of foreclosure placed immense pressure on them to maintain the early life advantages the high-quality schools their children attended offered them. Parents were equally concerned that residential instability would result in their severing ties with important social networks and institutions in the community, further depleting their social capital. In fact, most parents worked hard to avoid any disruptions to their children's education. Thomas, a 55-year-old married father of two children, explained that despite his ongoing financial troubles he was determined to keep his son enrolled in private school. According to Thomas:

> Part of the reason we are in this situation [foreclosure] is because I took out a loan against my home to pay for my son's private school … I was making the payments, but I was just late. This affected everything I needed to pay! There wasn't really a whole lot of money left over.

Like most parents affected by foreclosure, Thomas was fearful that moving to a new home would acutely affect his son's scholastic performance, possibly causing him to develop low self-esteem and diminish his sense of self-worth and self-confidence, which were crucial in his academic pursuits. Several studies concur with such concerns, indicating that changing schools has a negative impact on a child's educational achievements and that most parents in these situations tended to move to inferior schools (Been, Ellen, Schwartz, Stiefel, & Weinstein, 2011; D. E. Davis & Shin, 2009; Pettit & Comey, 2012; Weinstein, Schwartz, Been, Ellen, & Stiefel, 2011). The struggles children experienced tended to stem from variations in curricula across various geographies, and children who change schools often struggle or take extended periods of time to get accustomed to new teaching styles, instructional languages, and textbooks (Mehana & Reynolds, 2004). As a

The Impact of Foreclosures **249**

consequence, children's academic performance tends to suffer in the interim as they acclimatize to their new schooling environment (Rumberger, 2016).

As middle-class Black parents, Thomas and his wife were committed to long-term planning to give their son the best chance in life even if that meant going into debt. From a neoliberal perspective, Thomas and his wife treated their son's education as an investment in his human capital (Lipman, 2011). In their analysis of strategies used by Black middle-class parents to raise their kids, Rollock, Gillborn, Vincent, and Ball (2015) categorize this approach as "determined to get the best." Parents who fall into this category often relocate to areas with higher-quality schools, especially when the children are young, in anticipation of their formative years in school (Rollock et al., 2015). Like most parents in the present study, these parents viewed the high cost of private school as a meaningful investment, "partly because they view high achievement as a means of avoiding or at least minimizing racial disadvantages in the future" (Rollock et al., 2015, p. 49). For some parents, notable educational achievements were understood as the key to offering their children future opportunities and life advantages that would otherwise be out of reach. These advantages include attending prestigious colleges and working in highly respected professions where Black people are underrepresented.

Fortunately, all the children in this study were able to remain at the same schools despite some families losing their fight to remain in their houses. Louise, a 45-year-old divorced single mother with one daughter, explained that even though her home was foreclosed, she sought to minimize the impact on her daughter by not having to relocate her to another school. She commented:

> My daughter already had to endure enough change to no longer be in a home that was occupied by a two-parent household. That was a significant amount of change in her life already. There didn't have to be as much impact, so I tried to make that as minimal as possible in terms of affecting her.

Parents were fearful that a move would invite a heightened level of discontinuity in the children's learning environment, which some scholars suggest may acutely affect their learning, particularly if the moves are frequent or occur during the early stages of a child's development (Mehana & Reynolds, 2004). A number of research studies have documented the negative effects of involuntary displacement on a student's academic success (Hanushek, Kain, & Rivkin, 2004). The findings indicate that students who switch schools record lower math and reading proficiency scores than students in more stable school environments (Isaacs, 2012).

Discussion

Foreclosures and the stress of financial hardship have the potential to profoundly impact a child's schooling and education. The increased levels of anxiety and depression among troubled homeowners could cause parents to interact negatively with their children and could lead to a lack of emotional support at home. The results from this study suggest that some of the benefits associated with Black people owning homes are quite different from the realities they encountered. The idea that Black people have the same rights and protections afforded to them as their white counterparts was not supported by their experience, considering Black people lost their homes at an unprecedented rate. Black homeowners were provided high-priced loans with the highest possible interest rates, which made it impossible for them to avoid foreclosure (Bocian & Ernst, 2008).

The detrimental experiences of foreclosure during childhood have the potential to fester in adolescence and adulthood. Consequently, these interactions also have the potential to impair Black children's ability to succeed in school and indirectly create unequal learning outcomes. It is clear that foreclosures destabilize Black families and communities, and a longer-term inclusive plan will be required to keep these families housed. Perhaps as important as keeping families housed are policies that reflect a vested interest in averting the long-term effects that home foreclosures can have on Black children by ensuring that they are afforded the educational benefits required to secure a decent quality of life.

According to the American Dream, buying a home is supposed to be a very exciting time in a homeowner's life. Homeownership is presented as a viable opportunity for Black households not only to accumulate wealth but also to access better amenities, high-quality schools, and better social environments in which their children may thrive. Historically, homeownership has paved the way for a new beginning for disenfranchised minorities, a way out of poverty, and an opportunity to develop a sense of belonging and have a better chance at life.

However, as was found, the expanded access to homeownership became a source of pain and subsequent agony for many Black households. The imminent threat of foreclosures caused families to alter their way of life, which included making changes in family routines and traditions, living without utilities, and losing the ability to make healthy life choices for themselves and their children. The results of this study also demonstrate that foreclosures have a profound impact not only on a child's well-being but also on their academic performance. In mitigating the effects of these challenges, parents adopted an array of strategies to safeguard their children from the fallout of the housing crisis. But while some of the sacrifices were effective in the short term in that they were able to maintain a stable environment for their children, others were ineffective since they were unable to help homeowners avoid foreclosure and maintain ownership in the long term. These sacrifices, although demonstrating the great lengths to which some Black homeowners would go to maintain a stable living environment for their children, only delayed the foreclosure process and limited the availability of educational remedies available to these families.

Conclusion

This chapter is a timely intervention at a moment where Black households are becoming highly mobile, but little consideration is given to understanding the economic circumstances that enable them to access certain kinds of communities. It would appear that in "good times," when the economy is robust and there is relative social cohesion, neoliberal society wishes to embrace a perspective of cosmopolitanism as promoting mobility and equity across fluid transnational spaces and boundaries. Yet, as neoliberalism contributes to the "superdiversity" of urban and suburban communities (Vertovec, 2007), at the same time, this study recognizes that these gains are not without cost, as demonstrated by the significant financial burden placed on racialized families, especially Black households. We must, too, acknowledge that race exists at the very core of these perceived injustices around equity and entitlement. Indeed, our conclusion is in line with the critical cosmopolitan perspective put forward in this volume that extends beyond the embracing of diversity to unearthing the conditions of entitlement and inequality that provoke people to converge or clash with others in societal contexts where resources are circumscribed and increasingly contested.

This work also extends the discussion on cosmopolitan environments in demonstrating how Black households achieve community through homeownership. It illuminates the nuances of those experiences once individuals have access to these spaces, examining in particular the burden placed on Black youth. In this chapter, I have highlighted how achieving community through homeownership for Black households is not as straightforward as may appear on the surface as a result of anti-Black policies in housing finance that places Black homeowners and their children in precarious living conditions. In good times, these discriminatory policies are less visible, and neoliberal societies may convince themselves that they represent an "equal opportunity" viewpoint that is interested in promoting those who have been historically disenfranchised into positions of empowerment. However, when—through mismanagement, greed, unforeseen global developments, or a combination of these factors—economic conditions become more constrained, a different viewpoint comes into play, one that undermines people on the basis of race and social background. Indeed, factors related to race are weaponized by those in control and read into institutional risk assessment around trustworthiness and predictability with regard to questions of belonging—and homeownership. This chapter argues that better policies are needed to eradicate the inequities in the housing market in order to improve the lived experiences of Black households and the schooling of Black youth in these putative "integrated" spaces.

References

Aalbers, M. (2016). *The financialization of housing: A political economy approach*. London, UK: Routledge.

Appiah, K. A. (2006). *Cosmopolitanism: Ethics in a world of strangers*. New York: W. W. Norton.

Been, V., Ellen, I. G., Schwartz, A. E., Stiefel, L., & Weinstein, M. (2011). Does losing your home mean losing your school?: Effects of foreclosures on the school mobility of children. *Regional Science and Urban Economics, 41*(4), 407–414. doi: 10.1016/j.regsciurbeco.2011.02.006

Beck, U. (2006). *The cosmopolitan vision*. Cambridge, UK: Polity Press.

Bocian, D. G., & Ernst, K. S. (2008). Race, ethnicity and subprime home loan pricing. *Journal of Economics of Business, 60*(1/2), 110–124.

Brown, W. (2017). *Undoing the demos: Neoliberalism's stealth revolution*. Brooklyn, NY: Zone Books.

Collins, C. C., & Berg, K. A. (2019). Losing a little part of yourself: Families' experiences with foreclosure. *Journal of Family Issues, 40*(13), 1832–1859. doi: 10.1177/0192513X19848795

Davis, A. Y. (2012). *The meaning of freedom: And other difficult dialogues*. San Francisco, CA: City Lights.

Davis, D.-A. (2007). Narrating the mute: Racializing and racism in a neoliberal moment. *Souls, 9*(4), 346–360. doi: 10.1080/10999940701703810

Davis, D. E., & Shin, M. (2009). The lives of Sesame Street: The impact of foreclosures on young children and families. *Contemporary Issues in Early Childhood, 10*(2), 182–184. doi: 10.2304/ciec.2009.10.2.182

DeVault, M. L. (1991). *Feeding the family: The social organization of caring as gendered work*. Chicago, IL: University of Chicago Press.

Dickerson, M. (2014). *Homeownership and America's financial underclass: Flawed premises, broken promises, new prescriptions*. New York: Cambridge University Press.

Ford, J., Burrows, R., & Nettleton, S. (2001). *Home ownership in a risk society: A social analysis of mortgage arrears and possessions*. Bristol, UK: Policy Press.

Gilmore, R. W. (2007). *Golden gulag: Prisons, surplus, crisis, and opposition in globalizing California*. Berkeley, CA: University of California Press.

Gilmore, R. W. (2017). Abolition geography and the problem of innocence. In G. T. Johnson & A. Lubin (Eds.), *Futures of Black radicalism* (pp. 225–240). London, UK: Verso.

Goetz, E. G. (2007). Is housing tenure the new neighborhood dividing line? In W. M. Rohe & H. L. Watson (Eds.), *Chasing the American dream: New perspectives on affordable homeownership* (pp. 96–110). Ithaca, NY: Cornell University Press.

Hanushek, E. A., Kain, J. F., & Rivkin, S. G. (2004). Disruption versus Tiebout improvement: The costs and benefits of switching schools. *Journal of Public Economics, 88*(9), 1721–1746. doi: 10.1016/S0047-2727(03)00063-X

Harvey, D. (2009). *Cosmopolitanism and the geographies of freedom: Wellek Library lectures*. New York: Columbia University Press.

Isaacs, J. B. (2012). *The ongoing impact of foreclosures on children*. Washington, DC: Brookings. Retrieved from https://www.brookings.edu/wp-content/uploads/2016/06/0418_foreclosures_children_isaacs.pdf

Kingsley, G. T., Smith, R. E., & Price, D. (2009). *The impacts of foreclosures on families and communities*. Washington, DC: Urban Institute. Retrieved from ttps://http://www.urban.org/sites/default/files/publication/30426/411909-The-Impacts-of-Foreclosures-on-Families-and-Communities.PDF

Kotz, D. M. (2015). *The rise and fall of neoliberal capitalism*. Cambridge, MA: Harvard University Press.

Lacy, K. (2007). *Blue-chip Black: Race, class, and status in the new Black middle class*. Berkeley, CA: University of California Press.

Langley, P. (2008). *The everyday life of global finance: Saving and borrowing in Anglo-America.* Oxford, UK: Oxford University Press.

Leong, N. (2013). Racial capitalism. *Harvard Law Review, 126*(8), 2151–2226.

Lewis, N. K. (2018). *A dream denied: The fight against the mass eviction of families in Chicago and Jacksonville, USA.* (Doctoral dissertation). Retrieved from ProQuest Dissertations Publishing, Kingston, ON, Canada.

Lewis-McCoy, R. L. H. (2014). *Inequality in the promised land: Race, resources, and suburban schooling.* Stanford, CA: Stanford University Press.

Lipman, P. (2011). *The new political economy of urban education: Neoliberalism, race, and the right to the city.* New York: Routledge.

Mahmud, T. (2012). Debt and discipline. *American Quarterly, 64*(3), 469–494.

Martin, R. (2002). *Financialization of daily life.* Philadelphia, PA: Temple University Press.

McCormack, K., & Mazar, I. (2015). Understanding foreclosure risk: The role of nativity and gender. *Critical Sociology, 41*(1), 115–132. doi: 10.1177/0896920512463413

Mehana, M., & Reynolds, A. J. (2004). School mobility and achievement: A meta-analysis. *Children and Youth Services Review, 26*(1), 93–119. doi: 10.1016/j.childyouth.2003.11.004

Nettleton, S. (2001). Losing a home through mortgage repossession: The views of children. *Children and Society, 15*(2), 82–94.

Oliver, M., & Shapiro, T. (2013). *Black wealth/white wealth: A new perspective on racial inequality* (2nd ed.). New York: Routledge.

Osuna, S. (2017). Class suicide: The Black radical tradition, radical scholarship, and the neoliberal turn. In G. T. Johnson & A. Lubin (Eds.), *Futures of Black radicalism* (pp. 21–38). London, UK: Verso.

Pettit, K. L. S., & Comey, J. (2012). *The foreclosure crisis and children: A three-city study*: Research report. Washington, DC: Urban Institute. Retrieved from https://www.urban.org/sites/default/files/publication/25151/412517-The-Foreclosure-Crisis-and-Children-A-Three-City-Study.PDF

Robinson, C. J. (1983). *Black Marxism: The making of the Black radical tradition.* London, UK: Zed Book Company.

Rohe, W. M., & Linbald, M. R. (2014). Reexamining the social benefits of homeownership after the foreclosure crisis. In E. S. Belsky, C. E. Herbert, & J. H. Molinsky (Eds.), *Homeownership built to last: Balancing access, affordability, and risk after the housing crisis* (pp. 99–142). Washington, DC: Brookings Institution Press.

Rollock, N., Gillborn, D., Vincent, C., & Ball, S. J. (2015). *The colour of class: The educational strategies of the Black middle classes.* London, UK: Routledge.

Ross, L. M., & Squires, G. D. (2011). The personal costs of subprime lending and the foreclosure crisis: A matter of trust, insecurity, and institutional deception. *Social Science Quarterly, 92*(1), 140–163. doi: 10.1111/j.1540-6237.2011.00761.x

Rothstein, R. (2017). *The color of law: A forgotten history of how our government segregated America* (1st ed.). New York: Liveright.

Rumberger, R. W. (2016). Student mobility: Causes, consequences, and solutions. *Education Digest, 81*(8), 61–64.

Schneider, W., Waldfogel, J., & Brooks-Gunn, J. (2016). Mothers' and fathers' parenting. In I. Garfinkel, S. McLanahan, & C. Wimer (Eds.), *Children of the great recession* (pp. 173–205). New York: Russell Sage Foundation.

Shapiro, T. M. (2004). *The hidden cost of being African American: How wealth perpetuates inequality.* New York: Oxford University Press.

Shapiro, T. M. (2017). *Toxic inequality: How America's wealth gap destroys mobility, deepens the racial divide, & threatens our future.* New York: Basic Books.

Springer, S., Birch, K., & MacLeavy, J. (2016). *The handbook of neoliberalism*. New York: Routledge.

Tarasuk, V. S., & Beaton, G. H. (1999). Women's dietary intakes in the context of household food insecurity. *Journal of Nutrition, 129*(3), 672–679. doi: 10.1093/jn/129.3.672

van Ham, M. (2012). Housing behaviour. In D. F. Clapham, W. A. V. Clark, & K. Gibb (Eds.), *The SAGE handbook of housing studies* (pp. 47–65). Thousand Oaks, CA: SAGE.

Vertovec, S. (2007). Super-diversity and its implications. *Ethnic and Racial Studies, 30*(6), 1024–1054. doi: 10.1080/01419870701599465

Vertovec, S., & Cohen, R. (2002). Introduction: Conceiving cosmopolitanism. In S. Vertovec & R. Cohen (Eds.), *Conceiving cosmopolitanism: Theory, context and practice* (pp. 32–41). Oxford, UK: Oxford University Press.

Weinstein, M., Schwartz, A., Been, V., Ellen, I., & Stiefel, L. (2011). Foreclosure and kids: When losing your home means losing your school. *Poverty & Race, 20*(2), 3–5.

16

SHELTERED IN PLACE

When Walls Trump Bridges

Suzanne de Castell

This chapter is not a research report; it is a researcher's story.[1] And though it is not about linguistic and cultural diversity, nor directly about "cosmopolitanism," it is about some changes needed to support it, and some of the often overlooked, invariably unmentionable things that stand in its way. It is also a way of trying to make sense of a failed undertaking. That is a hard thing to do, because failure is distasteful, aversive, particularly for those doing well by a system. Talk of it borders on the impolite and mostly gets us nowhere. As Paul Rabinow (1986) long ago observed, "One of the most common tactics of an elite group is to refuse to discuss—to label as vulgar or uninteresting, issues that are uncomfortable for them" (p. 253). An always-impossible story, it is in Spivak's (1990) memorable terms, "non-narrativizable" (pp. 143–145). The extent to which public education plays a legitimating role in the production of socially structured failure speaks to the importance of making other stories possible. We might need ways to tell and listen to stories of failure, of things that aren't working in education today, to make sense of—and not be driven to distraction by—our experiences with it.

Public education's ability to provide all children, across all communities, with access to the skills and knowledge needed to participate in democratically regulated social, cultural, and vocational life is an aspiration increasingly difficult to realize under present-day conditions in both K–12 and postsecondary education. So it's helpful to keep in mind that public education systems have *never* met this challenge and that throughout public schooling's successive transformations, measured educational outcomes have continued to demonstrate a clear and undeniable relationship between income and achievement that long predates today's distinctively digital "divide" (Counts, 1932; Gorski, 2005).[2] Parents purchasing their children's educational success has its own very long (and very patriarchal) history that has, until women became involved in what has now

DOI: 10.4324/9780429327780-16

256 Suzanne de Castell

been designated "college admissions scandals," merited neither criminal proceedings nor public scorn. Under the power of false assumptions, can we be surprised that parental income is "the single greatest driver of student achievement ... the metric most predictive of a child's educational success"? (Hanauer, 2019, n.p.).[3]

Can we interrupt this "income/outcome equation"? Understanding that inadequate access to digital tools and resources is just the most recent manifestation of deeply structured inequality and cannot therefore be the cause of it, might these powerful digital tools and methods nevertheless be deployed as "levers" to interrupt and change its long-entrenched patterns?

This question drove a project initiated in 2013 to build a working relationship between a technology-focused faculty of education and the high-needs public schools in its immediate area, attended by students with little or no access to narratives of possibility in which a university education plays any part. Teachers and faculty lived and worked close by, yet the faculty of education was primarily involved with schools (though not *these* schools particularly) as sites in which teacher education students could be placed for the extended periods of classroom experience required to graduate, or as sites for faculty and graduate students to carry out their research. With district standardized test scores of these immediately located schools being consistently among the lowest in the province, it seemed long past time to get together.

A partnership development initiative between the faculty and the school district was initiated to mobilize the faculty's expertise and its technology-rich resources to help teachers in nearby high-needs schools make the "paradigm shift" to digital pedagogies for 21st-century literacy and learning. Contending, as agents, with globalization's ubiquitous impact in its lived, localized forms, everyone, whatever their conditions, nowadays requires access to some means of (digital) reception and production. Culture, politics, health, environment, education, and entertainment—all have been transformed by globalization, and all are accessible online, even where little may be accessible in one's lived reality. Students have no less need now for network access than their predecessors had for universal access to public libraries: at least a hope, if not a promise, of both mobility and place.

The Divide is Not Digital

For the last decade, most of the attention paid to "21st-century education" (21CE) has consisted in efforts to define, specify, characterize, and describe what a technologically supported refiguration of public schooling can, should, or must consist in. Most often, these efforts have been in the service of promoting and advancing "21st-century skills, technology and learning." Now well into the century, most educational administrations in the developed world have to a greater or lesser extent embraced the 21CE agenda. As the implications and impacts of what can properly be called a new educational paradigm are becoming evident, so are significant obstacles and impediments to its realization. Less obvious are the ways in which this embrace of 21CE has been a diversion.

That effectively and consistently mobilizing technologies as pedagogical tools call upon resources not readily available in all schools is obvious, and access to tools has been a priority. This inequitable provision of resources has been—misleadingly—labeled a "digital divide." But the divide is not digital. The digital is far from divisive, and indeed there is nothing more integrative than code (de Castell, 2011, p, 234). Digital technologies provide, for the first time in human history, a master code, a code of all codes, capable of representing knowledge of any and all kinds. Such a digital code promises a common language bridging qualitative and quantitative studies, human and physical sciences, philosophy, music, art, and mathematics, work and play, leisure and learning, body and mind. Digital competence is, in sum, a fundamental literacy requisite for participatory citizenship under conditions of globalization.

Educational inequality persists, to be sure, in uneven access to digital devices for classroom use and, maybe more importantly, in an increasingly dysfunctional pedagogical mismatch between traditional means and innovative ends. This is less about machines, though, and more about the numbing effects of a pervasive culture of poverty. Indeed, lack of technology, technology support, or a specific kind of technology, are often raised as barriers to digital pedagogies when they need not be. Even in the most privative conditions today, many people have nonstandard but functional technologies in everyday use (cellphones, game consoles), and whatever conduit can be had can serve educational ends, if teachers know how to use them and schools allow their use. Support for teacher upskilling in digital pedagogy is far less available in under-resourced schools than are the technologies it requires.

Having secured sufficient resources to provide both tools and teacher support,[4] our partnership grant could contribute the requisite means, from hardware to workshops to tutors and teacher release time, to see whether (and how) we could apply faculty knowledge, skills, and resources for both "upskilling" for teachers and individualized tutoring support for students. Three full years of funding would make it possible to track and document changes on all sides—further, this time span would allow teachers interested in pursuing a purpose-built graduate program to complete their studies. This key feature of the project design was informed by studies of the value-added when teachers pursued advanced studies in education (Sahlberg, 2007). Eleven faculty members, the school district, two other faculties of education, and several community agencies signed on to a partnership, and we were off.

Three years became six, and the project was, finally, ending. A span of six years means there are far too many stories to tell in a single chapter, so what follow are "impressionist vignettes" (Van Maanen, 1988) about beginnings, middles, and ends, scripted—because *all* stories are only ever partial accounts—to make visible some of the contours of the wall that was built between us, in the context of what became a "partnership" in name alone.

Research and Redirection

Beginnings

The fall of 2015, with a new school year ahead, saw a day-long project "kick-off" meeting at the faculty of education, with representatives from each partner organization. The goals, rationale, and intended outcomes for the project were reviewed, and there followed breakout group discussions where individuals shared their current research and identified projects envisaged for the future and how these might connect to the key objectives of the partnership project. That startup meeting was intended to provide any needed information and assurances, and to refamiliarize partners with the partnership's research goals to which we had all signed on. The next step was to work with the school district to facilitate our applications to both school district and university ethics boards for approval of the projects described in the proposal. We were taken aback, however, when we were advised that the district ethics board would not approve the project as written. That original proposal, now funded, to which partners had signed on, had been for a whole-school, cross-curricular digital literacies program. To make a positive difference to its neighborhood schools, specifically at two high-needs schools closest to the faculty, the integration of technologies school-wide across academic, social, and physical education had been key, as had outreach to the students' caregivers and community.

First, the school district research officer advised that we should specify each aspect of the study separately, which meant decomposing the whole-school intervention into "subprojects," each in a different content area led by an individual faculty researcher. The district assigned each of what became five separate projects to five different schools. Undeterred, we pressed on, even though the entire shape of the intervention was already fundamentally reconfigured, undermining its aspirations to build bridges between the faculty of education and its educationally disadvantaged local community.

At a follow-up meeting on December 15, 2015, between school board representatives and faculty researchers to finalize research sites, determine the school board's contributions, and set dates for projects to begin, further changes to the research program were communicated to us.[5] During that same meeting, one district research staff member asked how critical the teacher PD and action research components were to the project. Then one of the superintendents asked whether the teacher education piece of the project was "really necessary," and objections were voiced to giving "some teachers development opportunities that were not available to all." This would have been the second very good time to stop and reconsider the prospects for a research-driven, technology intervention-focused partnership.[6] Instead, we set to work developing online open-access modules teachers could use to support the digital literacy programming that remained a focus.

A third meeting was set for mid-January 2016, in anticipation of a project start date two weeks thence. Meanwhile, the faculty research team had been

Sheltered in Place **259**

unraveling—some members took up faculty positions elsewhere, some went on leave, others directed their efforts at projects that could proceed while the digital literacies project was stalled and, it seems in retrospect, stymied.

Losing the Plot

At our next meeting with district staff, we'd hoped to clarify how the district could support teachers' technology access and release time for professional learning. Following a brief update on the various subprojects, one superintendent expressed the view that the subprojects were having little to no impact, and that the board was not hearing anything positive from teachers or principals. We were advised that technology funding in this district was to be used for Chromebooks, not iPads, and that to protect students' personal data, teachers could not use any apps that collected user data—nothing that tracked student progress, for example. Thus informed, we were now directed to work more closely with school principals. Previously, we had asked to partner directly with schools but were told all interaction with schools was to be directed through the school board—though school board staff seemed disengaged, far too busy, uninterested, and unimpressed. Trying to engage teachers directly as researchers in the project, we were told by them that only district-initiated research would be approved and that teachers were not permitted to initiate their own classroom research projects.

With most of the project funding unspent, and with the division and dispersion of its research team members, this would have been another right time to terminate the project. Instead, we scaled back to one digital literacies initiative in the largest high-needs school. With the remaining researchers positioned alternately as providers of school iPads and as rather pesky and unproductive petitioners, rather than as valuable (and well-resourced) collaborators in an agreed-upon educational initiative, the now much-scaled-back work proceeded through the school principal instead of the board. While several subsequent attempts were made to reach out to school district staff,[7] key district staff had since changed roles, retired, or moved on, and no one remained of that original team.

Transforming Pedagogy: A Good Story

Within what was already an increasingly eroding structure of distinct and separately located "subprojects,"[8] the specific project described here focused simply on encouraging the use of iPads to support digital literacy development. The longest-running and last-surviving of the subprojects, this one involved 10 teachers and 130 students between the ages of 6 and 9 across 6 elementary school classrooms over 2 years. We had the leadership and support of the teacher-librarian and principal, three research assistants, and, for one year of the study, six recently graduated teachers hired to support the project as part-time tutors. Data were compiled from teacher and student interviews, classroom observations, fieldnotes, teacher

260 Suzanne de Castell

questionnaires, focus group reflections with tutors, notes and minutes from meetings with school district staff, videotaped professional development workshops, and illustrative examples of student work. This Integrated Literacies program used a multiliteracies/multimodalities, technology-infused literacy framework focused on developing 21st-century competencies of critical thinking, problem-solving, communication, and collaboration by advancing teachers' curricular goals using digital literacy pedagogies.[9]

We began by hosting a whole-school teacher information breakfast, inviting all interested teachers to participate. The teachers who participated spanned Grades 1–4—although the research design had specified work with Grades 2 and 5 to be able to use annual Ontario Ministry of Education assessments through the Education Quality Assessment Office (EQAO)[10] to identify learning impacts. Research funds covered the release of five teachers to attend two half-day in-school professional development workshops led by the program designer, with three additional days of classroom modeling and support visits mid- and post-training in the first iteration of the program, in 2017–2018. In the second iteration of the program, in 2018–2019, nine teachers participated in two full days of workshops and lesson planning, with one full day of classroom modeling and support from the program designer. To invite feedback and enrich the data, an online survey collecting teacher responses was carried out at two points in the process. We provided the teachers with 50 iPads, 25 on loan from other projects and 25 to keep at the end of the project for teachers to continue their digital literacies programs. In light of research identifying tutoring as one of the most effective ways of helping students in high-needs, underachieving schools (Dietrichson, Bøg, Filges, & Klint Jørgensen, 2017), we recruited qualified teacher education graduates who had been unable to secure jobs during a period of teacher oversupply to assist in class as tutors, with each classroom teacher determining who needed that help the most. The tutoring program ran over two academic years, first with Bachelor of Education student volunteers and subsequently with paid Bachelor of Education graduates.

Research team members observed all instructional sessions, scheduling visits with individual teachers, observing classes, and conversing informally with teachers and students. They scheduled and supervised the "tutoring teachers," communicated with them about assignments and requirements, collected tutors' notes, and carried out group interviews. To support program sustainability beyond the project, a teachers' manual was developed in two versions: a glossy full-color print version given to each teacher who participated that used images of their own students and classrooms in the hope of making the content more meaningful and memorable, and a public-facing, online version using stock images.[11] This open-access "teacher's manual" was intended to help sustain teachers' digital pedagogy beyond the life of the project.

What follows is a selection of illuminating comments from teachers, students, and the school principal describing their experiences of that program. It's certainly possible to "cherry pick" from interview and survey and observational data, but we had solid evidence that both students and teachers were taking up and learning to use new tools.

Teachers said:

> We use iPads an hour a day/Kids really engaged/everybody's technology use has definitely improved, big time, big time/Technology fluency, yes 100%/I can't wait to do this more/I loved it and look forward to learning more/Collaboration really stepped up.

Students told us:

> We use iPads everyday [sic] … they helped me learning/I used the read … reflect strategies, got better at reading and writing/It was fun and we get to do different things on it and sometimes when were [sic] all done we can do *free choice*, and then um we I knew *how to search*, you just *swipe down*, and I know how to use *new apps*/It was helpful because we were taking turns and sharing and we were putting it in the middle so we could both tap./Helped me learn about lots of words, to sound out/Partner helped me learn be sharing and concentrating with my partner/Taught me to read/it actually helps me to learn stuff that I already don't know.

The *librarian*—a key person at the school who helped massively—wrote, "Thanks again for an amazing year with this program. We truly appreciate it."

And we heard from the *principal* that "for the most part we are doing very well and I see proof of implementation every day. We are very thankful for all that you have done for our school." Then after the program was over:

> We have been very impressed with the level at which the program has become embedded into the daily into the daily routines of the students AND teachers … At this point I have absolutely no concerns that the project will die on the vine—those that are using it are deeply committed to it. I think the addition of the training materials … will be a great supplement to the program as well—could be used as refreshers for already trained teachers as well as a guide for new teachers. Teachers are also able to support each other in how to use the program.
>
> *(Anon., personal communications excerpts, 2018–2019)*

What Does that Good Story Not Tell Us?

There's a widely acknowledged issue in quantitative research, originally designated the "file drawer problem" (Rosenthal, 1979), a kind of publication bias where findings of nonsignificance are quietly shelved in favor of studies reporting findings that achieve statistically significant results (Zagorski, 2006). This, in

262 Suzanne de Castell

turn, risks biasing public scientific and technical knowledge about the subjects of study (Ioannidis, 2005) and concealing findings that—while statistically non-significant—may tell us things about that subject that might be just as important to know about. In qualitative educational research, we have a comparable "good news" bias and a comparable disregard of informative but less "positive" research reports. And yet how reasonable is it to expect educational studies to present redemptive good news stories about advancements accomplished through research or policy or other educational interventions when we know that public education has largely been lamentably ineffective?

This small sample of the positive comments from teachers and students, supported by on-site observations, suggests that students *really did* become far more engaged and learned new skills and that their reading and collaboration abilities improved. So, seeing and knowing these things, we can tell a kind of good news story about this project—except it's not quite that simple unless you really don't want to see the problems. As we have already discovered, the way to keep numbers of those infected in a pandemic lower is simply not to test them—not to look. So, in the name of public educational hygiene, let's have a closer look at this good news. That means documenting and taking seriously the kinds of things that can and do go awry in undertaking a collaboration, especially between and among institutions that mostly don't "play well" together, and perhaps indicating some reasons for that. Documenting and studying these crossroads and intersections, no-go areas, obstacles, and redirections can make, it is hoped, an important contribution to understanding what makes it so hard for schools and universities to work together to effect the changes that are so very obviously needed, and so very clearly not happening.

From a researcher standpoint, what gets left out is the challenge of designing and implementing a program of school-based research when that program can be thoroughly reshaped, redirected, and actually impeded by district-level educational administrators. Why does Canada's federal research funding program require "partners" to commit to contributions of both human and material resources that are quite unenforceable in practice, if it is the district that controls researchers' involvement with schools and teachers, turning faculties of education into petitioners rather than collegial experts with knowledge, skills, and tools to share? What does it signify when a team of university-based researchers, who may themselves have educated a succession of district administrators, and who have spent, literally, years preparing an extensively detailed and hugely competitive proposal for adjudication (and prospective funding) by a team of highly educated and experienced reviewers for Canada's federal research council, find that mutually agreed-upon research design stripped away by school board administrators whose contribution, at the end of the day, amounted to time reading, responding to, and specifying revisions of the partnership proposal, then donating time for a changing group of four to five district staff to attend, in total, four face-to-face meetings? But there's a good deal more to this iceberg, and other perspectives to consider.

For research assistants, it remained difficult to visit classrooms implementing the program. Scheduling visits at a time convenient to all was impeded by access to the technology, which was never sufficient and always rationed. On several occasions, without being alerted in advance, researchers found substitute teachers in charge who knew nothing about the project, and their scheduled classroom observations abruptly canceled. Teacher uptake was—understandably—stalled when iPads weren't available, and the research team was able to supply just two class sets. The district provided no technological support, nor did we attempt further requests after several frankly discouraging meetings.

Meanwhile, the tutoring component, which had made so much sense in theory, was proving difficult to execute in practice. Backed by research reporting one-on-one tutoring to be the single most effective intervention to increase the educational achievements of underserved and lower-socioeconomic-status students (Dietrichson et al., 2017), and enabled by high teacher unemployment at that time, hiring unemployed teacher education graduates as tutors ought to have enabled us to assist students most at risk of being left behind as their teachers undertook some pedagogical innovation, helping both teachers and students make progress in the Integrated Literacies program. After lengthy and repeated efforts at outreach and recruitment, however, just six teachers were available. And although tutors' salaries were equivalent to that of a beginning public school teacher, few wanted to work as many hours as we had hoped to employ them for. Nor did they show much interest in attending the (paid) training sessions for the program.

We had directed the tutors to assist students designated by the teacher as needing special support in completing their regular classroom tasks. But in practice tutors were more often—and most typically—found working in a breakout area with two or three children, on whatever the teacher thought they most needed to work on. That also meant the tutors were far less often involved with either supporting students' everyday learning or supporting the specific learning tasks in the Integrated Literacies program and were most often used to help with "pull-out" students while the teacher conducted regular lessons with the rest of the class.

Where is the Teacher?

It's a phenomenon familiar to many classroom visitors, including researchers, that in the presence of another adult, teachers will absent themselves, whether to mark student work, or do some planning, or just have a bit of a break. The same can happen when technological tools and practices enter the room. Technology decenters instructional agency from the teacher, distributes attention across students' own desks, and requires—the great leveler—compliance with external control systems. Under these conditions, student attention isn't centered on the teacher any longer, and teachers may be unprepared to become engaged in educational activities over which they have such greatly diminished control and in which their participation requires an investment of significant effort and attention. Where teaching with technology is concerned, then, too often teachers can withdraw just at the very point students are getting engaged, missing a powerful "growth point" in their and their students' educational development. There is real work to do to help teachers understand their roles in technology implementation and to see how to get directly involved in it. It's real work for teachers to develop a new digital pedagogy, one that is quite different from the print-based pedagogy with which they are most familiar and confident. Understandably enough, we saw far more withdrawal than engagement from teachers, more willingness to step aside, to defer to students who are purportedly (but not actually) "digital natives," or to step out altogether, watching from the sidelines while students muddled along by themselves.

While some teachers treated digital tools as stand-alone pedagogical devices, however, not everyone did. Project teachers took up digital tools and methods to varying degrees and in different ways, composing a continuum from no impact to transformative impact. The least successful implementation amounted to no or minimal use of iPads for student learning, affording the program *no pedagogical impact* on the existing classroom routine. This was the case where the teacher's involvement with the technology was solely as a gatekeeper—for example, "allowing" students to use the iPads after they had finished their work if class ended early, or as a reward. The second kind of technology uptake was *program-restricted*: some teachers used the iPads for one or more of the centers, following the activities set out for that center; then the iPads were put away and the remainder of the day's activities returned to predigital business as usual. A third degree of implementation involved a *hybridized pedagogy*, combining digital affordances with traditional conceptions, contents, and methods: for instance, one teacher routinized his class's use of Apple TV for students to share their individual answers and explain their thought processes—albeit on traditional printed worksheets. The most impactful uptake of the program involved teachers in a completely different kind of pedagogy, a *digital pedagogy* properly so-called, that was interactive, multimodal, and collaborative. Demonstrated when, for example, pairs of students read, recorded, reflected together on, then uploaded their finished version for teacher comments (and parental access), digital pedagogy was *transformative* when teachers and students designed their own ways to apply these skills beyond the program, innovating new activities not set out for them using the tools and approaches introduced through the program.

The digital literacies program undertaken over more than two years did seem, based on what interview participants said, to have an impact on learning and to contribute positive educational experiences for teachers and students. Observations of classroom practice, however, while identifying all these points

Sheltered in Place **265**

along the continuum toward it, identified very few instances where digital tools and practices *transformed* "teaching and learning as usual," beyond the bounds of the program itself.

What, Then, Did We Accomplish?

Hoping to discover more about what may have "stuck" with teachers and students from their previous year's uses of digital technologies, and how and why it may have stuck, we asked to come back and talk with teachers and sit in on some classes of teachers who had participated in the Integrated Literacies program. We waited until the school got settled into the new academic year, then emailed the principal who was again enthusiastic and supportive but explained that the teachers needed more time to get up to speed. We asked again in October 2019, and the school librarian explained that she was preparing new machines (iPads) with the necessary Integrated Literacies program-related applications as well as starting to train occasional teachers who were covering maternity leave for previously trained teachers. We heard nothing further and decided to try again after the winter break. In January 2020, teachers across the province were gearing up for strike action that further disrupted plans for following up on the impact of the Integrated Literacies program. Still, a follow-up request was made in February 2020 to continue with plans to review the program implementation. As far as we have been able to determine, with no direct access to the school, there was almost no carryover of these new, reportedly engaging and effective practices to the 2019–2020 school year, disrupted first in Ontario by rotating teacher strikes and then entirely derailed by the very much global COVID-19 pandemic that saw schools closed down entirely. Ironically enough, it is precisely those digital competencies we were working to initiate and support that became most needed by teachers for whom online interaction had to do the work of face-to-face teaching.

Why Can't Schools Catch Up?

Some schools can and do make transformative educational use of digital tools. But many do not. And there is nothing random about the patterns of uptake and resistance that we have seen as we situate studies in their respective local contexts. After several years trying to help an education faculty's most underachieving, at-risk school, located just a few blocks from a university building full of technology experts and rich with technological resources for education, we conclude this story by describing some of the impediments we have confronted, none of which are "digital." These are powerful obstacles to sustaining a technology-based program in any high-needs school, however apparently practicable and successful it may appear in the moment, and make for powerful reasons why teachers may revert back to the same textbook-and-worksheet practices that had their students

266 Suzanne de Castell

so disengaged, badly behaved, not paying attention, not trying—and most of all, not learning.

In the neediest schools, teacher absenteeism and teacher turnover are unsustainably high. Of the ten teachers we trained, only three came back the next year. While we know in the case of more invested teachers, technology innovation/implementation "travels" with them, it also means in this school, Integrated Literacies program teachers were very much a minority and so could not rely on a supportive "critical mass" of like-minded colleagues.

Absenteeism and turnover in teaching, as in any workforce, are exacerbated by hardship, disadvantage, lack of support, and inability to be successful (Sibbald, 2017). Schools in communities of disadvantage, like many in this district, with extremely high numbers of students requiring accommodations and assistance, present teachers with exceptional challenges. For that reason, low socioeconomic status and low-achieving schools and districts will rarely be the first choice of teachers in demand for their skills and experience. Those just starting out, or those who have been unable to find positions elsewhere, may use such schools as a point of entry, to get a foothold, a place to stay only until they can transfer out. More young teachers, mostly women, generally mean extremely high rates of absence due to pregnancy—six of ten project teachers took pregnancy leave. In under-resourced, high-needs schools, working conditions are demanding, exhausting, and wearing, particularly for people who entered the profession with an interest, respect, and concern for children's well-being—and contribute to increased and unscheduled absenteeism. School administrators are constantly challenged to find substitute teachers who will cover unplanned absences, making it exceptionally difficult, and educationally disruptive for students, to release teachers from their classrooms, even when funds are available to cover the costs of substitutes. And when only a fraction of the teachers trained return to the same school the following year, there's little chance of impact.

Impact is a lot harder to measure in schools where student turnover is high. At this one, for example, with 50% of the student body changing between Grade 3 and Grade 6, tracking the impact of an intervention is well-nigh impossible for researchers. It is even hard for teachers to assess their own pedagogical effectiveness. Large-scale standardized assessment programs like EQAO may speak meaningfully about schools where classes are stable for most students most of the year, and for many students year after year. The data EQAO reports, however, can only mumble irrelevantly and unintelligibly to parents, teachers, and administrators in schools like this one,[12] where fully half the class were different students than those who'd started the year, where even just within the month before testing, four students left the school and where one arrived the day before the test, where a repeatedly evicted family moves every three months because it's the only way they can have a home.

The more profound if less obvious barrier signaled by this continuously and rapidly changing participant population is that these students' abrupt and sometimes multiple shifts of location during the school year are often connected to a trauma such as family breakdown, eviction, or moving from one foster home to another or to a shelter. Trauma and psychological distress would presumably account for some part of the 50%—more than half of a teacher's class—who have been formally identified as "high special needs" students. It's not much of a stretch to imagine how much of teachers' daily work is devoted to crisis management of one kind or another, simply trying to establish necessary basic conditions for learning.

As noted, teachers did not think of themselves as free to carry out their own research, let alone think of action research as integral to their pedagogical practice. And the district's lack of support for in-service graduate courses gave us no leverage with teachers. ("The Programs Department at [School District] already offers a number of different programs to their teachers for upskilling and does not fully understand the need for this teacher upskilling piece from [University]." Meeting Notes, 2017.) Although we stressed the value of research showing the real educational benefits of graduate teacher education, not a single teacher inquired about courses, or admission, or faculty specialization—it was as if the university might now be as remote from these teachers' interests and investments as it would predictably become for their students. Even our efforts to make technology pedagogy more accessible by creating and promoting teachers' use of open-source modules designed by two partnering faculties met with no uptake at all. This surely might seem surprising given teachers involved in the program expressed both an interest in learning, and a need to learn in order to assist their students. And yet …

To make matters worse, what we heard from our cadre of six tutors was that their education faculties did not prepare students to work in "unsuccessful" schools. In a focus group at the project's end, they specifically commented:

> We get one class, that one class, in child development, barely scratches the surface, in PJ, but they teach you like theories … autism … that was all theory. That's as much as we get; At [university] we were told you have to know your students, you have to have differentiated instruction, but it was all reading.

The purpose of the mandated extended practicum experiences integral to the province's teacher education program is to allow what might otherwise risk being "all reading" to become the kind of learning that takes root and enables informed practice. Theories that "scratch the surface" can be deepened by such experience, and students need to be charged with pursuing difficult knowledge about unruly subjects of all kinds—and to understand why that matters so much to their abilities as educators. And that can't happen if teacher candidates are not placed in schools where those experiences can take hold.

The tutors told us they felt completely unprepared for the school ("lowest school I've ever been in, shocking; School—looks like prison, but you can't put

268 Suzanne de Castell

things on the wall cuz kids rip them up"), the kinds of students ("they just don't care"; "They don't have the experiences we expect, they can't connect with their lives"; "they don't have the social skills/lifeskills to benefit"), their behavior ("I'm spending half the day just trying to get them to not throw scissors at each other"), and their families ("It comes from their parents").

These young teachers' lack of prior exposure to the school lives of children from communities of disadvantage produced a fundamentally very conservative, even privative, conception of things: "It's mostly behavioral; they have to have the basics covered then iPad integration would be helpful but ...; The questions were way over the kids' abilities—I think they're too young." The program for which these students were being judged "too young" by this tutor, incidentally, is one with which much younger children enjoy enormous success—the real question for us was why these tutors thought these children could not do the same thing. This significant underexpectation of students' abilities—and their families' abilities to support their kids' educational success—results in precisely the reversion noted previously to familiar nondigital pedagogies, as if these were somehow the "foundation" for digital literacies. But they simply are not (Thumlert, de Castell, & Jenson, 2014). Traditional text-based capabilities enable and support and extend digital media specializations, and vice versa; but there are many more starting points than these just-graduated teachers are imagining—and imagination is absolutely what's required to extend to the neediest learners[13] the resources virtually taken for granted by everyone else.

Educational (In)Justice: Bridging the Digital Divide

Even when we provided machines, training, teacher release time, online resources, and tutors, and even though teachers could clearly identify and attest to the positive learning outcomes they saw when using digital tools, those high-needs, at-risk students could not bridge that divide. And that's because *the divide is not digital*: it's about poverty, culture, and the tenacious hold of traditional practices, a kind of "paradigm paralysis" (Earl, Torrance, Sutherland, Fullan, & Ali, 2003, p. 7) that is both administrative and pedagogical and that keeps innovation under lockup, its students securely "sheltered in place" under the protective custody of the public school's establishment.

As Diana Brydon (2011) notes, "Universities today no longer hold a monopoly on knowledge production, the training of citizens, the provision of skills for the contemporary workplace, or the certification of professionals. Challenges to university authority and legitimacy come from many quarters" (p. 99). Challenges, though, are quite different from obstacles. Challenges can be taken up, addressed, responded to, met, or not. But challenges are not borders, they do not wall off discussion and close off questioning. To be sure, universities today have to engage with other stakeholders, with communities, with institutions not always allied. But the question should equally be asked: For what reasons are regional school districts not just in charge of teachers' most immediate educational management but also invested with final pedagogical authority and research leadership?

All students' experiences are mediated through institutionalized power relations, most directly by their teachers, next by school administrators as directed by regional school boards, and then by government. Any serious consideration of cosmopolitanism and public education must appreciate the impact that regional school boards have on every aspect of students' and teachers' shared, institutionally regulated, experiences and understandings of cosmopolitanism. This chapter has sought to illustrate impediments in both system and structure that can undermine educationally innovative collaboration between public schools and universities, and to show how district-level administration of teacher development can, with the best of protective intents, impede rather than promote regional schools' uptake of current and emerging educational research and scholarship.[14]

Sequestering teachers and students away from external influence is a kind of protectionism that is surely understandable for educational leaders in badly resourced schools already besieged by staffing problems from high absenteeism, high turnover, and teacher apathy. It is a response to what can seem like insurmountable problems of insufficient resources to improve the prospects for children and families in undereducated communities grown accustomed to the traumas of poverty. But that closing of borders means the persistence of business as usual and disregards evidence that professional education beyond local (district) provisions can become a powerful means of system improvement. It leaves public schools in the most troubled and repeatedly underachieving districts doing about as much as they ever have to recognize and embrace cultural and linguistic diversity and change, and it leaves faculties of education remote from, and powerless in the face of, the lived realities and current conditions of public education "in the wild."

Telling Stories ...

For every event, there are multiple stories that can be told and many ways of telling them. To conclude this one, having told a bit of a true story, and a bit of a good story, this last page turns to the question of what might be the *best* story to tell. A true story lays claim to veracity. A good story claims engagement. But the best story, neither altogether true nor necessarily engaging, is the one that makes a better outcome possible, one that identifies points for intervention, a story that catalyzes change. Only if a story can disrupt complacencies, challenge assumptions, infuriate or horrify or inspire efforts to *address poverty first*, before all else, before ability, or merit, or lineage, or language, or ethnicity, or identity, local or global or cosmopolitan—only then do we have the best story. And until we do that, every story about educational inequality is just a coverup.

Notes

1 This project is deeply indebted to many people—students and teachers, administrative and support staff, BEd student volunteers, tutors, teacher educators, and research assistants and co-researchers—none of whom are named here because telling stories like this one is a risky business, so best that only they know who they are.

2 Where the income/outcome pattern *has* been destabilized, it has been human capital and not financial capital catalyzing change, and pedagogy, not policy.

3 Multiple studies, Hanauer (2019) further explains, "have found that only about 20 percent of student outcomes can be attributed to schooling, whereas about 60 percent are explained by family circumstances—most significantly, income."

4 The study discussed here was funded by a Partnership Development Grant awarded by the Social Sciences and Humanities Research Council of Canada.

5 A policy study proposed as a component of the larger project was rejected by the district, for reasons that weren't provided, and we were advised that the documentary component of the project would not be permitted. This was the core of our project's knowledge mobilization activities for both research documentation and dissemination, designed to encourage parental and community engagement with the school and its activities.

6 We would have done better to heed the advice of Ippolito and Schecter (2012) that in embarking upon institutionally supported research, it is wise to "remain constantly vigilant with regard to what cost is too high" (p. 623). Sometimes the best thing to do is to return the funding, however plentiful and hard-won, and start over.

7 Specifically, we wanted to meet to settle how the district would discharge its agreed-upon commitment of $36,000 (CAD), as we were still hopeful that could fund more iPads for teachers and more instructional support. There was no reply to this (repeated) request, which was eventually abandoned. We were on our own from that point, and there has not since been a single inquiry from the board about the outcomes of our "partnership."

8 The story of each of these other projects, and their respective findings, is not part of this one. Hughes, Morrison, Mamolo, Laffier, and de Castell (2019) provide one such account.

9 The Integrated Literacies program has five key components that advance curricular objectives: Read, Record, Reflect; Word Work; Writing Workshop; Strategy Identifier; Guided Reading. Students are grouped according to their reading and comprehension abilities and rotate to a different center each day during an 80-minute literacy block. Critical literacies and social justice issues are infused into all components of the program, encouraging students to integrate critical reflection, innovative problem-solving, and exposure to world issues. A cross-integration of subjects and topics, including social studies, science, health, and math, is interwoven into each task, exposing students to grade-level literacy content and cross-curricular expectations that promote collaboration and communication, differentiating for the needs and abilities of learners.

10 The Education Quality and Accountability Office (EQAO) is an Ontario government agency responsible for measuring student achievement in reading, writing, and mathematics, based on the expectations and benchmarks outlined in the Ontario Curriculum, at critical points in students' school careers (Grades 3, 6, 9, and 10). EQAO reports, at school, board, and provincial levels, the percentage of students who test above the provincial standard in reading, writing, and mathematics, those standards being based on the Ontario Curriculum benchmarks and expectations for each grade and subject area.

11 https://drive.google.com/file/d/1bTe9dEqVnYKllOPDv4QNy49L0YTuIZ3e/view

12 In 2019, just 36% of this school's Grade 3s "met provincial expectations" in reading, down from 50% in 2018; 38% in writing, down from 56%; and 13% in math, down from 50%. Enthusiastic reports from students and teachers had led us to look for some

Sheltered in Place **271**

positive change, certainly not an extreme drop. How can this be made sense of? A salient fact—and one completely unrelated to the quality of education—is that on November 26, 2018, General Motors announced the closure of its car assembly plant in that city. The plant, in operation since 1907, was the largest employer in the region. By December 2018, massive loss of employment resulted in increased evictions and exacerbated economic and familial hardship. Maybe what went wrong between 2018 and 2019 had nothing to do with school, and everything to do with poverty.

13 The students at this school were born in Canada (93%) and spoke English at home (92%), and while they changed schools much more often than other students (49%), only 17% moved outside the school district, with 82% of this school's students remaining in the same school district since starting school, compared with 51% for the school board as a whole (Ontario, Education Quality and Accountability Office, 2019).

14 After this chapter was completed, proceeding from disclosures of years of bullying and workplace harassment at this school board, a formal inquiry was carried out, followed by the retirement or resignation of several of the district's superintendents, including some with whom we had attempted to advance this project (and with whom our meetings had proved both demoralizing and undermining). That such toxic conditions could persist for the reported dozen or more years does not mean that bullying and unsupportive leadership are found only in districts with the poorest socioeconomic status, though they may be more common there simply as a result of their offering relatively fewer desirable conditions and career prospects. However, teachers and parents in higher socioeconomic-status districts are far more likely to speak up, to challenge and oppose, to document and pursue change than those mired in a culture of poverty, where entitlement, empowerment, and voice are hard to come by and readily dismissed, overlooked, and silenced by school authorities. So the negative impacts on students of aggressive and bullying district leadership can be correspondingly far more severe in the very regions that most need positive change.

References

Brydon, D. (2011). Globalization and higher education: Working toward cognitive justice. In R. Foshay (Ed.), *Valences of interdisciplinarity: Theory, practice, pedagogy* (pp. 97–120). Edmonton, AB: AU Press (Athabasca University).

Counts, G. S. (1932). *Dare the school build a new social order?* New York: John Day.

de Castell, S. (2011). "One code to rule them all ..." In R. Foshay (Ed.), *Valences of interdisciplinarity: Theory, practice, pedagogy* (pp. 325–341). Edmonton, AB: AU Press (Athabasca University).

Dietrichson, J., Bøg, M., Filges, T., & Klint Jørgensen, A. (2017). *Academic interventions for elementary and middle school students with low socioeconomic status: A systematic review and meta-analysis.* Los Angeles, CA: SAGE. doi: 10.3102/0034654316687036

Earl, L., Torrance, N., Sutherland, S., Fullan, M., & Ali, A. (2003). *Manitoba school improvement program: Final evaluation report* (pp. 1–94). Toronto, ON: Ontario Institute for Studies in Education, University of Toronto.

Gorski, P. (2005). Education equity and the digital divide. *Association for the Advancement of Computing in Education Journal, 13*(1), 3–45.

Hanauer, N. (2019, July). Better schools won't fix America. *Atlantic.* Retrieved from https://www.theatlantic.com/magazine/archive/2019/07/education-isnt-enough/590611/

Hughes, J., Morrison, L., Mamolo, A., Laffier, J., & de Castell, S. (2019). Addressing bullying through critical making. *British Journal of Educational Technology, 50*(1), 309–325.

Ioannidis, J. P. A. (2005). Why most published research findings are false. *PLOS Medicine, 2*(8), e124. doi: 10.1371/journal.pmed.0020124

272 Suzanne de Castell

Ippolito, J., & Schecter, S. R. (2012). Using institutional structures to promote educational equity: A tale of two schools. *Elementary School Journal, 112*(4), 607–626. doi: 10.1086/664786

Ontario, Education Quality and Accountability Office. (2019). *Framework*. Toronto, ON: Author. Retrieved from https://www.eqao.com/en/assessments/assessment-docs/eqao-framework.pdf

Rabinow, P. (1986). Representations are social facts. In J. Clifford & G. Marcus (Eds.), *Writing culture* (pp. 234–261). Berkeley, CA: University of California Press.

Rosenthal, R. (1979). The file drawer problem and tolerance for null results. *Psychological Bulletin, 86*(3), 638–641.

Sahlberg, P. (2007). Education policies for raising student learning: The Finnish approach. *Journal of Education Policy, 22*(2), 147–171. doi: 10.1080/02680930601158919

Sibbald, T. (2017). The movement of teachers within Ontario school boards. *Canadian Journal of Educational Administration and Policy, 183*, 4–14.

Spivak, G. (1990). *The post-colonial critic*. New York: Routledge.

Thumlert, K., de Castell, S., & Jenson, J. (2014). Short cuts and extended techniques: Rethinking relations between technology and educational theory. *Educational Philosophy and Theory, 47*(8), 786–803. doi: 10.1080/00131857.2014.901163

Van Maanen, J. (1988). *Tales of the field: On writing ethnography*. Chicago, IL: University of Chicago Press.

Zagorski, N. (2006). *Keeping a lid on negativity: As research data increasingly pour into journals, should only positive findings be reported?* Baltimore, MD: The Johns Hopkins University Medicine, Institute for Basic Biomedical Science. Retrieved from https://www.hopkinsmedicine.org/institute_basic_biomedical_sciences/news_events/articles_and_stories/translation_bench_bedside/200610_lid_on_negativity.html

INDEX

21st-century education (21CE) 256–257
360-degree stories 11, 16; Prerna Girls
School 10–14
1994 Rwandan genocide 122–130, 134

Aalbers, M. 240
Abdi, A. A. 113
absenteeism, teachers 266
achievement gaps 102–105; sustaining
111–112
actor-network theory (ANT) 227
additive/subtractive bilingualism 138
addressivity 7
aesthetic cosmopolitanism 57–58
agency 48, 142–143
agonistic cosmpolitics 63
Aguilar Zéleny, A. S. 144
ambiguity 48
ANT (actor-network theory) 227, 230
Anthias, F. 86
anticosmopolitanism 56
antiracism 129; cosmpolitan antiracism 35
Anzaldúa, G. 8, 48
aporia 50, 56
aporic thinking 56
Appadurai, A. 4
Appiah, K. A. 5, 35, 225, 235
appropriation, queerness 47–49
Arora, A. 102
Aspinall, P. 77
Australia 25–26; globally mobile teachers
29–32; liberal multiculturalism 23;

SWS (southwestern Sydney) see SWS
(southwestern Sydney), Australia

Bakhtin, M. M. 6, 7
Ball, S. J. 249
battles of multiculturalism 59
Beck, U. 22, 44, 212, 225, 234, 239
Beerkens, M. 173
belonging 86
Benito Juárez Intercultural School
144–150
Bhabha, H. 61, 69
bilingualism, additive/subtractive
bilingualism 138
Black bodies 72; *black globality* 55
Black mixed-race pupils 70–71; prejudice
from Black peers 75–77; racism from
teachers 77–79; racism from white
pupils 73–75; racism in curriculum
79–81
Blackness 75, 167
Black people: homeownership
(United States) 242–243; impact of
foreclosure on families 243–250; racial
capitalism 241
blending 49
Blommaert, J. 7
border thinking 142
bottom-up perspective 23
Brah, A. 49
Braidotti, R. 88
Breckenridge, C. 61

274 Index

Brooks-Gunn, J. 243
Brydon, D. 268
busing, mixed-race school pupils 70

Campion, K. 71
Canada: Montreal *see* Montreal, Canada;
  Ontario, IBD (identity-based data
  processes) 102–103; Québec 86; settler
  colonialism 132; study abroad programs
  185; Toronto *see* Toronto, Canada; Truth
  and Reconciliation Commission of
  Canada (2009–2014) 122; video
  games 189
Canagarajah, S. xx, 7, 8
CGEIB (Coordinación General de
  Educación Intercultural Bilingüe)
  139–140
Chakrabarty, D. 61
chaosmopolis 59–60
chaosmos 60
Cheah, P. 47
Chieffo, L. 174
China: critical cosmopolitanism
  219–220; discursive construction of
  intercultural experiences 213–217; EMI
  (English-medium-instruction) 212;
  IHE (internationalization of higher
  education) 210; international students
  209; multisectional interpersonal
  othering 217–219; Shanghai,
  discursive construction of intercultural
  experiences 213–217
"China Discourse" 217
citizen of the world concept 61
classroom hierarchies, digital games
  197–198
climate change 35
Coalition Avenir Québec government
  97n1
Cohen, R. 141
colonial continuity 125
communication 226; intercultural
  communication 210
community 132
community-engaged approach xxii
community-led workshops 122
compulsory schooling age, SWS
  (southwestern Sydney), Australia 26–29
computational literacy 190–191
computational thinking 190–191
Conley, V. A. 59–60
Connell, J. 33–34
contact zones 6

Coordinación General de Educación
  Intercultural Bilingüe (CGEIB)
  139–140
cosmopolitan antiracism 35
cosmopolitan condition 22
cosmopolitanism 5–7, 9, 44, 50,
  53–54, 61–62, 225–226, 228,
  239; aesthetic cosmopolitanism
  57–58; critical cosmopolitanism
  see critical cosmopolitanism;
  discrepant cosmopolitanism 62;
  Mary's story (Sweden) 234–235;
  rooted cosmopolitanism 142; rural
  cosmopolitanism 23; vernacular
  cosmopolitanism 62
cosmopolitanism of the poor 6
cosmopolitanization 62, 225, 234
cosmopolites 60
cosmopolitan translanguaging 10–15
cosmopolitics 55
counter-cosmopolitans 225
COVID-19 55, 265
critical cosmopolitanism 62, 133–134, 141,
  211–212, 228; self-cultivated orientation
  toward 219–220
critical pedagogies 158–159
Critical Race Theory (CRT) xxiii,
  34–35, 106
Critical Whiteness Studies 103–104
cross-border allegiances, climate change 35
CRT (Critical Race Theory) xxiii, 34–35,
  103, 106
Cruz-Malavé, A. 42
cultural appropriation 45
cultural dichotomies: in formal curricula
  215–216; in institutional promotional
  discourses 213–215; in institutional
  student management 216–217
cultural immersion 184
cultural pluralism 54, 58
cultural reductionism 57
curriculum: cultural dichotomies 215–216;
  racism 79–81; research, superdiversity
  122–123

Dabashi, H. 33
Darling-Hammond, L. 104
data, IBD *see* IBD (identity-based data
  processes)
decolonial cosmopolitanism 34
decolonization 48
decosmopolitanization 56
Del Val, J. 152

Demack, S. 112
democratizing education 114
design, digital games 193–194
deterritorialization 88, 97
DeVault, M. L. 246
Dewey, J. 226, 227
De Wit, H. 173
DGBL (digital-game-based learning) 190, 192–195
diaspora 49
DiE (drama-in-education) 155, 157–158, 167–168; francophone minority language schools 160–161; liminal spaces 168; race 161–168
digital divide 200–201, 257
digital-game-based learning (DGBL) 190, 192–195
digital games 189; classroom hierarchies 197–198; design 193–194; digital divide 200–201; girls 195–196; impacts of 198–200
digital pedagogy 264
digital stories 9, 11; Prerna Girls School 10–14, 16
digital technologies 257
Discourses 210
discourses of difference 156
discrepant cosmopolitanism 62
discrimination 124; institutional discrimination 126
discursive characterizations, IBD (identity-based data processes) 108–109
DiSessa, A. 190, 191
disposition 30, 143
divergent modernity 212
Donald, J. 58, 60
double consciousness 73–75
drama-in-education (DiE) 155, 157–158, 167–168; francophone minority language schools 160–161; liminal spaces 168; race 161–168
Dwyer, M. M. 174, 184

economic racisms, homeownership 241
educational disparities 101–102
educational inequality 257
educational justice 268–269
educational policies, Mexico 139–140, 142
Education Quality and Accountability Office (EQAO) 266, 270n10
elitism, STSA (short-term study abroad) 182–184
ELL (English language learner), digital games 197–198

Ellsworth, E. 157–159, 165
Elusive Culture (Yon 2000) 56, 59
embodiment 157–158
EMI (English-medium-instruction) 209–210, 212
empathy, DiE (drama-in-education) 164–165
English 12; proficient English speakers, Japan 180–181
English language learner (ELL), digital games 197–198
English language teachers, experiences of 30–31
English-medium-instruction (EMI) 209–210
EQAO (Education Quality and Accountability Office) 266, 270n10
Eslami, Z. 193
Espace Paris Jeunes Mahalia Jackson 95
essentialism 211
Estrada, G. 140, 144, 151
estrangement 56–57
ethnic communities 54
ethnic diversity, Japan 180–181
ethnicization 28
Ethnologue 144
exoticism 106
experience 226–227
experiential othering 219

Fanon, F. 55
file drawer problem 261
financialization 240
focus groups 165–167
food insecurity 246
foreclosure, impact on Black families 243–250
formal curricula, cultural dichotomies 215–216
Forte, M. C. 24
Foucault, M. 156
francophone minority language schools: drama-in-education (DiE) 160–161; race in liminal spaces 161–168; superdiversity 159–160
freedom 55

game culture 194–195
game-making 199
game-making project 196
Gamergate 194
gap gazing 104
gaps, intentionally sustaining 111–112
gap talk 105, 112

276 Index

García, O. 8
Gee, J. P. 190, 210
gender normativity 46
General Office of Intercultural Education (CGEIB) 139–140
"Genocide and Crimes Against Humanity: Historical and Contemporary Implications" 122–123; making sense of testimony 130–133; mobilizing critical frameworks to address responses to testimony 123–130
GHHN (Global Hip Hop Nation) 89
Ghosh, R. 113
Gidwani, V. 23
Gillborn, D. 105, 112, 249
Gilmore, R. W. 241
girls, digital games 195–196
Glick Schiller, N. 61
global capitalism 5
global citizens, Japan 180–181
global competence 178–181
Global Education Agenda 2030 139
Global Hip Hop Nationa (GHHN) 89
global imaginary 6
globalization 22; side-effects of 234
global jinzai 172, 175–176, 180, 185
Global University Project, Japan 176
glocalization xxi
Goldberg, A. 190
"good news" bias 262
Gouldner, A. xxiii
governmentality 47–48
Grant, S. 23–24
Gregoriou, Z. 50, 58
Griffiths, L. 174
Grover, S. 191
Gutiérrez, R. 104

Hage, G. 23
Hall, S. 156, 162
Handsfield, L. J. 143
hijras 46
Hindi 12
Hip Hop 86–88; hiphoplect 95–96; NBS Studio 90–93, 96–97; social media 93–95; traditions and technologies 88–90
hiphoplect 95–96
Historian-Survivors 125, 134
Holliday, A. 211
homeownership: economic racisms 241; impact of foreclosure on Black families 243–250; United States 241–243
home values 240

homosexuality 41; *see also* queernesses
Honig, B. 44, 48
Horta, P. L. 6
housing markets 240
Huisman, J. 173
Hupfield, J. 110
hybridity 40, 106; queer hybrid relationality 41–45
hybridized pedagogy 264

IBD (identity-based data processes) 101–105; data as narrative 108–110; data as political tools 110–113; deep critical learning 113; democratizing education 114; identity 105–108; theorizing race and whiteness 103–104
IBE (Intercultural Bilingual Education) 138, 140–141, 151
identity xxiii, 58, 230; IBD *see* IBD (identity-based data processes); Mary's story (Sweden) 229–232
identity-based data (IBD processes) 101–105; data as narrative 108–110; data as political tools 110–113; deep critical learning 113; democratizing education 114; identity 105–108; theorizing race and whiteness 103–104
ideological becoming 6
idiosyncratic linguistic practices 95
IHE (internationalization of higher education) 209–210; *see also* China
imagination 4
immigrant teachers 31
impacts of digital games 198–200
inclusion 187
income, education and 256
India, English 12
indigeneity 23–24
Indigenous people, cosmopolitanism 23–24
inductive coding 213
institutional discrimination 124, 126
institutional promotional discourses, cultural dichotomies 213–215
institutional student management, cultural dichotomies 216–217
Integrated Literacies program 260–265, 270n9
intentional gaps 112
interconnectedness 34
intercultural 211
Intercultural Bilingual Education (IBE) 138, 140–141, 151

intercultural communication 210
intercultural experiences, discursive construction of 213–217
intercultural understanding 180
interest convergence 103, 106
internationalization of higher education (IHE) 209–210; *see also* China
international students: China *see* China; critical cosmopolitanism 217–219; cultural dichotomies 213–217; othering 217–219
intertextuality 213
Irving, A. 61
Islamophobia 111

Jabbari, N. 193
Jafri, B. 132
James, C. E. 23, 95
Japan: declining workforce 180; global citizens 180–181; *global jinzai* 172, 175–176, 180, 185; Global University Project 176; study abroad programs 181–182
Johnston, M. P. 75
Joseph-Salisbury, R. 71
judgments 142–143

Kahn, J. S. 60–61
Karatani, K. J. 34
Karera, A. 125
Kay, A. 190
Kehl, K. 175
Khan, F. A. 46
Khwaja Sira people 45
King, K. 42
Kumashiro, K. K. 105
KWL (Know, Want to know, Learned about) 123
Kymlicka, W. 58
Kyte, S. 123

Lacy, K. 242
Langley, P. 240, 243
language, Mayo people 143–144
language maintenance 142, 146–150
language revitalization 141, 144
Laniel-Tremblay, E. 180
Lather, P. 158, 159
Latour, B. 227, 235
Learning Opportunity Grant, Ontario, Canada 112
legitimizing voices, IBD (identity-based data processes) 111

Leiva, C. 8
Leonardo, Z. 156
Leong, N. 241
liberal multiculturalism 23, 35
liminal spaces 158; DiE (drama-in-education) 168; race 161–168
lingua franca xxi
linguistic/academic othering 218–219
literacy, multiliteracies project 157
long-term study abroad (LTSA), *vs.* short-term study abroad 174–175
loss of innocence, mixed-race school pupils 73–81
Low, B. 180
LTSA (long-term study abroad) 174–175

Malik, S. 70
Manalansan, M. F. 42
Martin, R. 240
massively multiplayer online games (MMOGs) 193
matters of concern 227–228
Matthews, J. 185
Mayo people 143–144
media 5
media representation 126
Medina-López-Portillo, A. 175
mestiza consciousness 48
Mexico: educational policies 139–140, 142; IBE (Intercultural Bilingual Education) 138, 140–141, 151; Mayo people and language 143–144; trilingual education 144–150
Mignolo, W. 34
migrant teachers 31
migration 234
mixed-methods approach 192
mixed-race school pupils 69–70; busing 70; prejudice from Black peers 75–77; primary school 72–73; racism from teachers 77–79; racism from white pupils 73–75; racism in curriculum 79–81
MMOGs (massively multiplayer online games) 193
mobility 7, 23
mobilizing critical frameworks to address responses to testimony 123–130
monoracism 81
Montreal, Canada: Hip Hop culture 86–88; hiphoplect 95–96; NBS Studio 90–93, 96–97
moral space, media 5

278 Index

Morgan, B. 143
Morris, J. 175
multicultural exoticism 106
multiculturalism 32–33, 56, 180; to cosmopolitanism 56–59
multiliteracies project, New London Group 157
multimodality 157
multisectional interpersonal othering 217–219
mutual learning models, teaching cosmopolitan antiracism 35

Nadal, K. L. 75
narratives, data as 108–110
national identity 231–232
Navarro, Z. 27
NBS Studio 86–87, 90–97
neo-essentialism 211
neo-essentialist cultural dichotomies 211–212
neoliberalism 26, 34, 239–240
Nettleton, S. 244
New London Group, multiliteracies project 157
New South Wales, Australia, compulsory schooling age 26–29
Nicholson, H. 165
normative negotiations, queerness 43
Nussbaum, M. C. 63

Ontario, Canada, IBD (identity-based data processes) 102–103
opportunity gaps, sustaining 111–112
oral history frameworks 133
Orrenius, N. 229
othering 211; experiential othering 219; linguistic/academic othering 218–219; politico-ideological othering 217–218
"Oulala" 95–96

Pakistan, gender identity 46
Pakistani transpeople 45
Papastergiadis, N. 24, 88
Papert, S. 190
Papunya Tula artists 24, 34
paradigm paralysis 268
Parekh, G. 112
parental income 256
partnerships in education 258–265
Patel, G. 46, 49
Pea, R. 191
pedagogical domestication, resisting 62–63
pedagogical encounters 165

pedagogical pivot points 165
Perlis, A. J. 190
PISA (Programme for International Student Assessment) 101
Piu Piu community, Hip Hop 90
pluriverse 61
Plüss, C. 88
political tools, data as 110–113
politico-ideological othering 217–218
Pollock, S. 61
positive power 156
postcolonial theory 33
power: conceptions of identity 108; role in constructing identity 107
pragmatism 226
Pratt, M. L. 6
prejudice from Black peers, mixed-race school pupils 75–77
Prensky, M. 190
Prerna Girls School, digital stories 10–15, 16
pride festivals 47–49
primary school, mixed-race school pupils 72–73
Programa Nacional de Inglés (National Program of English) 139
Programme for International Student Assessment (PISA) 101
programming skills 190
PRONI (Program Nacional de Inglés or National Program of English) 139
publication bias 261–262
Public Culture 61

Québec, Canada, Hip Hop culture 86
Québécois 93
queer hybrid ethics 48
queer hybridities 40, 47, 49, 51
queer hybrid relationality 41–45
queernesses 40–42; appropriation 47–49; cultural appropriation 45–46
queer problems 49–51

Rabinow, P. 255
race xxii–xxiii, 156; in liminal spaces 161–168; theorizing in IBD processes 103–104
racial capitalism 241
racialization 49, 73, 156, 241
racialized differences 73
racial mismatch 77
racism xxiii; Black mixed-race pupils 71; in curriculum 79–81; mixed-race school pupils 72; from teachers, mixed-race pupils 77–79; from white pupils 73–75

Ramanathan, V. 143
Rampton, B. 7
readiness, study abroad programs 175
reflective thinking 226
refugees 62; critical cosmopolitanism 24
relatability 131
relationality, queer hybrid relationality
41–45
relationships of transactional events, Mary's
story (Sweden) 232–233
resisting, pedagogical domestication
62–63
reterritorialization 88, 97; NBS Studio
94–95
Riot Games 194
Robbins, B. 6
Robinson, C. J. 241
Rodriguez, N. 51
Rollock, N. 112, 249
rooted cosmopolitanism 142
rural cosmopolitanism 23
Rwandan genocide (1994) 122–130, 134
Rwigema, M.-J. 122–123, 125–127,
129–131

Sánchez, C. 152
Santiago, S. 6
Sarkeesian, A. 194
Sassen, S. 43
scales of opportunity 26
scapegoating practices 124
Schechner, R. 158
Schecter, S. R. 95
Schneider, W. 243
school choice, SWS (southwestern
Sydney), Australia 26–29
school transitions, mixed-race school
pupils 73–81
segregation between international and
home students, China 216–217
self-identification 110
self-transformation 30
settler colonialism 132
settlerhood 132
Shanghai, China, discursive construction of
intercultural experiences 213–217
Shapiro, T. 243
sheltered in place 268
short-term study abroad (STSA) 172–
174, 177, 184–185; commitment to
the program 178; elitism 182–184;
expectations for 177–178; global
competence 178–180; vs. long-term
study abroad 174–175

side-effects of, globalization 234
Sidhu, R. 185
Silverstone, R. 5, 17
Simon, R. 127
Sivaramakrishnan, K. 23
Sleeper, R. W. 227
Sobe, N. W. 24
The social 227–228; Mary's story (Sweden)
230–232
Social Darwinism 34, 124, 128
social imaginaries 6
social media, Hip Hop 93–95
Sollange, U. 122–123
Song, M. 77
southwestern Sydney (SWS), Australia 22
Souto-Otero, M. 173
Spivak, G. 3–4, 17, 255
Spurlin, W. J. 48
Stanton, G. H. 128
state power 34
Steger, M. 6
stereotyping 162
Stone, D. 110
stories, digital stores and virtual reality
(VR) story telling 9
STSA (short-term study abroad) 172–
174, 177, 184–185; commitment to
the program 178; elitism 182–184;
expectations for 177–178; global
competence 178–180; vs. long-term
study abroad 174–175
student expectations, study abroad
programs 181–182
study abroad programs: paradigm change
in 181–184; short-term study abroad
(STSA) 173–174; STSA (short-term
study abroad) vs. LTSA (long-term
study abroad) 174–175
subalterns 3; worlding the world see
worlding the world
subjectivities, transnational queers 42–43
summer abroad programs 172
Sundström Sjödin, E. 227
superdiversity 5, 133; curriculum research
122–123; francophone minority
language schools 159–160
surroundings 227
sustaining achievement/opportunity gaps
111–112
Sutton-Smith, B. 158
Sweden 224; foreign-born persons 233
SWS (southwestern Sydney), Australia 22,
25–26; compulsory schooling age 26–29
Sznaider, N. 212

280 Index

Taylor, C. 107
teacher agency 142
teacher development 258
teacher education programs 267–268
teachers: absenteeism 266; mobility
(Australia) 29–32; racism toward
mixed-race pupils 77–79; support for
257; training of 267–268; turnover 266;
withdrawal when using technology
263–264
telesecundarias 146
testimony: making sense of 130–133;
mobilizing critical frameworks to
address responses to 123–130
That Kid (TK) 197
theater: DiE (drama-in-education) *see* DiE
(drama-in-education); liminal spaces
158; multimodality 157
thinking: computational thinking 190–191;
reflective thinking 226
third gender 46–47
third space 69
time constraints, DiE
(drama-in-education) 164
time-space compressions 54
TK (That Kid) 197
Todd, S. 63, 142–143
Toronto, Canada 59; IBD *see* IBD
(identity-based data processes)
town of Seagulls, trilingual education
144–150
transactional events, relationships
of, Mary's story (Sweden)
232–233
transactional realism 226–228, 235
transitional space 165
translanguaging 7–10; cosmopolitan
translanguaging 10–15
translingual practice 8
transliteracies framework 8
transnational queers 42–43
trans people 46–47
trans-semiotics 8

trilingual education 140–141; Mexico
144–150
Truth and Reconciliation Commission of
Canada (2009–2014) 122
Turner, V. W. 158
turnover of students and teachers 266

United States, significance of
homeownership 241–243
universalism 60–61
upskilling 195, 257

Vattimo, G. 56
vernacular cosmopolitanism 62
Vertovec, S. 141
video games 189; *see also* digital games
Vincent, C. 249
virtual reality (VR) storytelling 9
visual narratives 9
VR (virtual reality) storytelling 9

Wahlström, N. 227
Waldfogel, J. 243
Waldron, J. 44
Warmington, P. 112
Weems, L. 44–45
"We Out Here Live" (NBS Studio) 94
Werbner, P. 23
"West Indian" child 70
whiteness 34, 103–104, 156–157, 164
white people 157
white supremacy 159
Williams, D. 81
Wing, J. 190–191
Winnicott, D. W. 165
women, game culture 194–195
worlding the world 4, 15–17
World of Warcraft (WoW) 193

Yon, D. A. 156
Yoshida, A. 175
young Muslim males, education (Australia)
28–29

Printed in the United States
by Baker & Taylor Publisher Services